An Expedition to the
Ranquel Indians

TEXAS PAN AMERICAN SERIES

An Expedition to the Ranquel Indians

LUCIO V. MANSILLA

Translated by Mark McCaffrey

UNIVERSITY OF TEXAS PRESS

AUSTIN

*This translation is dedicated
to the descendants of the Ranquel,
Araucanian, Mapuche,
and Pampa tribes
and nations remembered in its pages.*

Requests for permission to reproduce material from this work
should be sent to Permissions, University of Texas Press,
Box 7819, Austin, TX 78713-7819.

∞ The paper used in this publication meets the minimum requirements
of American National Standard for Information Sciences—
Permanence of Paper for Printed Library Materials, ANSI Z39.48-1984.

Library of Congress Cataloging-in-Publication Data

Mansilla, Lucio Victorio, 1831–1913.
  [Excursión a los indios ranqueles. English]
  An expedition to the Ranquel Indians / by Lucio V. Mansilla ;
translated by Mark McCaffrey.
      p.   cm. — (Texas Pan American series)
  Includes bibliographical references and index.
  ISBN 0-292-75192-3 (cloth). — ISBN 0-292-75203-2 (paper)
    1. Ranquel Indians.   2. Argentina — Description and
travel.   3. Mansilla, Lucio Victorio, 1831–1913.
  I. Title. II. Series.
  F2823.R2M34613   1997
  982'.00498 — dc21   96-39454

CONTENTS

Acknowledgments ix

Introduction xi

Note to the Translation xiv

AN EXPEDITION TO THE RANQUEL INDIANS

PART I
1

PART II
71

PART III
165

PART IV
233

PART V
315

EPILOGUE
381

Notes 386

Glossary 406

Select Bibliography 408

Index 411

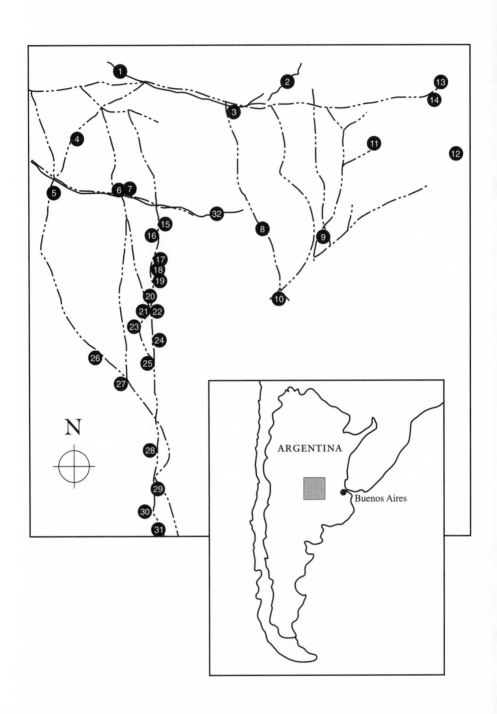

Places Mentioned in Lucio V. Mansilla's Narrative
and Expedition and Surveying Routes

(After the map in the 1947 Fondo de Cultura Económica edition
of *Una excursión a los indios ranqueles*.)

1. Río Cuarto
2. Río Saladillo
3. La Carlota
4. Chaján
5. Cuadril
6. Tres de Febrero
7. Paso del Lechuzo
8. Fort General Arredondo
9. Laguna de Langhelo
10. Tres Lagunas
11. Antiguo Melincué
12. Fort Chañares
13. Melincué
14. Melincué Viejo
15. Laguna Alegre
16. Monte de la Vieja
17. Zorro Colgado
18. Pollo-helo
19. Us-helo
20. Tremencó
21. Laguna del Cuero
22. Pozos de Bayo-manco
23. Lonco-uaca
24. Chamalcó
25. Utatriquin
26. Agustinillo
27. Laguna Bagual
28. Aillancó
29. Leubucó (Mariano Rosas)
30. Patamu
31. Quenqué (Baigorrita)
32. Río Quinto

ACKNOWLEDGMENTS

I FIRST BEGAN *to explore Lucio Mansilla's* Excursión *while studying films about Argentine gauchos at the Cinemateca Argentina in Buenos Aires in 1981. The capable staff members of that organization — fully creditable writers and researchers in their own right — considered Mansilla's book well worth the trouble of getting to know in depth and convinced me of as much. I am grateful to them for their persuasiveness, and to the University of California for the Humanities Research Grant that allowed me to travel to Argentina in the first place.*

Like the work of all writers, translations benefit both from exposure to an audience and from its response. The American Literary Translators Association provided me, through its annual conferences, with a forum in which I could "field test" the translation among other translators. This gave the project new vigor and provided me with much helpful guidance. A National Endowment for the Humanities seminar in American Indian Literature at the University of Illinois, Chicago, in the summer of 1994, brought me as close as I have ever been to a scholar's utopia. My thanks to the seminar's generous director, Dr. Lavonne Ruoff, for making my South American work welcome in a room full of North American scholars. The Newberry Library, the Huntington Library, the John Carter Brown Library, and the University Research Library at the University of California, Los Angeles, have, through their very professional and accommodating staffs, each proven to be more like a second home than a mere depository of great and rare books. Professor Rich Slatta, of North Carolina State University, was a source both of humor and insight as the translation proceeded. I am also grateful to Professor Janet Whatley, of the University of Vermont, for her support of this project.

I wish to extend a special note of thanks to Dr. Armando Zá-

rate, escrupuloso conocedor de Argentina, *for his willingness, over a long period, to constantly deepen my sense and knowledge of his country. Such generosity cannot truly be repaid except by the translator's recognition that, without it, the book's innumerable voices would sound like data gathered from so many informants rather than like a people with a story to tell.*

A final note of thanks to Theresa May and the exceedingly patient staff at the University of Texas Press. It was they who decided in favor of publishing Mansilla's book in translation, a choice for which I expect readers will now be as grateful as was I.

INTRODUCTION

LUCIO VICTORIO MANSILLA'S *Una excursión a los indios ranqueles* first appeared in La Tribuna *of Buenos Aires in ir-
regular, although almost daily, installments between 20 May and
7 September 1870. Mansilla had taken copious notes while on his
singular, eighteen-day expedition some six weeks earlier, and what
he did not fully compose in the field or at his post as commander
of the new army fort at Río Cuarto, he feverishly dictated as the
typesetters at* La Tribuna *stood waiting. The sixty-six chapters
Mansilla finished in this fashion, plus two more and an epilogue he
added as* La Tribuna *prepared to publish the work in its entirety at
year's end, comprised, essentially, the* Excursión *as it is still known,
and still read, in Argentina today.*

*Whatever genre scholarly consideration may finally determine
best suits Mansilla's creation, the book can be said to claim certain unquestionable achievements. It is one of very few works of
either North or South American letters which present a vivid and
sustained firsthand account of noncombative coexistence between
American Indian and white civilization, on Indian land, during any
nation's period of consolidation. Noted in its own country for its
wit, adventure, and narrative ingenuity, it brings original insight to
Western questions of "civilization and barbarism," immigration,
ethnic and racial diversity, and land ownership and tenancy. Mansilla's narrative tests the postulates of Argentine thinkers such as
Juan Bautista Alberdi and Domingo Faustino Sarmiento. The barbarism of frontier society, the superiority of European races, the
irreconcilability of the emerging nation with its indigenous populations — these were the bedrock suppositions which Mansilla bore
to the Ranquel settlements beyond the pampas. He himself did not
embrace these ideas. He chose instead, and largely alone, to es-
pouse dialogue and a candid, even Rabelaisian diplomacy — there*

was a kind of haphazard agape to his approach — as the best way to engage the "Indian problem." The Excursión *thus presents an eighteen-day dress rehearsal, complete with an arduous summit conference under the desert sun, Socratic point-counterpoint colloquia with the chiefs, elders, and braves, and hospitality on Ranquel protocol. It was all intended in Mansilla's mind as groundwork for a reconciliation between antagonists that never finally took place.*

The Excursión *is a gold mine of diversity. An epistolary serial narrative dedicated to a maverick Chilean writer and globe-trotter named Santiago Arcos, it was penned by a worldly-wise, forty-one-year-old Mansilla, scion of the Argentine commercial and governing elite and nephew of the deposed dictator Juan Manuel de Rosas. It is a military chronicle as well, one in which Colonel Mansilla carries out an authorized and peaceful foray of his own design into Indian territory. The book also advances a testimonial tradition practiced since the arrival of the Spanish in at least two inflections: the expeditionary and captivity narrative and the missionary "relation." The book is furthermore a travel chronicle, the fruit of an extraordinary expedition headed by a quixotic colonel of the Argentine army. It differs in three respects from the military writings on the "conquest of the desert" that would follow Mansilla's narrative some nine years and many thousands of Indian and army dead later: it is about communication rather than conquest, it presents a multitude of vividly drawn characters, and its author was a literary celebrity.*

Mansilla's relationship to the inhabitants on both sides of the frontier line was perforce more intimate, certainly more complex, than that of any of the travel writers before or since his sojourn. He had, among other things, reputation, personal safety, and both a family and a military career to consider in undertaking and recording the expedition. Mansilla's book may therefore be said to occupy a place as a forerunner of the testimonial literature which, in part, characterized the works of the "Generation of 1880," of which Mansilla would become a member in good standing. Anecdotal, glib, long on self-indulgence and short on character development, this would be the literature of a leisurely, proprietary class of comfortable witnesses. Small wonder, then, that it should often have taken the form of letters, as it does in the Excursión, *or that it should frequently deliver shared confidences and pleasantries.*

The Excursión, *however, is incalculably more powerful than the*

*exiguous demands of its genre might suggest. In the first place,
Mansilla's strategies for dramatizing his interaction with the frontier society are ingenious. He weaves endless sub-narratives and
digressions through the basic expeditionary account: stories of
Christian captives long accustomed to Indian ways; asides in which
Ranquels cajole the colonel to meet with them after the* parlamento
*to drink; unfinished homilies to which he gives wry titles such as
"Morality Applied to Politics, or the Art of Waiting"; and tongue-
in-cheek translations, as in "the pleasure of a drink with you"
for the Ranquels' exclamatory "Yapai!" Secondly, Argentina, like
many nations on both American continents, stood in puzzled ambivalence vis-à-vis the indigenous peoples inhabiting land which
nationalist expansionism demanded for the nation. Of what integrity may a nation hope to boast, Mansilla's latent question seems
to be, if it does not know its own people, or if its people have no
voice in its dialogue with the rest of the world? It was one thing to
pose this question to one's peers over, say, absinthe in the safety of
a paneled drawing room or to brandish it as political badinage at
the jockey club. It was another to bring back living literary evidence of the answer it might draw in a tête-à-tête with the chief of
the Ranquel nation.*

In translation, the Excursión *delivers something new to English-
speaking readers. At the time Mansilla rode out with his eighteen
soldiers, scouts, and friars to break bread and talk peace with Chief
Mariano Rosas, Argentina was, like the United States, a young
Western nation locked into a scheme of relentless westward expan-
sion. It defined itself as sprung from white European colonists and
immigrants, and it acknowledged as its intellectual masters men
who pressed at every turn for the modernization of social and
political processes along lines of racial and economic privilege.
Alberdi wrote in 1852 that to govern was to populate, and Argentina's doors would soon be opened to staggering numbers of immigrants. Few voices other than Mansilla's were heard to say that
Argentina already had people, had a people, who could assume
stewardship of the land.*

*The leading ideologues of Argentine society had chosen in-
stead to confront the coveted territory's Ranquel, Araucanian, and
Pampa nations and tribes with ever more dire propositions of assimilation. The book explores, among other things, the disquieting
moral and ideological questions lost on those who went forward
with the making of a nation with no better preparation for the task*

than that which a rigid deference to property-based expansionism might be expected to provide. The Excursión *may finally be only a recording of the possibilities inherent in the meeting of Euro-American and Native American cultures without the threat of immediate armed confrontation. Even in this modest but unattainable purpose, however, it has had few equals on either American continent.*

NOTE TO THE TRANSLATION

This translation is based on the 1947 *edition of* Una excursión a los indios ranqueles *published as part of the Biblioteca Americana by the Fondo de Cultura Económica (Mexico City and Buenos Aires). The FCE edition, under the care of Julio Caillet-Bois, itself followed the* 1890 *edition, the one most carefully overseen by the author. The translator has here and there judged some of Mansilla's rather private digressions as meriting a discreet pruning and has applied the shears as sparingly as possible. Certain obscure allusions to local personages, especially those intended by the author to answer other newspaper writings, have also been deleted at no discernible cost to narrative flow. The translator of course assumes full responsibility for these deletions, which in any case amount to no more than a small fraction of the overall text as published in Mansilla's lifetime.*

I

A TREK, A SOJOURN, *and a pilgrimage,* Mansilla's Excursión *to the Ranquel tent camps also became a gathering place for the voicing of tales and testimonials which, if not for the author's loose and catholic sense of composition, might never have reached the printed page. With its camp-fire leitmotif and its soldier and gaucho storytellers, the* Excursión *also challenged the contentious if polarized vision of civilization and barbarism which Domingo Faustino Sarmiento's* Facundo *had thrust upon the embattled nation some twenty-five years earlier. Mansilla parried, not with an equally high-minded essay, but with his variegated testimonial from the people of the desert, be they Christian runaways or Ranquels, copper-skinned, or blue-eyed, or both. His book encompasses pampas and desert, the horse as propitiatory logo of nationhood, the Indian's ostracism, the Christian captive's dilemma, the gaucho's poverty, and the diplomat's Gordian knot.*

Such a broad narrative sweep gave Mansilla plenty of latitude for marking the progress of his journey in real time. Thus, the actual departure could wait until Chapter 4, leaving ample space for the host and commentator to establish the setting. In the first chapters, the Ranquels mill about the fort in the days before the party gets under way. One soon understands that Mansilla will be playing a cosmopolitan hand as narrator. If we wonder whether he will deliver the enemy's story or let the enemy deliver its own, the pathetic tale of Private Gómez, with its texture of haphazard heroism, its hallucinating protagonist, and the "thread binding the existence of loved ones," shows us that Mansilla at least is willing to step away from center stage.

The Gómez story occupies four chapters of what from the outset shows itself to be a rambling epistolary narrative. There are in fact two different soldiers' stories in the first fourteen chapters. The scheming, venal, and tragic characters who people these accounts may later seem deeply flawed, and hobbled by complexity, when Mansilla describes how simply the Ranquel people go about courtship. Mansilla also wears the anthropologist's hat, and the adventurer plays geographer. Not that the Argentina of 1870 was in any primal, new-world sense undiscovered or even largely uncharted. Rather, one could say that Mansilla had taken it upon himself to evince a certain mixture of propriety and humility in encountering the land, its features, and its people.

These many and sometimes conflicting allegiances, strategies, and demands make the narrative ground a shifting one, no less for the reader than for the writer. Yet the story proceeds apace. When Chapter 14 comes to a close, the traveling party of some twenty men has come to within a thousand meters of the first Indian settlement most of them have ever seen. In a vivid first encounter, three women riding a single, haggard horse approach the party. Each of them is carrying a watermelon, it being common knowledge among the Indians that the water in the lagoon where Mansilla's party had stopped was undrinkable. Mansilla holds his grandiloquence in check as the women impress their image upon us and the story finds its bearings.

MY DEAR SANTIAGO,

I don't know where you are or where this letter and, God granting me life and good health, those to follow might find you.[1]

For some time now I have known nothing of your whereabouts, have heard nothing from you, but because my heart tells me you are alive I must also believe you continue your pilgrimage through this world. Nor do I despair of someday sitting down with you in the shade of an old, rotted-out carob tree, in the grass beside a lagoon, or on the bank of a stream, to enjoy a guanaco steak, or a side of doe, or a cut of mare or mountain lion steak; or ostrich rump from an ostrich felled with my own bolas, which to me has always been the kind that tastes best.

Now as for ostriches, after journeying through Europe and America, living like a marquis in Paris and like a Guaraní in Paraguay; after eating *mazamorra* in the River Plate, *charquicán* in

Chile, oysters in New York, macaroni in Naples, truffles in Péri-
gord, and *chipá* in Asunción, I recall that one of the great aspirations of your life was to eat an omelet from the eggs of a pampean
ostrich, and to eat it in Nagüel Mapo,[2] which means "place of the
tiger."

Our tastes grow simpler with time, and a curious social phenomenon has been recurring since there has been a world to speak
of. Mankind collectively thrives on the creation of pleasures, of
new delights for the palate and new needs, while the individual
man thrives on his struggle to free himself from the tyrannies of
fashion and civilization. At twenty-five, we are the victims of innumerable superfluities. Not to have white gloves, new and fresh
as a daisy, is a great setback and can cause the most proper of lads
to be passed up for marriage. Many a meal is forsaken and many a
stomach martyred on the altar of decorum!

At forty, when the north wind and life's winter frost begin to
wither the cheek and whiten the hair, our needs grow greater and
what won't we do then for a jar of cold cream or a packet of make-
up? Later it is all the same: with gloves or without them, our cheeks
powdered or not, an ape in his Sunday best is an ape nonetheless.
The plainest, simplest, and most innocent things please best. No
hot spices, thank you, no truffles. One thing alone spares us all
harm, causes no indigestion, no irritation: a home-cooked stew.

We observe the same phenomenon within another order of
ideas. There are creative nations and races and destructive nations
and races. Yet, in the inexorable *corso e ricorso* of time and humanity, the world marches on; and a feverish restlessness sways
humanity from one perspective to the next without the ideal ever
dying.

Cutting my exhortation short here, dear friend Santiago, I will
tell you that I have beaten you to the prize.

I assume you will not care to quarrel with me about this or get
carried away with envy.

Recall that you once fought with your father and later told me
why you had reproached him.

"Do you know why the old man is upset with me?" you said.
"He's envious that I have been to Paraguay and he has not."

It happens that my military fate has placed me in command of
the Córdoba frontier,[3] once the border most beleaguered by the
Ranquels. As you know, the Ranquels are those Araucanian tribes
who, having migrated at different times from the western side of

the Andes to the eastern, crossing the Río Negro and the Río Colorado, have now settled between the Quinto and the Colorado at the headwaters of the Chalileo.[4] Recently I celebrated a peace treaty with them which the President approved, ordering that it be submitted to Congress.

I had thought that, this being an administrative act, congressional approval wouldn't be necessary, but then what does a poor colonel know of the constitutional game? Once the treaty was approved, certain difficulties arose with respect to its immediate execution.[5]

These circumstances, on the one hand; on the other, a certain inclination to hazardous and distant forays, a desire to see with my own eyes the world they call *tierra adentro*, so as to study its customs and ways, its needs, its ideas, its religion and language, and to inspect for myself the terrain where the forces under my orders would perhaps one day have to march[6]—that is what decided me, in recent days and against the urging of certain men who claimed familiarity with the Indians, to penetrate the settlements and to dine, before you should ever do so, on an ostrich egg omelet in Nagüel Mapo.

Our unforgettable friend, Emilio Quevedo, used to say when we lived together in Paraguay, "Lucio, if not Paris, Asunción!" And I say, "Santiago, if not an omelet of fresh eggs in the Club del Progreso, an ostrich egg omelet in the tent of my compadre, Chief Baigorrita."

Say what they will, if happiness exists, if we can identify and define it, it lies at the extremes. I can well understand the satisfactions both of obscurity and of glory. But who can fathom the pleasures of all that lies halfway between: the satisfaction of indifference, the satisfaction of being just anything at all? I can understand someone saying, "I wish I were Leonardo Pereira, a rich and powerful man," but not, "I wish I were a shopkeeper from across the street, Juan or Pedro, any old Joe with no notoriety attached to my family name."

I can understand someone saying, "I'd like to be a bootblack or sell lottery tickets."

I can understand Romeo and Juliet's love, as I understand Silva's hatred for Hernani, and I understand the magnanimity of forgiveness, but I fail to grasp feelings which arise from nothing energetic or forceful, nothing terrible or tender.

I can understand there being people who say, "I wish I were

Mitre,[7] favorite son of fortune and glory, or just an acolyte at the San Juan church!"

But that anyone should say, "I'd like to be Colonel Mansilla," this is beyond me. For who is that old boy, anyway?

To General Arredondo,[8] my immediate superior at the time, I owe, dear Santiago, the immense pleasure of having eaten an ostrich egg omelet in Nagüel Mapo, of having touched the extremes once again. Had he not given me permission, I'd have been left with the mere hankering to go and not beaten you to it. I will always be grateful to him for having shown me that deference, and for having confided to me he thought it a risky undertaking, proving thereby that he was not indifferent to its outcome. It takes a friend to refuse to let another die an obscure and pointless death.

The new border of the province of Córdoba is no longer where you left it when you last passed through San Luis. The new line lies at the Quinto, that is to say, it has advanced twenty-five leagues. At last you can cross the Cuarto to Achiras without drawing up a will and making your last confession.

Many thousands of square leagues have been conquered. How lovely the land lying between the Cuarto and Quinto rivers for raising cattle! Indian barley, common beans, clover, and grasses all grow lush and fresh among the pasture lands; great hollows such as the Gato Gorge; long, plentiful streams such as the Santa Catalina and the Sampacho; deep and inexhaustible lagoons such as Chemecó, Tarapendá, and Santo Tomé provide an incalculably bountiful source of wealth.[9]

More than six thousand leagues have I ridden in a year-and-a-half's time to survey and study this land. No stream, spring, lagoon, hill, or dune did I leave unobserved as I personally went about determining approximate positions and getting the lay of the land, it being my understanding that a soldier's first duty is to know the whole span of land in which he one day must needs operate. Indeed, can there be a sadder lot than that of a commander who, given a duty to carry out, is then entrusted to some poor country fellow, who may guide him well but cannot suggest the first strategic idea?

The new border of Córdoba begins at San Luis and, following the Quinto River, continues on to Ramada Nueva, my own name for the new extension. The Ranquels call it Trapalcó. *Trapal* is cattail and *co* is water, and it comprises the watershed of the Quinto. Following the judicious plan of the Spaniards,[10] I established this line by placing the main forts on the south side of the Quinto. On an international border this would have been a military error, since obstacles should always be placed at the vanguard so that the enemy be made to overcome them first. But in the war with the Indians this problem takes on a different character, for this is an enemy who must be confronted with obstacles not to getting in but to getting out.

The foremost fort on the new border along the Quinto is called Sarmiento. There the road begins, passing through Laguna del Cuero and leading on to Leubucó, the center of the Ranquel settlements. It was from there I set out.

I will continue tomorrow.

Today I have dallied in certain details which I felt might not be altogether uninteresting to you. If this should hold true as well for the public with whom I am sharing this letter, I shall sleep as contentedly and peacefully as a schoolboy who has studied his lesson and knows it well.

But how can I tell?

So often we believe we can rouse our listeners to laughter and then they just sit there unmoved.

Which is why I hold that all human wisdom is contained in the inscription on the temple at Delphi.

 FOR SOME TIME I had been mulling over the idea of going into Indian territory.

My dealings with Indians coming and going to and from Río Cuarto to carry on peace negotiations had awakened an indescribable curiosity in me.

It takes going through certain things, finding oneself in certain positions, to comprehend the vigor with which ideas may take hold of certain men; it takes all this to understand how a mission to the Ranquels could become for a more or less civilized man like myself as vehement a desire as a secretariat in the Parisian embassy could be for any middling minister. Time, that great instrument of endeavors good and evil, whose course we should like to hasten by anticipating events—only then to be sunken or devoured by them—had led me to enter into a number of relationships which I may dare call intimate.

The Indian woman Carmen, twenty-five years old, lovely and astute, was attached to one of the last commissions with which I pursued negotiations.[1] She became my friend and confidante, strengthening these ties through the baptism of an ill-begotten baby daughter who accompanied her, the ceremony for which took place in Río Cuarto in full regalia and with a great many people in attendance. I left the children with an indelible memory of my munificence that night when I threw twenty-five Bolivian pesos into the air for them to scurry after, all to the inevitable chorus of shouts: "We cleaned old godfather out!"

No one who has not yet had the pleasure of being an "old godfather" can easily understand how unforgettable such a night can be, especially for any sorry mortal of negligible historical import and no title by which his name might pass to posterity, engraved in flaming characters in the golden book of history.

Wait, you have been an old godfather at some time. You know.

Carmen's addition to the Ranquel commission or embassy as an interpreter, which is as good as saying secretary or minister plenipotentiary, was not without its purpose. Mariano Rosas[2]— no mere boy, after all—has studied the human heart and knows the likes and leanings of the Christians. By an instinct common both to civilized peoples and to savages, he places great trust in the effect of a woman on a man, even if she stand reduced to the saddest of circumstances.

So it was that Carmen was dispatched with her packet of official and confidential instructions by the Talleyrand[3] of the desert and for some time exercised her charge with considerable craft and skill. Not so well, however, that I should fail, despite my natural guilelessness, to sense the complexity of her mission, so that had I been contending with another Hernán Cortés,[4] it might have been perilous, indeed fatal, for me, gravely discrediting my frontier government.

I will spare you the endless details, though they would give evidence of the blandishments to which the diplomacy of a frontier captain is susceptible, especially where secretaries of the caliber of my comadre Carmen are involved. I will only say that this time Mariano's book of human experience went up in smoke, it being Carmen herself who initiated me in the secrets of his mission. In short, we became close friends, and I owe the creditable reputation which preceded my triumphant entry into Leubucó to her good offices.

I secured one further intimate connection in the final negotiations.

Chief Ramón, leader of the Indians of Rincón, had sent an elder brother of his to me in testimony of his desire to be my friend.[5] Linconao, as this man is called, is an Indian lad about twenty-two years old, tall, vigorous, of pleasant countenance, graceful bearing, and gentle character. He distinguishes himself from the other Indians in not habitually asking for handouts.

The Indians live among the Christians feigning poverty and need and begging. They will use the same song and dance to mooch a ration of salt as they will for a good poncho or a pair of silver spurs. To deal with such a commission means, to a frontier captain, wasting about four hours a day listening to the likes of these. Now, as I with my sanguine-bilious temperament am not the most abiding fellow in the world, it has become apparent to me that a sense of duty can fundamentally modify human nature. In some of the parliaments celebrated at Río Cuarto I more than once overpowered my interlocutors, whose ritual exordium was "you need great patience to deal with the Indians, brother."

I don't know whether you have any sense of what a parliament in Christian territory is. I say in Christian territory because on Indian land it is a different ritual.

A parliament is a diplomatic conference.

The commission announces itself in advance through the interpreter. If twenty individuals comprise the commission, all twenty introduce themselves. They begin by extending a handshake in order of rank and thereafter take their seats, with rather enough aplomb, on the chairs or sofas offered to them. The interpreter, that is, the secretary and translator, sits to the right side of the commission head. The latter speaks and the interpreter translates, it being noteworthy that even though the plenipotentiary understand Spanish and speak it with perfect ease, the rules do not change.

As long as the parliament lasts, the commission must be given gifts of liquor and cigarettes.

Never do the Indians refuse drink, and as for cigarettes, they do not smoke at table but will accept tobacco as long as it is given out.[6] But they neither drink nor smoke unless they first fully trust the good faith of the gift-giver, or until the latter has drunk or smoked first. Once trust has been established, all precautions cease and they throw their heads back and drink the proffered liquor down with no further preamble than that which their own preoccupations dictate. One of these revolves around neither eating nor drinking anything without offering the first fruits to the mysterious spirit they believe in and adore though they pay it no outward homage. They take a small pinch of whatever they must swallow or drink and exclaim, as they toss it off to one side, "This is for God!"

They more or less ward it off this way. They believe that the devil, Gualicho, is everywhere and that by giving the first offering to God, who is the stronger of the two, they accomplish the exorcism.

The parliament then begins with an endless series of salutations and questions, as, for example: How are you? How are your chiefs, officers, and soldiers? How has it gone with you since the last time we met? Has there been any news from the frontier? Did you not lose some of your horses along the way?

Whereupon the messages ensue, as for example: My brother, or my father, or my cousin has instructed me to tell you it would please him to know that you are well in the company of all your chiefs, officers, and soldiers, that he very much wishes to meet you, that he has heard many good things about you, that he has learned that you seek peace and that this proves you believe in God and possess an excellent heart.

Sometimes each interlocutor has his own translator. Other times they share one. In the least significant of parliaments, the translator's work calls for utter probity. He must have a great memory, exceptional vocal chords, and boundless calm and patience. For it is nothing at all to have to repeat the same thing ten or twenty times before coming to the point.

When the greetings, compliments, and messages have ended, matters of importance are brought forward and when these end, the chapter on complaints and requests, a fertile one indeed, begins.

Any parliament will last a couple of hours. Ordinarily, several of the speakers will be snoring before much time has passed. Since the only one who bears responsibility for the matters aired is the delegation head, those accompanying him state their business and, having no further interest or stake in the doings and no license to leave, start yawning and finally fall asleep, at which point their potentate, sensing the folly of it all, requests permission to finish and withdraw. He promises, though, to return soon, as he yet has much to say.

Linconao suffered a powerful attack of the pox at the same

time as a number of other Indians did.[7] They brought me news of
this, and since he was an Indian of some prominence and much-
recommended character, an Indian to whom I had taken a liking, I
resolved at once to go see him.

Using tents which I had given them, the Indians had set up camp
on the banks of a lovely stream that fed the Cuarto. There on a
cool, green strip of land bespeckled with wildflowers, they had
pitched their tents in two rows that sat white and buoyant upon
the verdant ground. Each awaited me with somber, sodden, and
terrified countenance. The human spectacle stood in stark contrast
to the gay face of nature and the fair countryside. Linconao and
other Indians lay writhing on the ground in their tents, desperate
with fever. Their companions waited in a group at a distance. They
did not have the nerve to approach the pox victims, much less
touch them. Behind me came a cart I had brought along expressly
to carry them.

I first went over to Linconao, then to the other afflicted ones. I
spoke to all of them, rousing them, and called several of their companions over to help lift them to the cart, but as none of them
obeyed me I had to do it myself with the help of the soldier who
was pulling the cart.

Linconao was naked, his body ravaged with horrid virulence by
the pox. I will confess that upon touching him I felt one of those
shudders that rocks our fragile and cowardly nature whenever we
face danger. When my hands came in contact with his grainy skin,
it was as if a poisoned file had cut me, but the first step had been
taken and it was neither noble nor worthy, neither human nor
Christian, to retreat. So Linconao was hoisted to the cart by me,
his body brushing against my face.

Here was a true triumph of civilization over barbarism, of Christianity over idolatry.[8]

The Indians were profoundly impressed; they fairly babbled in
praise of my daring and called me their father. They have a truly
panic fear of the pox which, whether by cutaneous circumstance
or because of their blood, attacks them with lethal fury. When the
pox appears among the Indians, the tents get moved from one
place to another and the terrified families will flee great distances
to avoid the infested sites. Fathers, sons, and daughters, mothers
and loved ones are left to their misfortune, nor is anything done
for them other than to place several days' supply of food and water
around their beds.

The poor savages see in the pox a scourge sent from above by God as a punishment for their sins. I have seen numerous cases of it and survival is rare indeed, despite the excellent ministrations of our division surgeon, Dr. Michaut.

Linconao was attended to in my home. A patient and affectionate nurse cared for him there and all took an interest in saving him, which happily we were able to do. Chief Ramón has conveyed to me his most ardent gratitude for the care lavished on his brother, who for his part says that after God I am his father, for he owes his life to me.

All of these circumstances, then, plus the considerations mentioned in my previous letter, were pushing me towards the desert. Once I resolved to make the expedition, I maintained the utmost secrecy about it. Everyone watched the preparations, everyone conjectured, no one guessed it.

Only a certain friar friend of mine knew my secret.

And this time the moralist's maxim—that one should tell no one that which he wishes kept secret—did not hold true. The fact is that humanity, say what you will about it, has many good qualities, among them loyalty and discretion.

I assume you concur with me and with that I will say good-bye until tomorrow.

 THE FRANCISCAN FRIAR Marcos Donatti alone knew my secret. I had divulged it to him on the way from Fort Sarmiento to Tres de Febrero, another fort on the extreme right of the border line that follows the River Quinto.

Friar Marcos is a priest whose evangelical virtues combine with his wonderfully gentle character. He used to travel the length of the two borders of my command, saying mass on makeshift altars, baptizing, and preaching the holy word to the poor wives of poor soldiers. Every woman who heard him made her confession forthwith.[1]

It was a beautiful night, a night in which the stellar world shone in all its magnificence. No shroud of clouds hid the moon, and now and then as we neared the bluffs along the Quinto, whose winding course the road follows, we would see her portrait in the moving mirror of the river. The Quinto rises in the upper Córdoba sierra, runs in a curve from east to west and, like the Segundo of Córdoba, replenishes with its rich waters the great pastures of Villa Mercedes, only to disappear among the impassable gorges of Amarga.

We were approaching Lechuzo Pass, famous for its frequent use during the sadly memorable era of Indian depredations. There is a hill about half a mile wide there. It is thick with broad, dense trees. By a certain rational instinct to forestall danger, the fantasy-prone traveler will hurry through these woods. Lechuzo Pass, with its all too foreboding name,[2] is an excellent place for an ambush and the subject of many a strange tale of Indian deeds and misdeeds.

We crossed it at a trot, horses and riders alike whipped by branches; emerging from the woods I spurred my horse on and, with a "C'mon, Father" to Brother Marcos, took off at a gallop, followed by the good Franciscan. He had then and has now no other flaw than to have once abused an excellent Moor I lent him.

My assistant and the three soldiers accompanying me stayed behind and heard nothing of our conversation.

Father Marcos's imagination was full of ideas he had gotten from the gauchos who have gone to live among the Indians, whether by choice or as captives. He considered my enterprise extremely dangerous, not only because it imperiled my life, but because of the Punic faith of the natives. "Very well, Colonel," he said, "but don't leave me behind when you go. You know I am a missionary."

I have kept my promise and he his word.

We prepared for the trek at Fort Sarmiento, where a commission of Indians led by Achauentrú was for the moment in residence. Achauentrú is a diplomat of stature among the Ranquels. He has himself described his services to me.

As you can imagine, preparation came down to just a few things. Essential to any trip through the pampas are your horses. A good mount is everything, for there is no end of animals to rope, ostriches, doe, guanacos, hares, mountain lions, armadillos, or *piches*, or *matacos* to hunt.

When you have food to eat in the open country, you have everything.

Despite this, I made more formal preparations. I had to pack two loads of gifts and another of some very rich beef jerky, as well as sugar, salt, mate, and coffee. If anyone took any other sweets along they must have eaten them on the first day, because we never saw any of it. The rest of getting ready consisted of properly putting together saddle and gear for everyone going along, lest there be travelers without hopple, bridle and bit, and other essentials. Nor did we spare any pains in grooming the horses and trimming their hooves.

When I get ready for a trip one thing concerns me above all else: the horses. As for the rest of it, anyone going along can take care of all that. It goes without saying that no one who wants to be on good terms with me would ever think of traveling without a couple of good water skins. And rightly so. Water is usually scarce in the pampas and nothing discourages and demoralizes like thirst. I have lasted seventy-two hours without eating, but never more than thirty-two without water. Our country folk have an incredible endurance in this regard. Truly there is no fatigue they will not endure. They'll bear any inclemency, be it sun, rain, heat, or cold, with never so much as a whimper. And, just when they seem saddest, they'll break into some flip little tune. We are a privileged race, a wholesome and solid one, docile to all teaching worth our while and all progress that suits our spirit and genius. On this matter, dear friend Santiago, my opinion has changed greatly since the days when, three thousand leagues removed from here, we so passionately discussed the unity of the human species and the historical fatality of the races. I believed then that the Greco-Latin peoples had come into the world not to practice liberty and teach it through their institutions but to battle constantly for it. And, if memory serves me well, I used to cite noble Spain, struggling since Roman times, now to throw off foreign domination, now to create free institutions for herself.[3]

I see things differently now. I believe in the unity of the human species and the influence of bad governments. Politics, powerful springboard to human action that it is, nurtures and modifies our customs imperceptibly and prepares and consummates great revolutions that either raise the edifice on lasting girders or undermine it altogether. Moral forces dominate physical ones constantly and hold both the key to, and the explanation of, social phenomena.

Only when packed and ready did I announce to those forming my company that the following day we would head south along the Cuero road and that there was a chance we might reach Leubucó before we rested our horses.

Later I had the Indian Achauentrú called in and related my idea to him.

He showed great surprise at my resolution and asked me if I had sent word of it ahead to Mariano Rosas. He tried to talk me out of it, suggesting something might befall me and that the Indians, though good people who loved me greatly, nevertheless respected no one when drunk. I made my own observations to him. I described to him the need I saw for peace talks with the chiefs and the immense good that could come of a classic show of confidence such as I intended to give them.

A single thought had taken hold of me above all others: to prove to the Indians through an act of sheer boldness that we Christians are braver than they and more confident when our honor is at stake.[4]

The Indians accuse us of bad faith and endlessly tell stories in which they try to prove that we deceive and distrust them.

Achauentrú knows. He understood not only that my resolve was unshakable and that I would most certainly leave the next day, but also some of the reasons I presented. He therefore offered me many letters of recommendation and as a special favor requested that I send a scout ahead from the Cuero road to warn of my arrival, first so that the Indians would not be alarmed, second so that I would be properly received. To that end I asked for an Indian guide and he gave me one named Angelito, who was nothing of the sort. A name and the man who bears it are decidedly not the same thing.

After speaking with me, Achauentrú went to have a talk with Father Marcos and his companion, Father Moisés Alvarez, a young Franciscan from Córdoba blessed with noble traits and whom I respect for his character and love for his good heart. They all returned shortly, were quite upset, and said that, to a man, the Indians and the translators considered my expedition too daring, too fraught with danger and obstacles. Evidently, what tormented their thoughts the most was their own fate, should I be mistreated or held captive in the desert. Later I sent word back to them (for they were staying behind as hostages) not to worry. If the Indians mistreated me, the hostages would not be harmed. If they killed me, the hostages would not be sacrificed. Only if the Indians should refuse to release me would the hostages then also be denied the freedom to return to their land, passing instead into my possession and that of my officers and soldiers. I believe there were eight of them, while nineteen would be traveling with my group.

I entreated the fathers to make them understand that these were just and moral ideas.

They quieted down. Having dealt with them for months on end

without ever once deceiving or misleading them; having treated them the way God made me—sometimes good, sometimes bad, for my mood depends on my stomach and how well I happen to digest my food—I had won their complete trust in my word. Indeed, how many times did their expressions of confidence not reach my ears in and about the dispensaries. "That Colonel Mansilla, him good, him not lie, not cheat poor Indian."

The day and the moment of departure arrived at last. Fort Sarmiento was in revolt. Soldiers and women surrounded my house to bid me farewell—*sans adieu!*—and wish me Godspeed. They perhaps believed inwardly that I wouldn't return. Warmth and understanding and respect will exaggerate the peril to which those not unobliging to us may seem exposed. Fear reigns more freely in the imagination than in the things that finally must happen. Just when everyone expected to see the horses and mules lined up and us choose, saddle, and pack our mounts and get under way, the bugler sounded a double-quick call, an unusual one for that time of day.

The word spread instantly: Indians!

For a moment every face looked visibly shaken.

The soldiers ran with their weapons to the stables.

Almost immediately there sounded the troop call and just as quickly the garrison's forces fell to, the Twelfth Battalion was mounted on its handsome mules and the Seventh Cavalry on good mounts with its complement of riflemen.

At the same time that the troops had been hurrying into formation, the mess officers received orders to take up arms, and the women to gather in the clubhouse El Progreso en la Pampa, which the chiefs and officers were building and which has a fine billiards table and other comforts.[5] The Indians were told not to leave the ranch they were lodged at and the mess officers to take custody of Indians and women alike.

While all this was going on inside the fort, a great commotion reigned on the outside, where horses, cattle, everything, every four-legged creature, was forced from its feeding area and rounded up. The Indians had unquestionably invaded, or so went the scuttlebutt. Achauentrú was stupefied by it all, and didn't know whether the raid was an outgoing or an incoming one. When everything was ready, my second-in-command received orders to head out with the troops and march one league south, where I conducted a general review.

I had to see before I left how quickly the garrison could pull together, so I staged this whole alarm and had a laugh on the Indians, who for their part had a truly wretched time of it, not knowing what was going on or what to believe.

Let it be said in praise of all those who at that time were garrisoned at Fort Sarmiento that I had the military satisfaction of seeing everything carried out with calm and dispatch.

May God watch over my comrades-in-arms, my brothers in danger, sacrifice, and glory, while I am away; and may He watch over you as well, dear Santiago, and keep your mood easy and your stomach a living tribute to Brillat-Savarin.[6]

 EVERYTHING WAS READY by five in the afternoon. My people received orders to hand over all weapons but their sabers, which were to be placed unsheathed between the saddle bags. My assistants and I carried revolvers and a shotgun. As great as my desire was to approach the natives with neither fanfare nor ostentation, I could not bring myself to do it completely unarmed. The time might come when we would have to give up our lives, and it was only fitting that we sell dearly. There is an idea to which no man, save a saint, is finally resigned, and that is to sacrifice himself with the submissiveness of a lamb.

When all weapons were turned in, I had the horses and mules brought out. I formed four squadrons, gave each a string of horses, and left one in reserve. I gave orders to pack gear and saddle up, and half an hour later, with the sunset of the last day of March retreating radiantly on a distant horizon, I placed foot in stirrup and climbed into the saddle.

Several chiefs and officers had saddled up to accompany me a certain distance.

I left the fort amidst the rousing cheers and kindly smiles of the soldiers, and not one of them but worried some at our leaving, particularly Achauentrú, who rode over to embrace me, recite his litany of caveats, and remind me for the thousandth time not to forget to send a scout ahead announcing my arrival.

The Cuero road runs through Fort Sarmiento, which is the new name for the old and well-known Arganas Pass.[1] Actually a network of trails, this road runs southeast or, as they say in the savvy language of Córdoba, south and down.

They have a peculiar way of naming certain things, though only in practice do the advantages become clear. They call west "up," east "down." This allows for greater ease and clarity of expression because of the similarity of the words east and west. For example, if to get from point A to point B or, to put it more clearly, from Villa del Río Cuarto to Fort Sarmiento, going across the countryside, you were to ask a local scout for directions, he would point the way as follows: Looking southward and pointing with his right hand, he would say, "Head straight south on this line and travel down some, but just slightly down."

Now those are directions that anyone used to traveling in the open country can use to make straight as an arrow for his destination. If to get from Río Cuarto to Achiras in November, for example, when the sun tends to set towards the south, you were to ask directions here, the answer would go something like this: "Go straight up, line yourself up with the sunset and right where you see that peak, that's Achiras."

How can you go wrong with directions like that?

This custom of the Córdobans of calling east down and west up has given our provinces their designation as being either upland or downland, and the inhabitants as uplanders and downlanders. Besides the advantages this way of speaking offers, there is an underlying geographical circumstance. To go west or east from Córdoba is to go, in effect, either up or down, since the land rises further and further above sea level as one travels our country from coast to sierra; the land folds visibly, so that the westbound traveler climbs and the eastbound traveler descends.

I mentioned that the Cuero road is a great network of trails, a *rastrillada*, and I want to explain what I mean by that. *Rastrillada* is the name we give to the sinuous, parallel grooves which the Indians, with all their comings and goings, have worn into the ground. These ruts resemble the first tracks of wagon wheels in virgin terrain, are generally deep, and form a truly broad and solid roadway. There is no other in the midst of the pampas. To stray but a foot from them, to leave the trail, often poses a real danger, for it is not unusual to find, right beside the well-worn trail, a kind of sinkhole or bog in which a horse and rider may be entirely buried.

Guadal is the name we give to this soft and shifting terrain which for want of frequent treading has not been packed firm. The word is not in the Spanish dictionary, though we have taken it from our ancestors. It comes from the Arabic and means *water* or *river*.

The pampas are full of these obstacles.

Many is the time an entire military column has simply vanished while in pursuit of the Indians!

Many is the time a negligible stretch of land has allowed the enemy to mock the advances of some otherwise quite fearless captains in those endless pampas!

Many is the time the Indians themselves have perished under the saber blades of our brave frontier soldiers after falling into the miry *guadal.*

So vast are the pampas that even the most seasoned riders sometimes get lost in them.

The Indians' horses are something special in the pampas. They run through the sandy mire, fall and get up again and, incredibly, are never overcome by the herculean fatigue of it. They are trained on that terrain and are used to it.[2]

The quagmires are damp and then again they are dry, a swampy muck or loose sand. Only the eye that has seen them over and over again can know the *guadales.* Now the grass, now the color of the ground are the sure signs. But generally, they are an ambush for Indians and Christians alike. A horse that goes in there unaccustomed to them will struggle for an instant to get out and with such monumental effort that even on the coldest days it gives up, prostrate and sweat-covered, nor is there spur or whip that can get it back on its feet. Horses ultimately acquire such a fear of the *guadales* that often no power on heaven or earth will goad them forward should they step on the shifting borders of the trail. And mind you, the horse is the bravest of all the quadrupeds destined to serve man. At spur, a horse will bolt like lightning across the highest cliffs.

How unlike the horse is the mule! Never does she lose her aplomb. Whether along pampean trails or on the dizzying ridges of the sierra, our hybrid is ever cautious. The horse darts like lightning; the mule tests before proceeding. She places one forehoof, then the other, and is so wary that only where her front legs have gone will she place the other two. There is no use warning her of danger. She will obey neither spur, rein, nor strap. Her instinct for self-preservation is her sole mover. One need not try driving her. She goes where she wants to go. If she dies going over a cliff, it will not have been out of blind boldness, as it would for a horse, but merely out of miscalculation.

When the open land is covered with water, it becomes more

crucial than ever to keep strictly to the horse trails, for the damp terrain makes the danger of the *guadales* an imminent one at every step.

When we left Sarmiento it had rained plentifully. There is a break in the terrain half a league from there where the land falls away to a ravine that is all quagmire. I called a halt there, said my farewells and parted with my comrades and, after some general words of counsel to those coming with me, headed out, with my guide on the left following one track while I followed another.

How sorrowful to leave loyal companions! I read it in their faces, though they tried to hide behind affable smiles and warm handshakes. You see, only we soldiers know what it is to see friends depart for dangers that hold here a fall, there a death, while we stay behind. . . . And only the soldier knows what it is to see his brothers return from combat, whole and unharmed, on a day when it has fallen to him to wait behind while they go! There are mysteries in the human heart, utter abysses of love, abnegation, and generosity, that words will never quite explain. There is naught for us but to know this and keep still, which is why a gaze, an embrace, a motion of the hand say more than the most artfully wielded pen can ever describe.

We were still short of crossing the ravine when night caught up with us. The moon was tarrying, the sky was blanketed in clouds, the stars were nowhere in sight. So we walked for a long while in total darkness, falling, and getting back up each time we erred our course and stepped to the edge of the *guadales*. The mules carrying the jerky and gifts for the chiefs gave us great labor. They no sooner fled danger than found it again and fell. One of them was carrying the sacred ornaments of my friends the Franciscans[3] and we proceeded, praying every step of the way that no one would shout, "The mule with the priests' stuff just fell!"

We had to muzzle all the mules and lead them along by their halters. We lost time doing this and it was late when we reached Laguna Alegre. Our mounts were so exhausted from the night trek through more or less four leagues of darkness and water that I resolved to stop and await either clearer skies or moonlight.

We camped . . . and soon the fire glowed and soon everyone with me formed a circle around it. As we sipped our mate, each one of us told a more or less soporific tale.

We had anything on our minds but the Indians.

I told my story. A certain Private Gómez who died in the glori-

ous Paraguayan War was the subject. There is something fantastic
and awe-inspiring about his story. If I am in the mood for it tomorrow, and if you are not tired of my digressions or in a hurry to
reach Leubucó, I will tell you his story, too.

 THE CAMP FIRE is every poor soldier's delight
in the aftermath of fatigue. Military rank dis-
appears in its glow. Superiors and subordinates
converse fraternally, laugh heartily. Even the
cook and the aides who only brew the mate will
dip their spoon in the crock now and then, so to speak, whether to
back up their chiefs and officers or gainsay them, whether to talk
horse sense or nonsense.

As my assistant, Calixto Oyarzábal, finished his story, to the
chagrin of his audience—for Calixto is a prize rascal who could
make an Englishman laugh out loud—the company all looked at
me. It was my turn.

I was in good spirits and, after a few barbs at Calixto, I began
my tale, which goes roughly as follows:

Private Gómez came from Corrientes. He was one of those who
stayed in Buenos Aires when Urquiza first marched on it and the
Rosas dictatorship was overthrown.[1] Gómez was perhaps thirty-
five years old; he was tall, robust, and had a certain graceful sway
to his gait. His complexion was somewhere between white and sallow, with that peculiar hue of the tropical races. He spoke with a
Guaraní accent, as they generally do in that area. In short, a congenial and manly sort was Gómez.

He marched to the Paraguayan War[2] with the First Battalion,
First Regiment of the National Guard, which left Buenos Aires under the orders of Commander Cobo, if memory serves me. Gómez,
at any rate, belonged to Captain Garmendia's grenadiers. One day
a directive appeared in the General Orders for the Second Army
Corps of Paraguay, to which I belonged, saying: "Private Manuel
Gómez, four years front-line duty for insubordination."

Later an officer in my command arrived with a message: "I have
come to hand over high-ranking personnel to you." After taking
care of a few errands, I had the "personnel" brought before me
for interrogation, recrimination, and assignment to whatever company would best suit him.

It was Gómez and, as I saw it, his slim build made him ideal for the grenadiers.

José Antonio Garmendia and I often dined together in Paraguay, and following the afternoon muster he could always be found in my area, along with Maximio Alcorta, another good friend of ours who, excellent comrade though he is, is as passionate for the ugly sex as he is for the fair one and has a bedeviling knack for sending us, every now and then, people who have his highest esteem but who soon display a shiftier side.

Garmendia and I were eating together the day they sent us Gómez. As we sat at the table—or so we call a *yatay* log in the army—he told me that Gómez had been a private in his company, that he was a good man, indeed a humble and obedient sort, and that his transgression had been caused by drunkenness. He added that Gómez was prone to lose his head when inebriated; lose it, that is, to the point where he would become frenzied if contradicted. The best thing to do at such times was to treat him gently, as Garmendia said he had done always with success. In short, Garmendia recommended Gómez to me with all the energy a great heart such as his—everyone close to him loves him for it—can muster.

Gómez's manly presence and Garmendia's recommendations predisposed me, I scarcely need say, in favor of the newcomer. I in turn recommended him to the captain of the grenadiers, informing the latter of everything Garmendia had told me.

Time passed . . .

Gómez performed his duties in strict obedience. Circumspect and quiet, he minded his own business, bothered nobody. He had the officers' admiration and, with the figure he cut, commanded the soldiers' respect.

I can see him now. On Saturdays I would review the troops, and there would be Gómez, statuesque and foursquare, serious, melancholic, his rifle gleaming, strap shining, and all his gear splendidly arrayed.

He soon regained his rank.

Some five months had passed.

One day, an August day as I recall, I was walking the length of the shadow cast by my lodgings, which consisted of a handsome covered wagon. This was in the famous Tuyutí[3] encampment. What I was thinking about I don't recall in the least. Perhaps love claimed my thoughts at the moment, or glory—those, at any rate, are the two great subjects of a soldier's reflections. I only recall that as I turned, a voice shook me out of the abstractions into which I had plunged. I looked behind me and there at about six paces stood Gómez at attention, saluting, rocking forward and back, then to the left, then the right, as though threatening to lose his center of gravity. His eyes shone with a fire I had never seen in him.

I knew at once he was drunk.

It was the first time since he had entered the battalion.

Moved both by affection and by Garmendia's warnings, I spoke to him as follows:

"What do you want, my friend?"

"I came to see you, Commander. I want to request liberty . . . sir."

"And why do you want liberty?"

"I want to go to Itapirú to visit a sister of mine who came from La Esquina to see me."

"But son, you're not clear-headed right now."

"Sure I am, sir. Nothin' wrong with me."

"All right, then, wait a while and I'll sign you a pass. How's that?"

"Good, good."

With that he began a laborious about-face and tried to salute properly. Then he spun on his heels and withdrew.

Evening came and with it Garmendia. I told him Gómez had gotten drunk for the first time. He said he had probably done it to overcome his fear of speaking to his commander, as Garmendia had known him to do several times when Gómez was in his battalion. As we were both curious about Gómez, we decided to find out how long he had been drunk when he came to see me.

I called for the captain of the grenadiers and asked him a few questions, which yielded precisely the conclusion Garmendia had come to, namely, that Gómez had drunk in order to summon the courage to approach me. Starting with his company sergeant and working his way up to the captain, he had requested permission to speak to me from each of them, one by one, and had been stone cold sober each time. Otherwise they would have refused him.

The day after this incident Gómez was clear-headed again. I was about to call him over but noticed at parade formation that he had drawn guard duty. I decided to wait. When he had finished I called for him and asked him if he still wanted liberty.

He could only answer with silence and red-faced shame.

"For how long do you want your liberty, Private?"

"Two days, Commander."

"Fine. You can leave now. Be back tomorrow at assembly."

"Very good, sir."

With this he saluted respectfully and later that day set out for Itapirú. Two days later, as the troops assembled, as they cheerfully assembled, Private Gómez was back in camp after his visit with his sister. He had had more than a whiff of firewater and was carrying bread-cakes, cheese, and cigars which he quickly proceeded to pass out to his brothers-in-arms.

I got my share, too, an excellent Goya cheese[4] which his sister, whom I did not know, sent along for me.

There is nothing in the world so good, so pure, so generous as a soldier!

Time passed.

We marched from Tuyutí to Curuzú to launch the famous assault of Curupaití. Came the memorable day and, at late hour, my battalion received orders to advance on the trenches.

The order was carried out.

It was all hell and all fire. The men who weren't falling dead were falling wounded and every survivor counted his life in minutes. Bullets showered on us from all sides. Crowning the grandeur of that solemn and terrible canvas of blood was the thunderous din in which we fought, as the cannons blasted ceaselessly on. A mere five minutes into the fray my battalion's losses were already serious and many dead and wounded lay covered in blood shed intrepidly for their country's flag. While riding from one end to the other I found Private Gómez. He was wounded in one knee but kneeling on the other and firing away.

"Withdraw, Private," I told him.

"No, Commander," he answered. "I'm still all right," and continued to load his rifle as I went on my way.

Returning from the outermost point of my right flank back to the left, I again passed Gómez's spot. He had taken a second bullet, this one in the other leg, and was now lying prone and firing.

"Private, for God's sake pull out. That's an order," I said.

"I will when you do, Commander," he answered and, letting an oath fly, added, "Paraguayans, look out!"

Drunk with the smell of gunpowder and blood, he fired and loaded his rifle in split seconds, as if unhurt.

Here was a man with the bravery and serenity of a lion.

I ordered several men with lighter injuries who were withdrawing to take Gómez with them and continued towards the left flank.

The assault was a prolonged one . . .

As I was delivering an order I was hit in the shoulder by a piece of shrapnel and did not return to the trenches. A few minutes later the army withdrew, bespattered with the blood of heroes but covered with glory.

To take roll we had to inquire after the fate of each and every comrade in the battalion, one of the saddest military ceremonies. It is a review in which the living answer for the dead, the whole of limb for the wounded. Who has not felt a tightness in his bosom after combat as this solemn act proceeds?

"Juan Paredes!"

"Present!"

"Pedro Torres!"

"Wounded!"

"Luis Corro!"

"Dead!"

Oh, but that word "dead" has a sting you have to feel to understand in all its bitterness. All the usual inquiries and investigations carried out during review led us to conclude that Private Gómez had died and we left it at that. Visits ordered to all of the blood hospitals turned up no sign of him. For my part, I had serious doubts whether Gómez was dead. He was wounded, I believed, and a prisoner.

The soldiers all said, "No, sir, Private Gómez is dead. We saw him lying face down when we were pulling out of the trenches with the flag."

I felt the death of my soldiers as one feels eternal separation from loved ones, but I must confess that of all the soldiers who succumbed on that day of imperishable memory, it was Private Gómez whom I missed the most. The attitude of this obscure man, outstretched on his stomach, wounded in both legs and fighting with the sacred ardor of the warrior, was etched indelibly in my memory, nor will it ever fade. I will lose it only when the years have made me forget everything.

That is all for today. Tomorrow I'll pick up where I left off. Today I simply told you the death of a living man. Tomorrow I will tell you the life of a dead man.

If you found today's part interesting, you'll find tomorrow's so as well.

The men around the camp fire hearing my story saw it that way.

 THE ARMY AGAIN took up its position in Tu-
yutí, my battalion its familiar place. Talk of the
assault on Curupaití was for some time the order of the day, whether to criticize it or to remember the heroes who fell there. With the passing
of time, new battles, other dangers, we gradually forgot the noble
victims.

Only the memory of our loved ones persists in the spirit; there is
neither pain nor joy before which their cherished image fades.

From time to time, the hospitals of Itapirú, Corrientes, and
Buenos Aires would send us fresh platoons of men whose glorious
and mortal wounds had healed. It was a time of bitter daily fighting, when humanity and science performed true miracles. A time
of innumerable and horribly mutilated battlefield wounded who
returned mere days later, poised with renewed vigor to wield the
avenging sword. Corpsmen and trusted officers of their choosing
made periodical reviews of the hospitals, took note of the sick and
wounded and tended to their needs as best they could. I had frequent news from the hospitals in Itapirú and Corrientes. Our patients were faring well. I expected the release of some of them any
day now.

It was perhaps these concerns which, on a certain morning, occupied my thoughts as I took my customary walk along the para-
pets of the battery upon which our eloquent and fateful cannons
stood, their mouths aimed at a little hillock called Yataití-Corá. As
I walked, an aide approached me with news:

"There is one new release from the hospital, sir."

His face betrayed surprise.

"Who is it, then?"

"One of the dead, sir."

"Which one of the dead?"

"Private Gómez."

I literally jumped from the parapet with joy and anticipation.
Word of Gómez's revival had already spread through camp. When
I reached Rancho Mayoría, a group of onlookers was blocking the
doorway. They let me through and I went in. There, leaning on his
rifle, his knapsack strapped to his back, stood Private Gómez. His
clothes were in complete tatters, his face was pale, he had grown
very thin and was hard to recognize.

He did, in fact, look risen from the dead.

I embraced him and ordered at once that we throw a dance that night in celebration of the resurrection of a comrade and the return of our first casualty.

The battalion was in an uproar. Everyone wanted to see the private at the same time. Some signaled to him with their heads, others with their hands. The ones who couldn't see him well climbed atop the coping. No one dared interrupt me to speak to him.

"So how have you been doing, man?"

"Fine, Commander."

"Where are his release papers?" I asked the officer in charge of Rancho Mayoría.

He handed them to me, and when I noticed they came from a Brazilian hospital, I turned back to Gómez.

"You mean you have been in a Brazilian hospital?"

"Yes, sir."

"And how did you survive Curupaití? When I ordered you to leave the trench you were wounded in both legs. You couldn't move."

"Commander, when the rest of the company pulled out with the flag and I saw that nobody was coming for me, because they couldn't see me or hear me, I dragged myself the best I could and hid under some straw. I figured I'd make my move at night."

"And how did you get away?"

"When our people pulled out, sir, the Paraguayans came out of their trenches and began to strip the wounded and dead. I was alive, but badly wounded. When I saw that they were killing off some of the wounded who were pretty much gone but still in pain, I decided to play outright dead. I figured they might leave me alone. They never touched me. They were walking around nearby but they never saw me. Later on, when it got real dark, I pulled myself together and got halfways up and pulled myself along by my rifle. This rifle here, sir."

A profound silence reigned at that moment. Nobody dared breathe lest they miss a single word of the private's story.

"And when did you get away?"

"That night I didn't, 'cuz I don't know my way around and kept getting lost and it was awful hard to walk on account of the pain from the bullets I took. But soon as morning came I knew where I had to go, 'cuz I heard the bugle in the Brazilian camp. I followed the steam from a steamboat and came out at Curuzú. There were lots of wounded there getting on the boat. They put me on with them and took me to Corrientes and that's where I've been in the hospital but I'm pretty much all better now, Commander. I come back here 'cuz I been just achin' to see the battalion again."

"Hooray for Private Gómez!" I shouted.

"Hooray!" they answered, rascals every one and never happier than when they get stirred up and you let them raise a ruckus.

They took Private Gómez away in triumph, ribbing him a thousand different ways as they went. His unexpected arrival boosted our spirits and gave rise to general revelry for hours to come.

These scenes from military life, though frequent, are indescribable.

Garmendia came by that afternoon to share mess with me— lean roast and some wheat meal. He had by now heard from one of his aides that Private Gómez was risen. Garmendia has the fiber of a soldier and was childishly gladdened by the Gómez episode. He asked me straightaway:

"Where is he? Call him in, let's ask him how he escaped."

I told him everything the private just related to me, but he insisted on seeing his face, so I had Gómez called in.

Under Garmendia's questioning he repeated what we all now knew, with a few new details, such as that he took strips of clothing from one of the dead to tie his own wounds with the night he hid out. He also said he was sad and ashamed, because in the first moments of gunfire, on the day of Curupaití, Ensign Guevara had slapped his face, thinking he was frightened. "C'mon," the ensign had said, "stop staring down the barrel of your rifle. Fire the damn thing!"

He said he wasn't scared at all. When the ensign hit him he was only cleaning the barrel of the rifle. The scare came later when the Paraguayans left their positions and started stripping and killing the wounded. He had no strength then to defend himself and was afraid they'd finish him off before he could face them. He related all this with a captivating innocence that bespoke a heart of tempered steel. Garmendia had relished this as fully as he had Gómez's first revelations. For my part, I felt proud to count such a child among my ranks.

I confess I loved him.

That same night, under Garmendia's interminable questioning, Gómez also revealed that he once suffered from hallucinations. He told us in his faltering way, as best he could, that he had had a sweetheart in Buenos Aires when he was younger. He said she had been unfaithful to him and that he had been in jail for stabbing her.

A kind of somber shadow darkened his face as he recalled this, while his lips smiled ever so slightly.

Curiosity now sparked our interest in this crude, strong, and vigorous sort, so common in our country for that matter. Probing for the motives that had prompted our Argentine Othello to raise his hand against a woman, we managed to glean that his sweetheart had broken neither spoken agreement nor solemn oath. In his dreams, it turns out, he had seen her in his rival's arms. Now, he utterly detested his rival. When he awoke, the man wasn't there, though Gómez had seen him plainly, indeed, had stabbed him in the heart and, brought to by his sweetheart's screaming, awakened completely to find the two of them alone and his knife stuck in his beloved's chest.

This tale must be indelibly burnt into Garmendia's memory, because later that night he asked me several times whether I intended to commit it to paper. My spirit was at that time dwelling on other planes of endeavor and I never did write the story. Were it not for my excursion to the desert, Gómez's tale would remain unpublished in the archives of my memory.

There are doubtless some who believe that I am spinning fantastic yarns as the pen flies, just to keep the ink flowing and enhance the effects of these poorly wrought letters.

And yet it is all true.

The abyss between the real and the imaginary is not so deep.

One's visions can turn into a kindly or terrifying reality.

Ideas are precursors of facts.

There is greater likelihood that that which I think may be, than there is certainty that any event will repeat itself.

The old schools of philosophy posed it the opposite way.

The past proves nothing. It can serve as an example but cannot teach.

See how I wander into the forests of pedantry, where I fear I may get lost.

We spent a pleasant night thanks to Gómez.

Other impressions served as fodder for the next day's conversation. There is without question nothing more fertile for head and heart than two armies stalking each other, their cannons and rifles volleying from sunup to sundown.

For some time Gómez ceased to occupy both Garmendia's attention and my own. Yet what a dogged personality! One morning as I rode back to the redoubt, I passed as usual through old Mateo Suárez's camp. I never went through without either pulling someone's leg there or having my own pulled. As I rode by don Mateo's lodging, I learned that something unpleasant had happened in my battalion.

"Out riding around, eh, while they're killing off your mess officers back at camp?"

"Bad joke, old timer."

"Bad joke? Go find out for yourself."

Anxious and confused, I spurred my horse and left at a gallop. I was at camp in a moment.

There was no need to interrogate anybody. A man with his hands tied was roaring like a wild animal inside the brig. That tore the veil of mystery asunder for me.

"Untie that man!" I shouted with an inexplicable mixture of wrath and sorrow.

They untied him at once, the roaring ceased, and we heard only:

"I want to speak with my commander."

The field commander came forward and in a couple of words explained what had happened.

"Somebody murdered a mess officer who was visiting Ensign Guevara's quarters."

"Who did it?"

"Private Gómez."

"And who saw him?"

"Nobody, sir, but we suspect it was him; he's drunk and he's going around mumbling something about 'I swore I'd kill him. Nobody slaps this face . . . '"

I was horrified! I filled out a report without mentioning Gómez. Here I will conclude for today.

What may hold no interest in and of itself can nevertheless pique the curiosity of friends and readers alike, depending on the method followed in the telling.

For now, Private Gómez remains under arrest.

 A MAN HAD been murdered in broad daylight under a noonday sun. It had happened in a space no larger than one hundred square rods, amidst four hundred human beings with eyes to see and ears to hear. The body lay there in a steaming pool of blood, nor had anybody touched it when I entered the redoubt; and nobody, absolutely nobody could, on the unmistakable evidence of his own senses, say: So and so is your murderer. Nevertheless, everyone had a feeling it was Private Gómez and some said so outright, though none dared swear to it.

How strange and prophetic the instinct of a crowd!

As soon as I filed my report, which was limited to an account of the deed and a request for permission to proceed with a court-martial, I set about conducting my own investigation. The answers I received convinced me that Private Gómez was indeed the assassin.

Consider the man who in seeing his homeland threatened by the foreigner will march straightaway to the nation's borders with a song on his lips; who crosses rivers and mountains, harrows cannon fire, climbs walls, sacrifices everything—his time, his will, all that is dear to him, even his life; a man who springs to his feet when they shout "Get up!" at him; who marches when they shout "Forward!" and dies where he is standing when they say "Die where you stand!"; and dies perhaps in the sweetest moment of his existence, with tender letters from mother and sweetheart still fresh in his thoughts, letters hopeful in the immense goodness of God, in the ever-nearer return home. Does not such a man deserve that at one solemn instant of his life something be done on his behalf?

That something I did. And to dispel all doubt as to the author of the crime, I had the suspect brought before me and proceeded to interrogate him in the paternal and despotic manner of a superior. I had deluded myself into thinking I could draw the terrible secret from him effortlessly. The private was still under the deleterious influence of alcohol, yet lucid enough to answer all of my questions accurately.

"Gómez," I said to him affectionately, "I want to save you, but to do it I need to know if it was you who killed the man who was visiting Ensign Guevara."

Saying nothing, the private fixed his eyes on mine and made a gesture as if to say: Wait a minute while I try to remember.

I gave him some time, and when it seemed to me that the memory of something was coming to him, I pressed him.

"Come on, son, tell me the truth."

"Commander," he answered with utmost serenity, "I did not kill that man."

"Why are you deceiving me, Private?" I added, making a show of anger. "Would you lie to me?"

"No, sir."

"Swear to God."

"I swear, sir."

This scene took place far from any witnesses. The private's last reply left me speechless. I sank into meditation, resting my troubled brow on my left hand as though begging an idea of it.

I could think of nothing.

I ordered the private to retire.

He saluted, turned about, and left my presence, wearing the same expression he had when he came in. The guards were waiting a few steps away and escorted him to confinement. I called an assistant and dictated orders that Ensign Alvarez proceed at once to draw up charges.

Alvarez was the least apt of the officers for uncovering or proving whatever had happened, which is why I settled on him. Not because he might refuse me—he wouldn't—but because he had one of those impressionable imaginations that is inclined to believe anything having bizarre or unusual overtones. The private's sworn word notwithstanding, I had my doubts and was resolved to save him even if Alvarez turned up some vehemently damning evidence. So again I undertook my own investigation both to learn the truth and to mystify Alvarez. I let several people in on this on the sly. Alvarez, for his part, got right into the thick of things. He was soon as befuddled as he had ever been.

He started by searching the corpse and having it medically examined. These first formalities concluded, he came to tell me that some money had been found in the victim's pockets—twelve pounds sterling, I believe—and to ask me what he should do about it. I told him and added rather offhandedly:

"Didn't I tell you Gómez couldn't be the killer? He would have stolen the money."

This old trick had the desired effect.

"That's what I say," replied Alvarez. "There's something going on here."

Later he said a bloody knife had been found near the scene of the crime, but since there are a lot of knives like that one, there was no way to know if it belonged to Gómez. Alvarez said he would find out later. He believed that if Gómez had his knife, he clearly could not be the killer.

Although it was true that the disappearance of the private's knife could prove something, it could just as well prove nothing at all. It was nevertheless better if he still had it. There was another private, a man by the name of Irrazábal,[1] who had been my assistant for a long time and whom I trusted completely. I used him to find out if Gómez had his knife on him or not.

Irrazábal was on guard duty and did not keep me waiting. Gómez not only had his knife, it was strapped to his waist. I'll skip an infinity of details which would bog me down forever.

Alvarez continued his probe of the facts, becoming more entangled with each statement he took. He finally lost his grip when Gómez flatly denied having killed anyone, claiming instead that the bloodstains he had on his shirtsleeve came from the cattle slaughter.

In point of fact, he had that morning been in the army slaughterhouse with a company squad that was on slaughter detail. To confuse matters even further, he had gotten a small cut on his left thumb with another soldier's knife. Still, without anybody having said anything conclusive against Gómez, the battalion's conscience whispered now, as it had all along: Gómez did it.

As it turned out, two camps formed around the Gómez incident. One was made up of officers and educated soldiers. The other, less enlightened group was by far the majority. The minority held that Gómez did not kill the mess officer. It was even whispered that the latter had had a heated quarrel with Ensign Guevara, and some insinuated that Guevara owed him a lot of money.

Alvarez was fit to be tied, what with so many contradictory versions and opinions. What especially bewildered him, however, was the fact that my opinion, at all times and against everything that surfaced in the Gómez case, was in favor of the accused.

The charges were drawn up in short order, as there is only the briefest of waiting periods for such things in time of war. I attended the trial as a spectator, but when I saw the animosity which some harbored towards my protégé I felt thoroughly disgusted and went back to my camp in a fit of anger. Those who witnessed the questioning told me that our hero stayed a serene course throughout, answering every question with perfect poise.

Before he returned from the trial I knew what Gómez's fate was to be. Immediately I went to work on his behalf, but in vain. I accomplished nothing. The tribunal's sentence was confirmed and the next day came the awful order that Gómez was to face a firing squad in the presence of his battalion and under full martial regalia.

There was nothing left to discuss or think about but the final moments of the brave but unfortunate Private Gómez.

How fickle a thing is clemency!

To prepare Gómez they sat him in a chapel and called for a priest to hear his confession. Everyone had accused Gómez and everyone was sorry to see him die.

The private never blinked at his sentencing. Afterwards, he fell into a kind of lethargy. Several times I approached the tent they were holding him in, spoke aloud to the sentinel but couldn't get Gómez to raise his head.

Father Lima, the confessor, arrived at length.

Gómez was a Christian and received him with that abiding resignation that brings valor to the anguish of the final hour. The priest stayed with the convict a long while, left him alone for a while as well, that Gómez might withdraw again into his soul. Then he came to where I, awestruck by the greatness of a humble soldier, sat waiting. I spent the night in vigil with the priest. Neither of us could sleep. Duty prevented him. An intense, true, imponderable pain prevented me. I wanted, and did not want, to speak with Private Gómez for the last time.

I decided to go ahead and do it.

Poor Gómez! When he saw me stoop into the tent, he tried to stand and salute but couldn't. It was too small a space.

"Don't bother, son," I told him.

He seemed motionless.

"Commander," he murmured, and I thought I could hear a bitter reproach in his voice, as if to say, "You're going to let them shoot me."

"I did everything I could to save you, son."

"I know that, sir," he said, and his eyes misted up, as did mine. We embraced.

When I got hold of myself, I asked him, "How could you do it?"

"Drunk, sir."

"And why did you deny it when I asked you the first day?"

"You asked me about a mess officer and I thought I had killed Ensign Guevara."

"That was what you meant to do?"

"Yes, sir. He slapped my face for no reason the day we attacked Curupaití."

"And what did you tell the tribunal?"

"I don't know, sir. I thought it was the ensign who was dead. They asked me so many questions I got mixed up."

I left . . .

I asked the priest to find out from Gómez what Gómez wanted. He said he didn't want anything.

I had him ask if there was anything he wanted done; if there was, I would be glad to do it for him. He said that I might collect his pay when it came around, repay the sergeant of his company one peso he owed him, and send the rest to his sister.

The night passed slowly and sadly.

Day dawned beautiful. The battalion was somber. No one was talking. All awaited eight o'clock in a mournful silence. The grim and fatal hour arrived. I had been ordered to preside over the execution.

I did no such thing. I could not. I was sick.

My second marched out with the battalion and drew up a firing squad. I stayed in my cart. The drum was beating lugubriously. I covered my ears with both hands. I did not want to hear the dread report of rifle fire.

Later they told me how Gómez died.

He filed ahead of the battalion in military dignity, repeating the priest's prayer.

He knelt before the flag, which, surely out of sorrow, hung limp. They read him his sentence. He turned to his comrades with a somber air and said in a firm but bitter voice, "Compañeros, this is how our country rewards a man who is willing to die for her."

His exact words, as innumerable witnesses can tell you.

They tried to blindfold him but he refused.

He knelt. . . . There was a gleam . . . the rifles were aimed . . . a single explosion . . . and Gómez had entered the next life.

The battalion returned to its barracks and the rest of the squadrons to theirs. Not one of them but was impressed by the terrible example, not one but shed a tear for Private Gómez.

A few days later I had an apparition. Beyond any doubt, there are immortals out there.

 CLOSE BY MY REDOUBT lay the palm grove of Yataití, site of many an honorable entry in the annals of Argentine warfare. Private Gómez was laid to rest there. On his grave I ordered a crude pine cross be placed with this inscription: "Manuel Gómez, Private, Twelfth Line Battalion."

For several hours the memory of Gómez dwelt sadly in the thoughts of my good soldiers. Then, little by little, they let go of it, quietly forgetting the morning's morose impressions. If his name was mentioned at all the next day, it was no longer prompted by the pain they had suffered.

Neither love nor hate, sorrow nor joy can altogether absorb the existence of any mortal. God alone is everlasting.

The crowd at length forgot, as you can see, the private's tragic demise.

I set about carrying out his final wish.

I called the first sergeant of the grenadiers and, fanatically preoccupied lest the dearly departed's last wish go unfulfilled, made strict observance of it, paying the sergeant the single peso that the private owed him. I confess that afterwards I felt ineffably relieved.

It is sometimes so hard to follow through on the little things.

That is why man should be judged not by his great deeds but by his small ones. The former generally involve his honor or good name, his self-respect or pride, his selfishness or ambition. The latter involve none of these powerful wellsprings of the human soul, but only the conscience.

With the debt to the sergeant canceled, it remained for me to assure the restitution of Gómez's personal effects to La Esquina. I reserved myself subsequent access to his back pay should the National Guard ever dispense it,[1] and resolved to send his sister the six or eight weeks' worth he had coming to him.

It had been some fifty-two hours since the instant in which Gómez, as I have described, felt in his intrepid chest the bullets of his own comrades, in compliance with an order and with the most dreaded duty of all. I had left my redoubt as was my custom and gone to the commander-in-chief's quarters. There were two doors, one that opened to the east, one that opened to the west. The latter of the two was open. General Gelly[2] was seated at a small table, writing with his peculiar, methodical pause. It was his habit to move the table according to the time of day and the door through which the sun entered. At this moment he was near the open door. I was sitting in a reed chair with my back to him.

What was I thinking about?

Probably, Santiago,[3] about the same thing that joker from San Luis was when he stood there extolling the pleasures of his country estate for you.

"I spend my time here," he said one lovely spring afternoon, standing on the veranda, with its sweeping view of the countryside. "I spend it thinking . . . thinking . . ."

And you, interjecting in your droll way: "About what? About what? . . ."

And the poor fellow answering: "About nothing . . . about nothing . . ."

The general was distracted from his writing again and again by officers bearing sundry requests and addressing him from the doorway. I went on thinking. . . . In the precise instant in which my thoughts were drifting towards who knows what fog bank, an echo from another world, an echo with a Corrientes lilt to it, reached my ears.

"I came to see you, General, sir, to ask if I could . . ."

My blood froze. I stopped breathing. . . . I tried to turn around. I couldn't move!

"I'm busy now," mumbled the general, and the uninterrupted scratching of his pen had an unnerving effect on me, like that of the chattering teeth of a dying man.

"General, could you just do me this one favor, sir . . ."

"I'm busy," the general repeated.

I felt a dreamlike sensation, like being lifted by the hair by an invisible force and taken to a height where eagles fly. I must have been as pale as the whitest wax. General Gelly happened to glance at me and, seeing the anguish to which I had fallen prey, asked me rather testily:

"What's the matter with you?"

I didn't answer . . . but I heard him . . . my light-headedness was passing. The general was confused. I must have looked more dead than sick.

"Mansilla!" he said.

"General," I replied and, making a supreme effort, turned and looked towards the door.

If I had been a woman, I would have let out a scream and fainted. My lips were silent; but, as though dangling from a spring like one of those skeletons that dance on stage, I arose gradually from my chair, rather as if to back away.

"Could you do me this one favor, sir?" we heard again.

General Gelly stood up and addressed the voice coming from the doorway.

"What do you want?"

I felt a cold sweat on my brow. I placed my hand on it as if to condense all my ideas or bring them into focus at once. Then I looked at the general and exclaimed in terror:

"Private Gómez!"

Private Gómez indeed stood before us, in the doorway of the general's quarters, with the same face he had the night I saw him for the last time.

Only his clothes had changed. He was wearing a full-length black dress now instead of a military uniform.

We locked eyes for an instant that seemed an eternity.

General Gelly again repeated:

"Well, let's have it. What do you want?" And, turning to me, asked, "Are you quite all right, Colonel?"

The apparition answered:

"I would like permission to keep vigil at my brother's grave."

"Your brother's grave?" replied the general, not quite understanding the request.

"Yes. I mean Manuel Gómez. He's dead now." And with this came a burst of tears and a black neckerchief to wipe them. As this exchange proceeded, I regained my senses.

"And where is your brother buried?" the general asked.

"In the Paraguayan cemetery."

Whereupon I took matters in hand—how could I help but do so—and spoke to the unfortunate woman:

"No, you're mistaken. Gómez is not buried there."

"I know," she mumbled.

I wanted to convince her of this.

"I am the battalion chief for the Twelfth, which was your brother's line."

"I know," she mumbled, visibly frightened and backing away.

"I have your brother's pay for you. Come to the battalion. It's in the redoubt on the right. I'll give you his pay and show you where the cross is."

"I know," she mumbled.

A long dialogue followed in which I strove to get the woman to come to the redoubt so that I could give her her brother's pay and show her where he was buried, but she was like iron. "I know" was all she would say.

General Gelly's curiosity was evidently piqued by so stubborn a character. He asked her a few questions of his own.

"Where are you from?"

"La Esquina."

"When did you leave there?"

"Day before yesterday."

"Where did you find out about your brother's death?"

"Nowhere."

"What do you mean 'nowhere'?"

"Nowhere."

"Then how did you know?"

She then proceeded to relate with perfect candor that she had dreamt they were taking her brother away to be shot. Since her dreams always came true, she had believed it and took the first steamer passing through La Esquina. She was here to keep vigil by her brother's grave and had gotten it into her head that he was buried in the Paraguayan cemetery.

I followed General Gelly's questions with a few of my own. Gómez's sister had had her dream at the precise moment in which Gómez was in the chapel receiving his last rites.

An invisible and magnetic thread binds the existence of loved ones, who live as one in the tenderest ties of the heart. And, as a great English poet has said, "There are more things in heaven and earth, Horatio, than are dreamt of in your philosophy."[4] I tried everything I could to get the woman to come to my redoubt, even luring her with the one real plum I had, her brother's back pay, but it was no use. The general gave her permission to keep watch at her brother's grave and dismissed her.

After exchanging a few words with him regarding the strange dream-come-true, philosophizing on life and death, I went back to camp alone. We immediately sent emissaries out to look for Gómez's sister. They found her, but it was no use fighting her; she was as unshakable in her resolve not to see me as she was in her conviction that her brother's cross was not in the cemetery in which I had told her she would find it.

That night there was a wake. It was attended by a good number of soldiers and women from my battalion and provided for by me. I learned through them that Gómez's sister blamed me, as head of the Twelfth Battalion, for her brother's death and that she was a person of some small means in La Esquina. They also confirmed, without exception, that God sent her word of her brother's execution in her dreams. The day after the vigil the woman disappeared from the encampment, nor did anybody have any idea of her whereabouts.

The only merit this camp-fire tale can be said to have, as it comes to an end, is that it is true.

It is not every story that can make such a claim.

Have my readers perchance stayed awake throughout? If so, that's more than I can say for the people around the campfire. When I finished, some were snoring and others (the majority) were sleeping. Our horses jingled their bells, the moon was sending some light our way.

"Let's ride, Córdobans!" I shouted. "That's enough story-telling!"

Everyone got moving, and a quarter of an hour later we were heading for an oasis called Monte de la Vieja.

Good night, if not good morning or good health, patient reader.

 LAGUNA ALEGRE IS an aptly named, perma-nent, freshwater lagoon situated on an elevated outcropping of land encircled by dunes and by a kind of underbrush that yields excellent fire-wood. Our mounts got a good bellyful of the abundant grass there at Laguna Alegre and it sat well with them, as I hope Private Gómez's story did with you, Santiago, and with the reader. If it did not, I may find myself forced to skip others slated for telling in their own good time.

We got under way.

We were heading due south.

The road, that is, the network of trails, crossed a field that was covered with prickly *chañares*. The moon was in descent, the skies were cloudy, the night was dark, and the horses, unable to see ob-jects clearly, balked at each step so as not to rear up. The riders in fact did all the rearing up, what with the horses twisting under us and keeping us all from falling fast asleep.

All travelers ponder some wonder or another, whichever one most catches their eye. We all have a favorite anecdote, something to tell, even if only that we have been to Paris, which imparts a certain veneer, one you won't find on every face. Don't try to tell me this is not true. Take a topic: say, the pleasure of travel. You'll find the opinion of the tourists—not to mention those who have not traveled—divided on the subject, for not everyone travels the same way, or for the same reason, or with the same results.

One travels to spend money, acquire a chic look and a chic air, and eat and drink well. One travels to display one's own woman, sometimes someone else's woman.

One travels to educate oneself.

One travels to gain notoriety.

One travels for financial reasons.

One travels to flee one's creditors.

One travels to forget.

One travels for lack of a better idea.

You get the picture. It would take forever to list all the deeper reasons for traveling. The same goes for all of the actual results of travel.

For example:

Is it not common to go to Europe to broaden our minds, only to forget what little we have learned on this earth?

Do we not journey to find a cure only to die along the way?

Do we not go out in search of wool only to come back fleeced?

Madame de Staël[1] has stated that, say what you will about it, travel is the sorriest pleasure of all. Be that as it may, I hold that when traveling in the open country, on clear or cloudy night, it is a pleasure to sleep. I, for one, sleep perfectly at a canter, a trot, or a gallop. In fact, I not only sleep, I dream. I can't tell you how many times Eloy Avila, a friend of mine from Córdoba, has sneaked up on me as we were riding and stolen my riding strap as I dreamt away.

It was perhaps three-thirty in the morning when we reached Monte de la Vieja. Daybreak would be very late, so I resolved to stop a while. I shouted orders to dismount and get firewood. The fire was glowing in a heartbeat.

One of the Argentine gaucho's talents is the speed with which he can find firewood and the knack he has for starting a fire. A gaucho can find wood where no one else can even see it, and build a fire on water. And speaking of unseen firewood, do you know, Santiago, what the *alpataco* tree is? It's a tiny bush that branches out underground and grows very thick roots. They may be green, but they have so much resin in them that they burn like grease. You know the *chañar*. Well, the *alpataco* is like that. It abounds south of Río Cuarto, particularly in the Sampacho area, and sometimes south of Río Quinto. It looks more like a common young carob tree. Indeed, it takes a trained eye to tell one from the other.[2]

The roast was on the fire.

We had the water heated up in nothing flat while the roast cooked and the tea brewed and heads nodded randomly off. There were no stories this time. There was appetite, drowsiness, and a few orders for when day broke. We ate, we slept, and when . . . I was going to say, "when the hillside songbirds warbled." But wait, there are no songbirds in the pampas! A few larger species perhaps, a buzzard here and there. Except for the aquatic birds, the small fowl stay near the settlements. Anyway, Monte de la Vieja is just a small stand of trees, not very old ones, either, whose ruined branches can scarcely shelter a few people. The first light of day was just breaking when all of the aides, on my orders, began their routines as Camilo Arias, a man of my complete confidence, called them out. It was completely light out by the time we left Monte de la Vieja for the next stop, where there was supposed to be firewood and, above all, water. Our course took us south and up, or south and a few degrees west. The night had been mild, so that the morning presented none of those climatic phenomena so frequent in the pampas as, for example, when after a heavy dewfall or a deep chill the sun rises hot.

We marched on.

The terrain showed little feature: ravines and draws, one leading into the next; hills topped with burnt brush here, with sprouting growth there; saltpeter beds that deceive the eye at a distance, their platinum surface like that of water.

My objective was to get to Zorro Colgado.

At an unhurried pace, six leagues represent two-and-a-half hours of travel. With pack animals, a necessity on long-distance treks, somewhat more.

It was ten or so in the morning when we reached Zorro Colgado. We stopped there long enough for the animals that had fallen behind to catch up. When they had drunk their fill, we continued in the same direction until reaching Pollo-helo, which in Ranquel means "chicken lagoon." Here we varied our course a bit, seeking due south, and proceeded thus a league and a half or so in shifting, heavy terrain. We fell and rose again several times, the pack mules did the same, and so it went until we reached Us-helo, where there is another stand of trees, a watering hole not unlike the last one, and a small lagoon of brackish though potable water, when it hasn't dried up.

The animals were pretty much done in by the league-and-a-half of quagmire they had traveled over. We stopped, built a fire, cleared space for a siesta, rested, drank mate, slept, and at length the pack mules arrived. They had fallen into a ravine and gotten the Franciscans' leather trunks wet. By three or so we were heading for Coli-Mula, which lies south of our previous course. This leg of the journey was more varied than the others; the land is broken here and there by great saltpeter shoals and by sizable stretches of thick brush. We caught a horse in a huge marsh sown with big, far-flung trees. The horse had only been there a few days and wasn't outlaw yet. When we reached Coli-Mula, which means red mule, we had come three leagues. I don't know how this place got its name. There are no trees. A nice, small, circular lagoon, it has excellent and abundant water that lasts a long time. I decided to rest there until nine at night and send two men ahead. The sky was beginning to knit its brow, a black line stretched along the horizon. The sun scarcely shone.

We were in for wind or rain.

I called Private Guzmán, a splendid criollo, and the Indian Angelito, wrote several letters, gave them my instructions, and sent them off after making sure they understood everything. They had special orders to go to Chief Ramón's tent camp, which is the first one, and tell him that I would bypass his camp. I didn't know whether Chief Mariano would look kindly upon me visiting a subaltern before visiting him. I would see Chief Ramón on my way back.[3]

The messengers departed.

As I concerned myself with these matters, others went about making a good fire and getting us ready for a night's camping. The messengers were not yet out of sight when fresh and robust gusts of wind announced an impending and inevitable storm.

The sky darkened.

Experience told us we had best give up the fire and the roast and get ready for a long night. The wind was blowing harder, heavy raindrops began to fall, night drew nearer or, rather, raced towards us. We were soon enveloped in total darkness.

The rain came pouring down, the wind whistled, electrical flashes glowed in the heavens at incommensurable distances, bringing the muffled sound of lightning to our ears. The horses had drawn together, rumps to the wind, and remained immobile. Each of us hunkered down and rigged some way or another to keep from getting soaked. There was no way to turn our backs to the rain or to talk; the noise of the downpour drowned out any sound leaving the neck holes of our ponchos and capes, which at any rate were pulled over our heads. It rained ceaselessly for two hours, a leaden deluge. Whenever the lulls in the rain would allow it, I traded words with Camilo Arias, who was crouched beside me. In one of these diluvian chats I told him, "The Indians could kill me, though it's unlikely they will. But they just might want to hold me hostage in hopes of netting a big ransom. If that should happen, General Arredondo should hear about it right away. Tell the boys"—I meant a certain group of five men, my confidential scouts—"that if I'm not wearing this kerchief around my neck, that's a sign I am in trouble."

It was a red silk scarf from India that I always wear under my hat for the sun and the dirt.[4]

"Now, it could develop that I have to give the kerchief away. If that happens, the sign will be that my beard is braided. You're to say nothing about this to anyone but the boys. And once we get to the settlements, see to it that you never come near me to speak. Use a go-between."

Camilo is like an Arab: he speaks little. He knows that words are silver and silence is gold.

"Good enough, sir," he said.

Which assured me he had understood. Now, I thought, a certain musketeer will reach London and speak with Buckingham.[5]

You'll find out in good time the extraordinary turn of events regarding my beard. And since it is still raining and I am drenched through to my shirt, I'll say so long until tomorrow.

 **10** MAN PROPOSES, GOD DISPOSES. It was impossible to renew the march at nine. The rain stopped after four hours, but the sky remained overcast, threatening a new downpour. The north wind roared as ever and lightning veined the boundless heavens. I thought we should eat. "Everybody up!" I shouted. "Let's go, on the double! Build a good fire, start a roast, get some water boiling!"

The assistants came out from under their cover and a moment later the green and resinous *chañar* was crackling. The roast was cooking, the water boiling; several men surrounded the fire to warm up, dry their rags. Looking at the sky, they tried to guess whether it would rain again or not. The fire was built and built well with great, glowing flames rising from its center. It was irresistible. A woman could sooner pass before a mirror and deny herself the ineffable platonic satisfaction of a look.

I abandoned the posture I had been in for such a long time and drew near the fire.

They gave me mate.

Overcome by the fatigue of the previous day and night, the good Franciscans were trying to sleep. Tender feet always blister first.

Capitalizing on the confidence and familiarity I enjoyed with them, I had them get up and take their place around the fire. We worried the roast along, spread the coals, stretched the meat out, and soon had it ready. Meanwhile, we dried out. We ate well and made our beds with a certain amount of difficulty. Everything was drenched and all the leather gear was soaking wet. Finally, we lay down to get some sleep.

We slept splendidly.

One does sleep awfully well when the body is exhausted. Anyone tossing and turning with insomnia on some plush and spongy bed who could have heard us snoring away on the Coli-Mula wetlands, what envy that person would have felt! Unquestionably, civilization has its advantages over barbarism, but not as many as those calling themselves civilized claim.[1]

Civilization, if I have an exact idea of it, consists of several things. It means using high stiff collars, patent leather boots, and kid gloves. It means that there will be many doctors and many patients, many lawyers and many lawsuits, many soldiers and many wars, many rich and many poor. It means many newspapers in print and many lies in circulation; many houses built with many rooms and very few comforts. It means a government composed of many people such as a president, ministers, and a congress and which governs as little as possible. It means a great many hotels, all of them very bad, all of them very expensive.

Take, for instance, the one I stayed in the last night I slept, or tried to sleep, in Rosario. It is the beds of that hotel, precisely those beds, which have prompted these rather commonplace reflections.

Good Lord! There was one of everything God made on the fifth day in those beds. As I recall, that was the day for "domestic animals, each to its own kind, and the reptiles of the earth, each to its own kind." The Supreme Maker, according to Genesis, saw that all of this was good, though I can't for the life of me see how the household creatures at that hotel have ever been in any sense good; least of all the night I spent there, in which I would swear on a Christian bible that they weren't just bad, they were horrid. So unbearable were they, in fact, that I feel compelled to ask: Rather than investing public funds in foolish wars, should not money be used to improve the condition of the people? Are there not road and bridge inspectors, school inspectors, inspectors of anything and everything, and so on? So why not hotel inspectors?[2] Are these establishments perchance not intimately related to public health? Are they not host to cholera, yellow fever, and so many other things God created on the fifth day and which He in his primitive and innocent backwardness thought were good and therefore bequeathed them as inheritance to an ungrateful human race?

The horse bells were jingling; each man was getting ready to climb on his horse, his sorrows forgotten around the fire:

> *Y en el oriente nubloso*
> *La luz apenas rayando,*
> *Iba el campo tapizando*
> *De claro oscuro verdor.*[3]

Making the most of the fresh morning, we galloped while on our right, in the distance, the first mountains came into view.

I intended to get to the Cuero early.

No sooner had we left Coli-Mula than I knew I wouldn't make it. The land was covered with water and broken everywhere in high dunes and deep shifting ravines. We would have to march slowly. The horses could have withstood a brisk march, but not the mules. And yet, no matter how slowly I went, they lagged behind, falling under their loads and costing us time in uprighting them.

Beyond a place called Ralicó, where there is water and firewood, the land rolls noticeably, forming several steep dunes. That is the point from which the mountains of the Cuero river lands can first be sighted. The landscape begins to change and the eyes grow less weary than in the broad expanse of the desert, which is solitary, sad, imposing, and monotonous as a calm sea.

Without contrast there is existence, but no life.

To live is to suffer and to revel, to abhor and to love, to believe and to doubt, to change physical and moral outlook.

This is so great a need, that when I was in Paraguay, dear Santiago, I will tell you what I often did when weary of looking out on the same thing every day from my redoubt in Tuyutí: the same Paraguayan trenches, the same forests, the same marshes, the same guards. Do you know what I would do? I would climb atop the merlon on the battlement, turn my back to the enemy, spread my legs, bend over and, looking directly between my legs, stand in momentary if upside-down contemplation of things. It has a curious visual effect and is a method I urge you to turn to when bothered or tired by the sameness of life in old Europe, which thinks itself young; which believes itself to be ahead and lives in ignorance, incontestable proof of this being, as Théophile Gautier[4] would say, that Europe has not yet been able to invent a gas to replace the sun.

America, that is, the Americans (I mean the North Americans), are going to leave her behind if she does not take care.[5] For the time being, we are solving our hardest social problems by cutting each other's throats—nor do Malthus's theories and figures on population growth for one moment alarm us.[6] We have great political theorists who daily prove to us that pain can be not only an anesthetic but a remedy; that tyranny and civil war are necessary because their inevitable, fatal consequence is freedom. They can demonstrate this with a few, quick words and with frightening clarity. It has gotten so that our young people have their own political axioms and, far from letting go of them, they will stand blindly by them and indeed are willing to prove them, prematurely, citing first A, then B.

If you came back to this distant country, you would be amazed to see the progress we have made. For instance, you would be wasting your time to try to look for a windmill. The pine tree on General Guido's estate is, by some miracle, still standing. Civilization and liberty have razed everything else.[7] Paraguay no longer exists. The last statistics after the war show one hundred forty thousand women and fourteen thousand men. We accomplished this great deed with the help of Brazil. Between the two of us we sent López to the hereafter. Hardly what you would call meager accomplishments for such a short time.

The best lessons are learned in blood; thus is born the pain that enriches.

I tell you these things because they bear on matters at hand. I'm not just chewing the fat. You'll see later on that all this is related, and far more than it seems, to the Indians. Are there not those who hold that it would be better to exterminate than to Christianize them and use their manpower for industry, labor, and common defense, what with all the uproar about the threat of excessive, unchecked immigration?

Let us be on our way . . .

After the dunes of Ralicó, we come to the Tremencó watershed. It is two lagoons, one fresh water, the other salt water. Both tend to dry up. From Tremencó we go to Médano del Cuero. From there to the Cuero River itself it is two leagues. This lagoon is perhaps one hundred meters in diameter. Its water is excellent and, with a little digging for springs on its south side, a great many animals can slake their thirst there during the worst droughts.

A famous Indian named Blanco has lived at Laguna del Cuero for some time. He is the scourge of the borderlands of Córdoba and San Luis, the terror of travelers, teamsters, and horse drivers. By and by I will tell you how I threw him out of El Cuero with the help of a few gauchos. If I hadn't done this, I would have had to meet him in his own historic domain. This episode has its social interest and will enlighten many who never leave the cultured neighborhoods of Buenos Aires as to what our beloved country is. There is something for everyone here: a black man, for instance, who kills a whole family for love and revenge; a white man who kills a governor, also for love and for freedom, having first lent his virile might to the service of tyranny. Meanwhile, I can tell you that the land between Río Quinto and El Cuero is different. Rich, abundant, and varied pasture; *porotillo*, clover, you name it. Inexhaustible water, timber, immense mountains. A wise and hardworking cattleman would make his fortune there in a few years.

But it is thirty leagues from El Cuero to Río Quinto.

Hang a bell on the cat's tail. From there to the first permanent tent settlements it is another thirty leagues, and the Indians always hunt game around El Cuero. As I wait for the mules that have fallen behind, I reflect here on the shore of the lagoon as to whether it might not be better to run the big new railroad they've got planned through here.

Don't think the Indians are not aware of this.

They receive and read *La Tribuna*, too.

You laugh, Santiago?

Give time some time.

 I OWE IT to narrative fidelity to register one detail before going on.

We found nearly fresh tracks in Ralicó. Who could have come through here at this time of day with six horses, driving four and riding two? Only Private Guzmán and the Indian Angelito, the scouts I had sent ahead promptly upon reaching Coli-Mula.

The soldiers took one look at the tracks with their expert eyes and started in: "Look, here's the chestnut, these other ones are from the wall-eyed, here's that dark bow-legged horse." And all this with consummate savvy and no more effort than it might take you or me to spot a friend coming in the distance.

The truly unsurpassed trackers come from San Juan and La Rioja.[1]

There was a Riojano in the Twelfth Battalion. He was a tracker for General Arredondo in the war against El Chacho[2] and was so wily that he could tell from an animal's tracks not only whether it was thin or fat, but whether it had one good eye or two.

Clearly the storm had kept the scouts from continuing on their way. They had slept in Ralicó and had only a couple of hours start on me. If they didn't hurry, or if they hurried too much and wore out the horses, we would reach the first tent camp at Rincón almost at the same time.

God has given each creature its instinct, mind, accent, soul, in short, its character. I confess this incident vexed me to no end. Either I stayed behind one day so that my messengers' mission would achieve its desired effect, or I carried on with no further thought of them, running the risk of arriving first.

It should be noted that two roads lead out of El Cuero. One goes through Lonco–uaca—*lonco* means head and *uaca* means cow—and the other through Bayo–manco, whose meaning will become clear when I concern myself with the Ranquel language. Which of the two roads had the scouts taken, that was the question. There would be no way of knowing this from the roads around El Cuero, which would be submerged. Concealing my annoyance and wondering what I would do if my conjecture proved right and we could not track the messengers, I arrived at El Cuero.

We spent yesterday there waiting for our pack mules, dear Santiago.

Here we are again on the banks of the famous Cuero.

Those who have rendered an image of the pampa, imagining it in all its immensity one vast plain, how mistaken their descriptions have been! Poets and men of science alike have got it all wrong. Their idealized pampa, which in deference to the truth I would call pampas, in the plural, and the real pampas, offer two entirely different perspectives.[3] We live in ignorance even of the physiognomy of our own homeland. Distinguished poets and historians have sung homage to the *ombú* and the thistle. Where are the *ombú* in the pampas? Where is the thistle? Are they in fact natives of America, or of these zones? Who among those who have lived for any time in the country; indeed, who among those who have traveled these lands in an observing spirit, can have failed to notice that the *ombú* is always a sign of an inhabited home or vacant settlement, or that the thistle is found only in certain places, it having first been sown by the Jesuits and only later propagated?

These mountains running along the Cuero extend for a great many leagues from north to south and from east to west. They reach the Chalileo River, cross it, and make their intermittent way to the foothills of the Andes. Blanco the Indian lived in these hills. Neither chief nor tribal leader, he is what the Indians call a gaucho Indian. That is, an Indian answering to no law or leader, to no great chief and certainly no petty chieftain; an Indian who is lord of his own realm; ally one day to the adversary, its enemy the next; at large today in the mountains, riding herd tomorrow with another chief; a marauder raiding and invading for months on end, then a trader working in Chile, as has happened lately.[4] The whole of this Indian's power—and he is feared like no one else along the borders of San Luis and Córdoba, lands he knows intimately, as indeed he knows the rest—consisted, in the time of this story, of some eight or ten raiding cohorts. He generally took them along on his attacks, though sometimes he joined the great raiding parties. Since in those days the lands south of the Quinto and Cuarto were the same thing, Indian domain, the invasions often came twice a week, with a day in between, and sometimes daily.

More often than not the hero of these valorous deeds was Blanco the Indian. Innumerable times was the road from Río Cuarto to Achiras the site of his robbing and cruelty. Upon my arrival in Río Cuarto, Blanco the Indian was all the talk. You could not go anywhere but the havoc his plundering had wreaked was on every tongue. Who had not had cattle stolen? Who did not grieve the loss or captivity of a loved one?

Here was an Indian of terrible repute.

I was, consequently, his rival.

I resolved that before I advanced the border any further I would drive him out of El Cuero, inconvenience him, alarm him, rob him, anything along those lines. But I didn't want to use soldiers for this. Discipline has its drawbacks as well as its advantages. I cast about for a way of counterattacking, keeping in mind a maxim of the great captains: defeat the enemy with its own weapons. I wrote to my friend don Pastor Hernández, head of the Río Cuarto military command and a diligent, hardworking, and incisive fellow, telling him I needed to hire half-a-dozen rascals and that I preferred skill over daring; thieves, in other words.

Hernández did not keep me waiting. A few days later six men

hailing from the hills arrived at my door bearing a letter. The leader of the pack was called El Cautivo.

The Pharisees who put Christ to death could not have looked more like outlaws than these six. Their clothes were ragged, their faces mean, they skulked, they were shifty. You had to have a keen sense of civic duty to bring yourself to deal with them. They entered my quarters. Conducting a social study of sorts, I offered them seats. It was not easy to get them to accept, but at length I managed it and they sat down. Each of them placed his hat on the ground beside his chair as he took his seat.

They all lowered their heads.

I began the conversation with certain questions, such as what is your name, where do you come from, where do you work, have you ever been a soldier, how many lives do you owe? Then, with trust established, I continued, "So, you want to hire on?"

"Whatever you say," replied El Cautivo in that secretive way the Córdobans have.

"You men are savvy, aren't you?"

"You bet, sir."

"You do different kinds of work?"

"We do 'em all, sir."

"How much do you get?"

"That's up to you, sir."

"Get more than eight pesos a month?"

"No, sir."

"Well, I am going to pay you ten. I'll fix you up with food, clothes, and horses."

"Whatever you say."

"Sure, but we're talking about hiring you to steal."

"And how would that be, sir?"

"We'll go anywhere you send us," they all said at once.

"Hmmm, have you got the nerve for it?"

"Sure we do."

"Good, because I'm talking about robbing the Indians."

Silence. And there you have it. That's your country for you, and the reason for the *montoneros*⁵ and a whole lot more.

The colonel was hiring them to steal. They'd bring him the dawn's early light if he asked for it. They had no problem with that; they would shed their blood, risk their lives, whatever. The ten pesos and the rest of it made no more difference to them than the money they earned honestly. They had a certain predisposition, a certain way of life, a weakness for wild and barbaric pack riding. They were probably saying to themselves, "Now that's what I call a colonel!"

But now we were talking about the Indians, the very ones who just a few months back had laid their homes to waste, and in an instant their outlook had changed. Was it fear? What was it? No, it was not fear. Ours is a brave and determined race. Fear of death is not the thing that sometimes contains a gaucho.

I have seen one of them holding forth like a philosopher as they led him to the firing squad. He was a sergeant. The priest kept urging him to confess but he didn't want to.

"You mean you're not afraid to die?"

"Father," he answered with poignant expressiveness, "death is a leap in the dark. You don't know where you are going to land when you take it."

This happened in Chascomús.

So, what was holding back our Pampa Volunteers, as they came to be called? What was stopping them? Alas, it's sad to say but true and say it we must, the better to teach the younger generations in whose hands the future rests and through whose hands we, the aspirants of intolerance and hatred, the dwarves of any meritorious patriotism, the heroes of a bygone age of gold, will find deliverance.[6]

It was their complete lack of a sense of duty, their horror of all discipline. They were smart enough to understand that any robbery they carried out on my orders made me their accomplice. Robbing the Indians changed the game, however. They would have to go as soldiers. They may even have imagined it was all a trick to recruit them. Or so I understood it.

I was about to send them away. But here they were, after all. I explained to them that they were free men; that they could hire on or not; nobody was forcing them; they could back out if they wanted to. Once convinced that they risked nothing more than their lives, they accepted and it was all arranged.

I gave them good horses, clothes, carbines which they made into blunderbusses, and a cavalry saber to carry between the saddle blankets. Then they departed.

They had orders to rob Blanco the Indian.

El Cautivo knew the Cuero River lands.

They could keep whatever they took.

They returned with something. One doesn't work and put one's neck on the line without some sort of reward, as even the least calculating will tell you. They repeated the excursion three more times until Blanco the Indian went away. He could not reckon how much backup the Pampa Volunteers might have. I confess that when I sent these devils on such a hazardous mission, I paused to consider: no great loss if they get caught or killed. This was one of the reasons why I had chosen not to use my own poor soldiers.

The Pampa Volunteers ended up robbing me, too.

I took them aside, though all I could say to upbraid them was:

"What am I supposed to do with you? I knew you were thieves when I hired you." Then I sent them back to Hernández.

You don't play with fire for long without getting burned.

The pack mules have arrived.

I now know for a fact I won't be sleeping where I wanted to be.

We will arrive tomorrow.

 BEFORE GETTING UNDER WAY, I decided to leave the mules behind. The heavy rainfall had slowed them down almost to a stop and it was torture for the Franciscans to follow along at slow strides. Father Moisés is not so awkward on a horse, but Father Marcos never did find a comfortable position.

Despite my apprehensions, we found the two messengers' tracks. They had taken the Lonco-uaca Road. My translator, a Chilean mestizo of Christian father and Indian mother, a very savvy man, too, whose secrets have been placed in my keeping, not by him but by others—which will in turn enable me to share with you his amorous adventures in the frontier country—thought it an opportune moment to make several observations. They were judicious and sensible ones; and as they included the possibility that the messengers, neither of them having any practical knowledge of the road they had taken, might lose their way, I thought it prudent to make a few recommendations of my own.

We were now about to enter the hills. We would be spreading out and would no longer be able to see each other. Winding trails awaited us, trails that one minute disappeared, the next broke into four, six, or more roads, all of which led into the thickness. It was at once very likely we would err the right trail, as it was most probable we would soon be discovered by the Indians.

A certain Peñaloza is generally the first person to greet the Indians and Christians who travel through these lands, which he alleges to be his and for the use of whose turf and water he believes himself entitled to payment.[1] There is nothing to be done but pay, because Señor Peñaloza takes great care not to collect his contribution when the travelers are greater in number or better armed than those of his camp. Further along there are other lords of the land, the water, the trees, the beasts of the field, in short, of everything that offers an excuse to live off one's fellow man's sweat. These interterritorial duties are levied in the most courteous and politic way. The Indians virtually beg the mounted contributor for money, show him the poverty in which the people live, the scarcity of work. If the peaceful method achieves its aim, that is the end of it. If the traveler is not moved, threats are used. These failing, violence.

Rather parliamentarian of them for as far removed as they are from the centers of civilization.

I indicated to my people how they were to march. I expressly forbade anyone to fall behind on the pretext that their gear needed straightening. I would make a two-minute stop every quarter hour so that we could stay as close together as possible. I described the wetlands of Chamalcó to them. I would stop there a while, long enough to change horses should anyone lose his way nearby. I entreated the Franciscans to follow me closely lest the devil spoil my day by getting them lost. Finally, I pointed out that as we now found ourselves in a place where danger could arise when least expected, and considering that we were not well armed, I wanted each and every one of us to conduct himself with moderation and cunning, and above all with sangfroid, which is valor possessed of judgment. This done, I ordered two soldiers to return to Río Quinto with two strings of horses I did not need. The soldiers were told to ride slowly. I scratched out a few words in pencil for General Arredondo and several subordinate friends from my frontier world, telling them I had reached El Cuero in good spirits and that we were starting into the hills.

Beautiful, ageless carob trees, *caldén* trees, *chañar*, and buckthorn, in whose impenetrable shade the lush and cool and verdant grass grows, cover these hills, which do not have the beauty of those of Corrientes, the Chaco, or Paraguay. Slender palm trees rising like phantoms in the thick night; vegetation pushing through, ever renewed by moisture; orange groves everywhere proffering their golden fruit; climbing vines whose intricate tendrils and immortal flowers dress the tallest trees to the very tops all the year round; fresh moss, mantle for robust trunks; sticky lichen glistening in the morning dew like a glazing of precious stones; the elegant, swaying cattails shaking their silken, white crowns in the wind; aerial flowers that feed on the sheer breezes, perfuming the atmosphere, gay nature's own censers; birds of a thousand colors singing their bliss day and night; teeming serpents sliding in every direction; insects by the millions humming their endless diurnal and nocturnal chorus; the ever-abundant water to comfort a thirsty traveler; and so, so many other things that reveal God's grandeur: Where are they out here? I wondered, as I soliloquized among the carbonized, rotted-out carob trees.[2]

And because under certain impressions we lift our spirits, there to find a vision of our nation, I thought for an instant about the future of the Argentine Republic on the day when civilization, which will come with freedom, peace, and wealth, invades lands such as these: bleak, destitute of all beauty, devoid of artistic interest, but suitable for agriculture and raising cattle. There is abundant pastureland, a lifetime supply of timber, and water for but little labor, given the inexhaustible artesian springs honeycombing the pampas like so many invitations to work.

Every dune is a great, absorbent sponge. Dig a little in between them and the water will flow.

The way I see it, our heads-of-state are precipitate in their thinking when, in their zeal to link the Atlantic and Pacific, they want to put the railroad through at Río Quinto. The Cuero River is the line to follow. Its forests offer timber for cross-ties, no matter how many, fuel for the voracious boilers of the impetuous locomotive.[3]

Our patriotic impatience can lead to great mistakes. Patient study will keep us from error.

I cannot speak as a sage, only as an observer. I have the charter of the Republic in my head, but I lack the theodolite and the compass. The perils of the job are more imaginary than real. I might at some point deal with this subject. For now I'll venture to say that with one hundred armed men organized a certain way, I would answer for the lives and success of the workers. I would have you ponder this great problem of commerce and civilization. In all my travels in India, Africa, Europe, and America, I have never seen anything more lonely than these hills along the Cuero. Mile after mile of dry trees, scorched by the blistering heat. Mile after mile of ashes lying in sand, rising at the least stirring of the wind. Land and sky, there you have the whole spectacle. It was enough to plunge the soul into darkness. Our mounts were getting thirsty. Chamalcó was near.

We arrived.

Danger joins, bonds, fuses; pulling together is a human instinct in the solemn moments of life. Nobody had fallen behind. The scout guessed there would be water in Chamalcó.

We waited a long while before letting the animals drink.

They rested. They drank.

We found a spring at the foot of a magnificently full and robust tree.

We changed horses and carried on until we hit a great span of dry land.

I inhaled expansively.

Europeans love the mountains, Argentines the plains.

This characterizes two tendencies. From the physical heights one better contemplates the moral heights. The freest and happiest peoples on earth are those who live on its peaks.

Witness the Swiss.

A short ways along we again entered the hills. The tops were rounder here. We could gallop and indeed needed to if we wanted to reach Utatriquín—another watering hole—in daylight. The night would be moonless until just at dawn. I hurried when the trees allowed it and we reached the stage of the trip we wanted to reach.

> *Era la tarde, y la hora*
> *En que el Sol la cresta dora*
> *De los Andes.*[4]

This water hole is a huge pond of dirty, muddy water, scarcely potable to the animals. Foreseeing it might be bad, we had filled two water bags in Chamalcó. I had marched well this time and gained more ground than I expected. I no longer had any reason to hurry. I could rest a good, long while, which would do both the horses and my dear Franciscans a world of good. I ordered everyone to unsaddle.

Father Marcos looked at me as if to say, Praised be God, for if He has placed me in these straits he has also come to my aid.

There was an abandoned corral; we camped near it. I ordered double watch on the horses, roused the party with some warm words of encouragement, and a short time later the fire beckoned ardent and bright. The talking started up without regard to station or rank.

I've said it before: the camp fire is the democratic tribunal of our army. An Argentine camp fire is not like that of other nations. It is a special camp fire.

We were drinking mate for coffee, for dessert. Night had spread its black sweat cloth over us for some time. A voice murmured well within earshot of me: "If the colonel would only tell one of his stories. . . ." It was my assistant Calixto Oyarzábal, of whom I spoke in an earlier letter; a good lad, smart, too. You only have to give him a bootstrap and he will pull himself up by it.

"Oh yes," said the Franciscans, the officers, and the other assistants when they heard this. "The colonel should tell a story."

I let them beg a while and then gave in.

Men get that from women.

And do you know what story I told, Santiago? One of yours, the story of the teamster. I bet you've forgotten it.

I'll have to tell you from five thousand miles away. The honorable public attending this colloquium will kindly excuse me.

"Pay attention," I said before I started. "This is a story you'll want to keep in mind when you're riding through the thick woods in these hills."

Everyone drew together, one stirred the fire; eyes gleamed with curiosity and looked at me as if to say, We're all ears now, so go ahead.

I took that as a cue and proceeded as follows:

There was a teamster, a man who had covered a lot of country. He had joined the *montoneros* in the time of Quiroga and the law was after him.[5] As he passed one day through Llanos de la Rioja, he was met by a posse of four. They tried to take him, he resisted, they tried by sheer force to overpower him, but he defended himself. He killed one, wounded another, sent three of them running. Just then another posse came into view. The group our teamster had beaten back warned this group and they hurried after him. The teamster fled, taking cover in the hills. He was riding a chestnut mule and a mischievous one at that. He was running her through the hills when her cinch slipped. This and the animal lowering its head to kick—it all happened at once.

Now this teamster was all gaucho, a real rider. He was in the saddle and out of it again just like that, for quite a while, until somewhere in there he got his considerably long and thick hair tangled in the branches of a carob tree. The mule was still up to no good. She slipped out from between his legs, which left him hanging there. And there he stayed like Judas, a long time, waiting for someone to help him out of his fix, but it was no use.

Night fell. The posse that was looking for him chanced to pass that way. His mind was working fast and he hit on an idea. He made a long, morose face and let them come near. It was a moonlit night and they could see him as he spoke out in a hollow voice: Long live Quiroga!

That posse lit out of there but fast when they heard the dead man speak. You might say they were in the grip of panic and terror. No telling where they rode to next.

And that's how the teamster got out of that one.

But how long could he stay like that? It was starting to get uncomfortable. He tried to free himself. He looked for his knife but had lost it when the mule kicked free. This was fate, truly. He had nothing to cut his hair with and long as it was he couldn't quite untangle it from the branches with his hands. A man as used to hardship as he was can resist the weight of his own body, assuming there was no other way out of it, not just for a day but for days on end so long as he had something to eat. Necessity is the mother of invention, but he had nothing. The mule had run off with everything in the saddle bags. Happily, he had a piece of cheese in his pocket along with a tinder box, tobacco, and paper.

Water was the least of a teamster's concerns.

He ate the piece of cheese.

Then he took out his pouch and rolled a cigarette, lit it, and smoked. No one came by, though the posse had surely let the word out and aroused people's curiosity. So he spent quite a few days right there until he got so hungry he ate his shirt and died of indigestion.

I went in through one door and came out by another, didn't I?

I don't know if the public will like this story. I can tell you it was applauded at the camp fire. I'm a *porteño* from the barrio of San Juan and nobody is a prophet in his own land, which is why Sarmiento, himself from San Juan, is president, in fulfillment of a prophecy I made in Paraguay.[6]

It was about eight o'clock when I finished my story. I gave my orders, they got all the horses rounded up, picked their mounts, and we were on our way. That night strange things happened . . .

But enough of storytelling.

 YESTERDAY WAS TUESDAY, a bad day to board a ship, get married, file applications, collect money from debtors, or commit suicide. Besides being dated on a Tuesday, this letter bears the number thirteen, a number of ill omen, a mysterious, enigmatic, symbolic, prophetic, fateful, in a word, cabalistic number.

Things with thirteen always turn out badly. Misfortune falls on parties of thirteen. When thirteen dine together, sooner or later one of them is hanged, dies suddenly, disappears inexplicably, is robbed, shipwrecked, ruined, or wounded in a duel. Finally, it is quite common that in a group of thirteen there will be a traitor. This has been occurring unfailingly since that famous supper at which Judas gave Jesus the perfidious kiss, which is why France, that most cultural of nations, has an industry that any day now may be introduced in Buenos Aires. It takes its name from its practitioners, who are called *quatorzième* (the fourteenth). The *quatorzième* cannot be just anyone. He must be young, no more than thirty-five, of pleasant bearing, good manners, well dressed, conversant in several languages, and abreast of all the latest in his day and time.

Let us say a person has invited several friends to dinner, whether at home, in a restaurant, or at a hotel, and somebody has fouled up the plans. Only thirteen have shown up to eat and they have waited the mandatory quarter-hour allowed the unpunctual. It is time to call the *quatorzième*. How, indeed, could just thirteen dine? Thirteen might well be moved to harbor suspicions and suspicions might occasion indigestion. So a lackey is dispatched to find a *quatorzième*. There being one in every neighborhood, it doesn't take long to find him. He is like a doctor. He comes in, bows, and genuflects, all of which is answered disdainfully. Immediately the door to the dining room is opened, or not opened, as the guests may already be in there or whatever, and then comes the announcement: *Monsieur est servi.*

The guests take their seats. How glad they are! The soup is still hot, steaming hot. Good, it did not get cold. Happiness beams from every face. Plates clang, glasses clink. Suddenly the host calls out, "Here he is at last! Sit down wherever you like, there won't be anybody else coming now."

Enter Monsieur de la Tomassière (or so Paul de Kock has chris-
tened the character he created, the annoying friend who is always
late). He takes his seat, begging everyone's pardon and insisting
this is the first time it has happened. Meanwhile, our *quatorzième*
has gotten a sign from the owner of the house, a sign that means
the same thing everywhere: you can leave now. Without so much
as a single word he has been eclipsed. He was perhaps about to
taste the soup when M. de la Tomassière arrived. When he gets
home he finds someone waiting for him at his door. They're standing by at another banquet. They've tried to find some other *quatorzième* but to no avail. On this night of many dinner parties there
are either a lot of inexact people or too many cautious hosts and
the demand for the *quatorzièmes* is great.

He goes. He arrives, same scene as before. Again he must give
up his seat before trying a single dish. Back again at his lowly man-
sion, another customer. He accompanies this one with the same
results he had at the earlier invitations. There are nights in which
the rounds of the poor *quatorzième* exceed all calculation. He has
earned his money well, for he is paid for each trip, but he has suffered the torment of Tantalus.

The civilization of Buenos Aires should seriously consider this.
I am not an alarmist. But I hold that just as we are threatened
by many diseases for want of municipal police, education has for
many years neglected to instill in our young a certain idea: that it
is among the greatest of social shortcomings to keep others waiting. I can recall an Andalusian fellow who lived as a guest at the
house of a certain aunt of mine for eleven years. One day he announced that he was returning to his homeland. It was about time!
His good-bye went more or less as follows: "Señora, you can't
complain. I've always been exactly on time for lunch and dinner."
Whereupon he left, having said a good deal at that, for the person
who has never kept a dinner waiting because he has never given
one does not know what it is to wait for a houseguest or a dinner
guest.

I believe I have explained myself well enough, dear Santiago. If
this thirteenth letter was not published yesterday, it was because
yesterday was Tuesday and had a fatal number.

When I moved out of Utatriquin

*The bright sun was extinguish'd, and the stars
Did wander darkling in the eternal space.*[1]

The night was quite dark. The hill was thickly overgrown and along the trail were many tree trunks and small shrubs. It was most uncomfortable for both horse and rider. We had to go slowly. We were prone to fall asleep. . . . Now and then a carob tree or *chañar* branch would snap back into the rider's face and rouse him from his drowsiness. The slower air of the march kept my company less dispersed than at other times.

Like the night itself, I was feeling heavy-lidded and kept quiet. I was thinking about the unexpected instant which sooner or later marks the chart of life, the passage from the known to the unknown, from sad reality to who knows what sadder one yet; to an unconscious state, the void, nothingness; I was thinking of what my days would be up to the solemn instant in which my eyesight and voice expire, I gather a final breath of life, and with all the strength my spirit can muster, I say to myself: Now I die!

I became engulfed in such thoughts and reflections, and when the horrid and wrenching doubt seized me, I remembered Hamlet:

> *. . . To die, to sleep.*
> *To sleep! perchance to dream.*

It was like I was dreaming. . . . I could see all objects enveloped in a fine mist of opaque transparency; the trees seemed incommensurably tall; I saw confused multitudes pass before me, dark cities, the earth and sky were one and the same, there was no space . . .

A lash in the face from the limb of an *espinillo*, in whose thorns my hat got caught, which in turn forced me to stop, started me from the fantasia into which the drowsy march had sunken me. Several soldiers riding close behind me were conversing. It seems they had been swapping tales of adventure. The one who was talking when I began really to listen to them was saying something like this: "I'm tellin' ya, they put me on the front lines for no good reason."

"Well don't they always!" I said. "It's just like you boys to say so. There's never a good reason for punishing you."

"Oh yes there is, Colonel, believe me."

"Now what would that be?"

"Well, see, I had this real rascal of a friend who I thought the world of and who I told everything that happened to me. At the same time, I was in love with a girl from Renca. She loved me pretty well, too. Her father was rich and was against me seeing her. I had

good intentions and would have married Petrona. That was her
name: Petrona. But good intentions are not enough if a man's out
of luck or poor. We had the love bug so bad that we finally decided
to go to Mendoza, get married there, and come back when God
should allow us to. That was where it stood. We got together
whenever we could. It was never easy on account of her folks and
the judge spying on us.[2] The judge was a rich widower, an older
fellow. He wanted to marry Petrona. Meanwhile, his youngest
daughter and Antonio were running around together. He hated
Antonio and was always threatening to put him in the army. One
day we finally set everything up, the getaway I mean, and it took
some doing, too.

"I was supposed to elope with Petrona.

"Antonio would go with me and watch the window where I'd
be going into the house. We had to be careful of the judge. The
window led into Petrona's father's room. He was a gambler, a
heavy gambler just like Antonio. Not too long before that he had
won himself a big wad of money. He had beaten Antonio out of
everything he owned and Antonio wanted his hide.

"Petrona left the window shut but not locked. Her aunt was
with her, sleeping in the same room. Doña Romualda, her mother,
was out on the farm somewhere. It was the perfect night for this,
because Petrona's father had friends over. Antonio had dropped in
on the get-together early and come by to tell me that the old man
was already winning big time and if we didn't hurry up we'd blow
the whole plan. Even though I had set it up with Petrona not to
move until the stars were highest in the sky, I decided to go in a
little sooner than that.

"Everything was set: I had horses and a little money set aside to
buy something on the road. We left Antonio's and went to Petrona's window. We pushed it open nice and easy and then I jumped
in without making a sound and left it open behind me. After I was
in the room I heard snoring. It was Petrona's father. Antonio figured he had left the party a little earlier than usual.

"When Antonio heard the snoring he said to me under his
breath, 'Let's get out of here, man. We can't do this today.' I didn't
want to hear any of that, so I just said, 'Shhh.' The room was dark.
I had to walk on my tiptoes and be very careful not to make any
noise. I got to Petrona's bed. She had heard me. She was holding
her breath, same as I was. If her father woke up we'd be in hot
water. She'd get a strapping, I'd get it with a knife. The old man

was as bad as they come. I never heard Antonio come in behind me when I was making my way to Petrona's bed. I had taken her hand and she was just about to get up when we heard the sound of silver and then a shout.

"'Ah, you rat!'

"It was Petrona's father's voice.

"Antonio just couldn't resist robbing him. The old man heard him and grabbed his poncho. I couldn't leave the way I had come in and it would have been dangerous to hide under the bed. Petrona's father was shouting for all he was worth. 'Thieves! Thieves!' Next her aunt got up. I tried to get away but I couldn't. Antonio was on his way out ahead of me and blocked my way and Petrona's father grabbed me. I fought with him for a while but he had me. His sister helped him.

"Petrona was half dead by now. Her father was furious because she wasn't helping out too, and told her to turn on a light fast. He said he'd kill her if she didn't. She had to do it.

"By this time Antonio had taken off with the money.

"Between Petrona's father and her aunt they tied me down pretty good. There were a couple of police nearby and all the shouting got their attention and they took me away. They threw me in jail so I'd say where the money was but all I ever answered was I didn't know and I didn't steal it. They asked me if anybody was in on this with me and I said no. They never untied me from the *cepo* all that time."

"So why didn't you say Antonio was the real thief?"

"What, and squeal on my friend? And lose Petrona whom I loved so terribly much? I'd rather be taken for a thief than tell on my friend. I'd rather be a thief than have them say Petrona was just some woman I kept around. I'd rather be a soldier than have all that happen. Besides, women are all the same, falser than Bolivian silver.[3] See, I found out about that time, I mean before they threw me in the army here, that to get out of being punished by her father, Petrona was going around saying how she always thought I was probably no good and that I didn't really mean it when I was planning to marry her and that all I really wanted was to pull that robbery. Who knows but maybe that's what did it and I finally spilled my guts, what with being in the stocks and all, and told them Antonio was their thief. He was long gone in the sierra by now and you tell me how they were ever going to catch a wild one like him. He's the better part gaucho, you know, and pretty spirited."

"And do you still remember Petrona, Macario?"

"Well, Colonel, I guess the worse the women are to us, the longer it takes us to forget them."

"And nothing ever happened between the two of you?"

"You know how it is with love, Colonel. When you least expect it . . ."

"Circumstance makes the thief," said Juan Díaz, one of my scouts and a quick-witted one at that. Just then the woods opened on to a lovely clearing. The moon was rising white and sharp and the stars were gleaming tremulously in the blue sphere. I stopped my horse, who wasn't obeying the spur now as he had been just a while before. Turning to my constant companions, the Franciscans, I asked them if they would like to rest a while. "It would be our pleasure," they answered. The good missionaries were exhausted. Nothing fatigues like an all-night march.

The grass was exquisite, the night was mild. A stop now could only do the animals good. I passed word on that we would rest for one hour. We hobbled the lead mares, the cowbells ceased their tinkling, and with them died the only sound disturbing the sepulchral silence of that lonesome place. We stretched out on the soft grass. I rested my head on a small mound and fell into a deep sleep with my poncho rolled up as a pillow.

I had a dream, a vision enveloped as though by a garland or a luminous aura in these verses of Manzoni:

> Tutto ei provo; la gloria
> Maggior dopo il periglio,
> La fuga, e la vittoria,
> La reggia, e il triste esiglio.
> Due volte nella polvere,
> Due volte sugli altar.[4]

I was a conqueror, a little Napoleon.

Suddenly, I felt something like my head getting away from me. I pushed with my head, tightening my neck muscles; the earth was moving and I was neither wide awake nor fast asleep. My makeshift pillow kept getting out from under me. I thought I was dreaming. I went to turn over and a black, furry, four-legged object ran out. . . . I had been using an armadillo as a headrest.

Heroes such as I have visions such as that, atop reptiles, and the chapters of our story must perforce close, each one, with a terrible caveat: *lasciate ogni speranza.*

Let us leave my people sleep for a while while I make a new headrest.

14 AFTER I FIXED myself a new headrest, I went back to sleep until Camilo, our brave and exact Camilo, came over to me and said "Colonel, sir" into my ear. I woke up.

I was just then having a dream that was like a bizarre look through a kaleidoscope.[1] I was in two distant points at the same time, on the ground and in the air. I was myself and at the same time I was that soldier, that tender and loving and self-sacrificing country fellow whose story we had just heard from his own lips. I was talking to myself but speaking as he would: "What a mean, cruel woman Petrona was!" And I was speaking as myself as well. "They slandered Byron but he was right: in every land the heart of a woman is rich in generous warmth. Whatever the circumstances of life, women will, like the Samaritan, give of the precious oils and the wine." Suddenly I was Antonio, the man who robbed Petrona's father, or the jealous judge, or Private Gómez resurrected on the frontier. The disorder, the instability, and the incoherence of all the images were peaking at the very instant I woke up. I had picked up the thread of the previous dream—I don't know if this is something that happens to the reader—and taken off, not, this time, on the armadillo that scooted out from under my headrest, but on an enormous glyptodon, which was me. So, with my spirit bent on reaching its vision of glory while riding reptiles, I traveled those blessed lands murmuring:

> *Dall'Alpi alle Piramide*
> *Dall' Mansanare al Reno,*
> . . . .
> *Dall' uno all' altro mare.*[2]

We were soon on our way on fresh mounts.

The night had a somber majesty. There was a gentle wind from the south and a little chill in the air. Still fairly stiff from my grassy bed, I was afraid I would fall asleep on my horse and it was essential that we take great care, since no sooner did we leave the clearing behind and enter the woods again than the branches of the trees started to snap back at us. The penumbra the moon gave off, as each moment the ashen clouds raced across the vast skies obscuring her, made it difficult to appreciate the distances of objects. More than once we pushed imaginary branches out of the way and more than once, too, caught real ones full in the face just when we thought ourselves clear of danger.

Isn't that how it goes on the pathways of life—in politics, soldiering, commerce, and love? Is it not a cloudy night as we ride the trails of thick-grown hills? When we think we've pushed the stone to the top of the mountain, we tumble halfway back down.[3] We think we've reached the longed-for beach and the angry vortex closes in. Anxiously we await the tender and amorous billet-dous and instead receive a perfumed and perfidious Dear John. We stand ready to kill but bow our heads in humiliation at the first compassionate gaze.

How true it is! Man cannot seem to see any further than his nose.

I called Francisco, our interpreter, to keep myself from falling asleep. One question leading to another, I ascertained that within a matter of hours we would reach the first tent settlements. He told me that shortly before our stopping place the road broke off in several directions. We should proceed very carefully so as not to mistake one of these roads for the other. He was a scout, he said, but had not come through here in a long time and could lose his way.

"Then let's not talk," I said. "We don't want to get caught up in conversation and forget where we're going." With this I suddenly stopped my horse, waited until the whole party was together, and cautioned them that any minute we would reach the place where several roads broke off and soon after that the first tent settlements. They should be careful, and whoever first spotted the roads or the tents should warn the rest of us of it. We marched in silence a while. Now and then we would hear the whinnying of a horse and constantly the bells on the lead mares. Suddenly there was loud laughter. It was Calixto, my jocular assistant, erstwhile revolutionary who, as was his wont, was telling tall tales and had just treated his comrades to a whopper.

"What's going on?" I asked.

"Nothing, Colonel," answered Juan Díaz. "It's Calixto. He's trying to get us to swallow one whole."

This liar among men had just sworn by all the saints in heaven

that a woman from the sierra had given birth to a male phenomenon—Calixto's own words—with two heads. That much had
nothing especially improbable about it. Where the story got out
of hand was when Calixto added that the boy—or should I say
boys—had the strangest quirks. He said they drank cow's milk
with one of their mouths, goat's milk with the other; they would
say yes with one head, no with the other; cry with one, sing with
the other; all of which tended to cause some truly hellish quarrels,
which in fact were entertaining.

"You are one colossal liar," I told him.

"Colonel," he answered, "if there is a liar it is the gazette I read
it in."

"And what gazette was that?"

"A piece of newspaper don Pedro wrapped a pound of sugar
in that he sold me the other day at Fort Sarmiento. Everybody
in the Seventh Cavalry read it at the stables. Ask Carmen, he'll
remember."[4]

And Carmen, another one of my assistants, attested to the fact,
correcting only certain details, to which Calixto replied:

"Sure, I probably forgot some of it; but most of it is true, it
really is."

"Father Marcos, when we get to Leubucó, do me a favor and
hear this liar's confession."

"I'd be glad to," the good Franciscan answered, ever gentle, attentive, and kind in his dealings with others.

About this time somebody shouted, "Here's the trail!"

I stopped, as did everyone following close behind me. The rest
pulled up one by one.

"We must be almost there," said Mora. "I'm going to take a
look, Colonel."

I waited a while. He came back saying that it was very dark and
that he could not make out the most traveled trail, the one we
ought to take. Indeed, a dark, heavy cloud totally eclipsed the wan-
ing moon and the stars scarcely flickered light in the fine mist rising
from the surrounding horizon. We had arrived at open space again.
It was not possible to descry the limits in the dark. I ordered straw
to be cut. My quick and agile assistants obeyed and dismounted.
We had beautiful torches made in the blink of an eye, and by their
light soon found the trail we were looking for. Angelito and Private
Guzmán's tracks were on it.

"They came through here not too long ago," the trackers said.
"Their horses are beat and they've each only got the one they're on."

"Angelito's on the piebald," one of them said.

"Yep, and Private Guzmán's riding the thick-maned Moor," added the other.

We took the trail. We must have gone another league or so. We could not see the first tents through the inky darkness. We arrived. . . . It was a pond of water between two dunes. We camped. . . . I ordered the horses to be well secured and lay down, not crying out with the poet,

Without a hope in life [5]

but, on the contrary, trusting in the goodness of God, who had brought me this far without incident.

It was peculiar that the Indians had not heard us yet; they are often abroad, they go to bed early and rise with the stars.[6]

The crepuscular light announced the dawn of a new day.

Let us sleep . . .

How easily sleep comes to us when we are not inconvenienced by civilization, not irritated by its endless annoyances; when we have only to stretch out where we are, with no fear of being kept awake, as we throw off our clothes or think about what justice and human generosity have just done, or intend to do, to us. I'll confess, in the name of all things holy, I have never slept better or more peacefully than on the sands of the pampas with my saddle pack for a bed. My other bed, the soft and spongy one made for civilized men, now feels Procrustean by comparison. Living among the savages, I have come to understand why it has always been easier to go from civilization to barbarism than from barbarism to civilization.

We are very proud. And yet, it is easier to turn Orión and Carlos Keen into Indian chiefs, than to turn chiefs Calfucurá or Mariano Rosas into Orión or Carlos Keen.[7]

I awoke to the sound of soldiers, who were pointing to tents here and there. Curiosity had me on my feet in the blink of an eye. The Franciscans and the officers got up as well. Nobody was thinking of sleep anymore. Beyond question, there would be news soon.

The nearest tent was about a thousand meters away from us.

We spied something red.

The soldiers, with their hawk-like vision, as good as the best pair of spectacles, were saying whether they were Indians or Indian women and counting them and laughing out loud. While these exchanges went on one of them said: "Three Indian women have left that tent. They're all on one horse . . . and they are coming this way."

And indeed, they weren't long in reaching us and stopped about one hundred meters from our camp. I ordered the interpreter to speak. He told them it was I, Colonel Mansilla, on a peaceful mission, and that they should approach. The women prodded the skinny nag they were riding—they were astride him like men and were huddled together—and came towards me.

I went forward to meet them.

They were all three young, two of them good-looking, one so-so. They were wearing their habitual clothes, which I will have occasion to describe later, and each of them had a watermelon. It was a gift in case we were thirsty. The water from the lagoon was undrinkable and they knew it. I accepted the gift and gave them twelve Bolivian reales, sugar, herbal tea, tobacco, paper, everything we could. We had precious little with us as the pack mules were still catching up.

I inquired about their husbands. They answered that the men had been out hunting with their bolas for several days. Why, I asked, had they not been hesitant to come near? They replied that they had recently learned from Angelito that a certain very good Christian was coming to their villages. Besides, they remarked, what did they as women have to fear?

The women, Lord, how safe they feel anywhere they go! And yet, where can they travel without risk? I have never seen anyone more cocksure than these women (for certain things, that is).

There was no doubt in our minds that by now the Indians had heard us. I ordered us all to saddle up. We would go as far as La Verde and wait there a while. There would be good grazing and excellent water. My interpreter went with the Indian women to the tent, made sure the men weren't there, and returned with a poncho full of carob fruit.

It is an excellent pastime to ride a horse while chewing or sucking this fruit.

So it was that as we rode we put our jaws to work.

We were no longer in the hills. The hills lay to the east, the west, and straight ahead of us in the distance. We had reached a field which, broken into rather steep dunes, lent the view a certain resemblance to the Arabian solitudes. Vegetation was scarce and poor. The mire was deep. The horses walked only with difficulty. The morning was most beautiful. We could see tents in every direction, but not a single Indian, not a sole rider. Nothing to be seen of what everyone most wanted to see.

"Indians, Indians, I'd like to see some," the Franciscans were saying. And I answered: "Patience, Fathers, who knows if this isn't just to scare us."

From one dune to the next, from one hope to the next, from one illusion to the next, we arrived at La Verde. It was about ten in the morning. It is a deep lagoon, about three hundred meters in diameter. Adorned by trees, it is hidden in the crater of a dune about sixty feet high. I ordered everyone to unsaddle and change horses. Although this will doubtless be of little interest to the reader, I stripped off my clothes and jumped into the water. I wanted to inspire confidence both in those following me and, more importantly, in the Indians if they discovered me there.

They must certainly have been prepared by now. And this is as far as I will go today. Tomorrow I will tell you the tribulations of the rest of the day, in which our dear Franciscans sidestepped certain untoward events.

T EMPERAMENTAL INDIANS, *profane Christians, and twisted dispatches mark the first "sightings" and exchanges between Mansilla's party and the Ranquels. When one hundred fifty Indians, among them many Christian fugitives from the Argentine civil wars, ride out of the woods with Chief Ramón and surround the visitors, Mansilla writes that he fears a slaughter. As the book goes on such threats will continue, not overwhelmingly from whole tribes or nations, but vehemently from small parties and belligerent individuals. Mansilla the soldier, therefore, remains on guard.*

At the same time, Mansilla the writer stands empowered by the many changes. The Indians are all over him and cursing him, then all over him and kissing him. He is sitting on the ground speaking with a mixed-blood named Bustos, Chief Ramón's own brother-in-law, when he is nearly run down by mounted Indians of the same chief's tribe. Later, the Ranquels show a frenzied admiration for him. He is the brave bull they acclaim, the conniving liar they distrust. The witches and the elders want nothing to do with him. The chiefs, the braves, and the younger Indians want fervently to touch him and to keep everything he and his men have.

This yawing, volatile instability, so seemingly deep-seated in the ways of the Ranquels, turns out to spring both from Ranquel protocol and from the excitement generated by the truly novel events being played out. Both the exiles from the wars and the Indians themselves obey Ranquel protocol, which dictates that one wait, embrace, eat, drink, and talk. The Ranquel way of life is to beg, give, take, revel, and raid. The better Mansilla and his men understand these fundamentals, the more complete the picture that emerges for them, even if it is their presence that lends that picture its special dynamics.

In any case, the book first appeared as serial letters in a Buenos

*Aires newspaper, and the format's characteristic surprises and un-
ravelings needed therefore to be doled out judiciously. There is no
lack of substance by which to pace them: the Indians' craving for
sugar and horse meat; the next two fireside stories, those of Crisóstomo and Miguelito; the sheepskin seats and rolled poncho pillows in the chief's tent; the ragged Christians ordered to fire a salute to Mansilla's party of dignitaries; roast crushed carob beans;
Mansilla's red Algerian cape; Molière's Le Bourgeois gentilhomme
and its parallels to Araucan oratory. The many narrative digressions and the generous splashes of local color obey both a journal-
istic imperative to sell the story and a philosophical one to bring
ethical integrity to Argentina's push westward. The book in fact
can be read as a wager that moral philosophy could demystify an
adversary who, as Mansilla expected, wanted nothing to do with
the extermination it was beginning to see was planned for it. He
would, with these weekly writings, hold the Ranquel ethos up to
his multifaceted looking glass and beam the reflections back to
Buenos Aires.*

 AFTER I BATHED and the horses ate, rested, and
cooled off in the deep waters of La Verde, I ordered everyone to saddle up and the march continued. We were by now so close to Leubucó
that it was quite surprising not to have seen any
Indians. Surely Angelito and Private Guzmán at this very moment
were resting in Chief Mariano Rosas's tent, and the chief must
know I might arrive at any moment.

My interpreter and I were deliberating as we made our way
through the shifting and altogether laborious terrain—so laborious, indeed, that the horses could not keep a trot going—when
upon clearing the top of the last of the many mounds that make up
the one great dune of La Verde, we spied an Indian, armed with a
lance and approaching at a gallop. My interpreter was alarmed. . . .
I could tell by a certain expression of surprise that came over his
face.

"What is it?" I said.

"Sir," he replied, "the Indians do not usually travel this territory
armed."

"What do you suppose is going on, then?"

He shrugged his shoulders, hesitated for a moment and finally answered:

"They must be afraid."

"But of what? I wrote to Mariano, and you yourself translated that message for Ramón and Baigorrita and explained it well to Angelito."

"Ah yes, but sir, the Indians are very distrustful."

The Indian was coming towards us, whirling his long lance, which had a great tuft of flamingo feathers adorning its top. I had intended to stop. But, forced to choose between the Indian thinking that I was doing so out of wariness of him or provoking his suspicions if he was only coming to look me over, I chose the latter, even though it might mean he couldn't then get close enough to study me well.

The choice between giving a scare and receiving one is never open to doubt. A great captain has said that a battle is two armies that meet and try to strike fear into one another. In effect, battles are won not by the number of those who die gloriously and fight bravely, but by the number of those who run or lose all initiative, who are terror-stricken by the thunder of cannons, the whistle of bullets, the clashing of shining sabers, the imposing spectacle of bloodshed, the wounded, and the dead.

The Indian brought his horse to a halt and, nimble as an acrobat, stood on its back while resting on his lance. He was coming from the south, the direction in which I was heading. I continued to advance, though slowing my pace somewhat.

The Indian remained motionless. When we were within rifle shot of him, he dropped like lead onto his horse's back and started in my direction at a full gallop, though clearly intending for us not to engage.

There are aptitudes that cannot be explained; practice alone imparts them. It is a sort of divination. Our country people have some incredible inspiration in this regard. I have had it happen when riding in the open country that Camilo Arias would say to me: "Some animals must have broken loose over there and they must be wild, judging by the way that buck is running"; and sure enough, in a matter of minutes there would come the intractable animals, running defiantly, their long manes afloat in the wind. How beautiful it is to see a colt like that in the open country!

Without once stopping, I sent my interpreter ahead to meet the

Indian with the order that he should have him come to where I was. As neither I nor the Indian was about to halt, we ended up parallel to each other but facing in opposite directions. To look at us, you would have thought that we had had a signal for stopping at the same time.[1] My interpreter began speaking with the Indian. They spoke for a moment and then he came back, saying the Indian wanted to look me over. I spurred my horse and, after giving orders that no one follow me, headed for the Indian at an easy canter. He was waiting for me with his reins pulled in and his lance poised. Twenty paces from him I pulled up, saying: "Good morning, friend." "Good morning!" he answered. We exchanged a few words through the interpreter, all of them intended to pacify, and the Indian turned on his horse and headed south as fast as he could go. I, for my part, rejoined my people and continued to gain ground a step at a time.

Mora, my interpreter, was wearing a long face and, as I found out, was in a mood to match. He confided in me the very serious apprehension he was feeling.

We were discussing the leagues of desert yet lying between us and Leubucó and whether we would take the Carrilobo road, which passes through Chief Ramón's settlement, or the one to the right, which goes through Laguna Calcumuleu, which by now must be nearby. All at once we spotted two Indians hiding in a narrow hollow. I couldn't tell whether one of them was the same one I had just spoken to. I asked Mora. He peered at them, observed for an instant, and answered with perfect aplomb, "It's someone else. That other Indian's horse was *gateado*."

The two Indians advanced on me decisively. Like the first one, they were armed. It didn't take us long to draw close to one another. Unlike the other one, these two were not trying to gain my flank.

"They're going to run us down!" said Mora. "They're going to run us down! And they've got good horses."

"Then let's run 'em down, let's run 'em down," said I, digging my heels hard into my horse. I told my people not to ride fast with me and headed straight at the Indians at full tilt. We would have met head on and like lightning had we not pulled up about fifty paces from each other. We approached one step at a time until coming within the toss of a lance of each other.

"Good morning, friends, how is it going?" I said.

"Good morning, *che*, friend," they answered.

And as they still had their lances poised I had my interpreter call their attention to it, telling them it was I, that I was on a peaceful mission and had no other people with me than those they could see right there. The Indians lowered their lances at Mora's first indication, and when he finished speaking to them and making special mention of the fact that I was not carrying firearms, they made a gesture to the effect that they would like to shake our hands.

That was all I needed. I rode up to them and we shook hands with true cordiality. I offered them cigarettes, which they accepted with marked satisfaction, and sent Mora to our company to get some firewater.[2] I was alone with them now. While he went and returned, we asked each other questions of little importance, for they did not understand Castilian and I could not make myself understood in the Araucan tongue. Nevertheless, I was able to ascertain that Mariano Rosas, the main chief, was, at that moment and in the company of a number of other chiefs, lost in bacchanalian revelry. Father Burela had arrived several days before from Mendoza with a big load of hard beverage.

Mora came back, my interlocutors took a few good belts and, with a cheerful farewell, went their way—in the direction of Ramón's settlement—while I went mine. Mora was still downcast, despite the candor of the Indians. He really wasn't all there. Who knows what could happen, he would say as we rode along, then he would mumble, "They're so untrusting, these Indians!"

Figuring one thing and figuring another, suspecting this and suspecting that, hoping for this and hoping for that, my caravan plodded along, engulfed in an immense cloud of dust.[3] Mora would say, "The Indians are going to think there are a lot of us." I remained impassive; I had a quiet hunch there was no danger. There are situations in which tranquillity cannot arise from reflection. It must come from the soul.

The land was once again a broken array of dunes stippled with small brush, thistles, carob trees, and *chañar*.

We were approaching the top of a hill.

Everyone, absolutely everyone riding with me looked avidly out along the horizon, trying to sight something. We were borne along on the wings of impatience as we climbed atop dunes, descended to the sinking lowlands, dodged thorny brush beneath the rays of the sun, which was at its zenith, while the distance grew with each passing moment thanks to certain mistakes Mora made. Then all at once several voices cried out: "Indians! Indians!"

Indeed, with my eyes fixed somewhere ahead of me and my imagination forewarned, I spied several squads of armed Indians.

"Let's stop, sir," Mora said.

"No, let's go on," I replied. "They might think we're afraid of them or don't trust them. We're better off pressing forward."

Though my horse was fairly tired, I left my party behind and, getting off the road (we had finally found it), galloped towards the largest group of Indians. Taking a look around me, I saw at that moment that I was surrounded by enemies or by curious onlookers. I would soon enough learn what they were.

My party rode up to where I was and told me we were surrounded.

"Move forward at a canter," I told them, and galloped on.

Several squads of Indians were on me as quick as a breath of air. The astonishment painted on their faces was indescribable.

They were all riding good, stout horses. They were wearing the wildest outfits imaginable, some with hats, others with kerchiefs both clean and dirty tied to their heads. Some wore woven tribal headbands, others ponchos. Some scarcely had more on them than our first father, Adam: a simple breechcloth. Many were drunk, most had red face paint on their cheekbones and lower lip, and all spoke the same resounding cry over and over: "*Winca! Winca!*" That is to say, "Christian! Christian!" and here and there some foul epithet in impeccable Castilian.

I pretended not to understand any of it.

"Good day, friend!"

"Good day, brother" was the sum of my eloquence, while my interpreter plied his assiduously, explaining who I was and the purpose of my trip. There was a moment when the Indians encircled me so tightly, looking at me as though at a strange object, that I couldn't move my horse. Some of them grabbed the sleeve of the jacket I was wearing and said, as one might say upon recognizing something never seen before, "Him Colonel Mansilla, him Colonel Mansilla!"

"Yes, yes," I answered, handing cigarettes out right and left and passing around the jug of firewater.

Noticing that my party had continued on its way and was putting distance between us, I resolved to end this scene. I told Mora, he spoke to them and, after the Indians made a path for me, we all galloped off together to join my company. Soon we formed a single group, Indians and Christians mixed together, and came to a dune at the foot of which is a small woods. It is called Aillancó.

My officers and soldiers did not know what to do with the Indians; they gave them cigarettes, mate, and many a gulp of firewater. *Achúcar*, sugar, was what they really wanted, but we had run out of it. The reserve was with the pack mules and there was no way to appease the Indians.

New groups of them arrived one after the other.

A scene like the one I have just described took place with each new group. Remarkable in all this was the good disposition the Indians brought with them and the ill will of the captive or refugee Christians accompanying them.[4] The affability, so to speak, of the one stood in stark contrast to the rudeness of the other. When this reached a certain point, I in turn spoke harshly, insulted grossly, and thus managed to command some respect from the poor devils, or miscreants, who, seeing we had come all but unarmed, were beginning to smack their lips and rub their hands together.

We arrived at Aillancó and, as there is a small lagoon there with excellent water, I ordered a halt, dismounted, and called for fresh horses. Fresh horses were brought. While we were saddling them there came a group of twenty-six Indians led by a white man in shirt sleeves and long hair tied with a headband. He had a manly, somewhat unfriendly look to him and rode a magnificent black dappled horse with a perfect saddle, handsome silver stirrups and silver plating, a great pair of spurs, also silver, that he jingled, and a very long lance that he waved around. He rode up to me, stopped his horse suddenly, and said, "I am Bustos."

"Glad to know that," I answered with a show of arrogance.

"I am Chief Ramón's brother-in-law," he added, crossing his right leg over his horse's neck.

"I am Colonel Mansilla," I replied, imitating his posture and adding, "How is Chief Ramón?"

He answered that he was good and that he sent regards to me and all my officers and protégés. He also wanted to know why, if I had come all the way into his territory, I was now going around it. I thanked him for the good wishes and replied that I was not merely going around his territory without a word. I told him I had sent the Indian Angelito and Private Guzmán ahead with a message the day before. He told me that was precisely what had surprised Ramón. They had told him that I would stop at his settlement before going on to Chief Mariano's. We exchanged further words on this topic and before long I understood that Chief Ramón had made a deliberate mystification of the message I had sent him. Neither the Indian Angelito nor Private Guzmán could have made a mistake. It was most improbable. I had made very sure before they left Coli-Mula that they had understood me perfectly. On the other hand, my letter to Chief Mariano was definite, nor was his settlement so far from Chief Ramón's as to leave the latter no time to warn him.

My dialogue with gentleman Bustos went on for quite some time because he spoke Spanish as well as I did.

I was alerted that all the horses were ready and asked if I wanted to change mine. I said yes, they should find another one for me. I offered Bustos a cigarette, got off my horse and, inviting him to do the same, told him I intended to reach Mariano Rosas's tent before long. While they were changing my mount, I laid a poncho out under a tree and the two of us sat and talked like a couple of old friends. They brought me my horse, and when I had one foot in the stirrup and was saying good-bye to Bustos, who I was sure had taken a liking to me, two groups of Indians arrived from two different directions. One came from Ramón's settlement, the other from Mariano's. Mariano's group was led by one of his lieutenants, an unsavory sort as we will see later. An Indian of no particular note headed the other group.

Mariano sent greetings. Ramón sent word he'd be coming out to meet me momentarily.

I sent the first away with thanks and stood by in anticipation of Ramón's arrival.

While waiting I continued my conversation with Bustos. My party was bantering and entertaining itself with the rest of the Indians and with three women who had just ridden up together on one horse, when we were set upon by a number of Indians who, lances raised, charged me shouting, "*Winca! Winca!* Killing *Winca!* Killing *Winca!*"

I took a look around and saw that my people were ready for anything and, masking my irritation, said to Bustos, "Do you think they intend to do something barbaric?"

The barbarians were upon us now. Bustos and my interpreter both spoke to them in their language, and the Indian women jumped all over them as if being trampled by horses were nothing to fear. The women took hold of their lances vigorously and yanked them from their hands. The Indians were foaming with anger. Happily, the incident went no further.

My interpreter's fears and ill omens were beginning to come true, but we had the bull by the horns now and there was no turning back.

Chief Ramón's "ambassador" returned.
Charged with what embassy?⁵ You will find out tomorrow.

 **16** RAMÓN'S AMBASSADOR RETURNED.
Instead of coming to me, he went to Bustos.
What did he tell him? I never did find out. My
interpreter was not at liberty to speak with me.
Not only did he belong to Ramón's settlement—
and Ramón's brother-in-law was right there beside me—but we
were closely surrounded by a great many Indians who, watchful
and curious, never took their eyes off me as they tried to penetrate
my thoughts. What no one could hide from me was that Bustos
and Ramón's envoy were not in agreement. The former was ver-
bose, demonstrative, and noticeably upset as he spoke. Mora took
advantage of a moment when Bustos was distracted and intimated
to me with a meaningful look that Ramón distrusted us and that
Bustos was defending me.

So it hadn't been wishful thinking after all. The man had taken
a liking to me. Now I had an ally. I therefore tried to win him over
altogether, affecting perfect ease, showing no sign I had any idea
of Ramón's mistrust, and acting as though I found everything that
had gone on thus far utterly normal.

The ambassador left again and Bustos and I continued our conversation. He kept trying to justify Ramón's strange and crafty way
of going about things, that is, his way of pushing me back while
pretending not to.

"Don't be afraid, friend," Bustos would say.

This galled me.

"No, there's nothing to worry about," I would answer.

The more he admonished me, the more I began to harbor suspicions. I was beginning to think I had been far too flippant in
assuming he was on my side. We were sitting there, chatting. He
told me he was born in the old Fort Federation, now Villa de Junín.
His mother was Indian, his father was named Bustos, came from
Rojas, and at one time was a commander in the National Guard.
My company, meanwhile, was handing out cigarettes, herbal tea,
matches, handkerchiefs, shirts, underwear—they were under siege.
The Indians asked for everything they saw and got whatever each
man had with him that he least needed. Suddenly, we felt a thunder

of hooves. Engulfed in billowing dust, some thirty mounted Indians came to a stop so close to me that one more step and their horses would have trampled me.

Bustos couldn't hold himself back: "Whoooaa!" he shouted.

I never moved, never changed position. I just knit my brow and stared daggers right into the head Indian. He came up to me face to face, put his right hand on his heart, and said:

"This man Caniupán! Captain for Mariano Rosas," and pointing to himself again, "this man brave Indian!"

I kept a hard look trained on him.

Along with shouts of "*Winca! Winca!*" there came other ten-gauge oaths.

"Let's get on our horses," Bustos said.

Mine was right at hand and, needing no further urging, I got up off the ground and mounted.

"Caniupán wants to speak with you, sir," said Mora.

"Tell him to speak all he wants."

Through the interpreter Caniupán told me the following: Mariano sent me and all of my officers greetings. He was very sorry he could not receive me on this day as I deserved. He would receive me the next day. Could I be so good as to make camp where I now was?

I gave a most politic answer, resigned as I was to spending the night in Aillancó and aware now that all these delays were deliberate. While this captain and I spoke, several Indians, in particular one Chilean,[1] interrupted us with their shouts and rode their horses up to me, sticking their hands in my face, so to speak. As far as possible, I did not acknowledge these blandishments, which in fact alarmed me quite seriously. Then an Indian knocked Father Marcos over, pushing him with the breast of his horse, and letting out a stentorian shout as he did it. The reverend father received this token of affection with evangelical gentleness, despite having been momentarily airborne. Father Moisés, his companion, was treated to a similar demonstration and endured it in kind.

The Chilean Indian was shouting something which I assumed to be death threats.

Bustos, who did not leave my side, again said to me, "Don't be afraid, friend."

"You're starting to get on my nerves with your 'Don't be afraid, friend,'" I said. "Tell me that when you see me go pale."

Several Indians who understood Spanish shouted together, "That Colonel Mansilla, him Christian bull!"

Caniupán then addressed me in an imperious tone: "Give me a fat horse to eat."

"So you understand the language after all," I said.

"Little bit," answered the Indian. "Give horse?"

"Yes, well . . . I am thinking about it."

He was going to answer, when Ramón's ambassador appeared for the third time. As he spoke with Bustos, every Indian's ears were tuned to him, for he was speaking in a mysterious tone. Bustos answered in monosyllables that seemed to me to mean only yes and no. He came over to our group.

"Chief Ramón says that you are not Colonel Mansilla," he said. "He says the colonel will be coming later with the rest of the people."

I called Mora.

"Go to Ramón's tent," I told him. "Assure him that I am Colonel Mansilla. Tell him to send an Indian who has been to Río Cuarto and let him look at me. You stay there as hostage."

"I will tell him that if I am lying he can cut my throat,"[2] answered Mora. Turning to Bustos, he added, "Friend, stay with the colonel for me in case he wants conversation with anyone."

The self-assurance with which Mora left my side in the company of the ambassador had an unexpected effect on the Indians. They quit harassing us, though some of the Christians kept it up. One of my soldiers got a little out of hand and laid a slap on the face of the boldest one of these.

"Shut your trap, viper!" he said.

The Christian tried to start more trouble, but neither his colleagues nor the Indians would help him. The soldier was a devil. He had been half laughing when he slapped the Christian and now, holding up his firewater, he was yelling, "Drink up, *peñi*" (*peñi* means brother) right in the face of men who looked like they could do him some serious damage.

Some Indians rode up on their own and told us that Chief Ramón was not in his tent but nearby in the hills somewhere. Mora was with him now and they were making preparations to receive me. Behind them came a messenger. He spoke with Bustos, who then relayed the message to me.

"Friend, get your people in formation and tell me how many they are."

I called Major Lemlenyi and gave him my orders. This done, I told Bustos, "We are four officers, eleven soldiers, two friars, and myself."

"Fine. Now, friend, have them stay in wing formation as they are."

Turning to the messenger, he said, among other things, "*Mari purrá wentrú*," words I understood to mean "eighteen men."

While all my people held their formation, my horses wandered loose. I was praying I wouldn't get stuck with no other horses than the ones we were riding.

Bustos sent the messenger back.

Following his suggestions word for word—in the first place, I had no choice in the matter; in the second place. . . . Now this reminds me of a certain story. There was this fellow who was explaining why he had not done something. "First of all," he says, "I didn't feel like doing it. Secondly. . . ." Upon hearing the first reason, one of his listeners interrupted him. "Your first reason is good enough," he said. "You don't have to say any more." I was going to say that following Bustos's suggestions I renewed the march with my phalanx[3] in wing formation and myself at the head between the two friars. We went about a thousand meters in the direction of the mountain where Chief Ramón was. Another messenger rode up, spoke with Bustos, and we countermarched to our starting point.

This procedure was repeated two more times.

It was getting annoying, and I told Bustos so without attempting to hide my foul mood.

"My friend," I said, "I'm getting tired of being played with. If they keep this farce up they can all go to hell and I'll go back to where I came from."

"Be patient," he told me. "These are their customs. Ramón is a good man, you're going to meet him now. At the moment the thing is to count all your people."

Bugles sounded.

It was Chief Ramón coming out of the woods with about one hundred fifty Indians. His group came to a halt about a thousand meters from our wing formation. They sounded a call, and all those who had been behind me fell in with him except Caniupán, who formed a wing of his own as though to cover my rear guard.

They sounded a march and entered battle formation.

There were perhaps two hundred fifty of them. An Indian followed by three buglers who were sounding the war call rode up and down the length of the line, proclaiming war.

It was Chief Ramón.

Two Indians and my interpreter rode up to tell me I should come forward. And Bustos, after having the Franciscans follow some eight paces behind me, placed himself on my left.

"Let's go," he said.

We marched, arriving about a hundred meters from the center of the Indian line, at the head of which was the chief, a bugler on either side of him and one to his rear.[4] Caniupán followed me at some two hundred meters.

A profound silence reigned.

We called a halt.

A single prolonged cry was heard that made the earth tremble, and when the two wings of the line we had before us came together to speak among themselves, they quickly formed a circle which enclosed us. We saw the blades of their long, feather-topped lances shine, as they do for an all-out charge.

My blood froze . . .

"These barbarians are going to sacrifice us," I said to myself. Acting on this first impression, I looked at my people: "Take as many with you as you can," I conveyed to them with the mute eloquence of silence.

A most solemn moment it was.

Another prolonged cry again made the earth shake. The buglers sounded the war call . . .

Nothing happened.

I looked at Bustos as if to say, "What's this all about?"

"Just a minute," he answered.

They sounded a march.

"Greet the Indians first, friend," Bustos said. "Then you'll greet the chief."

And like a regular cicerone, he began the ceremony with the first Indian on the left wing, the one which had closed the circle. The ceremony itself consisted of a strong handshake and a yell, a kind of hurrah which each Indian let out as he shook hands; all this amidst another, uninterrupted chorus of shouts they made by beating the palms of their hands against their mouths. The friars—the poor Franciscans—and all the rest of the party did the same.

What a hellish hullabaloo it was!

Imagine how my wrists felt, dear Santiago, after about two hundred and fifty handshakes. With the mob met and greeted, I saluted the chief with a handshake and an embrace. It was obvious he did not trust me not to stab him in the back when I embraced him. He twisted free and sat back on the horse's rump. The embrace was hailed with shouts, cheers, and bugle blasts for Colonel Mansilla.

I answered: "Long live Chief Ramón! Long live the President of the Republic! Long live the Argentine Indians!"[5] And the circle of riders and lances broke in every direction. The Indians scattered to the ceaseless blasts of the bugle, whirling their lances, breasting their horses, now falling, now getting back up, the most skillful riders showing their skill and daring by breasting their horses until in breathless exhaustion the sweat ran off of the animals like foam. The shouts of jubilation faded out into the open sky. Surrounded by Indians with their hands out, Chief Ramón and I took the road to Aillancó.

We arrived . . .

With our ponchos spread beneath the trees and a ring of listeners around us, we began our parliament, mate come and mate go, firewater come, firewater go.

I had to talk my guts out, which wasn't in character for me, but there was nothing to be done but play my part. I regaled the chief as best I could with what little I had with me. I had to roll and light his cigarettes myself and try the mate and the liquor before he did to inspire his complete trust.

Chief Ramón is the son of an Indian father and a Christian mother from Villa de la Carlota. He is predominantly of our racial type. Tall and muscular, dark-eyed, somewhat fair-haired and of wide brow, he speaks very quickly. He is extremely well-groomed and dresses like a rich *paisano*. He loves the Christians righteously and has many of them on his settlements and several about his person.

He is perhaps forty years old.

His entire look is that of a gentle human being and only in his gaze is one sometimes surprised by a flash of fierceness.

He is a silversmith by trade. He plants a great many crops every year and lays by copious stores each winter. In this his Indians imitate him. His father has relinquished to him the governance of the tribe.

We had a hard, straightforward talk. He thanked me with a visible show of emotion for all I had done in Río Cuarto for his brother Linconao,[6] who under my care had avoided a case of the pox, and asked repeatedly if he still lived in my house and when he would be returning home. I told him not to trouble himself about this; his brother was very well tended to. If I hadn't brought him

with me it was because he was convalescent, very weak, and because to ride a horse would have only caused him further harm. He
warmly entreated me to visit him at his settlement and offered to
introduce me to his family. I promised him I would do so on my
return. As we separated he offered to visit me again the next day.
Bustos left with him, though not, of course, without asking for one
small bottle of firewater.

I gave him my last one.

Mora stayed with me on Ramón's express permission that I keep
him as long as I needed him.

No sooner did Ramón ride off than the captain named Caniupán showed his face, insisting I give him a well-fed horse to eat.
The request had all the air of an imposition about it and I stub-
bornly refused. He insisted with a shove and I asked him who had
ever heard of any man who was any kind of gaucho giving his
horses away. I told him I needed them to get back to where I came
from, or did he think I was going to spend the rest of my life out
here where he came from?

He said something that stung.

I told him to go to hell.

Those who were with him mumbled something that could start
trouble.

I thought it prudent at this point to cut him a little slack. Acting
as if this were a transaction of some sort I very begrudgingly ordered he be given a mare. I had two well-fed ones with me for when
we ran out of jerky, which would probably be that night if we had
many guests. They gave him the mare, his people skinned it in a
heartbeat, ate it raw, and even drank the hot blood off the ground.[7]
The only leftovers at that banquet were the bellies of the animals,
which a few starving vultures greased their beaks on later.

Evening was coming on and our visitors were thinning out.

One of Mariano Rosas's sons arrived with a few cohorts. He
sent renewed greetings from his father. He wanted to know how
things had gone so far and to urge me above all else and in every
manner of speaking that I be very careful with the horses.

I made a dry retort.

The messenger left, the sun set, the horses were rounded up in
a closed circle, firewood was gathered, the fire was built, we sat
down around it, passed the tea around, and started to talk. In going over the day's events and exchanging ideas with Mora, there
was no doubt in my mind that the Indians feared a trap. Clearly

they were going to keep me stalled on the road with excuses until their lookout men returned and assured them that I had brought no backup forces.

I must be patient.

What a grand virtue conformity is! I was resigned to my lot. The friars and I philosophized a while; and as God is immensely good, he breathed trust into us, granted us a restorative slumber, and brought sleep upon us on that uneven ground as if it were a bed of feathers and rose petals.

 THE FRANCISCANS MADE their beds near mine as was their custom. We always slept that way. I had in fact recommended it. The generous abnegation of these young missionaries, their patient acceptance of danger and affable character, their unfailingly level-headed manner, even their agreeable physiognomy—everything that makes up the physical and moral person—inspired in others a powerful allegiance to them. It stands to reason, then, that these sentiments being bound up with my duty to watch over them, I should endeavor to keep them constantly by my side.

Sound body, sound mind . . . and sound snoring.

The reverends were a snoring duet, with Father Moisés as tenor and Father Marcos as bass. I was several times tempted to play a joke on them, but then they must have been so exhausted that to rouse them from a sleep that if not interesting was at least pleasant and restorative would have been unforgivable.

However, I could not stay asleep myself.

I tried dreaming with my eyes open, but after building a few castles in the air, I called an assistant and had him make a fire. When the glow of the flames told me my orders had been carried out, I at last sat up. I sat there bleary-eyed for a while, contemplating the star-speckled firmament whose flickering lights announced the proximity of the king of day. Then I heard the water boiling. I arose, sat beside the fire, and while my people slept the blessed sleep I stirred the kettle, along with Carmen, and drank down a few good tins of coffee with him. Happily, Carmen had saved a little sugar, speaking of which I had to endure an affectionate scolding from him about all the things I was giving away, for soon we'd be left with nothing.

I was absorbed in watching the fire burn, the wood carbonize and turn to ashes, and the water disappear, so to speak, when Carmen announced, "Day is breaking."

"Then wake up Camilo," I told him. "Tell him to come have some mate."

I then changed position, leaned back, and propped myself on my right arm, and nodded off for a moment. Camilo's "Good morning" got my eyes open and I sat lazily up. I stretched my arms out like wings and held them there for as long as it took me to get through a good yawn. I heard Camilo say, "Good day, friend!" as he sat down. I looked around the camp fire and saw a ragged, hatless Indian trembling with cold. He was curled up like a monkey beside the bag Carmen had the sugar in, licking the fingers of his right hand while sneaking the left into the bag.[1]

"How is it going, brother," I said.

"Good, brother," he answered, pretending to shiver and adding, after putting a handful of sugar into his mouth, "Poor Indian very cold."

I had them give him a *calamanco* poncho[2] I was carrying in my saddle bags. Continuing the conversation, I learned that he had spent most of the night near us; that his tent was immediately next to our camp; that when he had returned to it yesterday, after going around with Ramón's people, he had found his family had run to the hills with others saying the Christians were coming on a big raid; that Blanco the Indian, who had arrived from Chile at the same time as I came, was the source of the woeful tidings; that everyone was very alarmed, and that three large parties of scouts had been sent north, east, and west on the Cuero road, the Bagual road, and the Tres Lagunas road, each with fifty men, and that the alarm would last until and unless there came a new report.

This confirmed my suspicions.

Anything might happen now, I thought, if these so-called scouting parties get too close to the borders of San Luis, Córdoba, and southern Santa Fe! It's entirely possible they'll be noticed, their presence taken as an invasion, and our forces moved south. Then the scouts would come back with a false report. The Franciscans plucked me from these reflections with morning greetings. They took their places around the fire, whose pretty embers invited company. After the fathers came the officers, and then the conversation opened up in general, as each remarked how well he had slept.

There was no need for the Franciscans to swear to this.

The Indian was a sly one. He entertained us a while with a battery of stories, among them one about a relative of his who had lived without a head. There were others about some Indians supposedly of remote lands who lived on the steam from their soup kettles. Or, there was the one about the Indians who could run as fast as ostriches and whose calves were on the front of their legs. He tried to get us to believe that everything he said was true.[3] I don't know if he believed it himself, but he seemed to. I asked him several times if he had seen these things. He answered that he had not; his father told him every bit of it. His father of course had not seen them either; he had heard it from our visitor's grandfather. But why be surprised that a poor Indian would believe tall tales when my own Major Lemlenyi believed what some wiseacre had told him, which was that in Patagones[4] there are Indians who have a six-inch tail for which they scoop a little hole in the ground before they sit down so they'll be more comfortable.

Human gullibility often attains admirable proportions.

Truth and falsehood—there's plenty of room for both.

Pressed to do so, I could prove that lies are more commonly believed than is the truth. Machiavelli says that he who would deceive will always find one willing to be deceived, which goes to show that if there are not more liars it is not for lack of those willing to believe but for lack of those willing to lie.

Morning broke.

Word arrived that there was nothing new with the horses. However, the mare I was saving to eat had eaten a poisonous weed and died.

Our goose was cooked if the pack mules didn't arrive by afternoon.

When the sun came out, one of Caniupán's messengers rode up, made a very proper greeting, asked me if I had slept well and whether there was anything new or if I had lost any horses, and finally advised me that the captain would be coming to visit me in a while. I returned the greetings and answered that it was early. The messenger asked for cigarettes, firewater, tea, *achúcar, achúcar*. They gave it to him and he left.

Our visitors arrived a few at a time. I call them visitors but I should say onlookers, because rather than dismount they would drape themselves across their horse's neck and stare at us. Then as they left they would either say "Good-bye, friend" or ask for a cigarette. The announced visit arrived in about two hours, accompanied by some twenty Indians. He got off his horse after a polite salutation, gave me a message from Mariano Rosas, and took a

seat on the ground next to me. He requested a cigarette with perfect nonchalance. I rolled him one, lit it myself, and put it in his
mouth for him, so to speak.

Mariano Rosas was inviting me to change camps, to advance
one league. He also begged my pardon. The spokesman here took
it upon himself to excuse him confidentially. Mariano, he said, was
achumado. Drunk.

I ordered horses rounded up and saddled, and since the land was
very uneven there, a couple of the horses got sidetracked during the
operation and were stolen out from under me. I told Caniupán
about this and made it crudely clear to him that this was no way to
do things, and that it was Mariano Rosas's duty to capture the
thieves, punish them, and make them return the horses to me if
they hadn't eaten them. I put on quite a show of anger; among
barbarians you are better off being taken for a hothead than for
a fool.

Caniupán carried on as well. He assured me the thieves would
be pursued, taken, and punished, but he knew perfectly well that
no such thing would happen. And of course it didn't, so that I lost
my horses and had no other satisfaction than that of having blown
off some steam for a while.

They brought me word that everything was set to go. I relayed
this to my conductor and we got under way.

Never do the Indians canter to get anywhere.

When we reached the road we were to follow, Caniupán broke
into a gallop.

"Gallop, friend," he said.

Not wishing to be ordered around even in the little things, I neither answered nor galloped.

"Gallop, friend, gallop," the Indian shouted.

It was a kind of imposition and it couldn't have rubbed me
worse if I had been his prisoner.

"I don't want to gallop," I answered. Then, several from my
group, seeing the pace the Indians were keeping, came galloping
from the rear.

"Slow down!" I shouted.

The Indians went ahead forming one group. The Christians
stayed back, forming another. They slowed down to wait for us. I
stayed at a canter and when caught up with them dug my heels in,
gave a sharp crack with the riding strap, and shouted, "Let's gallop." We all took off and I mean all. The Indians galloped as well,
and Caniupán rode alongside of me. We were making our way to

Laguna Calcumuleu, which means "water that witches live in." It was a good mile beyond Aillancó and some six hundred meters from the foot of Leubucó Hill.

It didn't take us long to get there. It is a place of no distinguishing features, a small lagoon like so many others. Its one merit is that it nearly always has springs of good drinking water. Its borders are low-lying and here and there adorned with shrub. When we arrived there, Caniupán spoke.

"Here is where Mariano says you can stop," he told me.

"This will do," I answered. I brought my horse to a halt, dismounted, and ordered camp set up. The Indian watched as the men unsaddled the horses and turned them out a certain distance so they could eat better, and, when he seemed convinced I wouldn't be moving from there, he took his leave, cautioning me several times to be very careful of the horses. He left me alone at last, though a few of those whom I had seen arriving with him back at Aillancó did linger here and there as though spying on us.

It was time to eat something solid. With the fire lit and the tea brewing we tried to cook some roasts but the jerky had disappeared. We would have to tighten our gut and keep the coffee and tea brewing.

For the rest of the day there was an incessant traffic of Indians from north to south and south to north. They would stop, come close, look at us, and be on their way. Some stayed to have long talks with my people. The Franciscans were always the most solicitous of a word with them, offering them a swig from their jug of darnel wine,[5] though I have no idea how it was not long gone by then. I had resolved not to talk to anybody that day unless they were specifically sent by someone. Thus, I spent the day strolling along the shore of the lagoon. I would read Beccaria[6] for a while, then a critical essay on Plato, an immortal to whom they could pay the fanatical homage of having everything written on philosophy from his day to the present cast into the fire without the speculative sciences losing much.

As evening fell a new messenger from Mariano Rosas arrived bearing a litany of questions and suggestions, all of them ending with the, by now, sacramental warning: Be very careful of the horses. I received and dispatched the messenger unceremoniously, though I felt seriously concerned that so far I had had no news of Captain Rivadavia, who had been among the Indians for two months now by virtue of the treaty I had been negotiating with them over the course of a year.[7]

Night came. We built a big fire, ate one of the fatter mules and a few armadillos and, sated and content, sang, told stories, and slept until the following daybreak.

It was just getting light when I woke up. I called Camilo Arias and asked if there was anything new. There was not, he answered, though we had been surrounded by spies. I sat up in my soft bed of sand, turned my gaze right and left, behind and in front of me and, sure enough, they were still out there watching us sleep.

The sun got hot and the visitors started to arrive and inconvenience us with every imaginable request, so much so that I had to get angry in a polite way with my assistants Rodríguez and Ozarowsky, for at the rate they were going they would soon be down to their underwear.

"It is a good thing to give," I told them. "But it would also be wise not to let them think we do it out of fear."

As I was making these prudent observations on the conduct they should be observing, an Indian asked me for the kerchief I was wearing around my neck. Here was my chance. I chewed him out and sent him on his way. He grumbled like a dog, muttered a perceptible oath, and added, "Christian bad." Then he left. A short while later a new messenger came from Mariano Rosas. He brought five others with him. I flashed him a hard look.

"The general would like to know how you are doing," he said.

"You can tell him I'm sitting out here in the open," I answered.

"The general would like to know how things are going with you," he added.

"Tell him," I said, "to ask one of the witches who live in this water how things should be going for someone who has nothing left to eat but the mules he needs to get back home."

"The general would like to know," he continued, "if there is anything you need."

"Tell the general," I answered, interjecting a terrible oath, "that he is a barbarian not to trust a righteous man who comes to him unarmed and that the next thing he knows some unprincipled scoundrel will come along and cheat him blind."

This answer drew a gesture of surprise from the messenger. Noticing this, I added, "Go ahead and tell him. Don't be afraid." With that I turned my back on him. When he saw I had no desire to continue our conversation he took his horse and got ready to leave. Just then a group of Indians arrived from the north. They mingled with these and talked for a while. Later Mora told me they said there was nothing new along the Cuero and that beyond that they didn't know. As they were leaving, one of them started to ride between the two Franciscans, who were resting on the ground about two yards from each other. I yelled like thunder and jumped furiously at him to stop his horse. I had my hand on my revolver and was ready for anything.

"Hey! Don't be barbaric!" I told him. "Don't step on the good fathers."

The man, who, as it turned out, was not Indian but Christian, stopped right where he was, almost between the padres, and answered, "Why, I knew that."

"Well if you knew, why did you go that way?"

"I wasn't going to do anything to them," he said.

"Oh, so you weren't going to do anything to them, eh?"

He said nothing, turned around and spoke to the Indians in their language. They followed him out. The poor fathers had had a right awful time of it, thinking the *populus barbaro* was on the rise.

Strange phenomena of the human heart!

Nothing noteworthy occurred after this scene, but a few hours later the same man so harshly dealt with by me reappeared.

"Colonel," he said. "I brought you this lamb and some corn on the cob."

The uncultured man had yielded, it was only fair that I yield as well.

"Thank you, son," I answered. "You shouldn't have gone to the trouble. Climb down. We'll have some tea and you can tell me your life's story."

He got off his horse, hobbled it, sat down near me and, after a few words of appeasement with the Franciscans, told us his story.

At that instant someone shouted that several red shapes could be seen coming from the hills. We will soon find out what they were.

ALL EARS WERE turned to Crisóstomo.

"Colonel," he began, "man was born to work like an ox and suffer all his life."

This introit from the lips of an unschooled man caught the gathering's attention. I got as comfortable as I could on the ground; I wanted to pay close attention. I am convinced that real drama has greater merit than all the novels of the imagination.

I was saying as much to Behety just the other night.[1] I was asking him to make a one-hundred-fifty-yard sacrifice for me or, in the vernacular, walk a block with me. Behety agreed with me about the merit of true stories and paid me a compliment.

"You are celebrated for your sayings," he said.

"And for my misfortune,[2] like Sir Walter Raleigh," I answered and, speaking into my cloak, added, "That's the world for you. We struggle to make a name for ourselves at center ring and end up buffoons in a sideshow."

How hard it is to know ourselves!

Crisóstomo continued. "I lived in the valley below Intiguasi Hill."

This hill is near Achiras and its name, if my ethnographic and philographic memory serves me well, means "sun house" in Quechua. The Incas gave it its name in one of their famous expeditions to the east side of the Andes. *Inti* means "sun," *guasi* "house."

"I lived with my mother and father, minding the herds. We had a flock of pampean sheep and several others of goats. We also made cheese. We weren't doing so badly. There was an uprising and they drove out the *colorados*, who I had gone with because don Felipe"—he meant Sáa[3]—"roped me into it. I hid out in the mountains around San Luis for a long time and then when things quieted down I went home. The *colorados* had sacked our home. Poor people always get jerked around like that. If it's not one side that does it to them, it's the other. That's why we never get ahead. We kept working and saving what little we had left until I got into trouble . . ."

Here Crisóstomo frowned, and a tinge of melancholy darkened his wind-chapped and sunburnt copper skin.

"And how was that?" I asked.

"Women, sir, women! They bring all harm and no good," he said.

"Don't you have a woman now?"

"Yes, I do."

"Then how can you speak so poorly of them?"

"That's the way man is, I guess, Colonel. He spends his life complaining about the thing he likes the most."

"Well, go on," I said, and Crisóstomo picked up the thread of his story, which by now had everyone sympathizing with him and avidly curious.

"Another poor family lived near us. We were very good friends, saw each other every day. They had the loveliest daughter. Her name was Inés. When we'd be out in the late afternoon bringing the flocks in we'd meet by the stream that starts way up in the hill. And since I liked the girl I'd get her to talk and we'd spend a long time in conversation. One day I told her I loved her and asked her if she loved me. She answered she did without ever saying a word."

"What do you mean 'without ever saying a word'?"

"Well, Colonel, I saw in her face that she loved me."

"And then what?"

"We went on seeing each other every day. We'd go out for the flocks as early as we could so we could lay back and talk. We'd sit on the bank of the stream in a certain place where there were some really nice willow trees. We'd hold hands and just sit there for hours watching the water run. One day I asked her if she wanted us to get married. She didn't answer. She just drew a long sigh and the tears came to her eyes. She cried and she made me cry, too."

"She made you cry?"

"Yes, sir, she did," answered Crisóstomo, giving me a look that seemed to say, "You mean I can't cry just because I live with the Indians?"

I felt the sting of reproach.

"I didn't quite get what you meant," I said. "Go on."

He did.

"While the sadness was passing I asked her why she was crying, and she told me her father wanted to marry her off to somebody named Zárate who had horses and a lot of land. She said they had told her the night before that if she kept carrying on with me they'd slap her around. We got so wrapped up with talking and all that we didn't notice we hadn't even brought in the flocks till the prayer bell tolled.[4] We went out after them together. Night came, it got dark, it felt like rain, and we got lost. We spent the whole night outdoors . . .

"The next day, Inés didn't come to the stream. I went to her house, her father did not welcome me. He tried to pick a fight with me. Inés was there at the ranch and when she looked at me it was like she was saying don't answer my father, just leave. I obeyed her. The old man poured on the insults until I was out of sight. I took it and never answered him back. Her old lady came over that night and argued with my mother. I heard it all from outside. Later on when we were alone, I told my mother what happened . . .

"My poor mother! She really loved me, she got pretty cross with me, then she cried and finally forgave me. Several moons passed without our families seeing each other. One night the dogs started barking. I went out to see what was going on. It was a neighbor woman who was going over to Inés's house. They were doing something in a big hurry over there. A few days later Inés married Zárate and there was dancing and drinking at her house. By this time I knew what had happened to Inés the night the dogs were barking because my neighbor, who was a good woman, told me the whole thing and then asked me who I thought the little baby girl Inés had just had was from. It made me awful mad to hear the fireworks at the wedding, which they had in the San Bartolo chapel right up against the mountains there. I went to her house and asked for my daughter. They yelled 'Drunkard' at me, so I tore up a little in there and someone cut me on my way out. I was sick for a long time. I got better, went to look for my daughter but couldn't find her. I loved her so very much and I had never seen her. One afternoon I found out there was nobody else home, so I went to see Inés. She was there. She looked at me like she'd never seen me before. I asked her for my daughter and she told me I was drunk! I reminded her of the night we got lost. She just kept saying 'You're a drunk.' I started to cry, I don't know what from. She called me a drunk again and threw me out of the house. I stabbed her . . ."

And at this point Crisóstomo became pensive.

We were aghast.

"So then what?" I said, jarring everyone from the reflective abyss into which the unfortunate lover's last phrase had driven them.

"Since then," he muttered bitterly, "I have suffered much, Colonel."

"What did you do?"

"I went home, confessed to my mother what I had done, and to my father, too. They begged me to go to San Luis and got my saddle bags ready for me. I took two good horses and headed for Chaján, but when I reached the road to the Indian settlements I couldn't resist the temptation to turn south, so I came here."

"And you haven't seen your mother and father, or Inés, since?"

"Yes, Colonel, I've seen them several times on raids with the Indians. You have to go along with that if you want to live here, otherwise they don't give you anything to eat. We captured Inés with her husband and her parents on this one raid. She was spared on account of me. She cried so hard and begged me to leave her be and forgive her, and I felt sorry for her. She was pregnant and I got them to leave her alone. They took her mother and father and sold them to the Chileans for one load of drink, which is two small barrels of firewater. I heard they're on a farm near Mucum now."

Here Crisóstomo took a few breaths, as though he knew he would continue his narration.

"Have you gone on a lot of raids?" I asked him.

"Yes, Colonel. What are we supposed to do? You have to find a way to live."

"Do you wish you could go back to the Christian side now?"

"I am married to an Indian woman and have three children," he answered, his eyes saying nonetheless that he did wish he could go back, but that he wouldn't do so without his wife and children. Frankly, these paternal sentiments of his made me forget the man who stabbed Inés.

What unfathomable chasms of tenderness and ferocity the human heart conceals in its tempestuous depths!

"Don't leave yet, Crisóstomo," I said and, getting up, walked to an outcropping of rocks to get a better look at the shapes approaching us.

"It's two Indian women," some said.

"And there's an Indian with them," said others.

The shapes were coming at a good trot. They rode up, greeted us politely in Spanish, and asked for Colonel Mansilla.

"I am he," I answered. "Feel free to climb down."

The Indian hopped down at once. The women drew in the colored, beaded leather strap which they use as a stirrup and got down from their horse, though with some difficulty because of the tight blanket they wrap themselves in. The first visitor was a gentleman known as Villarreal, son of an Indian woman and a Christian, and husband to my comadre Carmen's sister. Carmen sent her regards and some presents—corn and watermelons.[5] The second woman was also sister both to Carmen and to Villarreal's wife.

Villarreal is a man of regular stature; his gentle and expressive face is enhanced by his big, fiery black eyes. He was dressed like a rich gaucho. He speaks Spanish fairly well and is a distinctly well-groomed person. His father, whose name he bears, was from Bragado. Villarreal is possibly thirty-five years old. He was in Buenos Aires in Rosas's time and is perfectly conversant with the customs of decent Christians. His wife is a magnificent Indian woman who has also been in Buenos Aires. She spoke to me of Manuelita Rosas.[6] She is some thirty years old. Her sister is perhaps eighteen and was single. Both women were splendidly dressed. They wore

beaded bracelets of silver and many colors, gold and silver necklaces, the red *pilquén* fastened with a lovely gold pin about a
hand's breadth in diameter, very large triangular earrings, and
wide, beaded anklets on their legs.

Villarreal's sister-in-law is very pretty. Dressed in a hoopskirt
and other such finery, she'd be one dark beauty that would set men
reeling. She dressed less modestly than her sister. When she lifted
her arms, one could see a covering of hair on her underarm and as
the folds in her shirt opened part of her bosom showed.

They handed me the gifts with a thousand apologies for not having brought more, but they didn't have time and my comadre Carmen was hurrying them. I thanked them for the consideration, had
their horses tended to, invited them to take a seat, and struck up a
conversation with them. As the afternoon waned I asked them if
they had any intention of spending the night with me. They said
yes, if it wasn't too much trouble. I ordered their horses unsaddled.
Crisóstomo's lamb was put on the fire and while it roasted we hit
the mate and the Franciscans' darnel wine. It was nightfall when
an envoy from Mariano Rosas arrived, bearing the usual message:
How are you, how is it going, have you lost any horses? I told them
there was nothing new and sent the ambassador away as quickly
as I could without inviting him to dismount.

I kindly asked Crisóstomo to spend the night with me. I had my
reasons for wanting to speak to him alone.

He stayed.

We sat around the fire. Gorging ourselves on the corn—it was
like royal fare to me—we talked on a long while and when it was
late, rolled out our beds and, like in the good old patriarchal days,
lay down together, so to speak, with only the clear, bluish, light-
bespeckled heavens above us.

I should clarify something lest the reader get the wrong idea: the
Franciscans, as agreed upon, made their beds beside mine.

 THE NEXT MORNING had a dim, colorless atmosphere to it. The undulations of the sandy
terrain formed whimsical mirages in the rever-
berating sun. Objects near to us were seen far
away, their dimensions grown. We saw great la-
goons of tranquil, silver-plated surface in the distance; colossal
trees, which were only small shrub scorched by the desert sun;

runaway colts pawing the ground that were birds of prey raising the fine dust with their wings.

A tiny cloud of a dark, earthen tone had been holding my people's attention for a while.

I was deliberating whether to kill another mule or send Crisóstomo to buy us a steer; there wouldn't be enough corn for everybody. Then I heard a shout.

"Indians!"

"No, they're coming too slow to be Indians."

"They're mules."

"It has to be our pack mules."

That last remark roused me from my indecision, got me up and on my feet and looking in the direction of the objects in dispute. I called Camilo Arias—he has the eyes of a hawk—and pointed it out to him.

"What is that, Camilo?"

His eyes are bright and pierce like a dart. He aimed his gaze at the horizon and after an instant's reflection answered with his customary aplomb, his air of profound certainty, "It's the pack mules, sir."

"Are you sure?"

"Yes, sir, Colonel."

"Everybody up," I shouted. "Everybody get firewood! Let's go, let's get a fire built! Here come the pack mules."

My assistants got moving and scattered to the four winds; and, by the time they came back with their bundles of wood, the little cloud had made its way toward us so that the least observant among us could plainly see it was the three men who had stayed behind and the four mules with the Franciscans' sacred vessels, the tea, the sugar, the drinks, and other odds and ends of scant value, which were the great presents I had earmarked for the main chiefs. The mules were moving along at that peculiar pace of theirs which is neither canter, trot, nor gallop; but it is fast. They call it *marchado* in our country vernacular. It is something like an English trot, a march which to the rider feels not so much like the mule is walking, but that it is sidling along like a snake. Every kind of equestrian march—the canter, the trot, the gallop—is tiresome and will wear a rider flat out. Only the *marchado* spares the body its joints, the back and waist their pains, lets you sleep comfortably on the back of the donkey or mule as if on a speedy skiff cutting swiftly through calm waters, leaving behind its foamy wake. As silly as it may sound, I would compare that wake to the track left in the soft ground by our hybrid quadruped, whose tail sloshes unfailingly left and right, like a ship's helm, as he moves along.

The long-awaited packs arrived, then, and while everything inside of them was laid out on the ground and the fattest pieces of jerky chosen, a fire was built, and a pot set on it to cook up a stew and boil the rest of the corn. The fathers went about opening their trunks, taking out the sacred ornaments, which were damp, and spreading them out under the sun most carefully. We had to do the same with some of the presents for the chiefs. The mules had fallen into the Cuero bog any number of times and gotten everything wet, despite it all having been bundled in fresh hide, and plenty of it, at Fort Sarmiento. I was very upset; I knew from experience how delicate the Indians' palate is. Many is the time I have seen them handle eating utensils—fork and knife—at my table, with admirable skill; I've seen how deftly they take the tip of the tablecloth in hand and wipe their mouth with it; I've seen the perfect balance with which they bring a goblet of wine to their lips.

I can recall quite clearly a feature of good breeding in Achauentrú, Mariano Rosas's captain. He was seated at my table. The assistant serving him passed him the sugar, and as the Indian could see there was no spoon in the sugar bowl, he took a quick look at the saucer under his coffee cup. When he saw no spoon there either, he looked at the soldier and as surely as the most mannerly gentleman would have done, called out, "Spoon!"

"Quick, man, a spoon for Achauentrú," I shouted, exchanging knowing looks with all present, as if to say: There is positively no reason why these barbarians can't be civilized.

They announced that the jerky was roasted, the corn boiled, the *pucherete* ready.

"Let's eat," I called.

Once we were all seated in a circle, lunch began. Our visitors had the seats of choice next to the Franciscans and me. The two squaws were most beautiful, with their skin shining like burnished bronze. Their long tresses, black as ebony and adorned with tribal ribbons, fell winsomely down their backs. Their short, even, naturally clean teeth looked like ivory. Their fingers were tiny like their hands, and shapely and sharp. Their little feet were perfectly cared for, the toenails carefully trimmed. That morning, when the sun rose, they had gone to the shore of the lagoon, taken a short bath and, somewhat chary of our presence, painted their cheeks and lower lips with carmine that the Chileans sell to them at the price of gold. María, Villarreal's sister-in-law, was a little more coquettish than her married sister and wore black beauty marks, a favorite among the women. To do this they make a kind of dye out of mud that they take from certain lagoons. It is a rather compact mud of leaden hue and is thick enough to slice like bread and dry in the sun or shape into a bun.

The jerky was delicious—no bread too stale for a keen appetite, as the saying goes—and the *pucherete* was excellent; the corn was sweet and soft as honey cake.

We Christians ate well; Villarreal and the women drank their fill of firewater.

Villarreal, in fact, drank till he was pretty much stewed.

The coffee gourd was coming around. There being no other dessert, and cognizant as I was of some recently arrived Indians who were gathering nearby, I called them over, invited them to sit down in our circle, and gave them a few good drinks of the hard anisette. It dawned on me then that I hadn't debriefed the private in charge of the pack mules concerning news he might have had along the way; and that he, not having been asked, had said nothing either. I was mulling over whether to call him then and there, when from certain exchanges among my helpers I surmised that something unusual had happened. I decided to question him.

"Call Private Mendoza over!" I said, *incontinenti*.

"Call Private Mendoza!"

"Mendoza! Hey, Mendoza!" we heard. "The colonel wants you." The private was there in an instant. He saluted.

"How did it go on the way here?" I asked him.

"Not so good, Colonel," he answered.

"Why didn't you say something?"

"Because you didn't ask me."

"I didn't think there was anything to report. You should have come forward."

The private lowered his head and said nothing.

"Well, go ahead and tell me what happened."

"Sir, when we were just about at a pond not too far at all from here, near the La Verde dune, an Indian, one of the really bad ones, rode up. He had four of them with him. He says, 'Me Wenchenao. My tent here, my land here. Who say you go through?' I says now I don't know, friend. Just let me on through. The Indians had their lances right up against our chests and stuck them in the rump of the mules to make them scatter.

"'No let through if don't pay,' he says.

"And what do I pay you with, friend? Can't you see we're carrying stuff for Chief Mariano?

"'Then better give. Mariano have plenty. Father Burela bring firewater plenty.'

"While we were working this out, one of the Indians unloaded one of the mules. Then some squaws came over with pots, filled them up with sugar and tobacco and paper, and wrapped it all in a poncho and left. Then Wenchenao spoke up again.

"'Go now, friend, but first give shirt, kerchief, underwear.'

"And they wouldn't let up with the lances or let us through until we gave them some of that."

"Well, that's some heroic deed, there," I said. "You let a bunch of lousy Indians loot three men?"

"What were we supposed to do, Colonel? If we'd have stood up for ourselves they'd have taken everything."

"You're right," I said. "You're excused."

He saluted, turned, and withdrew.

I wanted to make the most of having Villarreal and the other Indians present, so I put on a show of great anger and indignation. I got up from around the camp fire and walked up and down, exclaiming all the while, "Damn thieving hooligans," and I'd pepper this with certain threats, like "I hope they try something with me so I can just send them all to hell." Every single one of the Indians there heard me loosing lightning and fire flashes at them and they didn't say a word, didn't even move from where they were sitting. Only when it looked like I was calming down did Villarreal, who was a good three sheets to the wind by now, get up and come towards me. He was staggering and seemed hesitant.

"Have patience, Colonel," he said.

"Where am I supposed to find the patience for a pack of thieves like that?" I answered.

He kept asking me to calm down. I kept answering and by the time I had heard him out on the ways of the Indians and the difference between the ones that work and the ones that steal, we were the best of friends. With the show over, I asked for some more firewater and offered some to the Indians around the camp fire. Needless to say, Villarreal's wife and her sister added a few kindly exhortations of their own, all of which ended with the same phrase: "Be patient, sir."

Seeing that my guests were now getting a little stewed, I thought the moment opportune for ending the libations.

"Give more, give more, Colonel," several of them said all at once. They were in fact stewed and wanted to go all the way. I wouldn't budge. When they saw I was firm they cleared out of camp one by one.

Villarreal and his women asked for their horses.

They were treating me to a private lecture on the best approach to the Indians, and on Ramón's relevant character traits—he was their immediate chief—when one of Caniupán's scouts rode up, saying Caniupán wouldn't be long in getting here. He said they were preparing a big welcome for me in Leubucó and did such a song and dance about all the Indians who were going to be there and the fireworks we'd be shooting off that all I could do was rub my hands together in anticipation of the royal reception that awaited me.

At length Caniupán arrived with some forty individuals in parade dress, that is, mounted on proud, fiery steeds they had decked out in full Pampean finery, with silver-studded head and tail gear, cinches, stirrups, and bridles, all of it of Chilean taste.[1] The riders wore their best ponchos and hats. Some had cowhide riding boots, others the softer colt skin, and many of them wore spurs on their bare feet.

I broke camp, said good-bye to my guests and, escorted by Caniupán, took the road to Leubucó.

Tomorrow I make my triumphant entry there.

 THE ROAD FROM Calcumuleu to Leubucó ran parallel to the woods lying to our east, and pushed into them as if to open a meadow. This formed a great inlet. Every so often it would branch into a network of trails going off to the different settlements.

The desert was very much astir. The Indians came from all sides, always at full gallop and ever heedless of the natural obstacles of the terrain, where horses trained like ours or like English horses, and no matter how vigorous, would have collapsed from exhaustion in ten minutes of riding. They darted to the tops of shifting dunes and shot down through the sand like lightning; they disappeared in the hills of *chañar* and as quickly reappeared again; they would sink into the soft winding sands and easily break back out;

they would lean right to avoid one cliff, then left to refuse another; and so whether on the horizon or out of sight on breaking surfaces, they would spring up at our sides, so to speak, when we least expected them and fall in with our party.

At times we rode in formation. I would be at the front with Caniupán; his Indians would ride behind us followed by my people. Other times we dispersed.

It is impossible to ride as a single unit with Indians. They loosen their reins so that the horse will give all it can, though they never hurry a horse. Riders whose horse has a short stride therefore wind up at the back while the others ride in the front.

Indians always begin a march in order. Soon, though, they're scattered like flies, except in cases of war. At war they might fight as a unit or scattered, some on foot and others mounted, or all intermixed as circumstances dictate. In one combat which my forces had with them at Pozos Cavados, they fought intermixed. Being fewer in number, my people had dismounted. The Indians charged three times and were turned back each time by gunfire. Then, when we turned our heads, the ones on foot would grab the horses by the tail as they went by and, carried by the animals, quickly move out of the reach of our bullets.

In no march except the military march do Indians respect rank or order. Right or left, front or rear, it is all one to them. Captain, petty chief, or big chief are only the least Indian's equal. The terrain, the kind of march, and the horse decide each rider's position. Is the chief on a good mount? Then the chief will be in front, very much in front. Does he have a bad one? He rides in the rear. All the glory resides in having the longest galloping, proudest, and most enduring horse. We will see later how the horses they steal from us (for they have no race or breed of their own)[1] soon quadruple their strength under the Indians' peculiar and severe training, leaving us reduced oftentimes in war to a state of impotent despair.

Upon reaching the entrances to the woods, I could see that my people were lagging behind and that my horses could not endure a long, sustained gallop in the sand. Even when we stayed on the trail the horses were sinking in up to their knees. We had to stop.

"Let's rest here," I said to Caniupán. "The good fathers are very tired."

It was an excuse like any other.

Caniupán stopped his horse at once, as did I mine and those

following us theirs, one after another. The Indians ahead of us stopped as well when they noticed we were no longer riding. We now formed two groups in a cloud of sand. To gain both time and rest for my horses, I ordered everyone to change mounts. The Indians did not get off their horses. It is their custom to rest on a horse's back. They stretch out as if on a bed, with the animal's neck as the headrest and their feet crossed on its rump. They will remain there for a long time, sometimes for hours. They don't even get down to give the horse a drink, but take the bridle off and put it back on as they lie there. Besides being very strong, the Indian's horse is very tame. Is the Indian asleep? The horse doesn't move. Is he drunk? The horse keeps his balance for him. Did he just let the reins drop upon dismounting? The horse stays put. For how long? All day. It is rare to find an Indian who uses hobble, fetters, headstall, or halter. If he does carry any of these with him, it is in all likelihood because he is breaking in a colt, or a stubborn horse, or teaching one that he robbed on his last raid.

The Indian lives on his horse much as the fisherman on his boat: his element is the pampa as the latter's is the sea. Where would an Indian go without first saddling up or just jumping on bareback and going? To the next tent a few blocks away? He'll take his horse. To the stream, the lagoon, or the pond, all of them near his dwelling? He'll ride his horse. An Indian's tent may be completely bare. He can be as poor as Adam. There is one thing never lacking. Night or day, come radiant sunshine or drenching downpour, there is always a horse bridled and tied to the post.

A horse! A horse! My kingdom for a horse![2]

In a critical moment, an Indian will give every last thing he owns for a horse.

We changed mounts in a circle, team-roping them.

When not done clumsily, that is, when not done with a lasso, this is an enjoyable country operation. Each group of my people gathered around a given string of horses. The lead mare was hobbled. The other animals were milling around her. The group took ropes and passed them along until they formed a circle like a corral. They took turns going in, one at a time and by number, to get their fresh horse. Whoever was in charge of each circle would pick one of the less used-up mounts, point it out as, for example, number four—spotted gray, and the person with that number would gingerly approach the horse with bridle and bit in his left hand and, careful not to scare it, find a good angle. If the horse was not gentle, they would toss the gear onto its back. The more gentle and docile horse will almost always go still when it feels this.

Changing horses out in the open with a lasso, over and above the risk it poses—even the least skittish horse will spook, bolt, and run wild—is a wearisome operation requiring great skill and is fraught with danger. Of all the gaucho's or *paisano*'s exercises, lassoing is the hardest and most perilous. Anyone can learn to use the *boleadoras* passably well in a short time. You don't need to be much of a horseman; you don't even need to be strong. The lasso, on the other hand, demands complete mastery of the horse, manly vigor, and agility.

While we were changing horses, several Indians arrived from the north, from the outside as they say. We call the south the outside.

"Where are they coming from?"

"They coming from outside, hunting with bolas," he said.

It was the last scouting party returning, but Caniupán did not want to say so.

"What find in open country, brother?" I added.

"Very quiet going Cuero, Bagual, and Tres Lagunas."

"Then Indians trusting me now?" I pressed.

Camilo Arias interrupted the dialogue, advising me that we were ready.

"On your horses!" I shouted. We mounted, started on our way, and in a few short minutes were on the Leubucó hill.

A vast network of paths and trails crossed before us in every direction. We rode as a scattered galloping band. Corpulent carob, *chañar*, and *caldén* trees there from time immemorial and a thousand sprouting shrubs breaking the straight line of the trail forced us to keep our reins drawn tight lest we trip or entangle ourselves in their thorny and treacherous offshoots.

Our horses aren't used to running in the woods. We had to stop constantly on account of them, as they might roll, and on account of ourselves, as we could wind up gaffed and dangling from the limb of a tree. Our awkwardness was comparable only to the Indians' skill. While we could scarcely go a step without hitting some barrier that would cut our progress short or slow us down to a stop-and-go pace, they rode on unimpeded, swift as the wind. They were soon out of the woods. We lagged behind. I could not forget that I had the Franciscans with me and must by no means leave them along the road somewhere or expose them to a leisurely swing, very much against their will, from a carob tree branch. We had shown too much patience to throw it away now with, God willing, the journey's end almost within sight.

The Indians were waiting for me in a cove just outside the woods; there was a great expanse of dry land there, of barren, sad, and solitary dunes. A long ways off, the crown of a hill broke over the horizon like a black sash.

"That is Leubucó," they said, pointing to the black sash.

I peered at it and, I confess, stared as if I had just been told, after a long pilgrimage across the vast and desolate Tartar plains to the border of China: There it is, the Great Wall.

At last I am going to penetrate the forbidden enclosure. For the first time, the echoes of civilization will resound peacefully where no man of my ilk has ever set foot.

Great and generous thoughts bring me here; noble and lofty ideas impel me; my mission, I have told myself, is worthy of a soldier, a Christian, a man; I could foresee the day when these barbarians, subdued and Christianized, would lend their strength to labor and render bonded homage to civilization, through the efforts of this, her humblest servant.

Away ye aspirations of a lucid mind! You are harder to fulfill than the very visions of a dream.

Man is not rational in discourse but in achievement.

We live in the age of success.

We came to a halt where the Indians were waiting for us. I ordered we loosen our cinches, give the horses a rest, and then let them drink. That done, we got into two groups that no sooner formed than broke up, and got under way at a gallop, our eyes fixed on the black sash.

We were galloping on wings of impatience and apprehension. It had been no easy endeavor to arrive at Mariano Rosas's abode. Even barbarians know how to surround themselves with theatrical pomp so as to dazzle and delude the crowds. Suddenly a group of Indians ahead of us came to a stop.

"Something is up," said Mora. "Otherwise they wouldn't have stopped."

"What could it be?"

"I would say they've seen a parliament waiting ahead."

"With whom?"

"With General Mariano."

"And how many of these will we have to do before we reach Leubucó?"

"Who knows, sir? It depends on the honors the general wants to give you."

An Indian was coming towards us at an easy gallop. They had sent him from the group that was stopped. He wanted Caniupán. We came to a halt. He spoke with him in their language and then turned and took off at an open gallop in the same direction he had come in.

"Parliament coming," said Caniupán.

"I'm very glad."

"Now run up to, gallop."

"Good, run up to at a gallop."

And with this we broke into a gallop without a thought for anything else. Every so often I took a quick look back and could see my Franciscans hopelessly exposed to a furious spill. I slowed my horse down to let them catch up. As it was, Caniupán kept saying, "Putting fathers next to us." On we rode, gaining ground and raising whirlwinds of sand. Four of our riders rolled in a matter of seconds and we saw a many-colored cloud coming towards us. We cleared the crown of a dune from the backside and from there could clearly see a group of some fifty horsemen.

"That them, slow gallop," said Caniupán, drawing in his reins.

"Good, friend," I answered, keeping my horse even with his.

We went along like that until we came to within some six hundred meters of them.

"There him, brother, run up!" said Caniupán, flying violently at them.

I followed him and my people followed me, nor did the Franciscans fall behind. I don't know how they did it, but the fact is they kept up with me all the way to where Caniupán, marrying words to action, shouted, "Now stop, brother!"

Both groups, one coming and one going, drew in their reins at the same time. We stood about twenty paces from each other. An Indian came out of their group. An Indian came out of ours. They stopped at an equal distance from their respective groups. With one facing north and the other facing south, the one coming from Leubucó spoke first.

How long did he speak?

I would say that he spoke, without interruption and without swallowing any saliva, for five minutes.

What did he say?

We will learn this later.

The other one answered in the same manner and form.

What did he say?

This we will learn later as well.

In all, they asked each other, and answered, three questions.

I asked Mora what they had conversed about.

He said that one had offered his greeting and the other had answered for me; that one represented Mariano Rosas and the other represented me, as Caniupán had just ordered him to do.

"But Mora," I said, "do you mean they spoke all that time just to say hello?"

"You see, Colonel, they are both good speaking men." He meant orators.

"But Mora," I insisted, "how could they talk for a quarter of an hour without saying anything but the greeting?"

"Colonel," said Mora, "the reasons Mariano's parliament put forward turned into many more reasons and your speaker did the same in order not to look bad."

"How many reasons did Mariano's speaker put forward?"

"Just three!"

"And what were they?"

"They were how are you doing, sir, how has your journey gone, have you lost any horses. There is always something bad happening out here with the horses."

"All that palaver just to say that?"

"Yes, Colonel. You see, they took each reason and made ten reasons with it."

"What do you mean?"

"You see, Colonel . . ."

Mora was saying this when Caniupán interrupted us, proposing to me that I greet the commission which had just arrived. I deferred to his suggestion and began the greetings.

You must be patient until tomorrow, dear Santiago, you and the reader alike. Patience is a virtue which it behooves us to exercise in the small things. As for the great things, I agree with Romeo, through William Shakespeare.

 AT ONE OF our stops, I seized the opportunity to ask Mora again about the art of spinning two or more reasons from one. In his own way, he gave me a complete course in rhetoric. I have already noted that he is a perceptive man and if I haven't, this is as good a time as any.

The Ranquel Indians have three forms and manners of conversing. There is informal conversation, conversation in parliament, and conversation in junta.

Informal conversation is like ours: smooth, easy, free of ceremony and figures, subject to interruption by the one or several interlocutors involved, animated or vehement depending on the topic or the passions excited.

Conversation in parliament follows certain rules. It is methodical, the interlocutors cannot and must not interrupt one another. It uses a question-and-answer format, has its own tone and tempo, its own refrains and academic attitude, so to speak.

One could only compare its tone and tempo to the *villancicos* sung at religious festivities. It is somewhat cadent, uniform, monotonous as the murmur of flowing water. I don't know the Araucan language well enough to register an example. However, any penetrating reader—and you, Santiago, are far out in front in that regard—will understand me with a modicum of effort.

Here are some sounds whose euphony mimics that of Araucan words: *Epu, bicu, mucu, picu, tanqué, painé, bucó, có, rotó, clá, aimé, purrá, cuerró, tucá, claó, tremen, leuquen, pichun, mincun, bitoooooon!*

Let us assume that the sounds just listed have been duly pronounced with their accents, lightly and all but ignoring the commas, and that the last of them has been pronounced just as it is written, as an interjection that is prolonged for as long as the speaker's breath can hold it. Let us further assume that these made-up sounds represent actual, well-woven words, and that they mean something like the following: Mariano Rosas has sent me to ask you and all your chiefs and officers how you fared last night at camp. Or, to use Mora's terms, let us assume that this inquiry constitutes a reason.

Now, to turn one reason into two, four, or more reasons means to turn the phrase around so that active becomes passive, what was in front goes behind, the middle goes to the beginning or the end. In other words, to turn the phrase every which way. The merit of a speaker in parliament, his skill, his talent is measured by the number of times he can turn over each of his phrases or reasons, whether with the same words or others and without altering the clear and precise meaning of the original. These orators of the pampas are as strong in rhetoric as the grammar teacher in Molière who, at the behest of a bourgeois *gentilhomme*, wrote this missive to a lady: "*Madame, vos beaux yeux, me font mourir d'amour.*" The gentleman was not satisfied. "*Vos beaux yeux, madame, me font mourir d'amour.*" He did not like this either. "*D'amour, madame, vos beaux yeux me font mourir.*" This, too, failed to please him. "*Me font mourir d'amour vos beaux yeux, madame.*" At last the bourgeois was satisfied.[1]

The orator's flair resides in the perfect uniformity of his intonation. And, above all, in the greatest possible elongation of the final syllable of the last word. Were a woman singer to learn Araucan she would be the rage of the Indians. Range of voice, if she had it, would do it for her—that and certain other things which we will speak of in due time. One mustn't put everything in the pot at once.

This final, prolonged syllable is no mere fioritura oratoria. It serves as punctuation—the period, that is—for the oration. When one orator begins it, the other ponders his own phrase, prepares, adopts the attitude and gesture of the response, which at all times consists of lowering the head and focusing on the ground. There are orators whose chief distinction is their loquacity; for others it is the facility they have for turning a reason over. These for the chronometric evenness of their diction, those for their cadent intonation. For Indian orators in general it is the power of the lungs to sustain, as one would hold a note in music, the syllable that closes the speech. When two orators are speaking, their listeners pay attention in perfect silence, weighing the first concept or reason, comparing it with the second, this one with the third, and so forth, approving and disapproving with simple nods of the head. When the parliament is over, it is time for opinions and discussion of the craft and power of the speakers.

Conversation in parliament is always official in character. It is used in cases such as mine or for receiving formal visits.

So comic and ceremonious are these barbarians that it defies description. If the chieftain receives twenty chiefs in a day, he exchanges the same questions and answers with all twenty, starting with how is their grandfather, their father, their grandmother, their mother, their sons and daughters, their next-of-kin, and so on. This inevitable, sacramental series of questions is followed by other, secondary ones which complete the ritual. These concern news from the countryside and from marches. Here the horses always figure significantly, for they figure in everything the Indians do. They are for them what the price of public funds is for our merchants. To have good horses and plenty of them is like us having good land titles and plenty of them. An Indian's importance is measured by the number and quality of his horses. Thus, when they want to state the measure of an Indian's worth, what he represents and signifies, they don't begin by saying, He has so many head of cattle, so many herds of mares, so many flocks of sheep and goats, but rather, He has so many strings of dark horses, so many speckled, sorrels, bays, chestnuts, and grays, meaning, in other words, that he can put such and such a number of Indians on horseback. This in turn means that he can arm a lot of Indians for a raid and, if he is victorious, his share in the booty will correspond to the number of horses he has furnished, as we will see when we discuss the social, military, and governmental makeup of these tribes.

Mariano Rosas is renowned as an orator of note. When we reach his tent, penetrate the intimacy of his home, and relate his customs, way of life, and his ways of governing and taking action, we will have occasion to offer palpable evidence of this, proving that even among the barbarians eloquence wed to prudence can carry the day over valor and the sword.

To return to my interrupted discussion of the Ranquels' ways of conversing, I will add that following the questions and answers about the health of the family and the news from the countryside, there come other questions of no real importance. After belaboring them a great deal, turning them over again and again, and after much coming and going, they finally get to the point. When an Indian pays a visit for the purpose of asking for something, he does not just blurt out his thoughts all at once. He says hello, listens for everything that might please the host, returns compliment for compliment, offer and promise for offer and promise, and says goodbye. It almost seems as if he is going to leave without asking for anything. Then at the last second he spills his guts, though little by little rather than all at once. First he will ask for some mate tea. Could they give him some? He will ask for sugar. Could they give him some? He will ask for paper. As long as they accept and give, he will keep asking and somewhere in all of this he has asked for firewater, which is what he was after. Then comes the finishing touch. He asks at last for what most seems to interest him and, if not turned down, answers: Not give Indian all the rest; give firewater.

The Indian does not use this sly tactic solely with the Christians. Cunning and distrustful by nature and by upbringing, he proceeds this way in every circumstance of life. He has endless reservations about everything and no end of things reserved for himself alone. There is no Indian who does not possess one or several secrets. They may be unimportant, but he will not reveal them except where it interests him to do so. One claims only he knows of a certain lagoon; another one knows of a dune; still another a ravine; this one a medicinal herb, that one a poisonous grass, another a lost trail through the woods. Thus, unlike the Christians, who say, "I know of a lagoon, an herb, a trail that nobody else knows," an Indian will say, "I have a lagoon, an herb, a path that nobody knows, nobody has seen, nobody has ridden."

Truly I am awful with my digressions today. I had picked up my train of thought above and now see that I have lost it again. I might as well lose it all the way and tell you what conversation in junta is. It is a most grave and solemn act. It is very similar to what parliament is in a free country; to our own Congress, for example. Civilization and barbarism join hands; humanity will be saved as the extremes touch. And say what they will about the extremes being vicious, I say that it depends on the kind of extremes. Granted, it is bad, irritating, hateful to be extremely greedy, but who will fault a gentleman for being extremely generous? Call it a calamity for a woman to be extremely ugly, but what woman counts herself unfortunate for being extremely beautiful?

You see what I mean about digressing?

Let us return to the junta and see whether it resembles what I have said or not.

The junta is called, an orator designated. He is a kind of informing member who expounds and defends certain specified propositions against one, two, or more adversaries. Anyone can help him who wants to. The informing member is usually the chief. It is a studied speech he delivers, one similar in form and tone to those of the conversation in parliament, the difference being that in a junta they allow interruption, heckling, whistling, shouting, and all manner of mockery. There are some very noisy juntas but all of them, except certain memorable ones that ended with capes flying,[2] have the same outcome. After much talk, the majority wins whether right or not. It is much to the point here to observe that the results of a junta are always known beforehand, because the chief always makes sure to indoctrinate the most influential chiefs and captains of the tribe ahead of time. All of which goes to show that the constitutional machinery known under liberty as the legislative branch is no extraordinary modern invention. It goes to show that we somehow resemble the Indians.

Since Mora's explanations were of interest to me, I prolonged our stop until there was nothing left to learn in matters of Pampean conversation. "Let's go," I said to Caniupán, and without further delay we continued on our way to Leubucó. The Indians moved at a gallop. Rather than pick up their dust, I did the same. Toward the south a cloud, apparently of sand, was rising on the horizon.

"Riders," some said.

I studied it for an instant but could make nothing of it.

I was interested in learning to count in Araucan, so I went over to Mora and, momentarily free of ambassadors, messengers, and parliamentarians, seized the opportunity.

"What are the numbers called in Indian language?" I asked.

Mora did not really understand my question. He knew perfectly well what four meant, but not what a number was. I put my question to him another way and tomorrow my readers, and next week you, Santiago, will know how to count in a new language:

One—*quinyé*
Two—*epú*
Three—*clá*
Four—*meli*
Five—*quehú*
Six—*caiu*
Seven—*relgué*
Eight—*purrá*
Nine—*ailliá*
Ten—*marí*
One hundred—*pataca*
One thousand—*barranca*

Now, fifty is *quehú-marí*; two hundred, *epú-pataca*; eight thousand, *purrá-barranca*; one hundred thousand, *pataca-barranca*.

This proves two things: First, that in possessing an abstract notion of a comprehensive number of infinite units such as a million, which in their language is marí-pataca-barranca, these barbarians are neither as barbaric nor as obtuse as many people think. Secondly, that their system of enumeration is the same as the Teutonic, as is seen for example in quehú-marí, which amounts to fifty but is grammatically five-ten.

Let this comfort anyone mortified that our parliamentary system should resemble that of the Ranquel Indians. The Germans, justifiably proud to be the compatriots of Schiller and Goethe, also resemble them. Bismarck, that great statesman, surely counted the eagles of the conquering legions of Sadowa in the same way that Mariano counts his lances on returning from a raid.[3]

But now the sand cloud is advancing . . .

 THE SAND CLOUD had caught my attention before I started talking to Mora. It moved and advanced upon us, retreated, turned to the west, then to the east, shrinking, growing, shrinking again and again growing. It rose, it fell, and rose and fell again. Sometimes it had one shape, sometimes another. Now a spherical mass, now a spiral; condensed here, scattered there, dilating, outspread, then concentrated again and more visible, keeping its balance atop a column of air to an immense altitude, reflecting these colors here, those colors there, then others still. One minute it looks like the dust of a hundred riders, the next like the dust of runaway colts. Either stray gusts of wind have raised this curtain, or the cattle are kicking it up. We thought we were getting close to the thing and we were getting farther away. We thought ourselves farther away and we were close. We thought we had spotted distinct objects within its bosom and saw nothing, saw the quick, back-and-forth, up-and-down, hither-and-yon movement of something that went away as suddenly as it had come, saw it and thought it a trick our own eyes played on us. We were about to get there but were not getting there. The land broke into abrupt dunes. We went up, down, galloped, and trotted, our imaginations overexcited with the thought that we would soon cover enough distance to satisfy our curiosity. But no, the cloud drew away from the trail as if fleeing from us, tireless in the varied and whimsical shapes it took, fooling the keenest eyes, and giving

rise to endless conjecture, to argument, and wagering ad infinitum.

We rode on, confounded by the strange cloud. Then, far off in the direction of Leubucó we saw some puffs of sand. These momentarily took our minds off the cloud that had so preoccupied us. We soon realized that these swirls were from a considerable number of Indians who were coming our way at an open gallop. They have such a peculiar way of riding out in the country that they are not easily confused with anything else.

We turned our eyes once again to the larger cloud. It had gained our left flank and now took on a more familiar shape, that of moving, animate beings. Just then the puffs of sand shifted to the east, forming an immense circle that seemed intent on entrapping everything in its path. At the same time we spotted still other swirls of dust in the direction we were heading. There were shouts.

"Those over there are on a chase with their bolas!"

"The other ones are headed this way!"

And this from Mora: "Those dust clouds straight ahead of us, sir, must be from another parliament which is coming to meet you."

Will the formalities never end! I said to myself.

Caniupán had words for me as well.

"Big commission coming, run into."

"Fine," I answered, and pointing off to the left, asked him, "What is that?"

He peered in that direction, ran his eyes quickly along the horizon, and answered, "Them run down guanacos."

So that is what it was. The cloud that had claimed our attention, and was now all but on top of us, held within its bowels an enormous mass of guanacos. Their pursuers had little by little closed in on them and the whole thing threatened to carry us off with it. The earth shuddered as if shaken by thunder, there were cries in every direction, we felt a muffled sound . . . the huge mass of guanacos passed like a cyclone, blasting the atmosphere and leaving us enveloped in a nightfall of sand. Behind them came the Indians, whirling the bolas and converging all on the same point, a sort of plain that lay to our right.[1]

When the great wave of quadrupeds had gone by and the curtain of sand lifted, there was light and we renewed our gallop.

Just as Mora had figured, the dust we had seen before was from another parliament headed our way. This time not one but three Indians rode out ahead of it. Caniupán sent three of his own when he saw them. These crossed with the others a certain ways out, exchanged who knows what conversation, and continued, each group on its own way. The three riding toward us arrived and spoke to Caniupán, who then spoke to me.

"You form people, brother, them commission."

I called a halt, gave my orders, and we assumed battle formation with Caniupán's Indians at the rear. Caniupán himself rode on my right and at his indication I had the Franciscans ride on my left. Mora rode behind me. Once in formation we started to gallop. We went on for a while and when the oncoming party became distinctly visible on a small rise of land about two thousand meters from us, Caniupán spoke.

"That nice commission, brother, run to now."

"Run to whenever you're ready, brother."

Those coming halted. Caniupán's three Indians came back and the other three returned to their group.

"Stopping short time, brother," said Caniupán.

"All right, brother," I said, pulling in my reins.

He sent an Indian ahead to the other group, with what message I don't know. They did the same. Their herald arrived and spoke with Caniupán, who then said, "Now, brother, run to."

"Run to whenever you like, brother," and with this we took off at a full gallop. The other party did the same. They were in battle formation, three great red banners waving atop long poles at either extreme and at the center of the line.[2] We marched to within some four hundred meters of each other.

"Getting close now, brother," said Caniupán. "Running into."

"Running into," I answered.

And off he rode at a furious gallop. I did likewise and behind me, all heart and guts, came the good Franciscans. When we were all literally about to run into each other, we drew back simultaneously about twenty paces apart.

The head of the parliament sent his speakers forward.

Caniupán sent his out.

They stopped at equal distances from their respective groups, one looking east and one west, and the parliament began.

It lasted long enough to exasperate a saint.

The speaker sent by Mariano Rosas was a Cicero of the pampas. He spoke through every pore, stretched the last syllable of the last word as if his throat were a wind instrument, and knew the art of making fifteen reasons out of one.

The speaker Caniupán named to represent me was no slacker himself. It was therefore of no use to me to shorten my answers.

My representative contrived to multiply my reasons as much as his interlocutor multiplied his.

Mariano Rosas sent along the following messages:

He was very glad that I was making my way to his settlement. (First reason)

How had my trip gone? (Second reason)

Had I lost any horses? (Third reason)

How were I and all my chiefs, officers, and soldiers faring? (Fourth reason)

I answered their four reasons with as many again, but since Mariano's speaker made sixty reasons of his four, my speaker did the same with mine. After these interesting greetings were concluded, I had to shake everyone's hand. There were about eighty of them in all, among them many Christians. At each handshake, at each embrace, they stunned my ears with cheers and hurrahs. The clamor only stopped when the embraces and handshakes ended.

The recently arrived Indians mingled with Caniupán's group and, now a single unit in orderly march, we continued on our way. Soon we spotted more dust clouds.

"There other commission," said Caniupán, pointing them out to me.

"How glad I am," I answered, saying to myself: At this rate we won't make it to Leubucó today.

"There is Leubucó," said Mora as we climbed the crest of a dune.

I looked in the direction he was pointing and there, on the fringes of a forest, I could hazily make out the tent camp of the commander-in-chief of the Ranquel tribes, the settlement of Mariano Rosas. The dust cloud was quickly drawing closer. An Indian arrived and spoke with Caniupán, who sent one of his ahead as well. Then came three and Caniupán sent the same number. Right after that came six more, and Caniupán sent six. We gained ground quickly enough through all this sending and receiving and soon had in sight the new series of ambassadors into whose clutches we were about to fall.

"There commission, nice, plenty big."

"Oh I can see it is nice," I said.

He was right about it being big. They did in fact comprise a considerable group.

"Run into hard, brother," said Caniupán.

"Run into however you like," I answered.

"Make order halt, brother," he added.

I called a halt.

"Make formation, brother," he said.

I followed his indication. My party assumed battle formation, myself and the friars in front as before. Caniupán's Indians covered my rear and the others formed two wings, one on my right, one on my left. About twenty paces ahead of us, the three banners occupied the center of the line we formed. Caniupán rode beside me. Once in formation, we began the march at a gallop. Those coming also advanced at a gallop, and there were bugle calls.

"Commission run into us now," said Caniupán.

"So I see," I answered.

We galloped for several minutes, then stopped when we saw they had stopped. Several messengers came and went. They spoke with Caniupán, we resumed the march. At a certain bugle call Caniupán spoke, "Running into now, brother," and as usual he took off, setting the pace for me.

This time we were about to run head-on into each other amidst a hair-raising uproar that the Indians made by beating the palms of their hands against their open mouths. The soft, uneven, scrub-speckled terrain threatened to give every horse and rider an awful spill. We could not march in formation. We alternately broke up and regrouped. The poor friars. They commended their souls to God and followed us as closely as they could. Many riders spilled, some with the full weight of the horse rolling over them, and these were first-rate horsemen. And then, one of the ironies of life: one of the friars rolled and landed standing up.

The two parties advanced, were literally on the verge of running into each other when at a signal from the bugle they stopped, as did we. A scene much like the previous one ensued, wherein two orators concerned themselves for half an hour with my health and my horses. But this time it was all more tolerable, for Captain Rivadavia had ridden out to meet me for conversation while the orators compounded their reasons with vehement eloquence.

This brave and resolute officer—a prudent and patient man— had been representing me for three months among the Indians. I embraced him effusively; it was one of the most gratifying moments of my life. No one who hasn't sometime met a compatriot, a friend, on foreign shores or in remote and unfamiliar regions, desolate and uninhabited regions, and met him after putting his own life in jeopardy, can understand what my feelings were.

When the greetings—six reasons turned into sixty by each side—were done, it was time for embraces and handshakes. This time there was nothing to alter the ceremony but bugle calls. I gave a hundred-and-some embraces and handshakes. And with all my ribs and every nerve in my wrist aching, there arose a joyous din. The cheers rent the air. Everyone except my people scattered, shouting, skirmishing, sprinting their horses, showing off their finesse and skill. Here was a true fiesta, an Arabian fantasy.[3]

We marched for quite a while like that—one big, scattered, breakaway party of stunt riders. Some ran horse into horse in deadly breasting games, others rolled, still others made their horses dance. Here a rider jumps off his horse at full gallop and climbs nimbly back on; another one kneels on his horse's back while still another rides standing. Everybody is doing something to dazzle, some pirouette or other. At the sound of the bugle all gathered and we formed as before. Our two wings had grown with the new arrivals.

An envoy of Mariano Rosas had just arrived.

The settlement lay nearby. It was a matter of minutes before we would penetrate. The messenger went back.

"Walking little ways, brother," said Caniupán, drawing in his reins and slowing his horse down to an easy lope. I had to follow what he said. I slowed my horse down likewise. Another messenger came from Mariano Rosas and spoke with Caniupán, who then turned to me and said, "Stopping, brother."

He said something to Mora in his language and Mora translated for me. We were to dismount and await orders.

The reader will judge whether I had reason to fume for a while.

I am in possession of a virtue which I did not have before making this excursion and which modesty compels me not to name; and I repeat what I have said before: It is no simple matter to penetrate the dwelling place of Sir General don Mariano Rosas, as his people call him.

 WITH THIS STOP I found my bag of tricks was empty. The truth is that for a long time now I've been one to plan for everything but the main thing.

Man goes through periods of grievous error, unforgivable blunders, and sad mistakes.

As anyone knows who has thrown himself into life unprepared, there are good years and bad years, propitious months and luckless ones, rose-colored days and days as black as chimney soot. Years, months, and days when we get everything right, our spirit seems to have its proper geometry and all is smiles and praise. And, conversely, years, months, and days in which it all happens to us the other way around. We love and we're forgotten. We go to war and get wounded or left behind. We run for office and get beaten. We play and lose, eat food made with oil and it makes us sick, buy lottery tickets and don't even come close. In other words, there are times so dismal that even serendipity fails to see us through. Or, as the saying goes, times when if it weren't for bad luck we'd have no luck at all.

There must be something to this.

Certain tribulations—my own as well as those of others—have given me pause to ponder the justice of God. A discreet man should study the world and its vicissitudes in his own head and in the other fellow's head as well. And frankly, I am tempted at times to think that our beautiful planet is not so well organized.

Who is to say we are not entering a time of moral imbalance?

I am going to have to find somebody who is versed in matters of knowledge and conscience and have him point me to some treatise or other on terrestrial mechanics, something a Laplace[1] might write. For now, however, I will take refuge in a tiny volume called "Morality Applied to Politics, or the Art of Waiting." It must be very good. It is a small and anonymous book. I've been noticing for quite some time that the best books are manuals of unknown authorship. I would say you will find the reason for this in modesty, usually a noble sentiment. I hope to find the answer to many of my doubts in this little volume.

I have certain, rooted beliefs and convictions derived from I don't know where—some things have no traceable parentage—and I wouldn't want to lose them or have them become embroiled in the archives of my imagination. I believe in God, for example, as I am sure my worthy readers do, though there is always that damnable saying: Trust in God and take your time. I believe in justice and that noble souls must be just even to those who in turn deny them justice. Yet I see people in the streets every day desperately complaining that there is no justice on earth. And yet I often hear those who place and win lawsuits say: Well, justice is certainly doing well!

Even lawyers spend all their time crying out against justice. What, after all, does the existence of two different allegations on the same issue, both of them well proven, imply?

I believe in charity and, meanwhile, hear harsh words about my fellow man every day and see people taken off to the cemetery who haven't got a stone to lie under.

I believe in religion. I believe that patriotism, honor, probity, love of fellow man are religious matters. Meanwhile, I read in an Italian book the other day—these Italians go overboard when they're dealing with religion—that all religions seek to grow rich.

I believe in the Constitution and the law. And an old gentleman of much experience, who often gives me advice, tells me this: Everyone governs the same; it's not Rosas who can't do his part.

I believe in the people, and if they call elections tomorrow, watch how no one turns out to vote.

I believe in free will and every day see people who let themselves be led by the nose; and my notion of human responsibility is shaken to its most solid foundations.

As you can see, I believe in a number of very good, very moral, very useful things.

The storekeeper across the way there neither believes in nor understands any of that, but he enjoys himself.

He has good health, a steady income, a reliable clientele. Nobody bothers or threatens him, nobody tells him off. He is an unknown, but he is a power.

Luck figures into a lot of it. They did not coin the proverb "God grant you good luck, son, because knowledge won't get you far" for nothing.

And one's name has its weight in this as well. Rarely do you find one man who detests another man who doesn't know the first man's name. That is undoubtedly why the Brazilians change their names.

When I finish reading my little treatise, I am bound to be in good shape for curing myself of all my superstitions. Soon I will be a complete man, morally, that is. Then how much will you bet me that everything starts to go my way? I bet you that if I sue, I win; that if I take a voyage, I won't shipwreck; that if I buy lottery tickets, I will be a major winner; that if I wager a military campaign, I will be decorated; that if I come back out to Indian territory, what happened this time won't happen again and they won't keep me waiting so long.

Do you suppose it is true that experience is the mother of knowledge?

Doubtless that's why they say that it is not because he is devilish that the devil is so smart, but because he is old.

I forgot to mention in enumerating my beliefs that I also believe in that gent. I have seen him several times.

Could it be that my aged father is right in the advice he has given and still gives me, advice that I in my modern petulance have chosen not to follow? Why, if you want to know how he thinks you have only to find out how I think. Could it be that the chain of the moral world is formed by linking yesterday's bitter experience with today's disenchantment? Is that how we lend method and configuration to our lives, by following those who have seen and lived more than we proud philosophers have? Could it be that the most educated, most accomplished, wisest youth will always be a suckling babe, a pygmy, beside his father?

Santiago, my friend! Could it be that your father knows more than you do?

Could my father know more than I do, as up as I am, you might say, on social studies? [2]

I happen to be at home in that area. Knowledge of man is my forte.

But then the letdowns man has marked for me!

That is the argument I intend to use on my smart aleck of a son when he raises the flag of rebellion, which cannot be long in coming. He has already started with certain spontaneous acts calculated to undermine my paternal authority. He spends more money than he should, which makes him the object of private whisperings in the family, and he has started to study medicine against my advice.

Studying medicine without my consent! He is out of his mind!

I can only compare that kind of aberration, in a day and age when I can homeopathically cure anybody's hangnail, to an expedition to the Ranquel Indians.

In effect, dear Santiago, when you look at it with cold objectivity, doesn't my trip to the settlements seem like a waste of time? Wouldn't you say that I deserve all the delays that Mariano Rosas has put me through before letting me penetrate his dwelling place; deserve them, I mean, for my extravagance in coming out here in the first place? How much better it would have been if my immediate superior had refused me permission to make the trip! Had he done so, I would certainly have been a little chafed, but then that's the way we are: we don't see the hand that wishes us well but extend our own to someone who would harm us!

But let us approach Leubucó from where we left off yesterday. Seeing that the stop was going to be a long one and that our mounts were soaked with sweat, I ordered a change of horses so as to make our entry properly. It was still early and there was no telling how long we might yet have to stay on our horses. While they were changing, Captain Rivadavia introduced several political personages to me who were refugees in Indian country, the two most noteworthy being a Major Hilarión Nicolai and a Lieutenant Camargo. Both have ridden with Sáa's people and made their way to the settlements—a handful of soldiers all told—after the San Ignacio uprising.[3] I had been told the worst sorts of things about these men. Fearing I'd be the target of something iniquitous, I had taken every possible precaution against them, though in thinking about it I should have looked at the fact that they were Christians as a guarantee.

Say what you will about it, the apple doesn't fall far from the tree.

Later we shall see if I was on track or not amidst all the misgivings that warred within me. And let my example be of some use to those who judge men by commonplace, rash, impassioned rules when the great law of life and of God is charity. Neither the elderly Hilarión nor the bandit Camargo impressed me the way I had expected, nor did they greet me as I feared they would. Hilarión, for all of his cunning, and Camargo, for all of his roguery, are a couple of courteous and attentive men, especially Hilarión. Camargo is a crude sort of person. The former is perhaps fifty-five years old, the latter perhaps twenty-eight. One has a long, snow-white beard, the other a fine, jet-black mustache. One looks like an Englishman, the other bears the stamp of his native land. Hilarión is a kind of gaucho político. Camargo is pure compadre. Camargo can read and write perfectly well, is brave, bold, proud, and generous. Hilarión temporizes with the Indians but does not speak their language. Camargo, on the other hand, speaks Araucan, says what he means, is not afraid of death, and will slip a knife into the coolest of men. Yet, Camargo is a person capable of changing his ways, as we will see when it comes time to relate his life, his misfortunes, and the reasons why he became a federalist, which were due mainly to a woman.

These women have the diabolical power of doing whatever they want, which must be why the French say, *Ce que femme veut Dieu le veut*. They can make a unitarian out of a federalist and vice versa, which is about as much as can be done with a person. And, of course, they can make a fool of anyone at all.

My new acquaintances, the talk we had, and everyone changing horses made the unforeseen wait in the antechamber a little more bearable. I am sure my foul mood was poorly concealed, because every rational person there who was knowledgeable in the ways and customs of the Indians urged patience. "That's the way it is out here, sir. The general is a good man and wants to welcome you in proper form." There was nothing to be done but wait for the preparations to be finished. Splendid indeed was this going to be, judging by the time it took to get it ready. The Victoria Square pyramid in Buenos Aires—where they spend more on cardboard and linen for it than it would cost to line it with marble—takes less time to decorate than an actual, living chief of the Ranquel tribes.

I was getting a lesson in ceremonial protocol for my reception when a neatly groomed Indian youth arrived, all decked out in silver ornaments and riding a handsome mount. A small escort accompanied him. It was Mariano Rosas's oldest son, who on his father's orders had come out to greet and welcome me. The salutation consisted of a rosary of questions, all of them pertaining, as we already know, to the physiological state of my person, the horses, and news of the march. I made a politic answer to each question, a smile on my lips and a tempest of impatience in my heart.

This time they added a new question: How many men were with me and how many weapons did we have?

I dutifully satisfied their curiosity.

The reader already knows how many we were upon arriving at the tent settlement. It was our good fortune that the number had neither grown nor shrunk. No accidents had occurred. As for the arms we were carrying, they consisted of knives, sabers without scabbards set between our saddle bags, and five revolvers, two of which were mine.

The son of Mariano Rosas returned to give an account of his mission. Later another envoy came with orders that we could now start moving.

A bugle sounded.

Everyone who was scattered here and there gathered in the formation I described yesterday and we got under way. We were in sight of Mariano Rosas. I could distinguish his facial features perfectly, count each one of the members of his retinue, his following, the personages of his tribe. We were about to climb down from our horses when . . . a sudden surprise! We were notified we would have to wait still longer.

So we waited . . .

We waited all this time, why shouldn't you, my readers, wait until tomorrow or the next day?

Curiosity increases the pleasure of things forbidden and difficult to obtain.

 THERE ARE SITUATIONS in which a simple indication, no matter how discreet, has all the character of a military order. What was I to do when, with the utmost Araucan finesse, they motioned to me that despite being within pistol shot of my long-sought goal, I must now stop a while longer?

Go along with it. What else?

We stayed on our horses in the same formation.

This sudden, last-minute stop had formed part of nobody's imagined program, but had in Mariano Rosas's ceremonial court great significance. On previous stops, the real object had sometimes been to stall for time until the crowd settled down, and other times to comply with official and social duty as dictated by courtesy and good breeding. This time, the head chief, the secondary chiefs, the captains, and the Indians of importance—as they say in Indian territory—wanted to see me up close before I climbed down from my horse; study my physiognomy,[1] my gaze, the air about me, my aspect; make sure, for certain fundamental reasons, of my intentions by reading in my face whatever I was concealing in the inner recesses of my heart. And they wanted to do this not only with me, but with everybody accompanying me, even the two reverend Franciscans, holy men incapable of plucking the wings from a fly.

Within the dissemblance, the ingenious and studied wiliness, of the savage and the undercivilized, there is always something candid. They think that deceiving a foreigner is an easy thing to do. The pride of the ignorant constantly gives itself away, starting with their conviction that they know more than their neighbor. Whether taken individually or collectively, ignorance is the same in its manifestations: falsely proud and falsely bold.

Mariano Rosas thought he was fooling me.

With a slight effort of voice, we could have spoken to each other and he chose to follow the known procedure and send an ambassador, one who didn't understand a word of my language. This was a calculated move. The idea was to oblige me to use my interpreter even for the yes and no answers, which kept my followers exposed that much longer to a thorough scrutiny. While this went on, the old witches used details and reports they had received to read the horoscope, divine the future, relate my recondite intentions, and drive out the malignant spirit, the Gualicho.

Mariano Rosas's representative spoke. It was the same tired tune, with the added note that he was glad to see me reach his land safe and sound, that he and all his chiefs, captains, and Indians were at my service, that this was a great day, as what I was about to hear would testify. With this, a few ragged Christians, among them a Negro—a Rigoletto of sorts—discharged their rifles and carbines. A great many fireworks went off and there were intermittent shouts of celebration. Speaking through my interpreter, I answered with all the affability of a diplomat. My interpreter in turn addressed himself to a representative whom my stone-faced cohort Caniupán had assigned to me from the moment we left Calcumuleu.

There was no escape. With the two interlocutors outdoing themselves lest they be discredited in the estimation of their public, which was gathered before them, the greetings went on like a rosary. After I was greeted, complimented, and congratulated, they requested my permission to do the same with the Franciscans, who by reason of their position alongside me, the attention I gave them and, above all, the "crowns" they were wearing, were assumed to be second in rank. I acceded, and there ensued a dialogue like those we already know, with the usual proliferation of reasons and their final syllables drawn till the speaker had no breath left. I picked up certain words with great frequency: *chao*, father; *uchaimá*, great; *chachao*, God; and *cuchauentrú*, which also means God, with one difference: *chachao* conveys the idea of my father and *cuchauentrú* conveys the omnipotent. Its literal translation is "man great," from *cucha* and *uentrú*.

The Franciscans answered evangelically, offering to baptize, marry, and save any and all souls that might wish for the spiritual aid offered by their ministry. Happily, the interpreters did not altogether grasp their apostolic reasons and could not multiply them as much as the gathering would have liked.

After the Franciscans came my officers. The Indians requested my permission to interview them as well. At this rate, they would be interrogating, saluting, and welcoming the pack mules before it was over. Mora told me that for this phase of the ceremony one of my officers would speak for the whole lot of them. Again the same reasons, raised to the fifth power and couched in oratorical mimicry of great virtuosity.

While these parliaments took place, many of the old, strange-looking Indians walked mysteriously around my party. They were quiet and stared suspiciously; we were the new arrivals and must be studied. They came and went over and over again, carrying word of what they saw to the witches, who were conducting the exorcism. Of course it was their life or their hide if by chance, quirk, or black magic someone should fall ill or an Indian or highly prized horse should die. That is exactly how these divines end their days—sacrificed—if they have too little talent, foresight, or good fortune to guess right.

They call for them and consult them over every trifle.

If you would go on a raid, talk to the witches; is it going to rain or stay dry, talk to the witches; what is this sick man dying of, talk to the witches. And if the events foretold fail to occur, say good-bye to the poor old witch! Her witchcraft will not save her from the clutches of the bloody obsession, and she dies. That notwithstanding, it is a practice that abounds among the Indians, proof that charlatanism enjoys preferential status everywhere as fore-teller of human destiny and of the destiny of nations, though modern civilization is more indulgent. We send Mazzini to the guillotine—that's one less voice crying out for freedom; but as for the practitioners of the transvasation of the blood of Saint Genaro, just leave them alone.

An indescribable restlessness pervaded Mariano Rosas's settlement. Indian men and women on foot or horseback came and went in every direction. Something extraordinary was happening and it had to do with me. It couldn't help but catch my attention. Impatiently, I asked Mora what he thought it was. He had no satisfactory answer, didn't really know himself. Later I learned that the old witches had been a bit stirred up. Their prognostications had not been so good at first. I was the harbinger of a great and inevitable calamity. Gualicho, transfigured, was riding with me. Salvation required either that I be sacrificed or that I be sent promptly home. As you can see, all witches are the same. They base their necromancy on credulity, fear, the instinct for wonder, and popular anxiety. However, Mariano Rosas did not want to sacrifice me or send me back home as I had come, without me first setting foot in Leubucó. It was the recalcitrant ones, the old ones, the Indians who had never lived among Christians; Indians who, enemies that they were to all strangers not of Indian color or blood, knew no other language or customs. It was they who believed the prophecies of the witches. But, as I said, Mariano Rosas, who aside from being the chief knew more than anyone else there, did not share their opinion. The witches were therefore cautioned to make a closer study of the sun's course, the path of the clouds, the color of the sky, the flight of the birds, the juice of the bitter herbs they chewed, the smoke from the dung they burned, because the chief could see something else. He wanted to shake my hand and embrace me. He was convinced that Gualicho was not with me and that I was Colonel Mansilla in body and soul.

Mariano Rosas faced me in his wing formation at about twenty paces. Epumer, his older brother and campaign general, stood to his left. Epumer has vowed never to leave his land or invade or even travel to Christian land. After Epumer came the captains Relmo, Cayupán, and a few others, among them Melideo, whose name means "four rats," from *meli*, "four," and *deo*, "rat." The Ranquels customarily take such names, and note I say names, not nicknames or surnames. One such name I have already cited. Others might be "four eyes," "tiger skin," "ox head," and so forth.

Immediately after the captains, several Indians of importance occupied their respective places, followed by a small crowd and finally some Christians from among a certain Colonel Ayala's people. He had been one of Sáa's followers, a wayward politician but not a bad man at all. He always treated me warmly and considerately. The Christians were armed with carbines and rifles, though not exactly shining clean ones. It was they who took the very real and pressing pains to fire the salvos in my honor. Ayala led them. Father Burela, who, as I have said, had arrived from Mendoza two days before me with a load of liquor and other trinkets for the ransom of the captives, was present and had been given a place of preference. Jorge Macías, a former classmate of mine, was wandering around, poor fellow, like a stray dog.

Mariano Rosas's settlement consisted of a number of tents scattered about several hovels built by Ayala's people. There was a corral and several hitching posts as well. Leubucó itself is a lagoon of little interest—it means "running water": *leubu*, "runs," *có*, "water." It lies on a plateau near a hill in a wide canyon of low dunes. Its surroundings are most mournful. It is the most barren and sterile place I have ever seen, a place made for solitude. Great networks of roads and trails branch out in every direction from Leubucó, which is the central station. The roads go to Ramón's settlements in the hills of Carrilobo; to Baigorrita's settlement on the edge of the Quenqué Hills; to Calfucurá's settlement in Salinas Grandes; to the Andes, and to the Araucan tribes.[2]

I have stealthily and covertly gone about gathering a great deal of information about these places, information I will publish someday not far off so that the public may make use of it. I say stealthily and covertly because nothing so ill behooves a stranger or any suspicious person such as myself than to ask certain questions or show interest in learning the distances and directions to places where Christians have never gone, all of which the Indians endeavor to keep shrouded in utter mystery. An Indian never knows the way to Chalileo, for example, or how far it is from Leubucó to Wada. The greatest indiscretion a Christian refugee can commit is to divulge it.[3] I remember once in Río Cuarto, I was trying to keep some statistics on the population of the Ranquels and asked Linconao, who loved me dearly, several questions in front of Achauentrú. When Achauentrú saw that I was getting satisfactory answers, he got irate with Linconao and threatened him in Araucan. He said that when they got back to Indian territory he would tell Mariano Rosas that Linconao "was a traitor who had been saying those things." He then turned to the other Indians present and said, "You are my witnesses."

Of course, how was I to understand all of this? My interpreter explained it afterwards. Mora told it all to me under his breath, pleading with me not to get him mixed up in it and to discontinue my questions, which I did, scarcely better informed than before.

No further spells were cast, the horoscope told no new ill omens, the eagles no longer looked south but north, which meant that people would be coming from within to the outside, not from the outside in, or, in other words, that there would be no invasion of Christians and that there was nothing to fear.

The moment to welcome me had arrived.

It was about time!

An envoy emerged from the ranks of Mariano Rosas and spoke to me, again through an interpreter.

"The general says that you and your chiefs and officers may get off your horses."

"Very well," I answered.

And I dismounted, and with me the Christians and Indians following us. At that moment there arose a thunderous hurrah and a "Long live Colonel Mansilla!"

Everyone joined in as I answered: "Long live Mariano Rosas!

"Long live the President of the Republic!

"Long live the Argentine Indians!"

There was true jubilation, endless firing of carbines and rifles and rockets, endless and infernal hollering and palm-beating over open mouths. Jorge Macías came to me in tears and embraced me.

As no one had given me any sign, I stood next to my horse and stayed there.

I had learned my lesson.

There was another parliament.

I'll say it one more time: It is not as easy as you might think to go pay Mariano Rosas a *salem-alek*.

 I HAD GONE to great lengths to reach Leubucó and set foot in the doorway of Mariano Rosas's dwelling place. Now I was there, safe and sound, having incurred no further losses than the two horses and no close shave other than the scare we got near Aillancó as a consequence of the strange and fantastic welcome given us by Chief Ramón. To have expected any less would have been like trying to cross the ocean without encountering wind or waves, like walking the streets of Buenos Aires in summer without finding dust or in winter without finding mud, like washing your face without getting it wet, or, as I have heard it said, like eating eggs without breaking shells.

It seemed I had good reason to consider myself lucky or, to put it in more Christian terms, to give thanks to the Almighty, which is in fact what I did, exclaiming inwardly, "Praised be God!"

With my bridle still in hand, I was waiting for an indication as to when I should step forward and greet Mariano Rosas. Meanwhile, I made a quick review of all the dignitaries facing me, though with a show of great indifference for everything and everyone.

Barbarians are all the same. They do not like to admit that they have never seen certain things that catch their eye, and they do not like people who enter their dens to find the things in there unusual. In Río Cuarto I used to enjoy showing the Indians a clock I had. It

had an alarm, a barometer, an optical mariner's needle, a theodolite, and an eyeglass. They would look and look with intense interest at all these things and then, as if to say "This doesn't impress
me as much as you think," they would say, "In Indian territory
many nice things."

An Indian who must have been something like the chief's page
spoke with Mariano Rosas, and then directly with my inseparable
companion, Caniupán, who in turn spoke with Mora. Following
our established routine, the interpreter finally spoke to me.

"Sir, General Mariano says he will now receive you. He wants
to shake your hand and embrace you. You must also shake hands
with and embrace all of his captains so that they will know and
treat you at all times like a friend. You favor them with a visit, you
put great trust in them."

The messenger was sent back through the sequence with a short
but warm and cordial message from me. Mora then spoke with
Caniupán again.

"Sir," he said, "Caniupán says that you may now step forward
and shake hands with General Mariano. You are to do with him
and the others the same thing they do to you."

"And what the devil are they going to do to me?" I asked.

"Nothing, Colonel, Indian things. That's the way they are here,"
he answered.

"I assume it won't be anything barbaric," I added.

"No, sir. They are going to want to show you affection. They
are very happy to see you and a little lit up," he said.

"Fine, but just give me an idea of what they are going to do."

"They're going to want to hug you and lift you up in the air,"
he replied.

"Well, if that's all it is," I muttered to myself, "there's no reason to get upset." Then, as a chieftain will call out to his followers
in a supreme moment "Forward, men, forward!" I looked at
my officers, and at the Franciscans, who were beaming beatific
smiles at everyone who looked at them, and said, "Let's go greet
Mariano."

I advanced, they followed, we came to within handshaking distance of the chief and the salutation began.

Mariano extended me his right hand, I took it.

He shook mine vigorously, I shook his as well.

He embraced me with his arms crossed behind my left shoulder,
I embraced him.

He embraced me with his arms crossed behind my right shoulder, I embraced him.

He lifted me powerfully into the air and held me there, letting out a stentorian shout. I lifted and held him and shouted equally.

At each of these steps, the spectators drummed their open mouths with the palm of their hands, shouting, "Aaaaaaaa!" at the top of their lungs.

After I had greeted Mariano, an Indian, a sort of master of ceremonies, presented me to Epumer.

We did the same thing we had with his brother, all of it amidst an incessant and thunderous Aaaaaaaa!

Then came Relmo; same scene as before: Aaaaaaaa!

After him, Melideo, alias "four rats," a rock-solid Indian of regular stature, but as pot-bellied, as fat, as heavy as . . . who should I say? As my comrade Peña, the president's aide-de-camp.

Lifting and holding this man up was going to be a problem.

I could hardly get my arms around him. I made an effort; my self-respect as a man of strength was on the line. Not to do it would speak poorly of the Christians. I redoubled my effort and was rewarded with complete success, as witnessed by the Aaaaaaaa!, this one longer and more spirited than the previous ones. It was all right out of a comedy. I almost exploded, my lungs nearly burst. Letting out an earth-shaking scream with your body arched to lift a weight greater than your own off the floor is serious business from a physiological, organic point of view. But most of all it draws laughter. Try to picture my herculean task with Melideo. Here I was, following established protocol in the land I happened to be in, while forbidden by laws of racial pride and religion from backing off, retreating, or weakening in the least.

If only it had ended with Melideo! But no, after him came other chiefs and other captains and after them several Indians of importance. Finally, the Christian and Ranquel rabble. All you could hear were the continuous, resonating, pounding shouts of Aaaaaaaa!

The sweat was pouring off of me, I was as hoarse as a rooster on a cold July morning. My strength was spent. The air felt like it was a thousand degrees above zero and not transparent but dense. You could have sliced it with a knife. It laid on me like a boiler plate. If I didn't die of heat exhaustion, if I didn't scream myself to death, it was because Allah is great and sustains us with physical and moral energy when we are in need of it, so good is he!

While I was reviewing these barbarians I kept remembering Alcibiades's words of advice: Wherever you go, do as you see. And I thought to myself I should have brought him with me to the Ranquel Indians. It takes the best of men to embrace and lift and carry someone four times. This is serious exercise. Indeed, it could entitle a fellow to a place, one day, in the mausoleum of posterity as one of the great gladiators or wrestlers of the nineteenth century. I knew I'd be remembered for something. You know, though, the waves of time swallow many a reputation.

The Franciscans were required only to shake hands. The same went for my officers and assistants. We were occupied very nearly one hour in embraces, salutations, and sundry acts of Indian etiquette.

When I finished greeting, embracing, and lifting the last Indian, shouting Aaaaaaaa! with everything my wasted lungs had left, the crowd let out its final hurrahs and cheers and scattered to their horses. Jumping on, they had themselves a riot. They raced, sprinted, and did every possible charge and pirouette. I was proud of, and pleased with, myself. I had registered an achievement. Not only had I given palpable and unassailable proof of strength and vigor, but also there were certain phrases floating around which gradually convinced me that for the first time these barbarians could admire a cultured and civilized Christian such as I for his physical prowess, the one gift they most exercise and most envy and respect. From time to time certain echoes would reach my ears: "That Colonel Mansilla, him bull. That Colonel Mansilla, him lift plenty, him good man."

I would hear this, and then curiosity would get the better of them and they would come up to me and crowd me—lots of them—until I could no longer move from where I was standing. They looked me up and down, looked at my face, my clothes, the gold and silver knife I had on my side, with its tooled handle, my grenadier's boots, my watch and chain and the baubles hanging from it—anything and everything that caught their eye, whether for its shape or its color. And after looking me over, they would hold out their hand and say, "That Colonel, give hand here, friend." And not only would they give me their hand to shake, but they would hug and kiss me with their dirty, slobbering, alcoholic, painted mouths.

They made exactly the same overtures to the officers, the assistants, and the Franciscans. Several Indian women and white,

Christianized women—as opposed to just Christian women—came up to the friars, knelt before them and, taking hold of the cords of their habits, said, "Bless us, father." Their self-denial and their primitive respect truly touched me. What a great thing religion is, and how it consoles, comforts, and lifts the spirit! The Franciscans gave several blessings, procuring at little cost the happiness of a number of sheep who had strayed, or were taken from, the flock.

The contentment was general. No, it was universal.

Nobody—and there were many drunken people there—showed us the least disrespect. On the contrary, chiefs and captains alike, the important Indians and the rabble, the isolated and captive Christians, absolutely everybody, treated us with consummate Araucan courtesy. Frankly, they were indemnifying us, and amply so, for all the stalling, the hunger, the raid, and the inconvenience they had given us along the way.

What else could these poor barbarians do but what they were doing?

Have we taught them anything that reveals the generous, humanitarian, Christian disposition of the governments that rule human destiny? They rob us, take us captive, burn our settlements, this is true. But what are they supposed to do if they do not have working habits? Did the dawn of humanity perchance present a different picture? What was Rome once? A gang of bandits, looters, rapacious and bloodthirsty traitors.

What, then, does our trumpeted civilization have to say?

But let us enter the tent of Mariano Rosas, who, before offering it to me, asked me what I wanted to do with my horses, have my own people take care of them or leave them in his care. And who, when told that my people had not eaten, called his son Lincoln—why the name I don't know—and ordered him in Spanish to slaughter and dress out a fat cow at once.

Mariano Rosas's tent, like all the other tents, has an entrance room. Let us rest in it until tomorrow so as not to alter the method I have set out to follow in this story. I am also stopping here for your sake, dear Santiago, and for the reader's, lest you be loathe to go on with me. A little bit is good, a lot is not, though opinions may well be divided in this respect, depending on the chapter.

Who, after all, tires of reading Byron, Goethe, Juvenal, Tacitus? No one.

And who tires of reading me?

Anyone at all.

26 OF THE TWO PROPOSITIONS Mariano Rosas made to me concerning the animals, I opted for the first on the principle that the owner's eye best fattens the horse.

I called Camilo Arias and gave him my orders. Mariano carried them out with numerous indications as to the best pasture, the water, what time of day they should be rounded up and corralled, as it would best suit our needs. He ended on a note of caution: we should exercise great care and vigilance day and night, for there were gaucho Indian thieves around. This showed me, first, that he knows the ways of the country and, second, that it is a good tailor who knows his cloth.

We passed into the entrance adjacent to the tent.[1] A tent is always made of hides, the entranceway of straw, usually corn husk. On another day, when we enter the tent, we will see how it is built and laid out. Today let us stay in the entrance which, like all of them, had a wooden frame and a flat, horizontal roof. It was about sixty square yards in area. Within they had prepared seats of great, thick, black, well-combed sheepskin. Two or three of them formed each seat, another two or three were rolled up to form the back. They were placed in two rows and the space between them had recently been swept and wet down. One row was for the recent arrivals, the other for the master of the house, his relatives, and visitors. The row they set aside for me faced east. On the right, in the first row, there was a seat raised higher than the rest. It had a wide back with two rolled poncho pillows, one on either side. This was to be mine.

Everything was perfectly planned for the most comfortable possible seating, whether you crossed your legs Turkish style, stretched them out, or folded them under. You could lie down, lean back, or take any posture you pleased.

Mariano sat face to face with me. Though he speaks Spanish as well as any of us, he had an interpreter brought in. It would be good for all present to hear my reasons and take them back to their *pagos* with them. This would create a popular atmosphere in my favor.

The parliament began like those theater posters from Rosas's time, which, after the usual "Long live so-and-so" and "Death to so-and-so" (and what a fraternal and civilized custom that was!) would say, for example, "Tonight's presentation will be *Clotilde, or Crimes of Love,*" which complemented the first part of the poster about as well as a pair of pistols on a statue of Christ.[2] That is to say, after the questions and answers *de rigueur*—how are you, how have you and all your chiefs and officers fared, have you lost any horses, for nothing happens in the country but misfortune—there came other, unexpected ones, though none of any interest.

I brought up the matter of the two horses stolen from me in Aillancó, as well as Wenchenao's raid on my pack mules. I vociferated, I apostrophized those who had shown me disrespect, and as I spoke it seemed to me my authoritative tone of voice was getting everyone's attention.

We had been conversing for perhaps five minutes, with Mariano's interpreter translating his reasons and Mora mine, when they brought in the food. A number of captives, both men and women—one of the women had been a servant of Rosas—entered bearing great wooden bowls made by the Indians and brimming with stewed beef made in an onion, corn flour, and *ají*-pepper broth. It was excellent, hot, succulent—and clearly great care had gone into making it. The spoons were made of wood, iron, silver, same for the forks; the knives were common. They served everyone, the recent arrivals as well as the visitors who had preceded me. Each of us received a copious plateful. As we ate, we talked.

It did not take me long to enter into their confidence. I was quite at home there, the more so for not having to set an example for my children. I ate like a barbarian. I made myself comfortable in the magnificent leather and poncho seat and said whatever nonsense I had on the tip of my tongue. I had the Indians laughing. Anybody who came near me I'd do something to him—pull on his nose or knock him in the head or give him a whack on the behind.

The more playful ones paid me back with interest.

With the first course out of the way they brought the next one, a delicious roast beef fit for a couple of Pantagruelian friars. I literally licked my fingers after this one. I'm telling you, a meal at a dining-room table is just not the same as a meal on the ground and in Leubucó. After the roast we were served a dessert of crushed carob and ground, toasted corn. It is good. They brought water in glasses, jars, and *chambaos* (a small jar with a handle). When the master of the house gave the sign—actually he shouted it impatiently several times, "A rag! A rag!" (the Indians have no equivalent word)—they brought several pieces of different kinds of cloth in different colors for us to wipe our mouths with.

When the meal ended, the drinking began. They drink like everybody else: through their mouths. But they do not drink with their meals. Drinking is a separate act. There is nothing else so agreeable to them. They will postpone anything for a drink. And just as a warrior making ready for battle prepares his weapons, they, when getting ready to drink, hide theirs. So long as they have anything to drink, they drink: for an hour, a day, two days, two months. They are capable of passing the time drinking until they burst. To drink is to forget, to laugh, to revel. When they are out of firewater or wine, they drink *chicha* or *pisquillín*. This time it was a wine party. The act of drinking is subject to certain rules which, like all human rules, are observed as far as possible. It begins with a *yapaí*, which is as much as saying, "The pleasure of a glass of wine with you?"[3] I wouldn't want our English colony to think that it bears no resemblance to the Ranquels. Yet, the invitation differs somewhat from our own. Normally, we begin by filling our guest's cup, then our own. We drink simultaneously after a more or less cheerful and cordial salute and eye one another over the rim of the cup to see who drinks more. It shows good manners of a classic style not to drink the cup dry, nor to appear obligated to accept the toast, since a toast means, for instance, to your health if not to your country or to the President of the Republic.

The Indians begin by saying "*Yapaí*" and by filling the vessel they drink from, usually an animal horn, to the top.

The person addressed answers: "*Yapaí*."

The one doing the inviting goes first, drinking until what the French call *goute en l'ongle*, that is, to the last drop, refills the glass, cup, jar, or horn exactly to where he had it before, passes it to the other party, who then quaffs it, saying "*Yapaí*."

If the *yapaí* was half a quart, half a quart must be drunk. Needless to say, nothing is more poorly regarded than a person who excuses himself, saying, "I don't know." Never would the Indians have trust in such a man.

Just as every well-directed meal has its presiding host, who rouses the guests and does the honors, in every Indian drink-fest there is one who has the say-so. It commonly falls to the one who has borne the expenses. In this case that was ostensibly Mariano Rosas but in reality the state, which had given money to Father Burela for the ransom of Christian captives. However, if Mariano Rosas had borne the expenses and was the master of the house, his brother, Epumer, was the host. Epumer is feared more than any other Indian among the Ranquels: feared for his valor, his daring, and his dementia when drunk. He is a short, fat man some forty years of age. He is quite fair and pink and pug-nosed, has full lips and prominent cheekbones, dresses stylishly, appears to have Christian blood in his veins, has killed several Indians with his bare hands, among them a half-brother on his mother's side. When clear-headed, he is generous and giving. When not clear-headed, he will stick his knife into the savviest of men.

This was the lad I had to deal with.

He carried an enormous, silver-sheathed *facón* slung in front of him and regarded me from under the brim of a Guayaquil straw hat with a wide, red hatband painted with white flowers. I carried a knife with a gold and silver sheath and hilt, and wore a wide slouching beaver-skin hat with a high brim. I did not take my eyes off the proud Indian. I looked straight at him when speaking to him.

We were all drinking.

"*Yapaí*, brother, *yapaí*, brother" was all that you could hear.

Mariano Rosas was accepting no invitations, claiming he was sick. He looked it. He waited on everyone, ordering the bottles filled whenever they ran out. Some he upbraided. Others he sent away when they became too much of a nuisance to me. He begged my pardon every two minutes. In short, he did the honors of his home in his own way and according to the customs of his land.

Epumer had not taken a liking to me, and the more he drank, the sharper and more direct did his barbs become. Mariano Rosas noticed this and was constantly stepping between his brother and me and joining the conversation. I was trying to find a way around the Indian but couldn't do it. I found him stealthy and intractable at every turn. His answers became so foul that Mariano had to ask me to excuse him, noting the condition he was in. Yet he never let up with his "Colonel Mansilla, *yapaí*!"

"Epumer, *yapaí*," I would answer.

And we would fill the horns with Mendoza wine[4] and drink it down.

My officers had had no choice but to leave the scene; it was either that or pass out from all the *yapaí*.

By now plainly stewed, the Indians polished off bottle after bottle with no regard for pace or protocol. "Wine! Wine!" they called out, their idea being to finish off, as they say, and Mariano had more wine brought in, and some fell down and others stood up, and some shouted and others fell silent, and some laughed and others cried, and some came to me and embraced and kissed me, and others threatened me in their language, saying, "*Winca* lying." I let myself be mauled and kissed and caressed however they wanted and pushed anyone to the ground who went too far with it, and since the wine had begun to take effect I was ready for anything. Still, I had the presence of mind to tell myself this: "You have to howl with the wolves if you don't want to be eaten."

My air, my manners, my frank disposition, my patience, my constant acceptance of every *yapaí* began to capture their sympathy. I realized this and made the most of it.

You have to seize the occasion by the forelock.

I was wearing a red cape, a beautiful but ill-fated red cape I had ordered from France. It was exactly like the ones the native Algerian cavalry corps officers wear. I have a certain weakness for the flamboyant and have for some time been unable to resist indulging it. I have a passion for capes as well, an innocent enough one, let it be said in passing.

In Paraguay I always wore a white cape.

I even slept with it.

My cape was my woman.

But then how dearly we sometimes pay for our innocent passions!

I have been turned away from the polls for wearing a red cape.

They have called me a red for wearing a red cape.

They have taken me for a party boss of insidious intent for wearing a red cape. So who says that the habit doesn't make the monk?

Figueroa is definitely right: "Say what they will about it, the habit makes the monk."[5]

I took off this historic cape, stood up, approached Epumer, and in friendly language told him, "Take this token, brother, it is one that I very much love." Saying this, I placed it on his shoulders. It made him identical to me and I saw in his face that my action had pleased him.

"Thank you, brother," he said, giving me an embrace that nearly burst me open. I saw Mariano Rosas's eyes flash, as eyes will when the heart is struck by the thunderbolt of envy. I took my handsome knife and giving it to him said, "Take this, brother; use it in my name."

He took it with pleasure, gave me his hand, and thanked me.

I had my lasso brought in. It was a masterpiece. I gave it to Relmo.

Pretty soon I would be giving away the shirt on my back.

I had my *boleadoras* brought to me. They were ivory with silver tethers. I gave them to Melideo.

I had my revolvers brought to me and gave them to Mariano's son.

I had three of the best hats, I had stockings, handkerchiefs, shirts—I gave away everything I had.

Finally, I had a barrel of firewater brought in and gave it to Mariano, who then said, "Brother, I want you to see how I am with the Indians. I am going to give this out to all of them in your presence. That is the way I am. Whatever I have is for my Indians. They are so poor!"

The barrel came and the divvying—by bottle, kettle, glass, cup, and horn—began. While Mariano conducted the patriarchal distribution, a man of his confidence, a Christian, approached me and spoke in a low voice.

"General Mariano says that if you have any more firewater please save a little for him. He plans to enjoy himself alone tonight once they all leave. It wouldn't be right for him to do it now."

How do you like the way the Indians operate?

I told him I had another barrel and that he should go ahead and hand out all the drink he had just received.

The orgy went on; it was a proper Bacchanal. Epumer was beginning to glow like a hot poker, terrible to behold. Mariano tried to take me out of there, but I refused. His brother wanted to drink with me and I didn't wish to abandon the battlefield and expose myself to the suspicions of the barbarians. I am strong and was relying on myself. If fortune failed to help me, well, it all has to end sometime, this battle of life—the pride and vanity, every bit of it—has to be over someday.

"*Yapaí*," said Epumer, offering me a hornful of firewater.

"*Yapaí*," I answered, horrified. I could drink a bottle of wine in one sitting, but a horn of firewater, let me see your best man do it.

At that instant and while Epumer tipped the horn, a soft voice spoke into my ear, "Don't worry. I am here."

Startled, I turned around to find myself looking into an infantile but energetic face.

"And who are you?"

"A Christian, Miguelito."

 MIGUELITO HAD CONCEIVED for me one of those electric passions which reveal the spontaneity of the soul, which are a refuge from great tribulation, which counsel and fortify, which balk at no sacrifice, which confound the skeptic and fill the believer with ineffable satisfaction.

We cross the stormy sea of life amidst anguish and pain, joy and pleasure, amidst grief and weeping, contentment and laughter; amidst disenchantment and doubt, belief and faith. And when we think ourselves strongest, discouragement overpowers us, and when we seem weakest, unguessed energies lend us the virile spirit of heroes. We go from surprise to surprise, from revelation to revelation, from victory to victory, from defeat to defeat. We are something more than a duality; there is something more complex, complicated, or indecipherable about us. And still, it is false that mankind is better in ill fortune than in good, better fallen than risen, better poor than rich.

The miser, basking in opulence, never feels duty-bound to the wretched.

The generous never ask themselves if what they give away today they will need tomorrow.

A coward is always strong with the weak, weak with the strong.

The brave neither oppress nor brook oppression; they may bend but never break.

The weak seek safe harbor, governance, the guidance of others.

The strong shelter and protect; they sustain themselves.

The virtuous are modest.

The vicious are audacious.

We are as God has made us.

That is why charity prescribes love, indulgence, generosity.

That is why human greatness holds fast to imperfection.

Such and such a man that I love may not deserve my esteem. Another whom I esteem is not my friend.

Reason is logic made inflexible.

The heart is inexplicable versatility.

Psychological problems are unsolvable.

Where does the plant's virtue of emission arise from?

The leaf? The cell? The petals? The stamen? The ovaries?

Mystery . . .

The plasticity of nature is generative.

Say biology and you have said reproductive organs, but how do the phenomena of life operate?

Great affection and great hatred both spring from the heart. From the heart spring sublime thoughts and sublime aberrations. That which moves me and that which horrifies me both come from the heart, as do my comfort and my anxiety.

But on what impulse?

What gladdened my life yesterday fills me with loathing today. What gave me life yesterday kills me today. Yesterday I thought I could not live without the thing I lack today, and today I discover within me the unexpected germ of resistance and suffering.

Like a lamp that is extinguished but does not die, so is our heart.

We complain about others, never about ourselves.

Are we severe in this? Are we ungrateful? No! We simply fail to understand ourselves.

If we understood ourselves we would not be unjust, longing as we do for the good.

> *There is a tide in the affairs of men*
> *Which, taken at the flood, leads on to fortune.*[1]

Make what you will of that, one thing is undeniable: if you can suffer and hope, you will risk anything. If you deny me this, you cannot deny me something else, namely, that when a man needs another man and looks for him, he finds him.

Our desperation is often no more than the effect of our febrile impatience.

Human solidarity is a tangible fact in politics, in social economy, in religion, in friendship.

Life is consumed in trading service for service. Harmony derives from a common belief: today is your day, tomorrow is mine.

Which is why the quintessentially odious person is the one who breaks the wise law of reciprocity and stains every inch of himself with the mark of ingratitude.

Dante puts such wretches in the fourth ring of the deepest hell. Those who enter there—*Vexilla regis prodeunt inferni*—are met by Satan's standard-bearers and the diabolical hosts pave the glacial den with their skulls.

How often indeed we find the man we need, and we were not looking for him.

The appearance of Miguelito in Mariano Rosas's tent is proof of this.

I was in danger and did not know it.

Miguelito cautioned me and I took heed. Forewarned is fore-armed.

Miguelito is twenty-four years old. He is smooth-skinned, white as ivory, and the sun has not browned his face. He has lively, black eyes as bright as stars, full, arched eyebrows, long eyelashes, a clear brow, a sharp nose, distinct, full lips, prominent cheekbones, a round face, long, straight black hair, regular size or a little on the short side, a broad back, and vigorous musculature. His eyebrows reveal pride, his cheekbones valor, his nose perspicacity, his lips sweetness, his eyes impetuosity, his brow resolve.[2] He was wear-ing coltskin boots, breeches with fringes, a striped *chiripá* made from an English poncho, a golden brown Crimean (*mordoré*) shirt, silver-buttoned suspenders, an ordinary straw hat with a broad red hatband. He had a painted, yellow silk neckerchief. His *facón* had a silver handle and his *boleadoras* were fastened to his waist.

I have already said that Miguelito is a Christian. I neglected to say that he is neither a captive nor a political refugee. Miguelito is with the Indians as a fugitive from justice. At twenty-four he has endured great hardship. He has a story, one well worth telling, and I will tell it before going on with my bacchanalian scene with Epumer. I heard it from him on the way from Leubucó to Chief Baigorrita's settlement several nights after meeting him.

I will speak as he did, say what he said.

"I was poor, sir, and my parents were, too.

"My mother lived from her work as a housemaid. My father raised game cocks. I raced horses.

"Sometimes my father and I would hire on together as highway laborers or to drive cattle from San Luis to Mendoza.[3] Other times we would do it separately.

"All three of us were born and raised in El Morro and that's where we lived. My old man was one cool gaucho. No one could rope like him or prime a fighting cock better. He was young and good-looking. I've never seen a livelier man. His only downfall was the booze. When he drank he'd get to spying on my mother, but she was a good, hardworking woman, poor Ma was, God rest and keep her.

"On top of everything else, my old man played a nice guitar. He read some and could write, too. I guess his first *patrones* had a lot of wealth on their hands and they taught him very well."

"What was your father's name?"

"Same as my own, Colonel: Miguel Corro. We're from the Corros of Punta de San Luis. They were people of means in Quiroga's time. But like I said, my mother and father and I were all born in El Morro, near the big hill on a ranch that is part of some land that always passed as ours, but I couldn't tell you whose it really was. If you know El Morro, Colonel, I can tell you where it is. It's just on the lower side of don Novillo's spread. I'm sure you know him, sir, he is rich like you.

"The house was almost always empty. My mother would go to town in the morning to work and stay there till after her *patrones* had finished their supper. My father and I never quit. He had his gamecocks, I had my racehorses to get ready. I had to walk them every day, morning and night. The old man and I liked to have a good time, too, so we never missed a dance. He really thought the world of me and always came looking for me to take me with him. So I was the one who would get him off the hook and make him and my mother make up when they fought. That's how we spent our time. We were poor but happy. We never seemed to run out of the few pennies it took to buy spirits and clothes. And horses. Man did we have horses! And always the best ones, too.

"In the house where my mother was hired there was a real sweet, nice girl who I always saw when I dropped by to talk to my ma. We were both kids and as soon as we'd see each other we'd start to laugh. At first I thought she was just playing around with me, but then I saw she liked me and I started making love talk to her. Then my mother found out and told me not to come around any more. I obeyed her and started to see another girl. This one came from a *paisano* family who were friends of ours. They had some animals and lots of stuff made of silver. I guess he played the slickest game of cards around. He could always draw any card he needed and he really raked in the money.

"The daughter of the people where my mother worked was called Dolores. The other one was Regina. Regina was a nice girl, but you'd be wasting your time trying to find another one like Dolores.

"I don't really know how much time went by after that. Maybe half a year. One day my mother found out I was coming over and talking to Dolores whenever I could and this time she got really mad and even though I was almost a grown man she threatened me. I laughed at her threats and kept on seeing both Dolores and Regina because I liked them both and they loved me. You know how us men are, Colonel. As many women as we see, that's how many we want. And the women don't need much at all!"

I don't recall what I said at this point to Miguelito or what I did next. I probably nodded in agreement and sighed. Miguelito continued.

"One day my father and mother told me that Regina's father told them that she and I could get married if we wanted. He would back me and what did I think about it. I told them I didn't care to get married. My mother was furious and even my father got mad, which he never did with me. My mother said she knew why; she said I'd pay, too, for not minding what she said. She said how could I think Dolores could be my wife. She said not only would she never be my wife but as soon as her family got wind of this they would have me put in the army. They were rich, you see, and good friends with the judge and the *comandante*.

"I wasn't taking anybody's advice and I wasn't afraid of anything. I kept things alive with Dolores, even though I couldn't get her to say yes. My mother was sad. She kept saying how something bad was going to happen to us. They let her go from her housemaid job at Dolores's and she blamed it all on me. Then all of a sudden they threw my father in jail and then let him out. Then they threw me in jail. They were just feeling that way, same as with my father. You know how it is when poor folks get on the government's bad side, Colonel.[4] But they let me go, too. On my way out, the lieutenant in charge of the police corps says, 'I know you've been makin' trouble out there.'

"'Trouble,' I says, 'what trouble?'

"'Meetings against the government,' he says.

"Now you tell me where he came up with that one, Colonel. It was all a big lie. The real deal was they were setting me up. My father never went with the *colorados* and neither did I. All we cared about was our work and we liked to be free, and whenever there would be an opening for a guard, we'd pay the commander rather than tote a rifle. That's the only way out of it. Otherwise, forget it, you're going in.

"One afternoon almost at sundown we were at home sitting by the fire. We heard horses coming. The dogs started barking and then we heard the sabers.

"We were saying like what's going on or what's not going on?

"My mother started crying and saying, 'This is all your fault.'

"You know how women are, Colonel, when it comes to anticipating bad luck, especially mothers. You'd think they can see it all before it happens like my old lady did that night. Because right after that the posse comes up and the head one gets off his horse and comes and makes my father go with him. He didn't even give him time to grab his poncho. They took him just the way he was.

"My mother and I spent a sad, sad night staring at each other. I was quiet and she was sitting on a chair beside her bed, crying. She didn't go to bed that night. Next day, soon as there was the slightest bit of daylight, I saddled up and rode straight into town to see what was up. They were accusing my father of a holdup and said if he didn't put up money for a stand-in, a *personero*, they would send him out to the frontier territory. Now where was I going to find money for a *personero* and who would want to go? When I went home I was feeling pretty sad to have to give my mother this news. But I was also thinking I could get them to spring my father if they would take me. I told my mother what was going on and what I wanted to do. She didn't say a word. She just got very mad at me and threw me out. I left and came back late. The dogs didn't bark because they knew me. I got all the way to the door of the ranch without her hearing me. I found her kneeling down in front of a niche we had there to Our Lady of the Rosary, praying. She was praying in a low, low voice. All I could hear was the end of the Our Fathers and the Hail Marys. I was holding my breath so I wouldn't interrupt her when I heard her say, 'Mother and Lady, pray for him and for my son.' Then I let my breath out. She turned around and I went in and hugged her.

"She didn't say anything.

"We couldn't talk to my father. They had him incommunicado. I hung around there for a few days to see if they'd let me talk to him. Finally they did. It turned out there was nothing at all to what they were saying about him. It was all a setup to do us a lousy turn. They wanted us out of there. They were starting with him. After that it would be me.

"It took money to get him out. We sold everything we had to do it.

"About this time the judge started visiting my mother and trying to get on her good side. I had to marry Regina because her father was the one who lent us the money to get my father out. From the day my father got out of prison—I got married that same night— there was no peace at home.

"My father was wearing a long face. All he could do was fight with my mother. He had gotten it into his head that my poor mother had been up to something with the judge to get him out of jail. He figured she still was. But what was a devout woman like my mother going to be up to, Colonel? I guess you know what a suspicious man is like. Well, that was my father all the way."

"And how were things working out between you and Regina?" I asked him at this point in his story.

"Like the devil," he said.

"But I thought you said you loved her and you liked her," I added.

"I do, sir, but I loved Dolores a whole lot and I like her more, too," he replied.

"And were you seeing her?"

"Every night, sir, and that's what brought all this on me and my family," he said bitterly, withdrawing into a cloud of melancholy.

Poor Miguelito! I exclaimed to myself. I admired the childish candor of a man who, because he had found a soft spot for me, had been poised with his knife to strike at the terrible and fearsome Epumer.

 ANY NARRATION TOLD simply, naturally, and with neither artifice nor affectation will find a sympathetic echo in the heart.

The ideal cannot be achieved unless we keep within the limits set by nature.

Or does the ideal not exist, or is it not true?

Or is there no plastic beauty: no features, lines, perfect human form?

Or no aerial beauty: accidents, fugitive phenomena, moral perfection?

Miguelito had captivated me.

He was like a novelesque apparition in the romantic tableau of my pilgrimage, in the hazardous crusade I had undertaken, consumed as I was by a fever of generous action and possessed of a set idea. I say set idea because man's abilities are limited and to do something useful, great or good, we have necessarily to circumscribe our sphere of action.

Seeing the tinge of sadness that darkened his endearing face, I left Miguelito to himself for a while. When the somber cloud of his memories seemed to dissipate, I spoke to him.

"Go ahead with the story of your life, son; it interests me."

He went on.

"I didn't live with my parents; they were pitifully poor and I had spent everything I had to buy my father's freedom. I had to go live with Regina's family.

"At first my wife and I got along fine. Her parents liked me and helped me find work. They lent me money too, and looked after me. The in-laws are always good to you at first. But then later . . . ! That's why the Indians have the right idea in not speaking to them. Do you know that custom, Colonel?"

"No, Miguelito, what custom is that?"

"When an Indian gets married and his wife's mother or father comes to live with him, he and they never look at each other even if they're together. They say the in-laws have the *Gualicho*. Next time you go into a tent watch for that. You'll see some blankets hanging there so the son-in-law can't see the mother-in-law."

What a custom! Not a bad idea, either, I thought. "Go on with your story," I said.

"Oh, they're nobody's fool, Colonel," he mumbled, and then picked up where he had left off.

"I hadn't been married to Regina for long when she and I started to get into it the way my mother and father always did. We fought every day like a couple of wildcats. My father-in-law jumped in the middle of every fight we had, sometimes my mother-in-law too. They always took their daughter's side. I had to leave the house whenever it got too bad. They would always call me a bum and a fool and a cheat. I'd be pretty sore and wouldn't come back for a few days. I spent my time with a lady friend, which was worse. That's the way the world goes, I guess. Then just to add to it, I would come home and Regina didn't want to be my wife any more. Her parents were advising her and she said she was out of sorts with me. This made me mad and I started losing my affection for her. Of course I was also seeing Dolores at night behind her parents' back. They figured I was married now and didn't suspect anything between Dolores and me. Anyway, I didn't really need Regina all that much any more.

"There's never a shortage of women for a man, Colonel, as I am sure you know. Just look around you here. You've got as many as you want. Now, there usually is a shortage of money. When there is money, a man can buy as many women as he can support. Mariano Rosas has five now. He used to have seven. Calfucurá has twenty. What a barbaric Indian, eh?"

"And how many do you have?"

"None. There's no need for that."

"Why not?"

"Because a single woman does whatever she wants to around here. Wait and see what Mariano Rosas says about the Indian women and the captives and his own daughters. Why do you think the Christians like it so much out here? There was bound to be a reason."

This got me thinking about the seductions of barbarism. Since there would be time enough for me to learn more about them and I wanted to hear the end of the story, I asked Miguelito if he straightened things out with his in-laws and his wife.

"I straightened things out and then again I didn't. We all got along sometimes, but other times they'd go one way and I'd go the other. Finally, Regina started to get jealous. I don't know how, but she found out about me and Dolores. Once she even threatened to have me arrested. It was all getting too tangled to unravel and besides they had to go and start talking about my mother, knowing I would overhear them. They said she was covering for me and I was covering for the judge. One night I almost lost it with my father-in-law. If it hadn't been for Regina, I'd have stuck my knife in him right up to the handle. You don't talk like that, that's all. That was low of him, because my mother was a God-fearing woman, Colonel. She worked like an animal all day long and her prayers were her life.

"Well, families always patch it up and we were no different, but only from the lips out. Inside was another story. I bided my time. My mother always told me: Be patient, son."

"And what about Dolores?" I asked.

"I was still seeing her, Colonel," he answered.

"And how did you do that?"

"Well, I'll tell you how and when I do you'll see how badly it went for me.

"I went to see Dolores on almost every dark night. I would jump over the garden wall and hide in the orchard and wait till she came. I always left my horse tied up on the other side. Dolores wouldn't always come but when she did we would stay there a long time making love and keeping each other company and then I would go back home. One day my mother said, 'Son, I can't stand living with your father any longer. His drinking gets worse every day and he goes on and on about the judge this and the judge that. He said if the judge comes by tonight he is going to kill him and me both.

And I don't dare send the judge away because I'm afraid some harm will come to the two of you. You saw what happened last time. With all the trouble out there now they'll use any excuse they can get to put you in the army.'

"I went to see Dolores after that. I was thinking hard. She and I spent that night same as always, telling each other our troubles. We said good night, I jumped over the wall, untied my horse, climbed on, and let the reins loose. The horse trotted straight in the direction of his stall. I was thinking about my mother. I was saying, 'I wonder if anything bad happened there tonight; I'd better go see her,' when all at once my horse stopped. It was used to me getting off at this one place to light a cigarette. There was a niche someone had there and they always lit a candle at night for the soul of some loved one I guess. I got off my horse. There was a small door in the niche. It was a very windy night. I was about to open the small door before I rolled the cigarette but then I thought what if I put the candle out, I won't be able to light up. So I left it closed till I had the cigarette rolled. Then I opened it and held the reins in one hand and leaned up because the niche was on a high rock. I was lighting the cigarette with my right hand when bang! bam! someone hit me in the face. I let go of the reins and the horse got spooked and took off. I thought it was the soul of the dead person from the niche and he didn't want me lighting a cigarette with his candle. I was scared stiff and took off running. I didn't know what happened and it didn't occur to me that nobody hit me at all, it was just the wind blowing that door shut on me. I was running for my life and going the wrong way. Instead of running towards my house, which was on the riverbank, I ran towards town. The night was as dark as the throat of a wolf. I had this feeling they were chasing me from in front and from behind. I heard noises all over. I've never been so awful scared, Colonel. When I got to town my blood was running warm again and I could see all right in the dark and I could hear. There were voices shouting, 'There he goes! Over there! Get him! Hit him!'

"When I turned a corner I ran into a bunch of them and didn't have time to get a good look. I stopped.

"They said 'Who are you?'

"Miguel Corro," I says.

"'Kill him! Kill him!'

"They fired their carbines and slashed at me with their sabers and I went down in a pool of blood. Luckily none of the bullets hit me or that would have been all for me."

Here Miguelito fell into a kind of daze, which he then came out of.

"Well?" I said.

"Next day," he continued, "I woke up at police quarters. I couldn't see very well, because the blood had dried over my eyes. I tried to get up but I couldn't. I cleaned my face and little by little started to see some light. They had me in the stocks by the neck and the feet. You know how the police are, Colonel: the lowest of the low-lifers and the worst of them, too. The only thing I could hear or see that whole time was people coming in and going out. I guess they were taking statements. Some police came in that night and threw me a bunch of boiled meat. I didn't have the strength to eat it. I had lost a lot of blood. Since I had my hands free I tore my shirt into strips and sort of tied my wounds, which were in the head and trunk. I was near a corner and could just reach some spider webs. Who knows what might have happened otherwise!

"I spent a terrible night. When the pain didn't wake me up, the rats and the bats did. Critters everywhere, Colonel! The rats chewed on my boots and the bats sucked on the clotted blood. Next day first thing they do is let me out of the stocks and two of them take me to where the judge is. They asked me my name, how old I was, and a few other things. They asked me where I was coming from the night they apprehended me and rather than get Dolores in trouble I made up a lie. I said from my mother's house. That only made it worse. Oh, I forgot to tell you that the judge wasn't the same one I knew, the one who used to visit my mother and who brought on all the trouble at my house. This judge was someone else from El Morro.

"That was all they asked me that day. Next day I made more statements and more the day after that and that's how they kept me incommunicado. They'd give me boiled meat and a horn full of water at noontime. I was about going out of my mind. I hadn't heard from my mother, my father, my wife, or Dolores. I thought they had forgotten about me and felt like hanging myself with my sash. Then one night I finally heard a conversation the guard was having, I don't know who with, and I found out I had killed the judge, or so they said. And if they didn't have me shot they would stick me in the front lines. I didn't understand any of it.

"One day, the soldier from the police guard who gave me my food and water made a sign to me like 'I have something to tell you.' I nodded to let him know I understood what he meant. He came in later and said, 'So and so's daughter says to let her know if you need any money. . . .' I was afraid it was some kind of trick they were up to, so I said, 'Tell her thanks for me, friend.' Then, as he was leaving, I said, 'Do me a favor, *paisano*, tell me what I'm being held for.'

"'You know better than I do.'

"'Do you know if my father is at home—Miguel Corro?'

"'Yes, he is.'

"'And my mother?'

"'She is, too.'

"'And where was the judge killed?'

"'Why, right near your house. It's no use pretending you don't know. It's all out in the open now.'

"I was dumbfounded and didn't ask him anything else. A few days later they let me have visitors. My mother was the first person I saw. Didn't I tell you the woman was a saint, Colonel? She told me what was going on. She was crying the whole time, poor thing. My father killed the judge in a jealous rage but no one saw it except her. They thought I was the assassin because they found me on foot in town in the middle of the night. My mother was really hurting. She said they were saying they were going to shoot me and how could they do that and this wasn't any fault of mine.

"I told her, 'My dear, dear Ma, I want to save my father.'

"She cried.

"Right then a guard came in and said she had to leave because it was getting dark. We hugged and kissed and cried. My mother left and I stood there as sad as a day without sunshine. She told me she would come back the next day. Maybe we could think of something."

Here Miguel stopped. He needed to take a deep breath if he was going to finish. He sighed. His eyes misted up with tears of tenderness.

I was moved.

 EVERY ZONE, EVERY CLIMATE, every land yields its special fruits, nor are science or art, even under intelligent human application, adequate to produce the chemico-natural effects of spontaneous generation.

The white and perfumed aerial flowers of the islands of the Paraná; the slender green palms of Morería; the towering, robust

Lebanese cedar; the banyans of India, whose blossoms fall to the ground and, rooting there, form vast galleries of thick and fresh foliage—they all grow in the conservatories of the London and Paris zoos, but how well? Musty, odorless, feeble, sallow; stunted and rickety; devoid of all their tropical splendor.

Our beautiful native plant is the same as it grows from within, as it thrives on contemplation and ecstasy, as it sings and weeps, loves and abhors, and dies in the present to live in posterity. The open air, the manly mastery of the horse, grasslands like the open sea, mountains jutting into the clouds, the struggle, the daily combat, ignorance, poverty, loss of sweet freedom, respect for strength; the unconscious longing for a better lot in life; the contemplation of the physical and social landscape of the homeland. These things produce a generous kind of person whom our politicians have persecuted and stigmatized and whom our bards have not had the fiber to sing, except to caricature.[1]

The monomania of imitation may yet strip us of everything: our national physiognomy, our customs, our tradition! They are making an operetta of us as a people. We have to play every role except the one we actually can play. They counter with institutions, laws, and someone else's gains. And they are right: we are making strides. Yet, would we not have made greater strides by studying our organizational problems upon other criteria and by drawing our inspiration from the real needs of the land?[2]

We are greater for our bursts of genius than for our cold and reflective contributions.

Where will this latter road lead us?

Somewhere, no doubt.

We cannot stand still when there is a social dynamics that makes the world move and humanity progress. But do the currents that mold us like so much soft wax into unseemly shape carry us any more swiftly and surely to wealth, respect, and freedom within the law than do our own turbulent, confused impulses?

I am just a simple chronicler, thank heavens!

I was impassioned by Miguelito. His noble figure wrenches certain thoughts from me despite myself. If unhusbanded and unaided our land can bring forth a soul as noble as his, it would then seem allowable that the nation's own clay, drenched as it is in the blood of brothers, might, if left unalloyed, serve to mold a people possessed of characteristic features, a people sanctified in the pride of its forebears and its martyrs, whose ashes rest forever in cold and unknown sepulchers.

Miguelito resumed his story.

"Next day my mother came with a bowl of sweet corn meal for me, some stew and tea and sugar. She built a fire right there on the ground, boiled some water and made mate for me. Dolores had sent a chore girl over with some money. She knew we were in trouble and said we shouldn't be afraid to use her if we needed anything. Meanwhile, my real wife wasn't around. That's what it is to marry when you don't really want to, Colonel, marry for money like the rich do.

"Dolores's chore girl told my mother that Dolores was sick and let on what it was and that it must have come from me. The old lady preached me a sermon then. She brought up all the times she had warned me and how I would never listen because that's the way the young are. She laid it right on the line: 'How are you going to fix what you've done now?' I was very ashamed of myself on account of what my mother said, Colonel, and she said it much better than I'm telling it right now. Why, her eyes were shining like the buttons on my suspenders. My poor old mother! See, she never did anybody any harm and she had watched Dolores grow up, so it made her feel bad to see her in such trouble. I kept thinking, 'If only I hadn't gotten married!' and just sat there and sighed. I couldn't think of anything else to do. A man gets so boneheaded when he knows he has done something wrong.

"I drank a full kettle of tea and ate all the corn meal, which was delicious. My mother could mash corn like nobody's business. She'd make it come out really nice. Then she healed my wounds with some remedies she had with her—plants from up the hill— and she took a clean shirt and some underwear out of a little bundle she brought with her and I changed. She rolled me about a whole night's worth of cigarettes, we sat down facing each other, and looked at each other a long time, and when she was about to leave the man who took the judge his pen came in with two police- men. He had some papers under his arm. They told my mother to leave. They didn't give her any choice about it, either.

"The judge read me my statements and some other ones I didn't get very well. Finally he asked me if I was confessing to killing the judge. I was stuck. They might find out about my father and I wanted to save him. What is a son for, wouldn't you say, Colonel?"

"You're right," I answered.

"You only die once," he went on, and it has to happen some- time.

"The notary asked me again what I had to say. I told him I was the one who had killed the other judge.

"He says, 'Why?'

"I was on the spot again. The notary gave me some time. I thought about it for a minute. I could say it was on account of a horse race, that he was the finish-line judge and called it against me and this made the speckled horse lose, which was this first-class horse I had. And it was true, Colonel. That was a mean and low-down trick they pulled on me one time, and from that day on me and my father had a bad time of it. They really played dirty with us. We lost every cent we had.

"Next he asked me if anybody had gone with me to do this killing and I told him no, I says I did it alone and he shouldn't bother blaming anyone else. He says what did I do with the money the judge had in his pockets. I says I never touched a thing. Probably the posse cleaned him out. They usually do. That's always been their way and then they turn and blame the guy who got in trouble over it.

"That was all he asked me. They left and put me in solitary again and kept me that way for days on end. They wouldn't even let me talk to my mother, but she came lots of times every day to see when they'd let us talk and bring me something to eat. I was bored with prison now and was just hoping they'd get it over with and put me out of my misery. My wounds had gotten worse on account of how clammy my room was and because all the little crawling things kept me awake day and night. That was no life at all.

"The notary came back one day and read me my sentence. I was condemned to die. How's that for justice, Colonel? I thought your doctors of the law were supposed to know it all! So tell me, if they know it all, how come they haven't figured out that I didn't kill the judge, even if I did confess to it? I suppose the new constitution is a great thing, but we poor always stay poor and a chain is only as strong as its weakest link. If the judge had up and killed me, what do you want to bet they wouldn't have ordered him shot? I've seen other things like that, Colonel, and I'm really still a boy.

"Anyway, the notary left me to myself.

"I spent a night like I never spent before. I don't scare easy, but I was getting the saddest ideas! Sad, sad ideas in my head and I was afraid to die. I was thinking about how if I didn't die my father would and that kept me going. The old man was so good and such a warm-hearted man to me! We worked and horsed around and fooled around with women and got into fights—we did it all and we did it together. So how was I not going to love the man and even give up my life for him? It's gone sooner or later anyway, you're going to do some damn fool thing or mix it up with somebody. That's all it ever takes to lay a poor boy out.

"I wanted a guitar so bad, Colonel. As soon as they took me out of solitary again that was the first thing I asked my mother to bring. She did, and I passed the time singing. The guards all came to hear me every day and we started making friends. If I had wanted to run, I could've. But I didn't want to get them in trouble, so I didn't. A man has to keep his word and they would always say, 'Now don't get us in trouble, amigo.' Every time my mother would come, they'd say it again. Then the guard would disappear and let me talk to her all I wanted. She didn't know anything about me being sentenced yet. I didn't want to tell her because I could see she was happy thinking they were going to let me go since they didn't have anything on me, and I didn't want to hurt her. But there's always someone willing to give you bad news and she finally found out. She made a beeline to me and asked what was going on.

"Now I was on the spot, Colonel, and with a good woman like that who loved me and all. When I told her the truth she cried like Mary Magdalen. The tears ran like a stream. We cried for hours the two of us. One question led to another till she got it out of me that I had confessed to killing the judge to save my old man. And then you should have seen her, Colonel, a woman who never got mad, get mad, not at me, because she kept hugging and kissing me and saying, 'My little boy,' but at my father. She kept saying, 'It was him, this whole thing is his fault and I'm not going to let them kill you on his account. I'm going to tell them everything.'

"All of a sudden she dried her eyes, stopped crying, got up and tried to leave.

"'Where are you going, Mamita?' I said.

"'To save my son,' and next thing you know she was on her way out the door, so I grabbed her petticoats and made her stay. I begged her over and over not to do anything, to trust in the Virgin of the Rosary who she was so devoted to and who could still do something to save me. I have always had a lot of trust in God."

"And you did well to. God never abandons those who believe in Him."

"That's true, Colonel, and that is why not only that time but others, too, I was saved."

"What did your mother do?"

"She gave in to my pleading and left saying she was going to light candles to the Virgin that night and the Virgin would protect us. And the little Virgin in the niche I told you about did save me like my mother hoped. She is really miraculous."

Miguelito paused.

I was left to my philosophizing.

Philosophizing!

Yes, to philosophize is to believe in God or to recognize that the greatest of comforts given to wretched mortals is to entrust their destiny to the mysterious, omnipotent protection of religion.

Which is why I join Fénelon in answering the cry of the skeptics by saying, "*Dilatamini!*"[3]

If there is an *ananke*, there is also someone who watches, sees, protects, keeps, loves, and saves his creatures, and does so unselfishly. You may take everything away from me, but if you don't uproot that one sweet, gentle conviction, my source of strength and comfort, what will you have taken from me?

 I WANT TO begin this letter with a flip display of personal erudition.

I too keep a vade mecum; it is a treasure like any other. But my treasure has one merit. I didn't inherit it from anybody. I put it together myself. Instead of spending most of my time passing the time, I have taken on certain useful tasks. In this way I have gathered, without realizing it, a tidy little fund, enough for me to justify crying out one day, *Anche io son pittore.*

Besides the merits just noted, my vade mecum has a further advantage: it is very handy and portable. I carry it in my pocket. When I need it I can open it, thumb through it, and consult it in a second. No one need worry about catching me unawares with my notebook in hand, like those literati whose study is a kind of inner sanctum, and woe to those who cross the forbidden threshold unannounced when the writer is pontificating!

Show some forbearance! What, would you be privy to the mysteries, wrest from the sphinx the dread arcanum, forsake your illusions?

Ah, you will find the sage in shirt sleeves, stitching a suit painted with the plumes of the forest bird—dark wings, red beak and feet, great black nails.[1]

All I know is what I have jotted down in my vade mecum, indexed and chronologically arranged.

It is nothing great, but it is something.

It has everything in it: ad hoc quotes in several languages I know both well and poorly; anecdotes, stories, travel impressions; critiques of books, of men and women; wars on land and at sea; sketches, outlines, profiles, silhouettes. In short, my memoirs to date in this year of the Lord, written in ten minutes.[2] If I were to publish these notes they wouldn't make as useful a book as an almanac, for instance, but they might still be somewhat entertaining. I don't think it would bother the public to read, for example: What points of contact exist between Epaminondas, the Theban statesman, and President Mitre?[3] What formal jacket was our current president wearing when he took the oath of office? How is his hairless pate similar to the head of Socrates? In what way does Orión resemble Roqueplan?

And then this Orión is a man about whom it can be said—and I'll take this phrase, not my own of course, from my vade mecum— that he is the quintessential *porteño*; that as man and writer he has Buenos Aires in his blood or, better yet, that he is the walking, thinking incarnation of this old and noble city; that there is not in all this ocean of mud a single reef that he has not cited; that he has learned politics from the inside out; that as a journalist and man of fashion he has enriched the literature of his land, and the tailors and the haberdashers; that his notions will be news in the provinces after they're forgotten here; that he would not have been named in brutal Rome's Who's Who, but that in learned Athens he would have been; that he knows everyone and knows everyone everyone knows; that he draws applause in Geneva and priestly Córdoba alike, where he speaks with the heretical openness of a Freemason; he draws applause in Rosario, the Californian city, speaking of universal fraternity; that he can be a prophet anywhere *ed altri siti*, except . . . I was going to say in his own land. He hasn't been able to make alderman there. He turns twenty-eight today, and I salute him with the sincere and intimate warmth of a brother in aspiration and pain, and if they say I am dragging him into my narrative, so be it.[4]

Yes, my friend Orión, I wish you "the strength of a serpent and the prudence of a lion," as a bourgeois *gentilhomme* would say, and I know you understand.

And with that, dear reader, I return to the matter at hand. What follows is Greek: Hellenic Greek, not Greek because you can't understand it.

Ek te biblion kubernetes.

I have studied Greek as well.

It was you, Santiago, who put the idea in my head. It was one of the lesser of the bad things I owe to your Mephistophelian inspiration.

To prove that I know Greek, like a schoolboy, here is a translation of that anonymous saying: "The world is not learned in books."

Now I am back to where I wanted to be. I have learned more about my country by going to the Ranquel Indians than I did in ten years of burning my eyes out reading studies, broadsides, gazettes, magazines, and specialized books. By hearing our *paisanos* tell their stories, I have discovered how justice is administered, how we are governed, and what our people think of our leaders and laws. This is why I pause perhaps longer than necessary to relate certain anecdotes, which surely appear as so many stories created to lengthen these pages and occupy the reader.

I wish Miguelito's story were only a story! Sadly, it happened just as I've told it, and if it holds our attention for a moment, it is because it is true. Truth holds powerful sway even over the imagination.

Miguelito went on.

"Imagine how my mother felt, Colonel. She spent everything she had on candles for the Virgin. She came to visit me every day. She said I shouldn't be upset because the Virgin wouldn't let us down in our misfortune. She said she had experience and had seen miracles more than once before.

"I wasn't upset except for her. I tried to hide it, but there was no way. She was too smart and saw through it. No matter how smart a kid is, Colonel, he cannot fool his parents, especially his mother. I mean, did I have my old lady fooled when I first started getting together with Dolores? Not at all! She knew it from the start and told me to take my business elsewhere. How sorry I am now that I didn't listen to her!

"Dolores wouldn't have suffered all that she did for me, but then we never mind our parents' advice. We always think we know more than they do. We finally come to regret it, but by then it's too late."

"It is never too late if you've got reason to be happy," I interjected.

He drew a sigh. "Well, Colonel, there are some diseases that have no cure."

"Have you heard from Dolores again?" I asked.

"Yes, Colonel. I'll confess to you. From what I've seen and what I've heard from the boys riding with you, you're a good man."

"You can trust me," I told him.

He continued his story.

"Whenever I can get away and I've got good horses, I cut out alone, take the road to Laguna Bagual, cut towards Cuadril, and wait overnight in the hills. I cross the Quinto and go into Villa Mercedes, where I have relatives. I stay there a few days and then in a couple of gallops I'm in El Morro. I hide up in the hills at a friend's place and visit my mother at night. Dolores comes to the house with the little girl. That's when I see her."

"So she had a baby girl?" I said.

"Yes, Colonel, didn't I tell you before we had gotten into trouble?"

"And don't you go see your wife?"

"My wife! She started running around with a landowner. And the bitch says she's waiting for news that I'm dead so she can get married. And she says they all want to marry her! Like she's some kind of beauty!"

"And other *paisanos* who are here, do some of them leave and go home like you?"

"Anybody who wants to can do it. There's no doors out here, Colonel, and everyone knows what time the lookout riders leave the forts, and then they almost never ride out to the front side. It's a cinch to cross the Quinto and the line and once the forts are behind you you're safe, because who doesn't have friends?"

"In other words, they're constantly coming and going from this side to the other."

"Why sure, Colonel. It's common knowledge around here. The Videlas take a whole string of horses when they feel like it. They go as far as Jarilla, leave the horses in the hills, and ride a fast mount to El Morro. They buy whatever they want there—sometimes they don't bother sending anyone, they just go in and buy for themselves—in their friends' stores and they bring letters back for everybody. Sometimes they make it all the way to Renca, and you know how far that is, Colonel." [5]

As Miguelito spoke I reflected on this country of ours. I could see the complicity of the frontier residents in the ravages of the In-

dians and our problem with hatred, our civil wars and persecution, all of it complicated by the problem of the security of the
borders. I listened with utmost interest and curiosity as Miguelito
spoke on.

"When you arrived the other day, Colonel, the Videlas had been
in San Luis. They were spreading the word that you and General
Arredondo were in Villa Mercedes. They said that people there are
saying that now there really is going to be peace."

I wanted to know the outcome of Miguelito's love story.

"Does Dolores live with her parents?"

"Yes, Colonel, they're good people and they're rich. When they
saw their daughter in trouble they didn't give up on her. They really
love my little daughter. If we can ever marry they're not going to
oppose it, or so Dolores tells me. But when will the other woman
die! Anyway, I can't leave here because the law will grab me, especially after the way I escaped."

"And how did you escape?"

"Well, I was still in prison. One day my mother came. She says,
'Your father says you should be on the lookout. He doesn't care
whose side he is on, but they asked him to come work for a day.
He's begging them off to see if maybe they're spies. As soon as he's
sure they're for real he'll join them on the condition that the first
thing they do is hold up the watchman and rescue you. Otherwise,
he won't join. That's where it stands now. There's nothing definite
yet. Tonight he meets the men and tomorrow I'll tell you what they
decide. I am backing your father. I want him to see this is the only
way we've got and I light candles to the Virgin so she will help us.
I dream about you every night and you're always out of prison in
my dreams. That's a sure, sure sign from the Virgin.'

"Next day my mother came back. Everything was ready. All
they needed now was somebody to give the call. They said that
Felipe Sáa would be coming under cover in two nights and he
would do it. And if he didn't come, the day was set, so whoever
was most fit to govern the people who were backing it would give
the call. Juan Sáa would be coming from Chile at the same time.
Well, Colonel, it all went as planned. One night when they sounded
the tattoo, a few who were waiting on the edge of town overran the
judge's house, some others took the command post, and my father
and some friends charged the police quarters. They had already
gotten all the guards drunk. Some of the guards tried to stand them
off but they were outnumbered. They came in, broke down the

door to the room I was in, and took me out. Once I was free my father said, 'Give me a hug, son. I didn't come see you before because I was ashamed to see you in prison for something your damn fool father did, and I didn't want them to suspect anything.'

"He made me so happy I almost cried. He had some white hair now and mind you he wasn't an old man. He was still young.

"El Morro was all a riot that night. All you could hear were gunshots, screams, and bells ringing. Some people died. I went around with my father and avoided serious trouble a few different times because I am not a killer. They wanted to loot Dolores's house on account of a rumor she was on Buenos Aires's side, but I wouldn't let them. They'd have had to kill me first. In the morning some people from the government showed up and we had to disappear. Some made for the Sierra of San Luis, others for Córdoba. My father headed for Rosario, because he could drive horses. I had to take one road or another so I took a different one—I galloped the livelong day, Colonel—and all of a sudden I look up and there's a posse. I took off, they ran after me, I was on a lightning-fast horse and no way could they catch me. I stopped close to the Quinto somewheres near Santo Tomé. You hadn't sent any troops out there yet, Colonel. I met up with some Indians, joined them, and came out here. And I'll stay until God or you, Colonel, get me out of here."

"Did you ever find out what became of your father?" I asked.

"He died of cholera," he answered bitterly. "Poor old guy! He really liked to work on a bottle of liquor."

And here concludes the true story of Miguelito which, *mutatis mutandis*, is the story of many Christians who have sought asylum among the Indians.

That is our country for you. Like any people in the process of organization, it presents the most contradictory pictures. Great and populous cities such as Buenos Aires, with all the pleasures and enticements of civilization: the theater, gardens, promenades, palaces, temples, schools, railroad lines, a dizzying everyday bustle— all of it on narrow, muddy, dirty, fetid streets that allow no view of the horizon or of the clear, blue skies with their harvest of shiny stars. I am suffocating in these streets and I miss my horse.

Beyond Buenos Aires, the open desert, great tracts of land where the proletariat vegetates in ignorance and stupidity.

Where are the churches, the schools?

Here, the noise of the throngs, the startling opulence.

There, the silence of poverty and chilling barbarism.

Here, everything heaped sickeningly together, driven by ego: a bunch of mollusks.

There, everything scattered haphazardly about, also driven by ego: pilgrims of a promised land.

Thesis and antithesis of the life of a republic.

They call that governing and administering.

And then for appearance's sake, they're calling for more people. They want immigrants!

It reminds me of all those wretched, helpless, and improvident married couples, whose sole comfort is the holy Word: Go forth and multiply.

III

THE WORD "BARBARIC" *comes to form a sort of counter-mantra in the journey narrative of the* Excursión, *so often and so freely does Mansilla use it. In its frequency it raises doubts as to how barbaric Mansilla actually believes the Ranquels to be. The late-nineteenth-century explorer mentality would perforce carry with it a colonizer's gaze, a benign pity for the primitive other, a fundamental paternalism. None of these is alien to Mansilla, although he seems to be offering his own body as collateral in a loan by which the Ranquel Indians open their way of life to him. Doing as these Romans do means, among other things, drinking oneself into a stupor in order to gain their trust. And their trust will be essential to the renegotiation of certain stipulations of a peace treaty whose details are scarce — we get a snippet in Chapter 38 — considering their importance in justifying the journey in the first place.*

The twofold purpose of drawing newspaper readers into the lives of the Ranquel people, while answering the political questions of the day — should the Indians be exterminated, what kind of settlements will the open country have, where will the railroads run and how will they be maintained — required that Mansilla imbricate two genres: the essay and the pastiche of stories. Chief Mariano Rosas collects from La Tribuna *those articles that concern the future of his people, and so he knows that the powers in Buenos Aires may want to build a railroad through Indian country. Mansilla is stunned when confronted with a chief who is prepared to challenge him on this issue, and he records the moment as a diplomatic snare. At the same time, he cannot as narrator forego mention of the chief's "great, sunken, sparkling blue eyes" or the boyhood captivity story which makes Mariano Rosas all but a blood relative of Mansilla himself.*

Overlapping again drives narrative strategy as Mansilla pens his splenetic descriptions of the Negro with the accordion. This "Rigoletto of the pampas" grates on Mansilla's nerves, though not without raising the specter of the "federal" dream for Argentina. Clearly, the narrator wants to probe the sinews of recent social and political history, but he finds himself drifting into the realm of the mystique surrounding his uncle, the deposed dictator Rosas. Even the "good Franciscans" riding with the party must be layered into the story using two registers of style. Mansilla portrays them as dutifully performing their baptisms and gently bringing the heathen into the fold. This makes the essayist's case for the auspicious advent of Christianity to the desert. We may just as readily remember them, however, flying off of their galloping horses and landing on their feet, or as sleeping bodies covered with sand on the morning of the first mass celebrated in Ranquel territory.

 WE WERE IN Mariano Rosas's tent when I met Miguelito for the first time.

The orgy had begun:

> *Este chilla, algunos lloran,*
> *Y otros a beber empiezan,*
> *De la chusma toda al cabo*
> *La embriaguez se enseñorea.*[1]

The Franciscans understood that this was not their scene and withdrew to the safety of Ayala's ranch. The officers had positioned themselves at a distance from which they could come to my aid if necessary. The assistants hovered inconspicuously near the entrance. Camilo Arias with a taciturn air ghosted into view from time to time, a shadow whose ardent, expressive, penetrating look told me from a distance: I am around.

As well-tempered as our hearts might be, there is no doubt that silence, solitude, isolation, and abandonment fuel danger in an imagination beset by fear.

That is why midnight bravery is bravery at its best.

There is something solemn about the darkness that slowly freezes the blood in the veins. I don't believe there is a single man in all the world who has not been afraid at night sometime. In the daytime amidst all the uproar and with witnesses, especially women, around, everybody is brave, or enough the master of himself to hide his fear, which is why I have sometimes said that bravery depends on the audience. A man who shows frank irresolution in the presence of a lady might as well have himself certified a coward.

Now, I have a deathly fear of dogs. They are my nightmare. Never mind a lot of dogs. Just let there be one and I won't go past it for all the gold in the world if I am alone. I can't help it. It calls for a heroism that is beyond me. When I was a captain in Rojas, I used to go hunting.[2] I would take my rifle in the afternoon and go to the outskirts of town. In the direction of the wetlands, where most of the ducks were, there was a ranch. Invariably I had to pass by it if I did not want to walk at least three miles to get around it. Well, no sooner would I decide to go duck hunting than I would remember the watchdog that lived at that ranch and instantly resolve to face it, bravely, in a showdown. I would leave my house and go to the critical spot. There I would make my strategic calculations, study the best maneuvers and the most imposing attitude exactly as if I were entering into battle and facing hand-to-hand combat. The damnable cur always recognized me as soon as he saw me. He pointed his tail, crouched back on his legs in assault position, tightened his jaws, and bared his two rows of sharp white teeth. That was all I needed. Ashamed of myself but also saying inwardly, "Discretion is the better part of valor," I changed direction and averted the danger.

One day I gave myself a good talking-to before going out. I called out my own name. I touched myself to see if I was shaking. No, I was all there. I felt like a man of action. Today I will walk by the dog, I said. So I leave, I march, I advance, I reach the Rubicon. Poor wretch! I shake, I balk, I struggle, I reach deep within me but to no avail.

I was not then, and am not now, a man who can fight with dogs.

I swear I hate them if they are not as gentle and harmless as lambs. I don't care if they are frisky little lapdogs.

Not only did my adversary recognize me, but he knew by my face that I was afraid of him. Mechanically, I lowered the rifle I had on my shoulder. Whether he suspected a shot was coming his way, or whatever reason he had, the dog turned around, backed up a ways, and stood there, as if to say: Fire your weapon, then we'll see.

Would the dog have reacted the same way to any other passerby?

Probably not.

I found out later he was tame.

But he had not taken a liking to me and once he knew my weak point he was going to have his fun with me, as I could have done, say, with a boy.

There is nothing amazing in this. Though they lack other faculties, animals have highly developed memories. Any horse, mule, ass, or dog can better our knowledge of the intricacies of a road we habitually travel. Birds get themselves from one country to another every year on migrations whose distances perfectly suit the birds' physiological needs. You have your swallows, who come back to the same nook in the same rooftop of the same tower after a long absence, year after year.

Which rules out all doubt: that dog, that damnable dog, knew what it was doing with me.

For a minute I almost had him backing down. Dream on, ye faint-hearted!

As soon as he looked like he might attack I turned tail, rifle and all, and ran. Of course he barked, which only increased my panic, so that long after he had forgotten about me I was still alone and forsaken somewhere out in God's country. And yet, if I had been in the company of a lady, that old dog would not have driven me away. The lady would have taken off running.

Women have a special gift of making us perform all sorts of foolishness. They can even get us killed. If it happens I am a woman's *cabaleiro servente* I will fight any dog, even a watchdog, for that woman, be she old and ugly or young and fair. Someone else might well commit suicide over a woman. A straight razor, a pistol, a leap from a tower—these things happen, no question about it.

There are heroes because there are women.

Better not waste too much thought on it, though. What would our fair planet be without them?

The immediate presence of my people, my own pride in refusing to be cowed or overwhelmed in any regard whatsoever by these barbarians, it all meant that under no circumstances was I going to leave the tent, Mariano Rosas's repeated insistence notwithstanding.

My main fear was intoxication. I wasn't so terribly afraid of a *loncoteada. Loncotear* is the Indian word for a beastly hand game of theirs. To play it, two people grab each other by the hair and force their heads back to see who can stand the pulling longer.

They play at this from the time they are small.

When they want to show a little Indian boy affection, they pull on his bangs. If the tears don't come, they have a way of praising him: "That one bull." To the Indians the bull is the prototype of strength and bravery. If they call someone a bull, that is one kid to watch out for.

The "*yapaí*, brother!" went on and on.

Epumer was out to get me, he and a little Indian fellow named Caiomuta, who never did give me his hand to shake. He said I was not there on good faith. "*Winca* lying" was his one, constant remark.

The wine and the liquor were running like water, spilled by the quivering hands of the inebriated, who roared like beasts and cried and sang and sank like stones, snoring as soon as they landed or retching like cholera victims. It was more sickening than it was frightening.

Everyone treated me with respect except Epumer and Caiomuta, who were teetering drunk. Every so often Epumer would reach down, grip the handle of his shining *facón*, and glower at me.

Miguelito spoke.

"Just watch out in front of you, Colonel. I am right behind you."

Whenever I refused a *yapaí* they growled like dogs. There was wrath painted on their wine-soaked faces and they mumbled angry words I couldn't understand. Miguelito spoke again.

"They're mad at you because you're not drinking, Colonel. They said you're doing it so you won't spill any secrets by drinking."

I then turned to some of those present and extended them an offer.

"*Yapaí*, brother," I said, and polished off the horn or glass. A deafening hullabaloo exploded *incontinenti* as they beat their open mouths with the palm of their hands.

Babababababababababababababababababababa!

It echoed, this yapping of toads, until the sound finally drowned in their throats.

As long as there was liquor, the saturnalia would go on.

Evening was approaching.

I did not want to be caught among that foul rabble after dark. Their bodies, polluted by consumption of horse meat, gave off a nauseating effluvium. They belched full and ripe, too, and each eructation seemed an emission from a pig fed on onion and garlic.

Wherever there are Indians, there is a smell of asafetida.

I tried to get up off the floor so I could slip out unnoticed. I could see most of the guests were passed out. Epumer stopped me.

"*Yapaí, yapaí,*" he said.

"*Yapaí, yapaí,*" I answered.

And one after another we followed etiquette and drank. The horn he was using held a quart. A dose of firewater of this size was enough to knock an elephant down, if elephants were given to drinking.

He half lost his head.

When I raised my drink to my lips I blessed myself in my imagination as if to say, God help me. I've never had such a drink. I saw stars, shadows of every color, a mosaic of muted hues as when sharp pain forces our eyes shut and squeezing our eyelids we see formless visions on our retinae. When Epumer stood up, I guess I made some kind of wisecrack. The Indian became furious. He tried to come at me with his bare hands. Mariano and the rest of them held him down. They asked me if I would please, please leave. I refused. They insisted, I refused, I steadfastly refused. They reminded me that when Epumer gets a glow going, he goes out of his mind and means harm.

"Nothing to get alarmed about," was all I could answer.

The Indian was struggling to tear himself loose. He wanted to lunge at me and his hand was on his *facón.* He kicked, he roared, he dug his heels into the ground, he stiffened his body and straightened it as if galvanized.

His eyes followed mine, mine were locked on his. As he struggled he finally pulled out his *facón.* It was a double-edged steel dagger with a silver hilt and handle. He was all but on top of me in half a second.

"Careful, Colonel," said Miguelito, stepping between us and speaking most gently to the savage in the Indian language.

"Careful!" shouted several people at once.

Affecting an ease that would speak honorably of my bloodlines and race, I answered, "Nothing to get alarmed about."

The Indian's final, supreme, convulsive effort exhausted what remained of his herculean strength, now attenuated by alcohol. When they felt him pass out, the ones holding him left his body to its own gravity and the immutable law was borne out: *E caddi, come corpo morto cade!*

The agitation subsided.

I wanted to know what cause or motive or what words of mine had so infuriated my adversary.

"Why was he so angry?" I asked.

"Because you called him a dog," someone answered.

"That's not true," said Miguelito in Araucan. "The colonel said something about dogs, but he did not call Epumer a dog."

No one contested this.

Apparently, in the joke I tried to play on Epumer to get his mind off the wrong kind of thoughts, I somehow interpolated the word *dogs*. To an Indian, as to an Arab, there is no greater insult than to call him a dog. Epumer misunderstood me and took offense. Thus his fit of fury.

Night was beating its dark wings. The drunken Indians snored, vomited, rolled on the ground in a pile. This one rested his dirty feet on that one's mouth, one his belly on the other's face. A number of Indian women and captives brought calfskins and made headrests for them, putting them in more comfortable positions. Others were still mumbling in indescribable, ineffable bacchanalian fruition. Mariano Rosas had one of his confidants ask me if I could give him the rest of the firewater I had set aside for him.

"Why, I would be delighted to," I said, capitalizing on this opportunity to quit the scene of my brave deeds. I left the entrance and set out for the ranch where my officers were lodged. I brought the firewater back to him.

Finally I stretched out, as tired as if I had just hauled a hundredweight on my back to the peak of Vesuvius.

What did I stretch out on?

On a coltskin pelt, my mattress on a poor makeshift bed of knotty, uneven sticks.

Sleep soon carried me to a world of fleeting peace of mind. I was enjoying it when a serenade awoke me. It was a Negro playing an accordion, a kind of Orpheus of the pampas. I had to resign myself to my fate and arise and listen to a *cielito* sung in my honor.

What a hard time this Negro was to give me!

 THE NEGRO SOON took his business elsewhere, for which I thanked the stars above. As festive poets go, as a bard, that is, he was no match for Aniceto el Gallo or Anastasio el Pollo.[1] He wasn't even a good accordion player. On the other hand, I have poorly developed phrenological tonal organs, so that I can say, with Voltaire, *La musique c'est de tous les tapages le*

plus supportable.[2] It is a twist of fate like any other. I am deprived of another innocent pleasure in life by the misfortune of having no sense of harmony. As you know, common standards would hold that a person cannot be good who does not love music and flowers, though that person may love many other things which delight and intoxicate the senses even more. There are people who honestly believe that artistic or aesthetic sensitivity are an essential part of being good-hearted. And yet, you will find such-and-such a fellow who loves music madly but is incapable of a simple act of generosity. You will find another who would spend a hundred thousand pesos on a genuine Rubens but would not make a sacrifice for his dearest friend. Such persons live in a kind of pleasant state of error, not unlike those who put morality beneath sentiment. It takes all kinds, I suppose.

As soon as I was rid of the man who had so cruelly torn me from the arms of Morpheus, I stretched out again on my hard and sinuous bed.

I was soon fast asleep, savoring the gentle narcotic and dreaming I was a conqueror of the desert. Lured by the echoes of civilization, the warlike Ranquels had laid down their arms and gathered into villages. Churches and schools had taken root in these forsaken lands and the word of the Gospel now drowned out all their troubled idolatry. Under the plow, under the fecund sweat of the brow, the earth brought forth her best fruits and bountiful harvests. The thunder of the desert invasions had ceased. Now the miserable barbarians thought only of multiplying and growing, making the most of the propitious seasons, saving and storing for a peaceful old age and having a sizable inheritance to leave their children. I was the respected and venerable patriarch, benefactor to all, and now the evil spirit, seeing me content with my good and useful deeds, with my Christian and humanitarian deeds, summoned me to take evil action and topple the government.

Mortal, the spirit called, seize these fleeting days! Don't be a fool! Forget your country, think about yourself! The glory of the good is an ephemeral thing, mere smoke and nothing else. It passes and nothing remains. Do you not have a wife and children? Well, fine. Do these human flocks not follow and obey you? Do they not love and respect you? Fine, then. Do you not have power? Are you not of flesh and blood and do you not love pleasure? Fine, then. Leave the path you are on. Come to your senses! Look around you, you fool! Listen to the voice of experience. Proclaim yourself emperor and have yourself crowned. Imitate Aurelian. You have a Roman name. Lucius Victorius, Imperator, will please the ear of the multitudes.

I heard the tempting admonishments with a certain mixture of pleasure and distrust. I was already thinking about the throne I would be seated on, the diadem I would wear, and the scepter I would hold when I ascended the Capitol steps. Would they be of solid gold or coltskin and *caldén* wood. Then a voice which I recognized in my sleep called at the door.

"Colonel Mansilla!"

At first I didn't answer. I recognized the voice, had only recently heard it. But I was not entirely awake.

"Colonel Mansilla! Colonel Mansilla!"

There was pitch-black darkness in the dilapidated ranch where I was lodged. My officers were snoring in untroubled sleep. A muffled, tumultuous noise made its confused way to our nocturnal abode. I sat up in bed and turned one ear to the door—a cowhide hung there through which I could see a crack—and listened again.

"Colonel Mansilla!" came the voice.

In the starlight I could make out a black, nappy-haired head and, spread between two red bands like shiny black beads resting on a lovely, protuberant bosom, two rows of ivory teeth.

It was the Negro with the accordion.

Just what I needed: a serenade.

To me it was like Mephistopheles calling.

"*Vade retro, Satanás!*" I cried.

He did not understand. Obviously not. Pure Latin at this time of night and alongside Chief Mariano Rosas's tent.

"Colonel Mansilla," he answered.

"Go to the devil," I retorted.

"General Mariano sent me."

"What does he want?"

"He says, 'How has your grace'—(verbatim) [3]—'been faring on your journey? Have you not lost any horses? How has your night gone? Did you sleep well?'"

This had to be a joke. I was perplexed for a moment. Then I answered.

"Tell him my journey has gone well. As for horses, Wenchenao stole two of them and is a scoundrel. If he wants to know how I've spent the night and how I've slept, he should let me rest and wait till the morning."

This said, I stretched out in a crooked line, so that my haunches and my shoulders fit the holes in my rough, uneven bed.

The face disappeared.

It was cold. The first days of April were chilly. I had few covers. It was not an auspicious arrangement for falling asleep. Groping around in the dark I found the tip of something that was either a poncho or a coarse cloth. I gave it a tug. It was like landing a whale dug fast into the muddy bottom. I finally got it, leaving one of my fellow travelers stripped of his saddle blanket. I pulled it over myself, wrapped it around me, curled up, covered myself up to my nose, and began to breathe heavily. I used my lips as a sort of valve so that my breath would come out condensed and the temperature surrounding my beleaguered humanity would rise. I was nearly asleep. There are ideas that seem to crystallize, ideas that will not simply evaporate. I could see my vision of glory. It was as though it were enveloped in a reddish mist.

The evil spirit hovered over it. I was emperor of the Ranquels, making my triumphant entry into Salinas Grandes. Calfucurá's tribes acclaimed me. Heralded over a hundred leagues of renown, my name filled the desert. They had built a great arc of triumph to me, a colossus like that of Rhodes, but with one foot in the mighty Andes and the other on the shores of the River Plate. In one hand it held a deformed goose quill, whose feathering shone like golden glass beads and whose tip sparked with letters of fire which only a lightning-quick eye could read. And the letters said, *Mane, thecel, phares*.[4] The other hand brandished a sword of incommensurable length, whose burnished steel blade flashed like a meteor and upon which there streaked diamantine letters which only an eye as quick as thought itself could decipher. And the letters said, *In hoc signo vinces*.

It was a monument of Egyptian size and structure and could well awaken bloodthirsty envy, Corsican vengeance, or a pharaoh's eternal hatred. Beneath it, quick as a thunderbolt and drawn by twenty yoked wild mares, a Tucumanian cart filed past.[5] It was bedecked with horse manes of many colors and from its bed arose a canopy of sheepskin pelts. Seated beneath the canopy was a youth of red-painted face. It was me! *Pape satán! Pape satán alepe!* I cried as I drove the horses with my endless whip. I was robed in a jaguar skin. The animal's arms formed the sleeves, legs, stockings, the rest of it formed the body and, finally, the head with its sharp fangs adorned and covered my brow in the manner of an ancient helmet. I don't know what had become of the tail. A strange being invisible to all but me was trying to stick a piece of straw into me. I looked at him as if to say: enough of costumes. He balked, then followed, not knowing what to do.

An escort in zigzag formation preceded me, also covering my rear guard. There were natives of all the southern tribes: Ranquels, Puelches, Pehuenches, Patagons, and Araucans.[6] Some rode dashing colts, others tame horses, these went on guanacos, those on ostriches, many on foot, some rode astride poles, an endless number on winged condors. For weapons they had lances and bolas; their clothing was mixed: some went gaucho, some in French style, some English, most were as naked as Adam. They sang a martial hymn to the sound of thick-reeded wooden flutes, and the words *Lucius Victorius, Imperator* arose with a crashing resonance amidst the repeated ba-ba-ba-ba-ba-ba-ba!

A new Balthasar was I, as I marched in conquest of a powerful city, quite against the counsel of my advisers, who said, "You will never breach that city victoriously. Its streets are paved with enormous monoliths and covered with bogs through which your cart cannot possibly pass." Stubborn, and I am so in my dreams, I did not want to heed the authoritative voice of my expert tutors. I had had myself crowned and acclaimed by these simple people, had overcome some obstacles in my life: why not endeavor to fight and vanquish a decrepit civilization? On the other hand, I was born in that eminent city and she would be proud to see me arrive at her gates, not like Hannibal at Rome but like another brave Camilo.

Thus I dreamt, half awake, half asleep, when a knock on the door again forced me to sit up in bed.

"Colonel Mansilla!"

"What is it?" I asked.

"The general says how did you sleep tonight?" the accursed Negro answered.

"Listen, man, you tell him I will let him know tomorrow."

I didn't catch what the messenger said next. A sudden, muffled roar drowned out his voice.

Once more I sought the posture that would best adapt to the bed which circumstances had afforded me. I was hoping not to be interrupted yet again. A chimerical hope! My veritable black beast had left and returned.

"Colonel Mansilla! Colonel Mansilla!" he called aloud.

"What do you want?" I answered, disgruntled and not moving.

"The general's son is with me."

This was more serious. I sat up.

"What can I do for you brother?" I asked.

"My father says to come," he said.

"Now?"

"Yes."

I called Carmen, my faithful valet; I asked for water to wash with, light, a comb, a toothbrush, anything that would serve as an excuse for stalling for time. Perhaps day would break. I could hear the noise from the nocturnal orgy and it didn't sit well with me to think of taking part in it in the dark. As is my custom when out in the country, I slept fully dressed and stripped down in the daytime for hygienic reasons and what not.

I was on my feet in a snap.

Carmen brought light, a candle of horse grease, water, a comb, everything I asked for, making one trip per item as he had to rummage around in the saddle bags to find things.

I performed my fastidious toilette as slowly as I could. Meanwhile, a number of curious onlookers, each a little drunker than the next, came to my door to watch me. Because it was taking me so long to leave the ranch, a new delegation was sent over, comprised of two of Mariano's sons. The older one spoke first: "My father says how are you, how is it going, how did you sleep, when are you coming, he is half stewed and wants to polish it off with you."

I answered most diplomatically, thanking them for their kindly concern and assuring them I would not keep the general waiting much longer.

I took longer to brush my teeth than I would have to polish a pair of grenadier's boots.

The Negro made an expert narration of this procedure. The rascal had been a slave on I don't know whose farm south of Buenos Aires, a soldier under General Rivas, a deserter, and was very familiar with the ways and customs of the civilized Christians. He said that what I was doing there was to keep my teeth from ever falling out. He railed at the Indians. "You are very barbaric," he told them and played his infernal accordion and sang and danced to its rhythms. He hurried me along now and then as well. "Let's go, master, let's go," he said.

I finally had to obey, and I say obey because that is precisely what I did. I no more wanted to drink firewater than I wanted to have my ear cut off. I left the ranch, leaving my comrades sleeping like babies. Father Moisés was snoring the loudest of all. Father Marcos had found lodging in Ayala's ranch.

The night was cold, the day still far off. The stars shone with that diaphanous winter light. The land was all frosted over as if sprinkled with tiny pebbles. A great, dying fire burned in the chief's entrance. Around it in heaps lay a number of Indians, passed out. Many saddled horses stood immobile where they had been left the day before, their reins hanging limp. Mariano Rosas, a vial in one hand and a drinking horn in the other, stood teetering with others among the gentle animals. They were babbling up a storm. Between one *yapaí* and the next, the name Colonel Mansilla was often heard.

Escorted by the Negro, Mariano's sons, and the curious onlookers, I went over to where they stood. When they saw me they did what all drunks do who have not completely lost their heads. They tried to hide their condition. Mariano Rosas made a speech to me in his language. I did not understand it but he was roundly applauded. I did comprehend, however, that he had spoken of me in the most affectionate terms, because as his peroration proceeded, many voices called out: "Him good Christian, him Christian bull!"

He ended by offering me a *yapaí*.

He drank first in accordance with custom.

He was drinking it down when a voice sounding quite nice to me spoke into my ear.

"I'm right here, Colonel, don't worry; and your comadre Carmen is here, too. She's over there in the entranceway pretending to be asleep so that she can hear everything."

It was Miguelito. I squeezed his hand and took the horn full of liquor as Mariano passed it over to me.

THE COMMANDER-IN-CHIEF of the Ranquel tribes is some forty-five years old. He belongs to a class of medium-built men, thin but possessed of limbs of steel. Nobody whirls the bolas, ropes, or takes a colt by the halter like Mariano Rosas. His long, black hair is now speckled with white. It falls over his shoulders and graces his wrinkle-furrowed brow. His great, sunken, sparkling blue eyes look straight out between long, thick eyelashes. Their habitual expression is melancholy, but they gradually enliven to reveal pride, energy, and fierceness. His small and finely accentuated nose is depressed at the tip and he has flaring nostrils, a sign of distrust. He is thin-lipped and almost never shows his teeth, a sign of astuteness and cruelty. He has a pointed chin and jutting cheekbones, as if the skin were stretched tight around them, which shows valor, and arched, full eyebrows between which there are always perpendicular lines, an unmistakable sign of irascibility. These are the characteristics of his naturally tawny physiognomy, which has been browned further yet by the inclemency of the sun and by the cold, dry, penetrating pampean desert air.

Mariano Rosas is the son of the famous Chief Painé. Settled strategically in Leubucó between the tribes of Chiefs Ramón and Baigorrita, he is the head of a confederation. He sometimes backs Ramón over Baigorrita, sometimes Baigorrita over Ramón, and he dominates both of them unfailingly. Divide and conquer is his motto. Thus Baigorrita and Ramón, though fierce fighters, diversely skilled horsemen, masters of every kind of rural task—and no less so than this Ranquelian Bismarck—ponder the prudence of his counsel, his mindful foresight, his persistent and conciliatory character.

In 1834 he was taken prisoner at Langhelo Lagoon, where Fort "Gainza," whose foundations I myself laid eight months ago when advancing the southern border of Santa Fe, now stands.[1] Mariano, some of the other Indians, and a few of the riffraff had stayed behind to take care of the replacement horses while his bellicose father conducted a raid well into Christian territory. The Christians in charge of security on the northern border of Buenos Aires, maneuvering wisely, went straight south when they heard the raid coming. There they planned to head the thieves off. They occupied and took possession of one of the main watering holes where the raiding party would have to pass with the booty, surprised the horse camp, took all the animals, and captured the Indians and riffraff alike. Mariano and his companions-in-misfortune were taken to Santos Lugares.[2] There they remained, shackled, imprisoned, and harshly treated. He was there for nearly a year, as he now recalls. They had given up hope for a better turn of events for themselves. However, as it is God's will that man ascend to the mountaintop when he least expects it, and fall to the abyss when everything around him smiles, one day they were taken before the dictator Juan Manuel de Rozas.[3] Through minute interrogation Rozas learned that Mariano, whose name at the time was the same as his father, was the son of a principal chief of great renown. He had him baptized with himself as godfather, gave him Mariano for a first name, his own Rozas for a surname, and sent him and the others to be peons on his *estancia*, El Pino.

They spent some years there, working hard and sleeping beneath the stars behind a *nandubay* corral. They were given useful and worthwhile training in country work: how properly to tame a colt and how to manage an *estancia* as it should be managed. Though they sometimes received a strapping when they had done nothing to deserve it, they generally were treated kindly. They were also paid rations and wages like any other worker. At length their love of family, the memory of the tent settlements, their longing for complete freedom, awoke in them the idea of taking flight no matter how great the risk. They waited for a moonlit night and, knowing they were trusted, took a string of choice horses, slipped away, and headed west. Not knowing their way around the countryside, they got lost. They remembered the name of a town, Bragado, that they had raided as boys but were afraid to approach the cattle farms to ask directions to it lest they be discovered and apprehended.

Their absence noted at El Pino, they were pursued, as they later heard from a captive woman, but were not caught. They met a detachment of police at the Márquez Bridge. They lied, saying they had come to trade and were returning to the tent camps.[4] When they reached Federación, which is now Junín, they had been wandering in the country for six days with no set direction, resting and hiding out in the swale grass and briar patches. They used the same scheme again to get through and it worked. There was peace at the time with some of the tribes living near the Toay River, which combined with our fugitives' story to produce the perfect effect.

That is the way Mariano Rosas told it to me, Santiago, and that's the way I am telling it to you. Mariano has the fondest memories of his godfather. He venerates him, speaking of him with the greatest respect. All that he is and all that he knows he has him to thank for, he says. He claims he has had no better father besides God. If he can groom and saddle a good running horse; if he can take care of all kinds of livestock—cattle, horses, and sheep—and raise a herd and keep good meat on their bones in any season; if he can rope, tie, and swing the bolas like a gaucho, he owes it all to his godfather. He says, too, that in addition to all these benefits he has him to thank that he is a Christian, for this has brought him good fortune in his undertakings.

I have already told you that these barbarians respect the Christians, recognizing their moral superiority. At the same time, they like to live like Indians, the dolce far niente, have the greatest possible number of women, as many as they can maintain, in short, be evangelists in so far as this assumes a certain mysterious virtue for being happy both in peace and at war.

True, civilization does the same thing, though it rather pretends not to. This is no doubt why someone has said that our attempt at civilization is oftentimes really no more than a state of refined barbarism.

Of course, I am blood nephew to Juan Manuel de Rosas, and you would think in hearing the Indian speak of his godfather and quasi progenitor that I might entertain illusions of giving him his catechism, as if nothing could be so easy. Well, man in his primitive state will make short work of the wisest fellow and all his wise books. Human vanity and foolhardiness, have they ever failed to earn their just desserts? In due time we shall see how diplomacy is the same everywhere, whether in London or Vienna, Buenos Aires or Leubucó. Let the whip and the saddle be cut from one and the same hide, I say. To be still more philosophical about it, you will find gratitude seated on its high horse whenever the self-serving run the parade.

Shortly after Mariano Rosas returned to his land, his godfather, seeing that the bird had flown and that the man who raises a brace of crows may someday find his eyes plucked out, sent a gift. He was not a man to leave loose ends. The gift consisted of two hundred mares, fifty cows, ten bulls of the same breed, two strings of speckled bays with their dark dams, complete saddle and gear with silver trim and tokens, pound upon pound of sugar and herbs, tobacco, paper, fine clothes, a colonel's uniform, and many red banners.[5]

Along with these splendid presents went a warm missive, which Mariano still possesses. It reads more or less as follows.

My dear Godson: You must not think I am angry at your departure, though you should have warned me so that I might have avoided the displeasure of not knowing what had become of you. Nothing could be more natural than

that you should wish to see your parents, much as you never
expressed such a desire to me. I would have helped you out
on your trip by seeing to it that you were accompanied. Tell
Painé that I feel deep affection for him and wish him well.
The same goes for his captains and Indians. Please accept
this small gift. It is all that I can send at this time. Turn to
me whenever you are needy. Don't forget my advice. It is the
advice of an affectionate godfather. May God give you good
health and a long life. Most cordially yours, Juan de Rozas.

This mellifluous and calculating letter carried an apparently insignificant postscript: P.S. Sometime when you are not busy, come
visit me with some of your friends.

A difficult, and more than difficult, an arduous thing it is to unravel the intentions of the most innocent mortal.

Let each reader comment on the letter and the postscript as he
or she likes. When it comes to my neighbor's thoughts, I always
keep in mind a saying by a certain moralist of note, who once confounded a statesman as follows: That law of God which forbids
rash judgment is not only a law of charity, but one of justice and
sound logic as well.

Mariano Rosas received the letter and the present, deliberated
on what to do, and as the best roll of the dice is not to roll them at
all (or, as Sancho Panza would say, If I get out of this one alive, no
more weddings in heaven), he resolved to thank his godfather for
the kind gift and not visit him. For this reason, and lest anyone ever
question his sentiments, he swore after consulting the old divines
never to leave his homeland again. He is bound by this solemn vow
to his home, to the land where he was born, to the woods where he
spent his childhood. Nor has Mariano Rosas, since his captivity,
ever set foot on Christian land. He fears that if he ever personally
comes on a raid he will fall prisoner.

I know this episode of his life because he himself told it to me.

When I conveyed to him General Arredondo's express and fer-
vid wish to meet him and that once peace was attained it would be
fitting that he pay him a visit in Villa Mercedes, Mariano Rosas
declined.

"That won't do, brother," he said.

"And why not?" I asked.

He then related in minute detail what I have just told. Note
therefore that the whole science of the Indians in their dealings

with Christians comes down to an aphorism that we practice every day: Better safe than sorry.

I have mentioned that Mariano Rosas was the son of Painé.

Painé died tragically.

In 1856, General Emilio Mitre, in order to save his division, had to leave most of his war matériel stashed in the desert. He rode as far as Chamalcó and countermarched from there. The Indians followed his tracks. Painé, commander-in-chief of the Ranquel tribes at the time, was leading them. They found a cache of munitions in the hills. There were grenades among them. One of them blew up. The cache flew and with it Painé. That is how the renowned chief died. His eldest son, Mariano Rosas, then inherited the government and the power. It is generally believed that among the Indians might prevails over right, enabling anyone to become a chief or captain. This is not so. They have their customs and their customs are their laws. Their hierarchies are hereditary. There is even abdication on the part of the father in favor of the eldest son if the latter is apt for command. This explains why Chief Ramón currently governs the Indians at Carrilobo even though his father is alive.

Among the Indians, like everywhere else, there are revolutions which depose those invested with supreme power. The rule, however, is as I have explained. It is subject to variance only when the chief or captain has neither sons nor brothers who can inherit his position. In that case they hold a plebiscite and the majority peacefully decides things, no more and no less than among any people for whom universal suffrage commands respect. Why, we have made more revolutions, bowing to one ochlocracy today and another tomorrow, swearing governors in and throwing governors out, than the Indians ever have out of the ambition to govern. It is a matter that lends itself to innumerable considerations that those who love rational freedom pursue and exterminate one another with implacable vehemence, trampling on institutions which they themselves have formulated, acknowledging and swearing themselves to be saviors, and all for the pleasures of power, while those who merely love their natural freedom never raise their lances in fratricidal wars.

Wait, though. I think I see why.

The barbarians do not pursue the best of republics. It seems they believe something of which we refuse to be convinced, namely, that principles are everything, men nothing; that there are no necessary men; that "if Caesar had thought like Cato, others would have thought like Caesar, and that the republic which was destined to perish would have been dragged over the precipice by other hands."

Mariano dresses like a gaucho, stylishly but not ostentatiously. When he came out to meet me he was wearing a golden brown Crimean shirt with a black braid, a silk neckerchief, breeches made from an English poncho, fringed leather stockings, calfskin boots, a wide belt with four silver buttons, and a light beaverskin hat with a wide red hatband.

Now that you know Mariano Rosas's origins, his face, what he wears, and other notes of particular interest, let us resume the story begun at the end of my previous letter.

Mariano had proposed a *yapaí*. I now had a horn full of fire-water in my hand.

"*Yapaí*, brother," I said and drank it down in one gulp so that I wouldn't taste it. It might as well have been castor oil. It felt like someone had dropped a hot coal in my stomach. The eruption came quickly. My mouth was a sewer head, spewing torrents of everything I had eaten. An intestinal revolution roared inside of me. I could hear the commotion only because I had ears. I could see nothing. I no longer felt like I was on the ground, but suspended in midair turning like a wheel on an axis though it did seem that my head was always tipped down, gravitating more than the rest of my body. I was being devoured by a horrible anxiety, nauseous retching, a bitter heaving of vinegar-like emissions, and an imponderable queasiness and disgust.

The dizziness passed.

The *yapaí* went on, the better to "lock it in," as a certain spiritual friend of mine and follower of Bacchus used to say upon entering the Club del Progreso, where, though already tipsy, he would ask the waiter for a cognac.

There are situations that resemble a fire on the high seas; all of the odds are against it happening. I now found myself in such a situation. To finish the party in style, Mariano Rosas wanted to *loncotear* with me. It was three o'clock in the morning. To get physical now after what he had just seen! I fought him off as best I could. The Indian was in no mood for joking. Seeing that I would have none of this *loncotear* nonsense, he hit on the idea of taking hold of both of my shoulders and shaking them with all his athletic strength, or just pushing me backwards. "Brother! Brother!" he said stridently, his tensed body vibrating like a rod. I contained him and pushed him back with a certain moderation. An abrupt movement on my part could cause him to trip. Were he to fall on his face, who knows but that his fellow carousers might not do to me what the mule drivers did to don Quixote. All things considered, I was in a tight spot. One of the times that I struggled to hold him up he tripped and very nearly fell flat on his face. He held fast to me with his powerful arms. I feared something was about to happen. I looked for his knife, found it, and gripped it vigorously so that he couldn't make use of it, and there we remained a while, he fighting to take me outside and I struggling not to leave the entrance. We broke, then we again locked arms. Again we separated and each time he came at me he stuck his hands in my face. I was tempted to call my officers and assistants; for, frankly, I feared a mishap. But somehow it bothered me to do that. If there were no dogs around to scare me, there were no hoopskirts to encourage me, either. The one instinct which that gathering awakened in me was that of self-preservation.

There was nothing left of the firewater but the smell.

The crowd wanted to finish itself off.

"Give me more firewater, Colonel," they were saying.

"A little more, brother," said Mariano.

Miguelito spoke to them in their language and, pulling me by the arm, said, "Let's go, Colonel."

I understood that he wanted to get me out of there. I followed him. The Indians dropped on to the floor, all piled atop one another. Miguelito took me in the direction of my ranch. Morning was about to break. The sky was covered over with clouds. The starlight barely shone through. We were in darkness. I walked not of my own volition but dragged by my guardian. I staggered along, losing my balance now and again. We reached the door of my ranch. Miguelito raised the hide.

"Go on in and get some rest, Colonel," he said. "I'll go keep them occupied."

I went in. A shadow entered behind me. By the dying light of the candle Carmen had brought in before, I thought I saw a woman. These women appear to us anywhere. They love us with no thought for themselves. And then we are so cruel to them afterwards! They give us life, pleasure, happiness. And all for what? So that sooner or later, filled with loathing, we will shout, "Will these foolish women never change!"

 THE CANDLE FLICKERED like a jack-o'-lantern. Searching for my bed where there wasn't one—the last vapors of my nausea made everything seem upside down and backwards to me— I tripped over the light, putting it out. In my mind's eye I could see chaos. I was groping for something to lean on so I wouldn't fall. My arms flailed like a windmill. I fell. I got up. I fell again, this time on top of my traveling mates.

Neither the friars nor the officers noticed the mass that several times came crashing down on them.

My hoarse voice, drowning in my throat, called for assistance. No one could hear me.

Groping like a palsied blind man I felt something smooth, soft, and silken. At the same time I detected the sound of hens as if in a dream. I had grabbed the tail feathers of a rooster or chicken and awakened Mariano Rosas's whole hen house. No doubt they had sought shelter from the chilly night and repaired to our dwelling, ultimately taking possession of my bed. I was so surprised that I let go of the bird and of whatever was holding me up. I fell down on my face and my mouth felt something soft and foul-smelling and cold. I thought I was asphyxiating and couldn't change position.

My legs felt dislocated, like a doll's. I made a supreme effort and stood up straight. I described two semicircles with my arms until I found a small, hot, polished hand which held me up, dragging me along inch by inch. An arm was wrapped around my body. I rested my unsteady head on a palpitating bosom and took several steps, like a wounded man. The hide went up in front of the ranch door and the dawn light flooded in, piercing my half-opened eyes. I could make out a number of voices.

"Where him Colonel Mansilla?"

"Him give more firewater."

"He's not here," answered a voice.

The hide suddenly dropped, leaving the ranch once again in complete darkness. I heard a sound of people grumbling in disappointment and a sound of fading footsteps. I felt something like a coarse, woolen cloth, brush across my face while somebody pushed me forward. I was not master of myself. I obeyed. I opened and closed my eyes. I saw the dawn's light enter the ranch again. Then I felt the cold. I was walking beside another person who was holding me up rather tenderly.

I fell asleep.

Some time later I awoke beside a big fire. Three women and three men were gathered around it, all of them Christians. They had made me a bed of coarse cloth and hides. Next to me was an Indian woman.

"What do you want to drink," she said, "mate or coffee?"

I recognized my comadre Carmen.

"Coffee, comadre," I answered, gazing at her with gratitude.

While preparing it she told me that when I got away from Mariano Rosas, she was in the entranceway, alert to anything that might happen. She slipped through the shadows of night, helping Miguelito get me to my ranch. As she was leaving, several Indians came by asking for me. She faked a Christian voice and answered that I wasn't there. Then, so that they wouldn't trouble me and would let me sleep, she had taken me to a neighboring tent where only Christians stayed.

I sipped at the coffee. Gradually, the narcotic effects of all the firewater began to wear off. The rose-colored dawn came through the cracks in the tent with its rays of fire. The roosters were crowing, the hens cackling, the horses whinnying, the bulls bellowing, the sheep bleating, all was astir as nature awakened. The notes of a poorly played accordion vibrated, and a voice that frazzled my nerves intoned these verses:

> *Señor Colonel Mansilla*
> *Let me sing for you.*

I was going to thunder at the Negro—it was him, the music man body and soul—when he entered the tent and, folding his instrument and pursing his lips, he interrupted his verses to speak to me.

"Good morning, master, has your grace had a pleasant night?"

It seemed wiser to take a polite approach.

"Yes, very pleasant, thank you," I said. "You can sit down, but only on the condition that you don't play your damned accordion or sing. I'm fed up with it."

He sat down.

They passed him the mate, and between sips he gave us the story of his life in a nutshell.

"Master," he said, "I am a federal. I was a casualty at the time our father Rosas fell. He gave us Negroes our freedom. They put me back in the army. I was with General Rivas but then I deserted and came out here. I don't intend to leave until the Restorer comes, and he will come soon because Juan Sáa wrote to us that he was going to find him. I fought in Ravelo's Negro company." Here he interrupted the story of his life to grace us or, in truth, punish us, with a song.

Que viva la patria
libre de cadenas
y viva el gran Rosas
para defenderla.[1]

I cut this wheezing short.

"Listen, man, I told you I don't want to hear you sing."

He stopped and, regarding me with a certain distrust, asked me, "Are you Rosas's nephew?"

"Yes."

"Federal?"

"No."

"Unitarian?"

"No."

"Then what are you?"

"What's it to you!"

The Negro frowned. Then, in a disrespectful voice and manner, he spoke.

"Don't treat me bad just because I'm a poor Negro," he said.

"Don't be insolent," I answered.

"We're all equal here," he retorted, adding something frankly indecent.

I grabbed a big piece of firewood and, raising my arm, said, "You'll find out." I was about to whack him with it when my co-madre Carmen held me back.

"Don't pay that drunk Negro any mind, compadre," she said.

She then addressed him in Araucan and the Negro, who had stood up, sat back down.

"I beg your grace's pardon," he said.

"Pardon granted," I said, "but take care you don't treat me again like you just did." He tried to unfold his accordion, but I would have none of it. To me it was like hearing a steel file scraping across teeth. Forced to give up his philharmonic passion, he chose to speak instead, offering his political opinions and describing the pleasures of life among the Indians.

"There's something for everyone here, Colonel," he said. "A man who behaves well is treated well, and General Mariano punishes the troublemakers by putting them to work in the public works."

I let out a good, hearty laugh.

"Public works?"

"Yes, master."

"And what public works would that be?"

"Ahhh! The general's corrals."

Just then Father Marcos entered, rubbing his eyes. The light from our pleasant camp fire had drawn him. He wanted water for a pot of tea. The good Franciscan took his seat around the camp fire and the talk continued. The Negro spiced things up with a few witticisms and asked me every so often to let him play his accordion.

"No and no," I repeated. "I would rather hear one of those cattle horns than your accordion."

His favorite air was the very popular "Arrincónemela." It reminded me of Buenos Aires and made me sad.

He begged me.

Obviously he needed his accordion like Paganini his violin and Gottschild his piano, but I absolutely refused. Not only that, but I threatened to alienate him from Mariano Rosas's good graces, if he did not wise up, by sending the chief a small cranking organ when I got back to Río Cuarto.

"Then," I said, "you would no longer be needed around here."

The sun rose. I needed to refresh my body. Remember, dear Santiago, that I have neither slept nor washed since we were in Calcumuleu. I asked if there was anywhere nearby to bathe.

They said there was—a big tufa-bottomed watering hole about two thousand yards away. Mariano's women and he himself bathed there early in the morning. I asked a Christian to point out the way to me. I then called an assistant, had a horse brought, abandoned the camp fire, jumped on bareback, and in one gallop was at the water. It was ice cold. The ablutions cleared my senses and retempered my body, erasing all signs of the bad night I had spent. I felt like a new man.

I made my assistant bathe himself. Unaccustomed to these daybreak plunges, he shivered with cold and his teeth chattered. Meanwhile I walked along the sand in long strides, provoking the reaction. It came. I got back on my horse and took the road to the tents. On the way back I saw a crowd of people and a big cloud of dust near the foot of the hill. They were running inside of a corral. I changed direction and went to see what they were doing. They had roped a fat cow and were getting ready to skin and dress it out. Mariano Rosas was there, fresh as a daisy. He had bathed before I did. No one who was not in on the secret would have suspected what kind of night we had spent. The ravages left on his body showed, nonetheless, in his sunken lower eyelids, which had a purplish tint. As I approached the corral he was twirling the lasso to rope the front legs. He wound it back in and, approaching me with the greatest warmth and courtesy, asked me if I had spent a good and comfortable night. I was as gallant and forthcoming as he.

"That fat cow is for you, brother," he said.

And quickly, he twirled the rope and gave it a masterful throw. Dismounting with great agility, he turned to me and said, "I have your uncle to thank for this, brother."

Lassoed and caught at the feet, the cow hit the dirt. I thought they would kill it the way the Christians do, that is, by stabbing it repeatedly in the chest and then slicing its throat amidst rending, earthshaking screams. They did it another way. An Indian whipped a bola at its forehead, knocking it senseless. They immediately cut its throat.[2]

"Why the bola to the head, brother?" I asked Mariano.

"So it won't bellow, brother," he answered. "Can't you see it's a shame to kill it that way?"

Let civilization comment as it will and answer its own question: Are barbarians who have a sense of kindness toward animals amenable or not to a generous redemption?

After they cut the cow's throat, they left it to the women, who skinned, quartered, and butchered it, gathering up even the blood. Mariano and I returned to his tent together, conversing like a couple of old comrades. Neither one of us made any mention whatsoever of the previous night's scenes.

Mariano was riding a dark horse, a favorite of his. It was saddled simply. It was a vigorous animal and bore General don Angel Pacheco's brand. We arrived at his tent, dismounted, sat down, and little by little the visitors started to arrive. There was much ado in the house, and I was the object of great attention. They brewed some mate for me and served me up a fat, succulent steak with the blood dripping off of it, English-style.

I ate the whole thing, burning my fingers first and licking them later as is the custom out here. What are they supposed to do without napkins or tablecloths?

Mariano asked me if he could leave me alone for a moment. He left, unsaddled his dark horse, turned it loose, saddled his Moor, tied it to the post, and gave a spate of orders. He came back into the tent rubbing a hobbling strap. "Brother," he said, "I like to take care of my things myself. They turn out better that way. Nobody handles my saddle and gear, or my horses, but me. My godfather was the same way when I met him. Thank God I am a healthy man."

After this we exchanged a few words of no interest. Finally he offered to introduce me to his family.

Tomorrow I will take you to the reception.

 THE DOOR TO Mariano Rosas's tent opened into the entranceway.

Several Indian women and Christian captives were sweeping with bishop's weed brooms, wetting down the floor with water poured from pitchers which they drew from a large wooden bowl they carried on one arm. On both the left and right they placed seats of very thick black sheepskin, set everything in order, bundled up all the horse gear, made the beds, hung the lassos, bolas, bridles, hobbles, and bits on forked *chañar* branches.

A pack of little Indians dragged the piles of trash and filth out of the tent on leather mats tied with leather tethers. The Indian women and captives lined these piles up symmetrically, which suggested that this was a frequent operation.

Several Indian women of different ages were combing their hair with straw hand brooms. They arranged their long and lustrous hair in two braids, three thick strands in each, tied off at the end with Pampa tribal ribbons. To better smooth and set them, they wet them with saliva. They also touched up each others' lips and cheekbones with carmine powder, shaded their eyelids, and painted their little black beauty marks with their special paste. They put on their earrings, bracelets, and necklaces, girded themselves well with broad, bright-colored sashes and, finally, used little, round two-sided leaden mirrors—the kind anyone can see in our city shops.

I was casting furtive glances into the tent and could see all this going on.

The Negro with the accordion came in, instrument in hand. Apparently the two were inseparable; there was no Negro without the accordion, no accordion without the Negro. He played a short air and sang some verses he had made up himself. He was also a poet as I have warned, though I did state as well that as a balladeer he was not on a par with Tyrtaeus.[1]

> *Señor don Mariano Rosas*
> *Your family awaits your return.*

So sang the master of ceremonies in Leubucó, our wandering Jew of political life, a man determined to live out his days awaiting the coming of the Messiah, the return of the Restorer.

Mariano smiled warmly and benevolently upon him, as men swollen with power will look upon their adulators and palace favorites. The Negro, who knew his place, did some pirouettes and danced. He looked like a satyr. His nappy hair stood up like horns, the bugging eyes were red from alcohol, his nose was flared and flat and full of secretions, his lips were fat and as pink as raw sausage. Things were going his way at the moment and he kept playing his accordion, looking devilishly over at me as if to say, Now I've got you. Good breeding forbade my showing displeasure at the choreography or at the musical display of this spoiled favorite of the master of the house. Indeed, Mariano Rosas looked over at me with a smile every now and then, so I smiled as well.

Everyone present applauded the Negro's buffoonery. He was radiant, he was jubilant. He sat down beside the chief, slapped his back, and embraced him. "Ah, fine bull," he exclaimed, full of admiration. "This is my father. I would give my life for him. Isn't that so, master?"

Mariano nodded in approbation and said to me under his breath, "He is very faithful."

Wretched human condition!

Man is the same everywhere. He looks to those who flatter his foolish pride, his self-love, his vanity. He flees and keeps a good distance from those who possess enough self-esteem not to debase themselves by lying. With good reason Dante has placed the adulators in Malebolge, the accursed pit, sunken to their nostrils in pestiferous latrines.

New visitors arrived. All were received with studied courtesy and in strict observance of protocol, which, as we know, consisted of a monotonous series of questions and answers.

There were seats for everybody, and as the greetings concluded, the introductions began. I had to stand, extend my hand, embrace, and answer in kind such questions and salutations as, How glad I am to meet you! How was your journey here? Have you lost any horses along the way? We are so happy to see you here! The Negro played, sang, danced and targeted whomsoever he pleased for his inane humor. Chief or captain, Indian or Christian—it made no difference to him. He had influence at court and could use and abuse his celebrated wit at will.

I called the Franciscans so that the recent arrivals could meet them. They came, and with sweet and gentle manner greeted one and all. A priest is something of an object of reverence to the Indians and the friars were accorded much respect.

Their presence notwithstanding, the accordion played on.

I was impatient to enter Mariano's tent and meet his family. As he made his rounds about the tent, hopping among the different seats, the Negro came to a stop beside me.

"Look," I said in his ear, "if you keep playing I am going to send Mariano a crank organ like I said as soon as I get back to Río Cuarto."

He gave me a look that said, "Mercy, no." Then he silenced the instrument and, turning to Mariano, said, "Everything is ready."

Mariano then motioned to me to enter his tent. He stood up, pointing the way. I followed, leaving the Franciscans in the entranceway with the visitors. We entered. His five wives, his three daughters and his sons, whose names were Epumer, Waiquiner, Amunao, Lincoln, Duguinao, and Piutrín were seated in a circle. At a certain distance was a group of captive women. The Indian women nodded their heads in greeting, the men stood up, gave me their hand, and embraced me.[2]

The captives greeted me with their gaze. I was moved.

Who, indeed, is not moved by the sad and tearful look of a woman?

Mariano showed me to my seat and took his own on my immediate right. There was another row of seats across from ours. Several Indians, Mariano's favorites, came in and occupied them. The Indian women arose and got things started. There were three fires in a line in the middle of the floor. On each of them large caldrons of stew were burning and plump roasts were cooking.

A tent is a sleeping quarters made of wood and leather. The top, the uprights, and the sides are made of wood. The ceiling and the walls are made of coltskin stitched with ostrich veins. The peak has a large opening through which smoke passes out and ventilation passes in.

The Indians never build their fires in the open. When they go on a raid they smother them. Fire and smoke betray man in the pampas and are his enemy. They can be seen from a distance. Fire is a lighthouse. Smoke is a watchtower.

Every tent is divided into two sections of niches on the right and left like the berths of a ship. In each niche is a wooden cot with sheepskin pillows and mattresses. Several coltskin bags in which the Indians keep their odds and ends are hung from the bedposts. One person spends the night in each niche. Of Balzac's theories on matrimonial beds, the Indians believe that the one that best serves domestic peace is the one that counsels separate beds.[3] As you can see, dear Santiago, the Indian's tent presents a more comforting sight than the gaucho's ranch. Yet, the gaucho is a civilized man. Or is he? What are the true characteristics of barbarism?

An Indian's tent has dividers in it for avoiding the promiscuity of the sexes: comfortable beds, seats, pots, dishes, place settings, a number of utensils which reveal customs and needs. A gaucho's ranch lacks everything. Husband, wife, children, brothers and sisters, relatives, drop-ins all live together and sleep intertwined. I cannot describe what this scene does to one's sense of decency.

Generally there is no door to a gaucho's hovel. They sit on the ground on hard pieces of wood or on dried cow skulls. They use no forks, spoons, or plates. They rarely make stew because they have no pots. When they do make it, they pass it around and each one drinks the broth. They have no pitchers. They use an ox horn instead and sometimes don't even have that. There is always a kettle because there has to be hot water for mate. The kettle never has a lid. It is work to take it off and put it back on. They get tired of that, pull the lid off, and throw it away. The roast is cooked on an iron grill, or a wooden one, and is eaten with the same knife one uses to kill one's fellow man. The roast burns the fingers.

How sad and disconsoling all this is! It tears my soul apart to have to say it, but our civilization, in order to rise out of its ignorance, must be made to undergo certain comparisons. Only then will it turn back upon itself and understand that this land is hard-pressed for a solution to its social problems. The fate of free institutions, like the future of democracy and liberty, will be uncertain so long as the popular masses remain ignorant and backwards.

God has bound effect inextricably to cause. Just as an elm brings forth no pears, those institutions will bear no fruit in which notions of good and evil, right and wrong are not universally lodged in every bosom. If we follow our present path, we may raise the scaffolding around the temple, but when we set the vault in place the building will come crashing down, burying all of us under its rubble. The builders will disappear and the demoralization of those who stood by watching their work will lead to anarchy. This is why the first duty of men of state is to know their country.

Five minutes after we first stepped into the tent they served the meal. They placed before each one of us a large wooden bowl filled with a corn and squash stew. We had place settings as well—spoon, fork, and knife—and water. The captive women were the servants. Some dressed and were painted like Indian women. Others concealed their nakedness in ragged and dirty dresses. How they stared at me, poor things! What ill-disguised resignation their faces betrayed! The one who seemed to fit in best was Mariano's youngest daughter's nursemaid. She used to be a maid in don Juan Manuel de Rozas's house. She was captured in Multias in Urquiza's time, when they sold on the San Luis and Córdoba borders what they robbed here.

I had eaten nothing but a steak since the day before. The stew was appetizing and well seasoned. I therefore dug into my meal as avidly as I did last night at the Club del Progreso. And, as they had not forgotten the hand cloths there, like they did forget the napkins here, I ate like a gentleman.

When the stew was finished they brought the roast, then the watermelon.

We were having dessert when the Negro reappeared with his inseparable accordion. He made himself at home beside Mariano and the music began. Fortunately, he had become very hoarse and could not sing. I hope you stay hoarse, I was saying to myself, and I looked at him, sort of motioning with my head in a threat to send the organ to Mariano. The satrap feared this and nodded in understanding. I let him continue.

The conversation went on as in a salon, each talking with whomever he pleased.

The Indians do not give cigarettes to Christian visitors. In order to smoke, I had to give my own away to everybody.

The Indian children lit them for us. Whenever they lingered, playing or wandering around, Mariano pushed them away. "Get out of here now, show some respect for your elders," he would say, almost verbatim. I noticed that in this regard the children were well behaved. Boasting about one of his sons, Mariano said, "This one is a real gaucho." Later they explained this to me. The Indian boy already knew how to steal hobbles and bits. Later he would complete his education by robbing sheep, then cows. It is an ascending scale. He introduced another one. This boy was no older than thirteen years old, and I am going by the year I am told he was born. His merit was that he already had a woman. His face was not unattractive, was in fact rather expressive. It showed premature excess, a consumptive in perspective.

We were smoking and chatting cheerfully when Epumer appeared wearing my red cape, the one that had caused all the trouble and headaches. I will admit it did not look so ugly to me. He greeted me courteously and spoke to me kindly. He asked for firewater and Mariano told him in his language that now was not the time for drinking. He sat down and took part in the conversation.

A face I had not seen since we arrived peeked through a crack in the tent and, unnoticed, motioned to me. It was a face whose presence there could very well cause me concern.

I made up an excuse. I spoke to my host, requested permission to leave, and withdrew, asking myself as I left what this could possibly be.

---

36 (*It would be better if the ladies did not read this chapter.*)

It was Camilo Arias's face.

I left the tent. From the entrance I glanced in the direction from which he had signaled. He was making a roundabout path toward my ranch. I hurried in ahead of him.

I motioned for those who were inside to leave, ordering Captain Rivadavia to tail the spies who as a matter of routine must watch my movements and eavesdrop on my conversations. I then instructed another officer to approach Camilo and inconspicuously tell him to come to the ranch.

As instructed, my faithful partner had not come near me since the day we reached Leubucó. Something serious or alarming, something I should not be unaware of, was happening. He was not one to break our agreement without good reason. He was as cool, as wily and as seasoned as they come. Our *paisanos* get that way early. Their errant and haphazard life shapes them so and to the highest degree. It is an amazing thing to see. From the time they are small children they cross the open country alone at all hours of the day and night on some nag or else prodding a team along. They will travel far from their home or settlement to bola-hunt ostriches, guanacos, or *gamas*, or to run down armadillos.

They sleep in the hayfields, brave the stormy weather all but naked with their bridle in one hand. They will arm themselves against any adversity, be it Indian, horse thief, or bandit.

No sooner had Camilo entered the ranch than I asked him what was going on. He looked around, made sure there was nobody else there and, still doubting his own senses, drew close to me and whispered in my ear.

"Blanco the Indian is back."

"So what?" I said, shrugging my shoulders.

"He is in the dispensary and says that Mariano Rosas may be making peace but he is not."

"Who is with him?"

"Some Indians and Christians."

"And what are they saying?"

"Same thing: Mariano Rosas may be making peace but they are not."

"Is that all they are saying?"

"No, that's not all. They're saying wait and see."

"And how did you find all this out?"

"By playing dumb and acting like I didn't get any of it. I went over to where they were and seeing as I know some of their language I managed to understand the whole thing."

"Very good. Leave now, and be careful of the horses tonight."

"Don't worry, sir."

He withdrew and I stood there thinking about what to do next. After a moment's reflection I decided I would tell Mariano Rosas what was going on. I called Captain Rivadavia and ordered him to announce my visit. Mariano Rosas sent word that I could enter whenever I wished. I went back to his tent, he dismissed his visitors, and when we were alone I apprised him of the situation. He tried to hide it, but I could see that, because he did not recognize Blanco the Indian's authority, the chief's conduct galled him.

"Don't be concerned, brother," he said. He then ordered one of his sons to call Camargo to the tent. While we waited, he told me some of the customs of his land.

"Brother," he said, more or less, "here in my tent feel free to come and go as you please, day or night, it doesn't matter. Make yourself at home. We Indians are open and simple people. We do not stand upon ceremony with our friends, we give what we have and ask when we don't have. We do not know how to work because we have not been taught. If we were like the Christians we would be rich, but we are not like them and we are poor. You have seen how we live. I did not wish to accept your offer of building me a brick house, not because I do not know that it is better to live under a good roof than how I live, but because what would the people say who did not have the same comforts as us? They would say I no longer live as my father did, that I have become delicate and weak."

There was no refuting such reasoning. I limited myself to listening attentively and with evident interest. He went on, explaining that among the Indians there is no such thing as prostitution of the unmarried woman. A single woman gives herself to whatever man she wishes. A man who wants to penetrate a tent at night goes to the bed of the woman he desires and speaks to her. Nobody—not her mother, her father, her sisters or brothers—say a word to her. It is not their affair but hers. She is mistress of her own will and of her own body and can do with it as she pleases. If she gives in, there is no dishonor, no criticism, no disapproval. On the contrary, it is a proof that she is worth something, otherwise they would not have sought or *can-canned* her.

In Araucan, penetrating a tent in the late hours of the night is called *can-canning*, and *can-can* is the equivalent of seduction. The French philologists are welcome to inquire as to whether the Indians took these words from the Gauls or the Gauls from the Indians. I only know that it is odd that among both of them *can-canning* and *can-can* relate to ideas associated with Cupid and his temptations.[1]

As we can see, the single woman is as free as a bird for the pleasures of love among the Indians. It will no doubt be thought that license is therefore rampant among them, that the Lovelaces abound and that one need only set his eyes on a woman to proclaim: I came, I saw, I conquered.

Nothing of the sort.

Freedom is a corrective in everything. Like the lance of ancient warriors, it heals the same wounds it opens. This is an old truth in the world. Freedom brings license, but license is its own antidote. As for the freedom of a woman, the same social observation has been made before, by whom I don't recall. French women marry to be free; English women to forsake their freedom. What are the effects of this? In France the number of seduced single women is greater, while in England that of married women is higher. Moreover, it is the jealous who, as a rule, are predestined for matrimony. Why? Because modesty is the great watchdog of love.

Does modesty exist among Indian women? The curious will perhaps ask me tomorrow. To spare myself the trouble of answering, I will say here and now that everywhere in the world, among civilized people as well as the most backwards savage tribes, women know by instinct that modesty increases the mystery of love. If this weren't so, why, one might as well become Indian first thing tomorrow morning, renounce the security of the borders, and let ourselves be conquered by the Ranquels.

Alongside the single woman, the married woman is a slave among the Indians.

The single woman has great freedom of action. She goes out when, where, and with whom she pleases and does as she pleases. The married woman depends upon her husband for everything. She can do nothing without his permission. On simple suspicion, on the mere sight of her speaking with another man, he can kill her.

Such is the unfortunate lot of these women!

And all the more so because, like it or not, they have to marry whomever can buy them.

There are three ways of marrying.

The first is the same as anywhere else: with the parents' consent and for love, with the additional stipulation that the parents must be paid. If in this kind of marriage the woman escapes from the husband after marrying him and takes refuge in her parents' house, the poor fool who married for love loses his wife and all that he gave to acquire her. The second way of marrying is to surround the chosen one's tent with several friends and bodily remove her from it with the help and blessing of the parents. In this case, too, one must pay, though more than in the previous case. If the woman later flees and takes refuge in the parental tent, they must give her back. The third way is like the previous one. The tent is surrounded by the greatest possible number of friends and, whether she or the parents like it or not, the woman is forcibly taken out. However, in this case there is far greater payment due than in the other two. If the woman runs and takes refuge in the parental tent, they may or may not return her. If, as is their right, the parents choose not to return her, the husband loses what he paid. And the fool who used muscle to marry grows wiser for the trouble.

Things are not so poorly arranged among the Indians. Love and violence pose equal risks. An Indian man can marry two or more women. Generally, he will have only one because marriage is serious business and costs a lot of money. It takes a lot of friends who can lend the gifts needed for the first kind of marriage, and the gifts and the manpower needed for the second and third kinds.

Only the chiefs and captains have more than one woman. The woman the chief married first runs the tent. The rest of them have to obey her, though there is always a favorite who gets by without doing so.

Widows, if they are pretty, play a great role among the Indians. They are as free as the single women in one sense, more so in another, for no one can force them to marry or steal them. They are therefore the happiest creatures in the world both among Christians and among Indians. Small wonder that there are women who risk marrying on the chance they will become widows. Chief Epumer is married to a widow and she is his only wife. I found her very lovely and interesting, and on one visit that I made she received me with the utmost kindness and charm. She is an Indian woman of surprising deportment and cleanliness. Who but a widow could tame a fearsome, powerful, and impetuous man like Epumer!

Mariano Rosas was just finishing our Ranquel lessons when his son returned with Camargo.

"Lieutenant," he said to Camargo, "go tell Epumer that I have heard that Blanco is here and that he is saying things he shouldn't be saying. Tell him Blanco is to come to the council that is to be called and that he should watch his mouth or else."

This "or else" meant that they should kill him if necessary if he didn't obey. Camargo soon returned with Epumer's answer. Epumer said that he had already heard what Blanco was saying and that he had had word sent to him to quiet down.

"You see, brother," said Mariano upon hearing this, "there is no cause for alarm. Don't pay that Indian any mind. I will make him knuckle under and, if not, I'll run him out. When he heard we were going to be invaded he left the Cuero lands without my permission and took everything he had and went to Chile. Now he finds out we're at peace and that there is no reason to fear an invasion, so he comes back. That is a fair-weather friend for you. He will not do anything. He is all talk."

Camargo confirmed everything Mariano said and added a few observations of his own, gaucho variety, as for example: "I just might hit that Indian poltroon right where he lives."

Captain Rivadavia came in to tell me the food was ready. I took out my watch and, showing it to Mariano, told him it was four o'clock. The Indian looked at it as if to say he was familiar with such objects.

"Very nice," he said. "I have a silver one, but I don't use it. There is no need for it here."

"This is true," I answered.

"Go ahead and eat, brother," he said. "It is getting a little late."

So I left the tent once more, ate, and when the sun went down, returned to the entrance.

Mariano was sitting with several Indians and, like them, was half stewed.

They offered me a seat, I accepted.

They were drinking firewater.

They offered a *yapaí*, I accepted.

They offered another, I accepted.

They offered another, I accepted.

Happily for my insides, the cup this time was a very small horn and the bottle of firewater was nearly empty when I arrived. Mariano was in a meditative mood, his eyes fixed on the ground. The other Indians were falling asleep. I was engulfed in thoughts I cannot recall when a man from my group staggered into the tent, a knife in one hand and a bottle of firewater in the other. When I saw him, my blood froze in anger.

"Get out, Rufino!" I shouted.

He ignored me and kept coming.

"Get out!" I shouted more forcefully than before.

Again he disobeyed me and kept coming. He held out the bottle to Maiano Rosas.

"Have a drink, General," he said. Mariano took it.

I took it away from him. The moment was a decisive one for me. If I let one of my own soldiers show me disrespect I was as good as lost. In one move I took the bottle from him, pulled my knife, and shouted at the gaucho more loudly than before. "Get out of here," I said, and jumping over several Indians I was on him.

Rufino finally obeyed and left. I walked back to where I was before. I felt extremely upset and was choking on my bile. Mariano, who had not moved from his place, proceeded to speak with a studied coolness and sinister expression.

"We are all equal here, brother."

"No, brother," I answered. "You and your Indians may be equal. My soldiers and I are not equal. That troublemaker showed disrespect for me by coming in here drunk and refusing to obey my order to leave. My soldiers must respect me here more than anywhere else."

The Indian frowned. His face wore an expression in which I thought I could read: the audacity of this man. I had not planned for this effect, though I did understand that if I let this drunkard get the better of me I would lose prestige in the eyes of the barbarian.

We remained silent for a long while.

Neither one of us wanted to speak.

He mumbled it again: "We are all equal here."

My answer, seeing that Rufino was causing a scene around my assistants' camp fire, was to yell out at them in a great show of anger. In reality I had recovered my serenity.

"Gag him," I shouted.

The Indian furrowed his brow more. I did the same and we remained silent. Miguelito drew us from the abyss of our reflections. He came to intercede on Rufino's behalf, offering to take care of him himself. It seemed an opportune moment to bend a little.

"Go ahead and take him," I said. "But be careful!"

Rufino heard this. "Nothing to worry about here, Colonel," he said, and started in with a "Long live Colonel Mansilla." I motioned to him to keep quiet and he obeyed. A moment later his convivial voice could be heard in a neighboring tent, where a drinking stand was set up.

"Them boys are happy," said Mariano.

"Yes," I answered curtly and, bidding him a good evening, I left him alone.

Night was drawing near. I had Rufino brought in and told him to go to sleep.

Rufino has his story, too.

He is one of those gauchos we think of as bad.

I SLEPT SOUNDLY and completely undisturbed. Man adjusts to anything; my hard and uneven bed felt like feathers to me. Had I not been without blankets, I could say I spent a delightful night. I awoke with the morning star, shouting, "Let's have a fire!" and raced through my ablutions by candlelight. I went outside. The camp fire was burning and the water was boiling in the kettle. I sat down to have some mate and enjoy the saws and yarns of my soldiers. Each one had an anecdote to tell.

Everyone had had something happen with the Indians. One of them gave away everything he had, cigarettes and all. Another one gave his boots away. This one his poncho, that one his shirt. Only one, a real bullheaded fellow from Mendoza, had the backbone to turn a deaf ear to the handout-seekers and stand his ground.

As morning broke, I set about instructing them in the conduct they ought best observe: on why immoderation, disrespect, and neglect of their superiors was here more than anywhere else counterindicated. They understood my reasoning perfectly and paid religious attention. I singled out Rufino for a harsh sermon.

This Rufino was a gaucho from Villanueva.[1] Nobody could stand up to him. The scourge of the countryside, he was seized and inducted for service in the Twelfth Line Battalion along with others of his stripe. The military command sent me very forceful recommendations concerning him. I was to exercise great caution with him, as he was considered a reckless man. I could see that he would be a bad element for the Twelfth Line, so I had him brought to me three days after he was inducted.

They had cut his long hair, put a kepi on his head, hung a jacket on him, and outfitted him with trousers. The gaucho had vanished under the recruit's uniform. He was a tall, well-built man of great restless black eyes, expressive countenance, effortless movements. All in all, there was a resolute look to him. I struck up a dialogue with him.

"What's your name?"

"Rufino Pereyra."

"Where are you from?"

"I don't know."

"Where were you born?"

"I don't know."

"Who were your parents?"

"I don't know."

"What kind of work did you do before you became a soldier?"

"Nothing."

"Do you know why you're in?"

"No."

"They say you're a thief, a rustler, and a murderer."

"If that's what they say . . ."

"But what do you say?"

"I am not a bad man."

"What are you then?"

"I'm a gaucho."

"But they wouldn't put you in just for that."

"The judges don't like me."

"Then you must not have accepted their authority."

"I don't like soldiering. I took off for the hills when I found out they were after me. I fought with their posses a few times and beat them."

"That's all you've done?"

"That's it."

"But you said you didn't work, and in order to live without bringing harm on your neighbor, you need to work. So I'll ask you again: what did you live on?"

"I gamble."

"So how can they call you a thief, a rustler, and a murderer if you're not?"

"I got blamed for things other friends of mine did who I didn't want to turn in, and as far as being a murderer, it's probably because I cut a few of the posse in fights."

"Do you want to make a deal with me?"

"Whatever you say, Colonel."

"Will you give me your word?"

"Yes, sir."

"Your word of honor?"

Rufino said nothing.

"Do you know what honor is?"

Again, silence.

"Honor means always keeping your word even if it costs you your life. Do you understand me now?"

"Yes, Colonel."

"Good. You're going to be my assistant, take care of my horses, be my trusted man, and I am going to have them release you from the Twelfth Line right away."

The gaucho said nothing.

"Are you willing to serve me properly? I cannot release you from the service outright. You will have to be a soldier. I will help you get what you need. What do you think? Do you want to give it a try?"

"Yes, my Colonel."

At last he had said it: *my* Colonel.

I gave the appropriate orders, and Rufino Pereyra was soon out and about in Villanueva like any other soldier. I was living in Belzor Moyano's house at the time. Rufino lived there as well. This amazed everybody, so great was the terror he inspired. One morning he was in the front hallway while I stood outside the front door talking to a police sergeant. I entered my room with the sergeant and Rufino came in behind me unnoticed. When I sensed his presence he had already sat down in a chair.

"Well, just go ahead and lie down on the bed, compadre," I said. "Make yourself at home."

He caught the sarcasm in my voice and sat up straight.

"Well now," I said. "So you knew you shouldn't sit down in your chief officer's presence or come in if he hasn't called you?"

And with this I yanked him roughly from his chair.

The gaucho got on his feet and tensed up.

"Well, if I don't know it," he said in his mountain accent, "why haven't you taught me?"

"For that wisecrack take this," I said, and gave him something we tend to use in the service when we need to get rid of a recruit who has no instinct for discipline or respect for his superiors. For several days the gaucho put on a long face, watching me out of the corner of his eye as if to study my body for the best place to stick a knife into it.

There was only one way to master him: belittle him and inspire full trust at the same time. I sent for him.

"Tomorrow," I said, "as soon as the morning star is out, saddle up my big chestnut, push the door to my room open, come in slowly, come up to my bed, call me, and if I don't wake up, shake me."

I prepared a roll of fifty Bolivian pesos and a letter for Commander Racedo, Twelfth Line Battalion, which was some five leagues away. "I am sending this with Rufino Pereyra," I wrote, "for the purpose of testing him. Dispatch him at once, taking care to note the time he arrives and the time he leaves."

I am a very light sleeper.

At the agreed-upon hour I heard the door to my room open. I pretended to be snoring. Rufino entered and, finding the room completely dark, walked slowly up to my bed.

"Colonel," he said. I did not answer. He called my name again, again I said nothing. He called a third time. I remained silent. He touched me and shook me. I finally answered as if from the depths of sleep.

"Who is it?" I asked.

"It's me."

"Look for the matches there on the chair next to the head of the bed and light the candle."

Rufino obeyed, felt around for the matches, lit one, and we had light. Without even sitting up I reached under my headrest, took out the roll of Bolivian pesos and the letter.

"Do you know where the Cabral Creek is?" I asked, handing them to him.

"Yes, Colonel."

"Take this to Commander Racedo and be back by twelve. It's ten leagues there and back. There's no hurry, so don't overwork my horse."

He did not answer. He squared, saluted, did an about-face, and left. I put the light out and went to sleep. I had retired very late. I had gone to a dance that night. I was sound asleep. I heard foot-steps near my bed, woke up, opened my eyes, and looked. There was Rufino Pereyra, back from his errand, a letter in his out-stretched hand. I took it, broke the seal, and read.

"He got here with everything at nine-thirty and is on his way back," Racedo's note said. From that day on I always treated Rufino with complete trust and he served me honorably in everything, even confidential matters.

Our country is full of Rufino Pereyras.

In two years Rufino, the bad gaucho of Villanueva, the famous bandit feared by all and accused of every iniquity under the sun, only slipped once: the time he walked in drunk on Mariano Rosas and myself. My adherence to my own standards of conduct, pur-poses, and rooted convictions, deriving as it does from my study of the human heart, compelled me to follow the tongue-lashing with sound practical advice, exhorting him warmly not to let it fall on deaf ears. He promised not to incur in the same error again so long as we were with the Indians.

The sun, a resplendent disk of fire, bathed the horizon in rich hues of purple and honey gold.

Morning had broken a while since.

I decided to go to the water hole to bathe. I got up, left the fire, and took the trail to the water. I had only gone a few steps when I met up with Mariano Rosas. He was on his way back from the water, as his wet hair and freshly washed face revealed. We greeted each other amiably.

"I am going to bathe, brother," I said.

"I just did the same," he said, "and now I am going to run my horse."

We rode in opposite directions.

As I returned from the water, he was on his way back. His horse was foaming with sweat.

He rode in, dismounted, unsaddled, and saddled another one that was hitched to the post. This done, he put a bridle on it and tied it to the post.

The Indians perform this operation every morning. When they steal our horses, they start by turning them loose in the hills so that they will get used to it there and get a taste for the grass. When they finish that, they saddle a different horse each day at sunup and gallop it hard on the sandiest, most broken, duned terrain they can find. This second education imparts an extraordinary vigor to our horses. Also, by standing tied to a post with nothing to eat or drink for twenty-four hours, they build up an incredible endurance for deprivation. Thus the superiority of the Indians in the frontier wars. Their whole strategy rests on flight, on eluding combat. They are thieves, not warriors. Fighting is their last resort. All their glory lies in carrying out a profitable raid and returning from it with the least number of Indians sacrificed in the name of work.[2]

How can our horses possibly compete with theirs? How can we hope to catch them when they have several hours head start on us?

We might as well try to catch the wind.

After Mariano tied his horse, we sat down beneath the entrance and agreed that it was time to take up official matters. Tomorrow we will have our first diplomatic conference.

THE NEXT DAY I received Chief Ramón's visit. He came with a large party. We had a hard, level talk, as they say in those parts. We drank several rounds in the Araucan way and agreed to meet at the border of Baigorrita's territory the day of the council, which would soon enough take place. Bustos, the mestizo who had shown me such good will in Aillancó, was with him. I gave him something from what little I had left. To the chief I gave my twenty-round revolver, showing him how to make use of it, how to load and unload it. He didn't seem so happy with the gun. It's nice, he said, but we have no use for it out here; we have no way of getting more bullets. I promised to furnish him with bullets if we had the good fortune to observe the peace treaty strictly and faithfully. He answered that he for his part would spare no effort in that regard. He called on Bustos to attest to the fact that he was a good friend to the Christians. "I have relatives in Carlota; my mother was from there," he said several times, always adding, "How can I help but love the Christians? I've got their blood in my veins."

After he left, I had Captain Rivadavia look to see if Mariano Rosas was prepared to talk with me about the matter at hand—the peace treaty. The purpose of my trip was to iron out certain difficulties which arose from the form in which it was accepted. He said the chief was at my service and that I should proceed to his tent whenever I wished.

I did not keep him waiting.

When I entered the tent he was lunching in the company of his wives and children. They all arose, greeted me attentively and respectfully, and before I had time to settle into the seat they designated for me, they placed a large wooden plate of some very nicely made corn chowder with milk in front of me, asking me if I liked it with or without sugar. With, I answered, and they brought it to me in a heartbeat in a little pouch made of Pampa cloth. I had not had lunch yet, so I ate the chowder forthwith. They offered more and I accepted.

The candid air about me, my primitive postures, my way of kidding around with the Indian children and the women had the best possible effect on the chief.

"You will have to excuse us, brother," he said again and again. When I looked straight at him he would lower his eyes, and when he thought I did not see him, he would look me through and through.

We spoke about matters of little importance while the corn chowder lasted, which was all there was for lunch. Several months before, he had sent me letters inviting me to be his compadre. Now he introduced me to my future goddaughter. She was a little seven-year-old Indian girl, the daughter of a Christian woman. She looked more Spanish than Araucanian. I sat her on my knees and fondled her. She did not shy away.

At last we got down to talking about the peace thing, as they say there. Mariano spoke first. "Brother," he said, "I want peace because I know what work is and I could take care of my family. Some have not wanted peace, but I have made it understood that it is best for us. If I have taken a long time to accept what you have proposed, it is because I had many minds to consult. It is not the same thing to govern here as it is among the Christians. There the ruler rules and the rest obey. Out here, you have to work things out first with the chiefs, the captains, and the elders. All are free and all are equal."

Clearly, from where Mariano Rosas stands, we live in a full-blown dictatorship and the Indians live in a full-blown democracy.

I felt it unnecessary to rectify his ideas.[1]

On the other hand, I might have been hard put to prove that government, authority, power, and disciplined, organized force are not all-powerful in our troubled republic, where each day brings another cry for heightened and fortified and protected power, never mind the dogged historical facts telling all those with eyes to see that most of our misfortune comes from the abuse of authority. As familiar as Mariano Rosas might be with this, what sense was there in wasting his time with a political dissertation? Because I was for the moment an ambassador (sic) and as such ought to take things seriously, I followed words of praise for his conduct with an explanation that the peace treaty must be submitted for congressional approval before it could be put into practice.

That the Indian might better understand what is meant by *executive power*, *parliament*, *budget*, and other such niceties, I used rhetorical figures from country life. And whether or not I was inspired, which does not generally happen to me—I only remember it happening once, when I gave up studying the guitar because of the phrenological depression on my skull where tone-sensitive organs would ordinarily be found—again, whether or not I was inspired, the fact is that Mariano Rosas was edified.

His yawning told me as much.

Were I to continue to display my oratorical skills, my knowledge of constitutional law, and the seductions which the civilized man invariably believes he holds for the barbarian, he might fall asleep on me. I therefore resolved to ask him a question: "And what do you think, brother, of what I have said?"

"What do you think I think? The treaty is signed by the President, the man who rules. It is not going to be easy to make the other Indians understand the things you have been explaining to me.

"We will call a great council," he continued, "and there, between the two of us, we will speak our piece."

"Meanwhile, brother," I said, "you can count on me if you need any help."

"I will count on you because I see that if you did not love the Indians you would not have come to this land."

Naturally, I assured him that the President of the Republic was a very good man; that he had worked himself gray to bring education to all the young children of my land; that he would not abandon them to their ignorance; that he has the character and tendencies of a gentle person and no love of war; and that at any rate the Constitution mandates that Congress maintain peaceful treatment of the Indians and promote their conversion to Catholicism. Congress would give the President as much money as he needed for these things and since they were very good friends there would be no fighting between them if they should hold different opinions, because together they governed the country.

"And tell me, brother," he asked, "what is the President's name?"

"Domingo F. Sarmiento."

"And is he a friend of yours?"

"A very good friend."

"And if you were no longer friends, what would become of the peace you have made with us?"

"Nothing, brother, because I cannot fight with the President even if he punishes me. I am only a poor colonel and my obligation is to obey. The President has great power, he commands the whole army. Besides, if I leave, another colonel will take my place and he will have to do whatever General Arredondo, the man I answer to, tells him to do."

"And is Arredondo a friend of the President?"

"A very good friend."

"More than you?"

"That I cannot say, brother, because, as you know, friendship cannot be measured, only proven."

"And tell me, brother, what is the name of the Constitution?"

Here my strategy went up in smoke. And yet, if the president can be Domingo F. Sarmiento, why, for that barbarian, should the Constitution not have some other name as well?

This was a little tricky.

"The Constitution, brother . . . . The Constitution is just called . . . the Constitution."

"Then it has no name?"

"That is its name."

"Then it has only one name, and the President has two?"

"Yes."

"And is the Constitution good or bad?"

"Brother, some say it is good, others bad."

"And are you a friend of the Constitution?"

"Very much so, of course."

"And Arredondo?"

"Arredondo, too."

"And which of you is more of a friend to the Constitution?"

"We are both very much its friend."

"And what is the Congress's name?"

"The Congress . . . is called . . . the Congress."

"So it has only one name, like the other one?"

"That's right, just one."

"And is Congress good or bad?"

"(Hmmmmm!)" [2]

I must admit this question left me perplexed. But I owed him an answer. I thought it over and planned a reply in good conscience and was about to make it when two dogs that were wandering around jumped on a bone and started an infernal ruckus, which interrupted our dialogue. Mariano stood up to scare them away.

"Get out!" he shouted.

I took advantage of the break and excused myself. Once back in our hut, I sat on the bed with my elbows on my thighs, my face resting in my hands, and sank for a long while into deep meditation.

"I have been wasting my time," I said from the echoes of my own spirit. It is not so easy to explain what a constitution and a congress are. Mariano Rosas understood perfectly well what a president is, first because he has another name—he could as soon be Domingo as Bartolo—and secondly because he commands the army. Consequently, my study of the Indian mind leads me to conclude that the people will always understand the rod of law better than they understand law per se. Symbols impress the imagination of the multitudes more than do allegories. Thus, anywhere in the world where there is a constitution and a congress, there is also greater fear of the president.

I met with Mariano again several hours later.

I could see that he was in a festive mood and made the most of it by asking him if we could have mass the next day. I conveyed to him the fervent wish on the part of many Christian captives and refugees in Indian territory to hear it said.

I took the good news to my Franciscans and like true apostles of Jesus Christ they were jubilant. We determined to say mass, weather permitting—that is, barring wind or dust—in the open air. We would lean the sacred altar against a giant old *chañar* tree whose enormous boughs would serve as a roof over us.

Tomorrow we hear mass.

 WITH SUPPER FINISHED and mass set with the Franciscans for between eight and nine the next morning, I had begun to get ready for bed when an unexpected visitor appeared at my ranch hut. It was my future compadre Camargo and one of Mariano Rosas's interpreters, a man from Mendoza named José who had married into the Indian tribes and adopted their habits and customs so thoroughly that one may well doubt whether he is Christian. There is something different about him, for out in Indian country they say he has worked out very well. They place every bit as much trust in him as they would in one of their captains.

José is bound by love, family, and wealth to the outlying country. The Indians, who know the human heart as well as your next-door neighbor does, realize this perfectly well. They therefore see him as one of their own. He and Camargo both had the instruments of pleasure in hand—I mean a bottle of firewater. I offered them a seat. They accepted, trying most painstakingly to hide their condition and offering me a taste of the brew after the requisite formalities.

I had to accept their *yapaí.*

However, we were alone and I felt rather less obligated to defer to them than on other occasions. They took this well enough. My status as colonel on the one hand, on the other our common religion and origins—circumstances which in every life situation foster a certain cordiality among people—assured them they were not abusing my hospitality. Besides, they counted themselves honored to be admitted into my quarters at such an unlikely time of night. They were content just to fraternize with me and drink by themselves, with my permission, which they requested with thoroughgoing gaucho ingenuity.

"Excuse us, Colonel," they said, "if we're not in such good shape. We want to finish this one bottle right here in your cabin. If that's not all right or if we're bothering you, we'll get out."

"Make yourselves at home," I said. "I don't stand on etiquette."

"We know that," they answered in unison. "That's why we came."

So saying, the very smooth-talking José, upon whom I had lavished gifts in Río Cuarto, embraced me.

"This man is like a father to me," he said to Camargo. Then, looking meaningfully at me, he said, "You know who José is, Colonel."

I guess I am finding out, I said to myself, knowing better than he what really counted here. A drunk's declarations are about as reliable as a woman's promises. It is a fool who holds his breath waiting for them to come true. On the other hand, kindness is no sin and I was as kind to my visitors as the time and place allowed.

I thank God each day for giving me a flexible character. I am as content and cheerful in the bare shack of the *paisanos* as I am in the palatial salons of the rich. I sit as comfortably in a plush easy chair as I do beside the common soldier's glowing camp fire.

The bottles, which did not have the virtue of inexhaustibility, were down to their last drops. José was by now dreamwalking in the Lord's vineyards. The stronger Camargo was still master of his senses.

"We brought some music along for you, Colonel. Excuse me for a minute."

"Why, thanks very much. You shouldn't have gone to any trouble."

Camargo helped himself up by the frame of the hut, leaned out the door, said something, and sat down again. Instantly there appeared—*horresco referens*—the Negro with the accordion.

"Huh?" I said. "Not that, Camargo. Give me any kind of music you want, but not the accordion, no, no. I'm tired of seeing that devil's face."

I then turned to the Negro.

"Get out! Get out!"

He refused to obey. He seemed stuck to the floor as his body moved left and right, up and down in curves. He was drunk as a skunk.

"Get out! Go somewhere else, somewhere far away!" I said.

Camargo, seeing that the Negro was getting my goat, stood up, took him by the arm, and showed him to the door. Delivered from the beast, from that truly black beast, I drew a sigh of relief. It was one of those drop-down-on-the-sofa-on-a-hot-summer-day sighs, when you have just slipped free of an afternoon visitor whose whole life is telling you about his latest lawsuit or his trouble with the authorities.

José was now fast asleep. Camargo sat down and fell into a kind of firewater-induced lethargy. I studied his physiognomy. He is what they call a handsome gaucho. He has long, bristly black hair and big, bright, slanted, lively eyes like those of a fiery horse. He has long, soft, thick eyebrows and eyelashes, a large, rather aquiline nose. His mouth is somewhat set back and he has a thick lower lip. He is white, as though well-bred, has pock marks on his face and a light beard. He is tall, thin, and muscular. His spacious, flat brow, prominent cheekbones, pointed chin, broad back and vault-like chest; his always bony and moist hands; it all reveals daring, vigor, and a rigidity that could verge on cruelty.

Camargo is one of those men whom one does not pass alongside of, when one is alone, without feeling a certain fear of aggression. The Indians respect him, as they respect anything strong and manly and anyone having little regard for life.

Camargo has little regard for life.

The knife scars across his hands prove it. His restless, turbulent, haphazard existence proves it. His days are consumed amidst and against firewater and incessant saturnalias with all the fighting that goes with them; amidst the roar of Indian raids and rebel riding. For if he is with the Indians today, he is with Elizondo or Guayama[1] tomorrow, and when they are routed he flees for the safety of the Indian settlements on his swift and indomitable colt. If I may say so, this is a gaucho who, in the heroic instances, vindicates the honor of the Christians. Whether face to face or from behind, one on one or among several, he will denounce the Indians as "barbarians" whenever he pleases. I have often heard him do it and he doesn't hold back.

"Just don't let me catch these Indians trying any moves on me. I'll stick a knife in the first one who does and he'll have to heal his wounds in the afterlife."

After studying this iron-man Camargo and the Semitic persistence stamped on his face, I decided to break his indeliberate silence and speak to him.

"How did you end up here?" I asked.

He is a vivacious conversationalist, but this time he only sighed, retreating further into his fog of painful memories.

"Come on, man," I said. "Tell me your life."

"Sir," he answered, "my life has been short and there is nothing in particular to tell. I am not a bad man, but I have been unlucky. I am from San Luis, near Renca. My parents were honest people of some means. They gave me plenty of love and a good education. I can read and write and do figures. I was sort of cocky as a kid. When I was hardly a man I had this idea there was nobody who could beat me at anything. Whenever I heard some gaucho was around playing the bad guy, I would go find him to see if he wanted to tangle with me.

"I wanted to be in the military service. My dream was to make general. I hadn't done anybody any harm, although I had a head full of trouble. I always went in for the boozing and gambling and fighting, but you'll never hear anybody say I hit 'em from behind. I fell in love with Commander N.'s daughter and she loved me, too. I was young. In fact you are looking at a twenty-two-year-old man, Colonel." (He looked thirty-two.)

"Besides all that, my parents had a little money like I said, so I was all in all pretty nicely set up. Commander N. knew I was seeing his daughter and didn't like it. He tried to run me down one day at the races. He came at me on his horse but I turned mine on him and next thing you know he was flat on his back, mount and all. It was a crazy thing and he never forgave me for it. From then on, he went around saying he would kill me. I was watching out for him. They tried to blame certain things on me but could never prove anything. Then a revolution flared up and they came after me. There were four in the posse and no way were they going to get me. I knew I was lead rider in that parade and shot out of there. I rode till I found the *montoneros*."

Here I interrupted him.

"And what were your ideas on that?"

"Ideas? All I wanted was to be happy and have a good time. Horse racing and women, those were my ideas."

"And what did you do while you were with the *montoneros*?"

"We raised hell. I rode some of the time with El Chacho, who was barbaric. After they killed him I stayed in the hills. When don Juan Sáa came, I joined him with some others. Then General Arredondo defeated us at San Ignacio and I came out here with Baigorrita's Indians."

"And what have you been doing since then? What kind of life have you had?"

"I went to San Luis under cover and brought my wife and some relatives and they are all here now."

"Have you gone on raids with the Indians?"

"On a few, yes, sir."

"Is it true you're to blame for the Indians having killed a number of Christians?"

"That is false. I have been in the homes of some low-down people, but I was against cutting their throats. Hey, if it hadn't been for me the world would be a few poor souls poorer."

Here our colloquy was cut short by the Negro with the accordion, who struck up a tune outside the door. Camargo got up and went out, and from certain words with which he underscored his suggestion that the Negro leave, I gathered that our luckless Orpheus of Leubucó had not been treated as artists generally prefer to be, even bad artists. The Negro took his music elsewhere. Camargo returned and, without coming back in, said good night from the other side of the door. "And excuse me, Colonel," he added.

It was time to think about getting some sleep. My assistants Lemlenyi, Rodríguez, Ozarowsky, and the two blessed Franciscans, who had all heard Camargo's story, were yawning mightily. I awoke José, called two assistants, and had him taken to a nearby tent. Meanwhile, as I prepared to spend a sleepless night what with a brisk, cool wind ushering the dirt in through every crack in the wall, I gave some thought to these Argentine lives, to these crude, half-primitive types so abundant here, who will sacrifice themselves or go to their deaths for a borrowed cause. For we have institutions and laws to spare but lack eternal justice. By eternal justice I mean justice which, in a spirit of guardianship, watches over the impoverished as well as the sumptuously rich and powerful.

Under these impressions I had a dream—I am a hopeless dreamer—*I had a dream, which was not all a dream.*

A dream!

Who in this country will hang a man who has ten million pesos?

THE NIGHT WAS long and wearisome and ice cold. The sand blew into the ranch everywhere, as if hurried through. When the morning light brightened the picture we formed—my officers, the friars lying on the floor, and I on my so oft-mentioned bed—I looked through an opening in my blankets that I had been using as a breathing hole. They had all disappeared under a yellowish cover, a sinister dune-like surface which rose and fell in rhythm with their breathing. What cares could possibly tyrannize them there? We shook the sleep, the sweet, enervating sleep out of our system. Once on our feet, we got moving.

The Franciscans took out the trunk containing the sacred ornaments and set about getting them ready for mass. I freshened up in the pond, had a light breakfast of mate and coffee, and went to take a look at the place the altar would be set up if the wind calmed.

The sky was clear and blue, the sun shone splendidly. Time slipped by unnoticed as preparations moved along. The neighboring Christians were called and, it being impossible to hold mass in the open air as I wished, we looked for a hut, though to a man we were disappointed. As true believers we realized that the immense majesty of God was best served either under the vast azure dome of the firmament, or beneath the massive vaults of any of the towering basilicas. Wherever man lifts his spirit to the Supreme Being, the grandeur of the spectacle should be such as to inspire an inward retreat. The mysticism of prayer is all the more fervent when the imagination bears the poetic suasion of the outer world.

The wind was incessant.

We had to resign ourselves to using the hut of one of Ayala's people,[1] a sergeant. They tidied it up as nicely as they could and in a matter of minutes the Franciscans had improvised an altar. The men and women began arriving and taking their places a few at a time. Poor souls, they wore the best rags they had. Kneeling, seated, and standing, they awaited the appearance of the priests in respectful silence. I looked at my watch. It was nine o'clock. It is time, Fathers, I said, and with my officers accompanied them to the chapel.

It could not have been more modest. The memory that He whose sacrifice we were about to honor was born in a stable and slept in the straw comforted me. The Franciscans had spread blankets and ponchos on the floor and walls of the ranch. The wind was no bother, the candlelight illuminated a wooden crucifix upon which the gaunt and mournful, blood-bespattered face of Christ stood out. The altar seemed to glow with its lace cloth and covering all painted with golden flowers. The shining custodia and silver cruets gleamed.

It was all very lovely and it prompted prayer.

Father Marcos would officiate, with myself and Father Moisés as servers, though I had only a vague and jumbled recollection of my altar-boy Latin. It was my duty, however, to set an example at all times.

We assisted Father Marcos in putting on his vestments and the mass began. Groups of curious Indians drew near to watch.

A profound silence reigned.

The metallic altar bells rang, inviting all to make an act of contrition for the blood of the Redeemer. It was the first time that the humble *Confiteor Deo Omnipotenti* had sounded its humble echoes among those barbarians, the first time in those desolate lands. Whenever the ceremony let me turn aside from the altar I watched the Christians. They were praying with intense devotion. There were several Indians among them. I noticed tears of regret or pain in some of the women. Others wore on their faces something vaguely resembling a glimmer of hope. All seemed intimately happy to have reconciled themselves with God, lifting their spirits to Him in the presence of the cross and the altar.

As the sacrifice went on I thought constantly of my mother. I remembered the childish suffering she made me undergo, taking me to mass every Sunday at the San Juan church so that I could help out at mass under her watchful eye.[2]

"Poor mother," I said, "how far away you are now."

I prayed to God for her and for all those I loved. And I thanked her for that suffering, for by it I was now able to experience the pleasure of extolling religion among the infidels by taking part in the august ceremony for which we had gathered. When it was over and the priests had given their blessings, the altar was dismantled, ponchos and blankets were taken off walls and floor, and the chapel turned back into what it was, a lowly hovel. The ornaments were put away, the trunk was returned to my ranch, and we immediately went with the Franciscans to thank Mariano Rosas. His tent was full of visitors who were having the afternoon meal with him. Each person had a bountiful plate of stew before him, as well as corn and squash. As always, the chief received us courteously, rising to extend his hand and motioning to us to be seated. Then he introduced us to all of his guests.

He had matters of grave importance to attend to, that is, the rallying of spirits for the great council soon to take place. The Indians are no different from the Christians in that respect; the success of affairs of state is always doubtful if the task of prior persuasion is not carried out.

The Franciscans withdrew and left me alone.

Mariano Rosas spoke sometimes about things in general, other times about particular matters. He is a calculating, suggestive, and insinuating speaker, though at times he raised his voice in excitement, staring hard at the Indian whom he was answering and gesturing with his arms, which was not his usual way.

They brought me food to eat and I ate.

The present conference had a long way to go, so I left, agreeing to set the date for the council later. I wanted to know it ahead of time because I planned to go to Baigorrita's lands for a visit.

I slept a good siesta, though Captain Rivadavia interrupted it to tell me that Mariano Rosas was alone and waiting at the entrance to his tent. He had asked if I would like to come in. I answered the call and we were just getting down to business when the Negro with the accordion came capering out from the tent proper, pumping away. This to me was like seeing a *iettatore*. I had no choice, however, but to listen to him. As I have said, the head of the household immensely enjoyed him. As long as the Negro was there, there was no point in talking about anything serious.

The chief was in an exclusively light-hearted mood. He questioned me at length about Buenos Aires and Rosas's family. His memories were indelible. It appeared that his whole objective came down to making sure that I was indeed the Dictator's nephew. He asked for a portrait, claiming that the one I had was the only one he lacked to complete his collection.

Sure enough it was.

He told the Negro to bring the portraits.

The Negro left and returned with a small, very soiled cardboard box containing photographs of Urquiza, Mitre, Juan Sáa, and others.[3] He gave the box back to the Negro and told him to put it in its place. The favorite took it and, happily for me, remained in the tent proper.

Then Mariano and I got down to business. Everything was set with the dignitaries of the desert. The council would be held in four days to leave fair warning time. Nothing unexpected would happen. I would reveal the purpose of my trip and Mariano would back me in everything. There was only one doubtful point. Why did I insist on buying *possession* of the land?

"As you know, brother," said Mariano, "the Indians are very distrustful."

"I know that, but you mustn't distrust the current president of the republic, on whose authority I have made this peace treaty."

"Do you assure me that he is a good man?" asked the chief.

"Yes, brother, I assure you of it," I answered.

"And why do you want so much land when south of the Río Cuarto, between Langhelo and Melincué, between Aucaló and El Chañar, there is so much unsettled land?"[4]

I explained to him that the security of the borders and the felicitous outcome of the peace treaty dictated that there be at least fifteen leagues of desert behind the new line and as much again beyond it. This would be land which the Indians would agree not to settle on or use for open bola hunting without passports.

He argued that this was their land.

I explained that the land belonged only to those who made it productive and that the government was buying possession of it, not merely rights to it. The government realized that the Indians had to live somewhere.

He invoked the past, arguing that in other times the Indians had lived between Río Cuarto and Río Quinto and that these lands were theirs.

I explained that the fact that they had lived in a place did not give them dominion over it.

He argued that if I were to live among the Indians, the piece of land I occupied would be mine.

I asked whether that meant I could sell it to whomever I wished.

He did not like the question because the answer would be embarrassing to him.

"Look, brother," he said, scarcely able to conceal his annoyance. "Why do you not tell me the truth?"

"I have told you the truth," I answered.

"Wait and see, brother."

He stood up, entered the tent, and returned carrying a pine box with a sliding top. He opened it and took out a number of stitched chintz pouches. It was his archives. Each pouch contained official notes, letters, drafts, periodicals. He knew each paper perfectly. He could point to any paragraph to which he wished to refer. He rummaged about in his archive, found a small pouch, unlaced the stitching, and took out a folded and wrinkled piece of newspaper. It came from *La Tribuna* of Buenos Aires and had been handled many times.[5] He pointed to an article he had marked off about the great interoceanic railroad.

"Read, brother," he said.

I knew the article.

"I already know what it's about," I said.

"Well, then, why are you not open with me?"

"What do you mean by 'open'?"

"You haven't come out and said that you want to buy these lands to run the railroad through El Cuero."

I was deeply embarrassed. I had foreseen everything except the argument just made to me.

"Brother," I said, "that will never happen, and if it does happen, what harm would come to the Indians from it?"

"What harm, brother?"

"Yes, what harm."

"I will tell you what harm. After the railroad goes through, the Christians will say that they need more land to the south. They will want to throw us out of here and we will have to go south of the Río Negro to alien lands. There are no good places to live between those lands and the Río Colorado or Río Negro."

"That will not happen, brother, if you and your people honestly keep the peace."

"No, brother. The Christians say it is better to get rid of us."

"Some believe that. Others, such as myself, feel you deserve our protection and that there is nothing wrong with you going on living where you live if you keep your commitments."[6]

The Indian sighed as if to say "I wish it were so!" Then he spoke again.

"Brother, I have trust in you. I have told you: fix it however you wish."

I made no reply. Scrutinizing his face I found nothing but his habitual expression. Mariano Rosas, like all men accustomed to power, had great self-mastery. It is pointless to try to read in his face the truth or falsity of his words. He says what he likes. He keeps what he really feels hidden in the recesses of his heart.

He went about putting his archive in order. That done, he closed the box and called out: "Negro! Negro!"

I shuddered.

I made up a pretext to avoid seeing his face and excused myself. It was getting to be time to eat. There were already some nice fat roasts laid out on the fire. They gave off an appetizing smell and I wasn't about to let them get burnt.

"Let's eat, gentlemen," I called out.

We took our places around the fire and the repast began. It happened that my comadre Carmen was around. I offered her a seat, she accepted, and entertained us for a good while with the story of her life and some of the particulars of Ranquel ways and customs.

Mariano Rosas had evening visitors who spent the night with him in splendid enjoyment of the pleasures of conversation and wine.

 MY COMADRE CARMEN lived in Carrilobo, near Villarreal's tent. Villarreal was married to her sister and Carmen had brought my goddaughter with her to visit me. We enjoyed listening to Carmen. She has a facility for Spanish and possesses enough wealth of expression to communicate her ideas, reveal her sentiments, and make herself understood.

She gave me several notions regarding the beliefs of the Indians. They never gather to worship God but hide in the forest and worship alone. God is neither the sun, the moon, the stars, or the universality of all living beings. Thus they are neither idolaters nor pantheists. They are monotheists and anthropomorphists.

God—Cuchauentrú, the Great Man, or Chachao, the Father of all—has a human form and is everywhere. He is invisible and indivisible. He is immensely good and must be loved.

Gualicho, the devil, is to be feared.

This gent, whom we depict with a horn and a tail, naked and spitting fire from his mouth, has no form at all for them. Like Cuchauentrú, Gualicho is indivisible and invisible and is everywhere.

Moreover, while the former has no thought of harming anyone, the latter always seeks to do his neighbor an ill turn. It is Gualicho who causes the raids that fail, who brings the invasions of Christians, sickness, death, and all the plagues and calamities that afflict humanity. Gualicho is in the lagoon whose waters are unclean. He is in the poison fruit and herb, the tip of the spear that kills, the barrel of the gun that intimidates, the darkness of the horrific night, the clock that marks the hour, the compass that points north; in short, he is in everything incomprehensible and mysterious. One must be on good terms with Gualicho, for Gualicho gets into everything. Let him get into the belly and there will be stomachaches; into the head and there will be headaches; into the legs and he brings paralysis; in the eyes and there is blindness; in the ears and we are deaf; on the tongue and we are dumb. Gualicho is extremely ambitious. One had best let him have his way in everything. From time to time horses, mares, cows, goats, and sheep must be sacrificed to him; at least once a year or once every twelve moons, which is how the Indians measure time. Gualicho is an old woman's worst enemy, especially an ugly old woman: he gets under their skin, who knows how or where, and he jinxes them.

Woe to the woman who falls under Gualicho's curse! They will kill her to drive out the malignant spirit. The poor old things endure extraordinary suffering because of it. If not sentenced, they are ever on the verge of being sentenced. All it takes is for something to happen in the tent where she lives. An Indian gets sick or a horse dies: It is the old woman's fault. She brought it down on the Indian or the horse. Gualicho will not leave the tent until the wretched woman dies. These sacrifices are not done publicly or ceremoniously. The Indian who holds that power over an elderly woman sacrifices her in secret.

As for the dead, the Indians have a profound respect for them. As there is no place more sacred than a sepulcher, there is no heresy comparable to exhuming a corpse. Like the Hindus, the Egyptians, and the Pythagoreans, the Indians believe in metempsychosis, the passage of the soul from the body after death and its migration over a more or less long period of time to other countries, where it gives life to other rational or irrational bodies. The rich are usually reborn south of the Río Negro and are to return from there, though there is no memory to date of anyone having returned. That is why they bury them with the best horse and most valuable silver riding gear that they have. They also sacrifice horses, cows, mares, goats, and sheep around the grave and in proportion to the wealth that the deceased has left or that his next-of-kin or friends possess. The horse and the buried riding gear are for the dead to have something to ride in the country where they will be reborn. The rest of the animals are meant as food for the journey there and back.

The women, too, are reborn, make no mistake about that. Some who have lived for a long time among the Indians hold that there must be a wealth of crafted silver buried in the desert as a result of their customs. For my part, I think that the Christians, having very little fear of Gualicho and being in no wise Pythagoreans, have taken it upon themselves to dig it up. In any case, my comadre informs me that funeral rites are not carried out with as much pomp as before.

She tried to explain why. "I don't know," she said, "whether it's because the Christians have always searched the burial sites or because silver is worth more now."

I am inclined to believe that the two reasons combined are causing the burials to be ever less lavish. The fact is that the Indians now have many needs. They are very fond of drinking. They like sweet mate tea. They smoke and wear fine clothes. It is easy to see how upon the death of a kinsman they would want to honor his memory by sacrificing horses, cows, mares, goats, and sheep and that they would keep the silver.

My comrade Carmen assured me that until the arrival of the Christians there was not a single instance of the looting of sacred burial sites.

Could it be that civilization corrupts?

The above notwithstanding, the Indians are driven neither by bloodlust nor by ferocity, proof of this being that they never sacrifice human victims to the ghosts of their deceased. They kill the old women, true, but they do so because they believe them to be possessed by Satan. Anyway, it is not such a great loss, or so some would say.

Seriously, however, there is a disquieting truth to register here, namely, that certain Christian refugees living among the Indians are worse than the Indians. I know one who in order to win a fearsome name for himself made a barbaric human sacrifice in holocaust to a member of his family.

I will relate this deed.

Bargas is a bandit from Córdoba who, for what crimes I do not know, lives in Indian territory, is married to several women, and lives the life of an Indian or worse. One of his sons died. So, what does he do? He pretends to subscribe to the popular belief that calls for the deceased's favorite horse to be buried with him so that he will have a way to get around in the afterlife. But Bargas, instead of a horse, sacrifices an eight-year-old captive boy, buries him alive with his dead son, saying that now his son will have a peon to serve him.

It can be seen from the above that captives are regarded as things among the Indians. You can well imagine their condition. They are the saddest, the most unfortunate of all. Adult or adolescent, young boy or young girl, black or white—it makes no difference. It is the same for all of them until they can win the complete trust of the Indians and ingratiate themselves. Their first days in captivity are a true *via crucis*. They must wash, cook, cut firewood in the woods with their own hands, build corrals, break in colts, take care of the cattle, and serve the brutal pleasures of concupiscence.

Woe to those who resist!

They will shoot them or whip them to death.

Humility and resignation are their only recourse.

Nevertheless, I have known heroic women who refused to let themselves be defiled, women whose bodies chose martyrdom over surrender. One of these women was covered with scars, but she had not given in to the erotic furor of her master.

She told me the story of her life with angelical candor.

"I swore," she said, "not to give myself to an Indian until I found one I liked and I still haven't found him."

She was from San Luis and I have her name written down in Río Cuarto. The poor thing is no longer among the Indians. I was fortunate enough to ransom her and I sent her home.

There are terrible dramas in the barbarian's world.

The more captive women there are in a tent, the more frequent are the scenes that awaken and unleash the passions, degrading and debasing the human race. A new captive woman, be she old or young, pretty or ugly, must suffer not only the connivance of the Indian but, worse yet, the hatred and intrigue of the women who have preceded them, the hatred and intrigue of the head of the house's women, the hatred and intrigue of the other women and servants. Jealousy, envy, whatever at once chills and enflames the heart, is turned on them. So long as there is any fear that the new arrival will conquer the love or favor of the chief, the persecution goes on.

Women are always implacable with other women.

It often happens that the Indians will feel sorry for the new captives and protect them from the older ones and from the Indian women. Yet, this too only worsens the situation unless they take them as concubines.

A certain captive, whose life I was looking into, answered one of my questions as follows: "Before, when the Indian desired me, things went very badly for me, because the other captives and Indian women mortified me terribly. They would lay their hands on me in the hills and beat me. Now that the Indian doesn't want me any more, everything is all right. They are all my good friends."

Simple words that sum up the existence of the captive woman.

I will add that when an Indian tires of a woman or finds himself in pressing circumstances—or merely on a whim—he can sell her or give her away to whomever he pleases. If this happens, the captive enters a new period of suffering until time or death put an end to her troubles.

Shortly before leaving Leubucó I happened to meet a Christian who was trying to arrange for the purchase of a captive from an Indian, if only to do her a good and kindly deed.

"The Indian is a very good man," the poor woman told him. "He will sell me as long as they don't take me away from here, but the Indian women are vicious."

This idea of taking her away requires some explanation.

There are two ways of selling. One is simply by changing masters, the other is by redemption. The latter is more expensive.

As I am sure you understand, dear Santiago, I did not learn everything I have told you in this letter from my comadre Carmen. I owe part of it to her, the rest to others and to my own observations. What follows, however, I do owe exclusively to her.

The night was mild and clear, an inviting one for conversation, and we needed only the starlight and the moonlight to read. I seized the opportunity to take a lesson in Araucan. Finally I came to understand certain words whose meaning I had sought for some time, such as the Picunche, the Puelche, and Pehuenche Indians. *Che* is a word that, depending on its context, can mean "I," "man," or "inhabitant." The four cardinal points are called *puel*, north; *cuerró*, south; *picú*, east; *muluto*, west. Thus, Picunche means "inhabitant of the east," or of a certain part of the mountains. Puelche is "inhabitant of the north." Pehuenche, following the same rule, means "inhabitant of the pines," the name given to the Indians who live among the colossal pines on the western side of the Andes.

After my Araucan lesson I asked my teacher, who, though she

had children, was neither married nor a widow, to tell me her life story, and tell it she did. It was all about her adventures with a certain young man, the father of my goddaughter, and she told it like the simplest thing on earth. It makes for an off-color chapter that anywhere else in the world would come under the name seduction. Among the Indians it is one of life's accidents, that is all. It is meaningless. The human species is subject to the laws of reproduction. There is nothing strange about a woman giving herself to whomsoever she pleases and becoming pregnant as a result. The only difficulty lies in getting married, since generally nobody wants the burden of someone else's children, even when they come from a legitimate marriage.[1]

To conclude this chapter, and apropos of women who wake up one morning with children, let me mention what a peculiar pharmacopoeia the Indians have. Astringents, purgatives, and cold water—that is it in essence. The cold water is their remedy par excellence. No sooner does an Indian give birth than she and the fruit of her womb enter a lagoon together, whether in winter or summer.

One final word before I leave the fireside and go to bed. This is an extraneous observation perhaps of some interest to the medical world. My former classmate, Dr. Jorge Macías, who has spent two years among the Ranquels and would still be there were it not for me, maintains that there are no consumptives among them and attributes it to the diet of mare's meat. If this were borne out and its basis confirmed, we could exclaim from this day forward: no more consumptives.[2] I dare not say whether this merits further investigation. However, I do recall that not so long ago, any number of physicians laughed when the medicine women prescribed ostrich craw.

 NEXT DAY I rose with the early bright and concerned myself with preparations for the march to Baigorrita's tent settlement. I sent a messenger ahead as Mariano Rosas had suggested and at two in the afternoon ordered the horses rounded up. They had them saddled in a minute. It had been days since we had ridden and we were all eager to shake the laziness out of our bones.

Camargo was to accompany me. His mission would be to stay close to me and observe what I said to Baigorrita. For all his talk of adherence and like-mindedness, my brother Mariano harbored distrust. My journey troubled him. He could not understand why I should inconvenience myself with a trip to Baigorrita's settlement if I would be seeing him at the council in just four days' time. The idea that there might be a scheme afoot to start a quarrel between him and his ally preyed on his mind. Camargo would therefore accompany me with explicit orders to attend all of my parliaments and interviews. Under no circumstances was he to leave my side. He would be my shadow.

For all this, my excursion to Quenqué can be explained, and quite plausibly. Baigorrita had invited me some months before to be godfather to one of his sons. I was, then, going with the Franciscans to baptize my future godson and, at the same time, to better familiarize myself with the desert by penetrating to where only very rarely will someone of my circumstances be found, that is, someone on military duty. By the same token, Mariano Rosas did have his reasons for questioning this. Not once but several times different administrations have used frontier agents to attempt to sow discord between him and Baigorrita, or between these two and Chief Ramón. The memory of what happened with Coliqueo's tribe remains fixed in the minds of the Indians. This tribe was part of the confederation I have mentioned before. It fought against Buenos Aires at Cepeda but took the opposite side at Pavón and fought against Urquiza. Coliqueo is thus to the Indians the epitome of bad faith and perfidious dealings. "God will not help him," Mariano Rosas told me in conversation, "because he betrayed his brothers."[1]

With these credentials, and so many others that I could cite to make my point that our civilization has no right to be so rigid and severe with the savage, since not once but many times—this group today, that group tomorrow, and all of us alternately—we have armed him to help us exterminate one another in fratricidal fighting (witness Monte Caseros, Cepeda, and Pavón). With these credentials, I was saying, the precautions and fears of Mariano Rosas are easily understood. I therefore took heart when notified that Camargo would be accompanying us and gave Mariano my thanks. It was my intention to utilize frank and truthful diplomacy. I judged this a duty of conscience and an inflexible rule of conduct as a Christian, a name whose good standing I must endeavor at all costs to uphold. Consequently, I had nothing to fear from the vigilance of my shrewd attaché.

It was two-thirty in the afternoon when we moved out of Leubucó, as cheerful, content, happy, and hopeful as we had been upon leaving Fort Sarmiento.

I have never crossed the vast plains of the pampas without feeling my heart beat with pleasure, so bracing is the manly exercise of riding there. I will say it in all candor: I prefer the air of the desert with its sublime and poetic solitude to these boxed-in streets, this anthill of busy people, these circumscribed horizons that block the star-covered firmament—unless I look straight up—and deny me the thrill of the tempest when the luminous lightning twists and the thunder rolls.

It was a beautiful day.

We were going slowly. The horses had suffered enough and longed for their climate, their grass, and their water. I should have been thinking less about going back to Leubucó than about returning to my frontier. On the other hand, the mule I had was loaded with what little was left for Baigorrita, and the journey would be a short one. Heading south out of Leubucó there is sandy terrain followed by small dunes and, finally, hills. Beyond the hills there is the first water, a small lagoon with several ponds bordered by cattails and vibrant vegetation along the shores. The land here is lowlying and humid. It is some two leagues of travel but fatigues the horses as if it were four.

We rested a while. Nobody was hurrying us. Camargo held his first conference with me there. Man of the world that he was, he understood that his role was perforce a less-than-honorable one and saw fit to make this known to me, that I might better read his attitude. After all, he was in turn being spied on, though by whom he could not say.

Reciprocal espionage is the order of the day in the court of Leubucó. Several times when speaking with persons recently come to Mariano Rosas concerning matters of no grave importance, but which could lend themselves to misinterpretation, I was warned.

"Speak slowly, sir," they said. "That man over there is listening to us."

Who was it? Sometimes a dirty, slovenly Christian who was hanging around looking absentminded. Other times a poor, apparently insignificant Indian crouched in the warm sun, someone to whom I had spoken without getting a reply, though he spoke and understood Spanish. This odious practice breeds gossip and endless petty intrigue. It keeps everyone at odds with each other. Outwardly they all fraternize, but inwardly they bear a cordial hatred for each other. It is Mariano's way of knowing everything that goes on around him, near and far. The visitors he receives every day, many of them coming from the same tent and settlement, are his secret agents. They spy on others and they spy among themselves. The most pitiful-looking Indian will in fact be his confidant and know his secrets. Hence the influence, exemption, and favor enjoyed by the Negro with the accordion. No wonder I felt an instinctive repulsion for him.

We renewed our march on fresh mounts.

Gradually the terrain became more rolling. We crossed a series of small dunes which got steeper by degrees. We spied the crown of a hill and, farther off, towards the southwest, the heights of Poitaua, which means "place from which one peers," or watchtower. We began to feel the cool afternoon breezes. We galloped on and entered the hills. There were *chañar* trees, thistles, and carob trees, but mostly carobs. This is the most useful tree the Indians have. Its wood is excellent for fire and burns like coal. Its fruit fattens and fortifies the horses like no other feed, lending them admirable strength and power. It can be used to make a foamy and soporific punch, or to make *patai* when ground alone or a pleasant and nutritious meal when mashed with toasted corn. The Indians always carry pouches with carob pods in them. They suck them on long rides, just as the Coyas of Peru chew coca leaves. It is food and it replaces cigar smoking as something to do.

Speaking of cigars, dear Santiago, I will take this opportunity to tell you that the Indians love tobacco as much as they do firewater. They prefer Brazilian black tobacco to any other. The Pampas trade in it and the Chileans bring them something they call tobacco. It is a plant I have not yet seen as such but which I have smoked, and it has the same effect as opium, that is, extremely strong.

All Indians know how to smoke, just as they know to drink. They would consider anyone poorly raised who did not know how to smoke. They smoke tobacco three ways: in pure cigar form, as a cigarette, and in a pipe. The pipe is their favorite. There is no Indian who does not have his long-stem with him. They make them themselves and have an ingenious way of doing it. They take a piece of white wood about half a foot long and an inch in diameter. First they make it into a parallelepiped. Next they give it a cylindrical point, then they drill it. They make a small hole on one of the sides and put a thimble in it with another hole that meets the long one.

Anyone interested in making an Indian pipe now has instructions. I recommend this kind of pipe for all aficionados of strong tobacco. As soon as the resin goes through them, almost all tobaccos are the same.

The Indians ordinarily smoke only at night, before going to bed. They fill the pipe, lie on their bellies, put it in their mouths, drop a live ember into the bowl, and draw as long as they can, swallowing all the smoke. They do this again immediately and then a third time. On the fourth drag they are overcome by a kind of nauseous convulsion. The pipe drops out of their mouths and they fall fast asleep.

We left the hills, descending along a gentle slope toward a ravine. We intended to stop there and spend the night on the shores of a small lagoon called Pitralauquen, which means "lagoon of the flamingos." It gets its name from the abundance of these birds always found there. When we halted and dismounted, the sun was setting behind the heights of Poitaua and its corona bathed the clouds on the distant horizon. Circular and one hundred meters in diameter, the lagoon was full of water. Hundreds of pink flamingos, white geese and swans, brown ducks, and widgeons glided gently atop the liquid surface.[2]

The Indians do not customarily kill aquatic birds, nor were these disturbed by our approach.

We camped near some low-growing *chañar*. We gathered the horses together and put a rotating watch on them lest we get raided. We found firewood and soon a beautiful camp fire brightened the picture.

The Franciscans were a little worn out. Their one thought was to rest. Meanwhile, there was a good roast cooking, so, like true veterans, they stretched out on the soft straw. My assistants and I took a bath, startling the restful birds who flew off in every direction and whose nests we inhumanely looted to stock up on eggs. The first stars were out when we got out of the water. We dressed in a hurry because it was cool now. The fire was burning about five yards away from us. We got ourselves over there and directly stopped shivering.

We were soon eating and Mora, my interpreter, entertained us with stories of his adventures. I have already told you about him in an earlier letter and, if memory serves me well, I offered to tell you his life story.

Mora is a common enough kind of fellow. He is of average height. Your everyday observer could take him for a dimwit, but nothing could be farther from the truth. He is about as gaucho as they come: shrewd, resolute, trailwise. He has never been known to get lost in the open country. On the darkest night he marches straight to where he wants to go. If hesitant, he gets off his horse, grabs a handful of grass, tastes it, and knows where he is. He knows the winds by their smell. He has admirable retention and a very well developed phrenological sense of memory of place. He never forgets a face or a place. Only upon close study of his face can his Indian blood be detected. His father was Araucan, his mother Chilean. He came to the tent settlements as a boy with his father as part of a trade caravan. He fell in love with an Indian, got involved with her, decided he liked her people's way of life, and joined Ramón's tribe. His father had been an interpreter for a border chief in Chile, as well as a farm peon and a roadhouse keeper. He lived with the Christians.

Mora is industrious and hardworking, has children, loves his wife dearly, has some means, and would leave the desert if he could take all he has with him. But how? It would be a difficult if not impossible undertaking. Mora has been at my service for several months and has shown himself to be faithful and decisive. He is a man of fine sentiments and very rational ideas who realizes that civilized life is better than that of the desert. But, as I have said, he is bound to the desert for life by ties of family, love, and property. He speaks a perfect Chilean Spanish, knows Araucan well, and is one of the most intelligent interpreters I have seen. Interpreting is a difficult art because the Indians lack the equivalents of certain expressions of ours. The interpreter cannot translate literally, but rather freely, and to do so properly must have a penetrating mind. Take, for example, this phrase: "If you have a conscience you must have honor." It cannot be rendered literally; the Indians do not have the moral ideas implied by conscience and honor. As Mora explained it, a good interpreter would say, "If you have a heart, your word must be good," or "If you are a good person, you will not deceive me." Of course Mora, notwithstanding the favorable portrait I have made of him, is no tenderfoot when it comes to taking part in the Indian raids. On the contrary, he leads the charges, which is why he has something to live on. People work one way here, another way somewhere else, as he told me when I remonstrated him. He, a white man born to Christians and baptized in Los Angeles, a man who could live honorably, instead has the existence of a marauder.

When Mora finished telling what I have more or less recorded in the previous paragraph, we were almost done with supper.

It was freezing cold.

We made the beds with our feet towards the fire. I put the two friars next to me—I always treated them like the apple of my eye—and tried to sleep.

All creation was still. The silence of the desert went uninterrupted but for the odd whinnying of a horse or the honking of the birds in the lagoon. Studded with sorrowful stars, the firmament wore the rising moon's corona of light.

IV

I RONY CAN UNDERCUT BOMBAST. *The desert dystopia of ragged civil war fugitives, cattle raiders, captive women, and ban-
ished mixed-bloods all but lashes Mansilla's balloon of statesman-
like eloquence fast to the ground. He knows by the time he begins
his interim trip to the neighboring chief Baigorrita's settlement in
Chapter 42 that the flights of oratory will be few and their effect
negligible. When he does open all his valves, the Indians go to sleep
on him. He is self-effacing enough to smile at this lesson, but it may
also have implications that sting. Mansilla cannot have helped but
to hope for a political impact beyond what the clarification of details concerning the delivery of horses and distribution of provisions might yield him. His constant reading in political philosophy
alone would drive him to greater heights than that. Yet the irony
with which every broken story he hears is imbued will not allow
any bust-atop-a-pillar aesthetics to falsify the narration. Were this
not so, clearly Mansilla would have hurried the story to the great
hilltop council in which he sits down to confer face-to-face with
Chief Mariano Rosas.*

*Persuaded by what he had found in the desert to cast his narra-
tive as only an apologist could, he knew that* les miserables *must
be seated at his table if the whole effort was to amount to anything
at all. The gamble was that the readers would care more for the
Indians, gauchos, and captives peopling the story — they were, after all, future Argentine citizens, or so Mansilla hoped — than for
the naysayers in the military high command and the legislature
who wanted the whole desert mess wiped clean once and for all. In
this respect, the mere appearance of Mansilla's newspaper accounts
dealt a first blow to the mentality of denial. Whether it is the dis-
reputable quadroon who spies for Chief Calfucurá but wins Mansilla's patronizing sympathy, or the forgotten flamingos and curlews of the Pitralauquen Lagoon, the printed transmission of a*

*complex, if derelict, frontier world finally comprises a canvas that
cannot be hidden from view.*

*There was a notion in the minds of many of the citizens of
Buenos Aires that the barbarian hordes would soon tear down the
city gates. For his part, Mansilla locates real barbarism in poverty,
cruelty, dissoluteness, and neglect. Still, the subtleties of character-
ization require that he qualify his judgments of character. What is
first heard and learned at night by camp-fire light feeds the percep-
tions that will empower the best discourse. It is an infinitely suggestive ambiguity about the Christians and the Indians that sustains the writer, not the preconceptions or certainties he — or the
reader — may bring to the scene.*

IT WAS SO COLD that even with the fire burning
all night I could not sleep. I tossed and turned.
How I envied my soldiers. They were curled up
like armadillos far from the fire, snoring away.
Life eventually becomes one vast game of
making do. I had plenty of covers and someone to stir the fire all
night long and could not sleep. They scarcely had anything to cover
themselves with and slept on like a bunch of holy men.

It felt like the night would never end.

I got everybody moving with the first light. I had them take the
horses on a warm-up walk, and as soon as the sun began to warm
us they would lead them down to the lagoon. I ordered the fire built
up bigger. They put water on to boil and started cooking some
steaks. We had tea and ate breakfast.

The ground shone bright and silvery on its surface. It had gotten
very cold and the frost was four lines thick in the dampest places.
With the sun came a pampa north wind[1] and the fog began to lift
in all directions. Gradually the frost burnt off. The sun beamed its
way through the watery veil that in vain sought to stop it. The solar
disk, cause and effect of all that constitutes the planet we live on,
was dissipating the very phenomenon it had helped originate.

It was now eight in the morning and the sky and horizon were
completely clear. The horses drank. We saddled up, mounted, and
headed south along the Quenqué trail, leaving the one to Calfucurá's settlement off to our left. We galloped until the animals
broke a sweat. It was all uphill through sandy underbrush. Then

we descended into a more hazardous zone before discovering off to the east the first tents of Baigorrita's tribe and a scattered few horses and cows. I called a halt, lest we frighten the vigilant and untrusting denizens of those parts, who, swift as the wind, rode straight to within rifle shot of us to look us over.

I sent Mora out to meet them. He spoke with them and instantly they came back with him to greet and welcome me. They knew nothing of my visit to Baigorrita's, but realizing that just days before I had arrived in Leubucó, they had figured it must be me by the order and manner of my approach. They had spotted me from the moment we first kicked up dust in Pitralauquen. The Indians are like the gauchos when it comes to picking things out at great distances. They sight objects with never an error and can distinguish perfectly between dust from a runaway animal and dust from running riders. When confused as to whether an object is moving towards them or not, they have a simple way of resolving their doubt. They take a knife by the handle, place it perpendicularly on their nose and guide their eyes along the blade, which serves as their visual reference point. If the object deviates from that point it is not stationary and must therefore be a tree, a bush, a cattail, or a thistle, whose proportions always increase in space with the erratic effects of light.[2]

This *carda*, by the way, is perhaps a species of cactus. It grows up to fifteen feet and produces green, granular acorns something like berries. You can find a little caterpillar inside the dry ones that is in fact the chrysalis of the horsefly. The *carda* is a great resource in the open country. Its wood is not strong but does burn admirably. It is like tinder. When the berries burn they form delightful little globules that look like fireworks and are a consummate delight to the imagination. You can watch a *carda* fire hours on end, as the insatiable flames devour all the wood you can throw them. The incandescent acorns gleam and vanish like diamonds in the quick-burning fire.

The *carda* has another recondite virtue. When the parched and weary traveler finds a leafy *carda*, he stops there like an Arab at a cool oasis. He pulls a stem and in the alveolar ridge between the leaves he can always find drops of fresh, pure crystalline water, the evening dew sheltered there from the unkind rays of the sun.

I spoke for a moment with the new visitors and after giving them tea, sugar, tobacco, and paper, marched on as they cut away from our party and headed for their tents.

We galloped a while until arriving at a densely forested hill with century-old trees. The brushfires had ravaged those giants. Some were carbonized from trunk to top and would crumble into a thousand pieces at the slightest push. I found good grass and decided to rest there. As it turned out, I would have been stuck there for some time regardless. It seems that a skittish mule was startled by the sound of a half-burnt stump that somebody knocked down when trying to pull a bough out of it for a fire to heat water. The mule took off and so did the horses. In the time it took to get them all together again we managed to have a few mates.

We changed mounts and as we were halfway to Quenqué and it was early, I went on with the march through the forest. It took us a good hour to get through. We came to lowlands, crossed a saltpeter field, and just then spotted dust clouds coming our way from some distant dunes. We reached them soon enough. Some of Baigorrita's people had come out to welcome me. We halted, sent our respective parliamentarians forward, exchanged a great many reasons, and took off again at a gallop as one group.

More dust clouds from the same direction told us that Baigorrita was now coming. He had some fifty riders with him. We were even with Caniupán's home. He was the Ranquel friend we had met at the border. He was a soft-spoken Indian and a gentleman, and one of the few of his kind who does not beg for everything his eyes happen upon.

Baigorrita used neither Ramón's imposing ceremonies nor Mariano Rosas's fastidious preambles. As soon as we could see each other's faces we stopped.

He came out alone, as did I.

We spurred our horses at the same time and casually embraced and shook hands, as if it were the thousandth time we had met. The group coming and the group going came together to form one. Baigorrita and I rode and conversed. A Chilean named Juan de Dios San Martín, of whom I shall speak later, was his interpreter. Mora was mine.

Baigorrita speaks no Spanish and scarcely understands any.

In another half hour we were at his tent, where some people had gathered to await us. Everyone greeted both me and my people with warmth and respect.

There is nothing to say in particular about Baigorrita's tent. It was smaller than Mariano Rosas's and bare. We entered. My compadre could not be called the paragon of cleanliness. There was at least one of everything God created in there: mice, bedbugs, fleas, and something worse yet. Every so often I would come upon some hapless little critter crawling in my clothes looking for some blood to suck. This is nothing new to a soldier. I took each one and quietly pulverized it.

We had a long and dreary conference. My compadre introduced me to his principal captains and to several elderly Indians considered important for the experience contained in their counsel. I spread some trinkets before them as gifts. To my compadre I gave my six-shooter, some Crimean shirts, breeches, and stockings. To my godson I gave two gold coins. The Franciscans and my assistants also presented gifts. The reception was so cordial and simple that everyone got along quite nicely.

After the greetings and official presentations came the conversation, with its liberal sprinkling of adages and witticisms. One very jovial and amusing Indian, an ancient, beloved, and revered friend of Baigorrita's deceased father Pichún, and every bit of sixty himself, saw that I had something covering my hands that he had never seen.

"What is that, *che*?" he asked in good Spanish.

They were my thick, beaver-skin gloves. I held them in the highest esteem. I have a weakness for taking excessive care of my hands. I was momentarily at a loss for an answer. If I said gloves, he would no more understand me than if I said *matracas*. I puzzled over the answer.

"Boots for my hands," I finally said.

The Indians eyes lit up as if he had made a discovery.

"Them nice. Good," he added, grabbing my two hands with his. I pulled one away, unbuttoned the glove, and with his help pulled it off.

He immediately put it on.

I did the same with the other one and gave it to him. He put that one on, too. His hands were smaller than mine and the gloves looked like mittens on him, something like the ones you can see hanging in the armory windows. The Indian looked like a monkey opening and closing his hands and was delighted. I let him enjoy them for a while and when it seemed to me he had worn my gloves long enough I asked him to give them back.

"Not giving," he answered.

This was not in my book of tricks. If I lost my gloves it would certainly ruin my hands.

"I will buy them from you," I said, seeing that he had closed his hands to hold on to his prize better. He shook his head no. I reached into my pocket, took out a pound sterling, and offered it to him, thinking I could awaken his greed. He took it but did not give me the gloves.

"Give me the boots for the hands," I said.

"Not selling," he said, "taking to council like Christian."

"Then giving back pound sterling," I said.

"Me poor Indian, you rich Christian," he answered.

And with that he kept the pound sterling and made a monkey of me. Everybody present hailed the Indian's trick with spontaneous laughter.

"What an old devil, eh?" said my compadre Baigorrita.

I had to bow to circumstance and declare myself a neophyte in matters of legerdemain.

The visitors began to leave a few at a time. I was tired and for certain reasons had to change clothes. I left the tent without ceremony. There were a lot of people outside, chatting gaily with my party as they went about threshing some carob beans. There were two harvests for the winter.

I was hungry. I called the Chilean, Juan de Dios San Martín, and said, "Tell my compadre to skin a cow for these people to eat," as if I were at my closest friend's cattle ranch. He was back in an instant. The cow was on its way. Soon two Indians brought over a lassoed cow. The women dressed it out, giving the lion's share to my people. The fire was on.

Rather than spend the night in my compadre's tent, I chose to sleep out in the open. Evening was near. His women rounded up the tamer cattle on foot. The dogs that went along with them were as skinny as they were big and were hard to miss. The sheep and goats were mixed together. When they got to the door of the corrals, the dogs separated the different animals and the Indian women the flocks, enclosing each in its respective pen. They carried the operation off like a child picking its favorite black and white beads out of a basket. Whenever a goat or lamb wound up in the wrong flock, the dogs would drive it back to its own.[3]

They announced that the roast was ready. I finished changing and took my place around the fire. As I sat down I saw a deathly face cross in front of me. It looked like an Indian.

Who was it?

 **44** LIFE PASSES UNNOTICED.
It is but the road to death, as the Arabian proverb has it. When we least expect it, winter is upon us and only then do we see, like the improvident grasshopper, that we have sung the summer blithely away.

Once our hair knew the playful touch of fine, ivory hands but now it has gone white. No one touches it anymore. Our eyes have lost their magnetic shine. Nobody looks into them. Our smooth, rosy skin is dry and sallow parchment. Nobody notices it. The flame burning in our hearts has scarcely the glow of a pale, sepulchral lamp, but then who could draw warmth from its feeble flicker? We have aspired but accomplished nothing for ourselves or for humanity. We have consumed an exuberant, robust existence, while numberless fortunate parasites fed on our substance and cried, "*En vain, hélas en vain.*"

Our one consolation: the ironic farewell we at last grant the world as we depart. Our epitaph:

> *Ci-gît Pirou, qui ne fut rien,*
> *Pas même académicien.*

If that is how a life must be spent, then how much more obliviously do we spend any given night.

My first night in Quenqué, in the open air and near my compadre Baigorrita's tent, was one of those nights. I don't believe I recall a single bit of it. I only know that I slept. My weary body felt nothing of the night air, no hard ground, no starving, restive dogs crunching the bones and leftovers of our fire, biting through them till their sharp teeth should find the hidden marrow.

The Indians do not feed their dogs, and yet they have many of them. There is a pack for every tent. The poor animals eat what creatures they can catch or, like the ostriches, what flies they can snatch from the air. It is unbelievable how hunger hones their skill at this. Just let a fly buzz anywhere near their noses; it will end up in their stomachs. They are very harshly treated. They are covered with bumps or, if not, have worm-eaten scars, their reward for going near a camp fire or skulking up to a butchered cow, if only to suck its spilled blood off the ground. Only the Indian women have any compassion for them. The dogs are their inseparable companions. They follow them to the hills and to the water. They round up cattle with them. They sleep beside them. Never do the dogs follow the men. The feast they had at my campfire has probably become legendary among them. Right now they are doubtless singing canine hymns in that same hoarse language they use to bay at the moon, or to worship it; hymns to the splendid generosity of certain strangers of unknown visage and raiment who spoke an unintelligible but pleasant tongue and who once passed this way.

Morning broke.

We said good morning to the Franciscans, arose, drank some mate, and prepared to welcome our visitors, who for their part did not keep us waiting.

My compadre Baigorrita had bathed very early. He was standing barefoot with his breeches rolled up over his knees and his sleeves pulled up, clipping a horse that was tied to a post. I approached him, said hello, and without interrupting what he was doing he returned an affable smile. Juan de Dios San Martín was around, and Baigorrita had him tell me to make myself at home. I thanked him. With one last snip of the scissors he invited me into his tent.

I accepted and we entered. Three fires were burning. The Indian women and captives were using them to make our lunch, which was stew and roast beef. My compadre and I took our seats facing each other. The visitors began to arrive. They formed two rows and the small talk was soon under way.

They were all people of a certain importance. As Juan de Dios San Martín was not a good enough interpreter, another Christian completely trusted by Baigorrita was called in. It was essential that all those present be well informed of my reasons. Juancito was the new expert's name. He came in and took his place between my compadre and me with his back to the entrance to the tent. He was a nappy-haired *zambo* about seven feet tall and fat as a greased turkey. He wore only simple Pampa breeches. His face bore the unmistakable marks of the grossest animal instincts. All of his features were deformed and he had plucked all his facial hairs out Indian-style and painted his lips and cheekbones. His eyes were lively but showed no ferocity.

I gave him my first reasons and he tried to translate them. He could not do it. His ears had never heard as cultured a language as mine and mind you I was making every effort to keep it utterly simple. He did not understand the first word of it. When he conveyed my reasons to Baigorrita, Camargo and Juan de Dios San Martín interjected.

"The Colonel didn't say that."

The visitors were growing impatient. They grumbled at the *zambo*. Ashamed and chagrined by his own imbecility, he was wringing his hands. His face and hands perspired as if he were in a sweat lodge. They gave off a peculiar, and revolting, greasy odor. When his confusion reached its peak, he went into a kind of concentrated furor and clammed up. Then, suddenly, he said, "I am no use here" and got up and left.

Nobody had a word to say about it.

The conversation continued as the other interpreters took up the slack. My compadre's wives, the Indian and captive women got moving and lunch was served. Each person was given an enormous wooden plateful of boiled meat, broth, squash, and corn, just as we had at Mariano Rosas's. I ate *sans façon*, adopting what postures suited me best. Figuring that what I was about to do would make a good impression on the man of the house and the guests, I took off my boots and stockings, took out the knife I carried on my waist, and began to cut my toenails quite as though I were alone in my own room doing my morning routine.

My compadre and his guests were delighted. This Christian colonel acted like an Indian. What more could they ask for? I was going native, assimilating to them. It was barbarism conquering civilization. The Lucius Victorius, Imperator, of the dream I had in Leubucó the night Mariano Rosas made me drink the horn full of firewater stood transfigured. When I finished the toenail-cutting procedure, I cleaned my fingernails, and to top the whole thing off picked my teeth clean with the knife.

They brought out the roast, water, and hand rags. Instead of using the house knife, I used my own. The Indian from the day before showed up wearing my gloves, sat down beside me, and decided he would play with my goatee, saying he most certainly was going to braid it. "It's pretty," he said. I let him have his fun.

After lunch they brought in some bottles of firewater and, *yapaí* come and *yapaí* go, we polished them off.

My godson, whom I had fondled the day before, came up to me. I stroked him. One of the captives spoke to him in his language and the little boy joined his hands and, flush with embarrassment, said, "Blessing."

"May God make you a good Christian, godson," I said. I reached for him and sat him on my knee, and he became as meek as a choirboy. I took out my watch and placed it next to his ear so he could hear the ticktock of the wheels. He didn't move. I put the watch back in my pocket. Then I noticed that certain tiny millipedic animals were walking on his head, so I began to delouse him.

I realize, dear Santiago, that these are hardly philosophical or instructive details. But what do you want, my friend? If I have no deeds of martial valor to sing to you, let me describe plainly all that I did and saw among the Ranquels. The cleanly and respectable public will kindly indulge me this, unless, as is only rarely the case, it prefers a lie to the truth.

Rien n'est beau que le vrai.

I will drag that saying in here and carry on with my story.

My godson was used to this operation. The Indians do it for one another, when the sun is going down, with an appendage which I will leave it to your perspicacity to guess.

There is no rule book of good taste, is there? A raw oyster is the tastiest of morsels to some. Vitelio would eat forty-two at a sitting to whet his appetite.[1] Some go for cheese that stinks and prefer the kind that walks. Still others cannot get either one down. So let us not wonder at the Indians' custom. I will repeat it ad nauseam: our civilization has no right to be proud. In Santiago del Estero, where the language and customs have a primitive flavor, the poor do the same thing as the Indians. Anyone wishing to see it need only take the northern mail stage and ride around that Argentine province. They do it in the Córdoba sierra as well, which is closer. That would be the more picturesque excursion.

My godson fell asleep. I rested his head on one of my thighs and let him be. The visitors were beginning to retire. Some lay down and went to sleep. Following my plan to make myself interesting, I did the same, but how was I actually going to sleep? Impossible! Bodies foreign to my own had me indescribably agitated. Still, I stayed in the tent pretending to sleep. I snored. My compadre ordered silence. The sight of me must have pleased him.

Suddenly I called for Rufino Pereyra in a weak and tremulous voice. He didn't answer; he could not hear me, nor did I think he would. Then, affecting great anger, I bolted up and shouted at the top of my lungs, "Rufino! Rufino!"

"I'm coming, sir," he called from a distance before coming flying into the tent.

"Why didn't you come sooner?" I asked.

"I didn't hear you."

I reprimanded him.

My compadre was calmly smoking his pipe surrounded by his three youngest children, who were sleeping. He looked at me as if saying to himself: Now here is a man. My contrasts were winning him over. Gentleness, harshness, ease, and irascibility speak highly to the savage mind.

"Bring me my shaving razor," I said to Rufino.

He left the tent.

"Compadre," I went on, turning to my host, "I am going to make a present to you. I see that you shave."

Not understanding me, he said nothing. The interpreters had retired. He called Juan de Dios San Martín, who came in with Rufino, who in turn had the straight razor and the four-sided strop for it, one of which was stone. I took it, showed him how to use the strop, gave both pieces to him. He took them and put them into a pocket on his leather sash after checking to see that it fit.

I left the tent. I changed clothes after Carmen helped me get rid of the intruders who had taken cover in my hair. I went for a walk because I needed to breathe the pure, free country air. I shot at some vultures and lapwings and after a while went back to the camp fire so that I could finally dissipate the effects of the firewater with some coffee. On the way I passed behind my compadre's tent and there saw, once again, the deathly face from the day before, resting with somber aspect against the side of the ranch—the kitchen, in fact—which stood out a couple of feet. There was another, younger face there with it, a strange and markedly Christian one. Curiosity drew me to them.

I spoke to them. They were silent.

"You don't understand?" I said, somewhat acridly. They answered me in Indian language. I could see they did not wish to speak to me, but the incident had sparked my curiosity. I cannot say why, but that first face definitely alarmed me. I went on my way, fully intending to find out who these strangers were. I entered my compadre's tent. He was alone with his children in the same position in which I had left him a while ago. He was cutting tobacco. And with what? Why, with the straight razor I had just given to him. What else?

He was using the strop to set the razor in.

That's what you get, I said to myself, for lavishing gifts on the uncouth. My compadre beamed a pleased and beatific smile my way as he regarded himself in the terse and lustrous surface of the blade.

"Nice," he said.

"True," said I, mumbling, "you won't cut your throat with it, either." I made a gesture with my hands like I was shaving and told him it was better for that. He understood but had an answer.

"Knife," meaning that the knife was more suitable for shaving. He called Juan de Dios San Martín.

I took my leave and went to tell my assistants and the Franciscans what had become of Rodgers's razor.[2]

 THERE WAS NOBODY at the camp fire. Everybody was behind the kitchen, the one place where there was no sun.

I was looking for someone whom I might tell about how my compadre Baigorrita had put my fine straight razor to use. So I went in search of my fellow pilgrims. I found them talking to two strangers. I took them aside, they formed a ring with me in the middle, and I told them the story, laughing out loud. "Bunch of animals," a few of them said, and after a moment of hilarity I asked who the men were they were talking to.

"We don't know," said some.

"We were trying to find out," said the Franciscans.

"Let's see about this," said I.

I walked over to them. The rest followed me.

"What's your name?" I asked the first one I had seen. He was a quadroon, maybe forty years old and tawny. He had a frightening face with great, black lackluster eyes, a flat nose with hairs coming out of the nostrils, a large mouth with a sardonic smile, and two rows of enormous, separated, crocodile teeth. All this was enclosed in an oval that began with a narrow, tapering brow under thick, hard hair that stood up like porcupine quills, and ended in a pointed chin turned slightly upward. He was fat and had not a single wrinkle in his skin. He wore a gold earring on his left ear, and had plucked his mustache and beard with tweezers, Indian-style, which had allowed the thinnest film of dust to enter the irritated pores, so that when he perspired, his unfriendly face looked much like it would have if he had had it tattooed with tiny pins and Indian ink. He wore rags, went barefoot, and on his callused feet his huge, encrusted nails stood out like fossil shells on limestone. He did not answer, but he turned his vague gaze on me.

I questioned him again.

Saying nothing, he lowered his eyes and stared at the ground. He drew his neck down between his shoulders as if to say, I don't know, what do you care?

"You're some kind of troublemaker, I'll bet," I said.

I turned to the younger one. "And who are you?" I said.

He looked like a quadrumana, a monkey dressed as a gaucho. He too had shaved in the Indian fashion. His clothes were new and of good quality. He was perhaps eighteen years old.

"I am Major Colchao's son," he answered.

"Major Colchao's son?" I answered, surprised.

A captive had approached our group. "He is my husband," she said.

"Your husband?"

"Yes, sir."

"How so?"

"The chief married us."

She proceeded to tell me she was from San Luis and had for some time been married to a very bad Indian. When he was killed in the last Ranquel invasion of Río Quinto, when I defeated them at Pozos Cavados, Baigorrita had given her to Major Colchao, one of El Chacho's rebel soldiers who had hidden out in Indian territory. She said that Colchao was a good man and that now she was happy.[1]

"Look here," she said. "Look what the Indian did to me."

She showed her arms and bosom, which were covered with hardened bruises and scars. "That's why," she added, her expression a mixture of candor and cruelty, "I prayed to God that Indian would throw up everything he ate. He had a bullet wound in his neck and everything came back out through it, but with the fluids in there and all . . ."

This unfortunate woman was making me sick. Her eyes were very beautiful, however, and there was an alluring lubricity to her face. She was slender and comely. Rather than let her go on with the repugnant story of her oppressor's agony, I asked her about Major Colchao.

"Who is he?" I said.

"You must have seen him, sir. He was the one who roped the cow we skinned and butchered."

I had taken him for an Indian. He was an insignificant man in whom my compadre had great trust. Colchao worked as his foreman.

"And you say this boy is Colchao's son?" I asked her.

"Yes, sir."

"And where do you live?" I asked the boy.

"In Estanislao's camp."

"Is that near here?"

"No, sir."

"How far?"

"A day's ride" (about thirty leagues in conventional Indian distances).

"And do you know that man?" I said, pointing to the quadroon.

"Yes, sir."

"Since when?"

"For three days."

"That's all?"

"Yes, sir."

"You just met him somewhere?"

"On the trail on my way here."

"Where were you coming from?"

"From Estanislao's tent."

"Whereabouts does that lie?"

"Over there" (pointing southeast).

"How was he traveling?"

"On horseback."

"How many horses?"

"Just the one he was riding."

"And where was he coming from?"

"From Calfucurá's."

"Is that the way over there?"

"That's it."

"And how many days does it take to get from Estanislao's to Calfucurá's?"

"Two and a half."

"Does that man speak Spanish?"

"Yes, sir."

Here I interrupted my conversation with Colchao's son and turned to the other man.

"So you've been playing dumb, eh?"

He said nothing.

"Say something, you idiot," I said.

"I'm ashamed to," he answered.

"You're probably some bandit," I replied. Then, with my back to him I lowered my voice and spoke to my helpers. "Check out his story."

I was going to leave but then an essential question occurred to me.

"Where are you from?" I asked him.

"Patagones."

"Aha," said Rodríguez, one of my assistants, "you told me a minute ago you were Chilean."

"He told me he was from Bahía Blanca," said someone else.

"He's some kind of troublemaker, for sure," I said. I started for my compadre's tent. He was right where I had left him, same posture, still cutting tobacco with the razor and talking to Juan de Dios San Martín. I sat down and had the interpreter ask him who the stranger was. He said he did not know. He had seen him but figured he was one of my people. Juan de Dios San Martín said he had not noticed any such man. I told my compadre that I wondered how he could take such a bum for one of my men. He shrugged his shoulders and ordered San Martín to find out who he was, where he came from, and what he wanted. San Martín left.

I stretched out on the floor as I would on a spongy sofa. My compadre went on cutting his tobacco unperturbed. We remained silent while San Martín found out what we wanted to know. He was my compadre's spokesman, his secretary, friend, servant, and confidant. He was in Río Cuarto several times as Baigorrita's representative. He is a Chilean *roto*, quick as greased lightning, sly, soft-spoken. He knows how to back off or lean on you as needed. He is thirty years old and can read and write perfectly well. He had several books, among them a treatise on geography. Faces like his are commonplace, unnoteworthy. He is a pure-blooded white man. He claims he is with the Indians in order to ransom certain relatives of his from Mendoza. This may or may not be true. I only know that among the women captives Mariano Rosas sent me in Río Cuarto, and whom I turned over to Father Burela, there was one who was seventeen and who claimed to be his cousin. She was very grateful to him. San Martín also appeared to be much enamored of a little fourteen-year-old girl who had *already* been my compadre's lover. He had sold her to San Martín, who said he would leave the Indian settlements as soon as he finished paying for her. She could be seen around there. She was pretty and reportedly very much a wide-eyed innocent. She was from Mendoza and dressed exactly like an Indian. Her fairness stood in dramatic contrast to her slovenliness. She laughed and played with all my assistants with infantile abandon and her "master" was not concerned about it.

Doubtless the life-or-death control he held over her allowed him this confidence. It is a barbaric institution; surely no one would deny it. Yet one must acknowledge that no one kills out of jealousy among the Indians. Moreover, infidelity is extremely rare.

As long as I am waiting for San Martín to bring back the news he has gone after, it occurs to me I might pose a question.

The virtue of conjugal fidelity, which cannot be conventional but rather must have as its basis one sentiment, love, where is it more secure, among the Ranquels or among the Christians?

I will keep my answer quite to myself.

I believe I will wait for San Martín, dear Santiago, and call your attention meanwhile to the kinds of people who take refuge among the Indians. You tell me. With secretaries, interpreters, and intimate friends of the sort I have just sketched for you, do you suppose the Indians know the Christians, their ideas, tendencies, and projects? Theirs is a world truly worthy of study. They live virtually on top of us, pounding at the door like Rome's enemy at her direst hour, and what do we know about them? That they rob us. That is enough, but it is hardly news to this country. You might as well say, "There is civil war in Entre Ríos." The public mind knows it, cannot see it but feels it. The public mind has a different question. What remedy will reconcile, with the least bloodshed, the fact of war with the right to make war? And why this question? Because so long as you show the public mind the cutting edge of a sword, human clemency will be justified in crying, "Fratricide!"

San Martín returned with word that the stranger came from Calfucurá's camp. My compadre was not in the least surprised.

"How come you don't keep an eye on the people coming and going and staying in your house days at a time?" I asked.

"Anybody who wants to come here can, compadre," he answered.

"And what if they are here to spy?"

"What is there to spy on?"

"Why, the things you do."

"We have been doing the same thing all our lives."

I made a sign to San Martín. He followed me out of the tent. My compadre kept on with his tobacco. He still had a roll from Tucumán to cut. San Martín had served me loyally on other occasions. I told him to find out more about the stranger and he left. No sooner was he gone than Father Marcos came to tell me that the stranger wanted a shirt and some breeches, herb, tobacco, and paper.

I had run out of everything, but where there are soldiers there are generous hearts. I called an assistant and told him to ask all his friends till he found a shirt and breeches, and whatever else the stranger wanted. He called a meeting, asking this one for one thing, someone else for another. He asked one for tea, the other for sugar, tobacco, and paper, and came back immediately with everyone's donation. I gave it all to Father Marcos, and the good Franciscan went away content, taking everything to his protégé.

I sat down to rest on a divan that the soldiers improvised for me out of saddle bags and ponchos. I was just nodding off when I heard horses approaching and the voice of a drunken Indian.

"Where him Colonel Mansilla?" he asked.

He was talking to the men standing behind the kitchen.

"Over there," they answered.

An Indian rode up, all but trampling me under his horse's hooves. I recognized him at once. It was Caiomuta, and seeing that he was drunk I affected contempt for him and said nothing.

"You, Colonel Mansilla," shouted the barbarian, digging his spurs viciously into the horse, breasting him and raising a cloud of dust that engulfed me. I thought he was going to run over me. Saying nothing, I rose to my feet and prepared to defend myself.

"You Colonel Mansilla," he again shouted.

"Yes," I answered dryly.

"Ahhhhh!" he said.

I remained silent and, as he backed off several steps, I advanced on him, covering my front with the fire from a burning pile of firewood that stood as an obstacle between us.

"You Indian friend?" he said.

"Yes," I answered and stepped forward to extend him my hand.

He refused it. "Me give friend hand no more."

"I am your friend."

"Why measuring land then with round gualicho?"

"Round gualicho" was my mariner's compass, which I had used countless times in crossing from Río Quinto to Leubucó.

"It is not for measuring land," I told him.

"You lying," he answered.

"I don't lie."

"Then what round gualicho doing?"

"I used it to find the way. It tells me which way is north."

"Why doing that if have road and scout?"

"Because I like to know right where I am going when I am out in the country."[2]

"*Winca! Winca!*" he muttered. Then, leading his horse in concentric circles so as to show off its reins and his skill, he let out a yell.

"Lying!"

Several Indians rode up, spoke at the same time, and surrounded me. "Giving shirt," they said.

"I don't have one," I answered dryly.

Caiomuta, his eyes full of malice, brought his horse nearly on top of me. Only with difficulty did he manage to stay on the horse.

"You rich, so give to poor Indian," he said.

"I do not give to anyone who is not my friend," I answered, frowning at him and calling him a barbarian. He drew back on his horse as though preparing to run me over. I stepped back. My helpers and assistants arrived and surrounded me.

"*Winca! Winca!*" roared the Indian.

Just then Juan de Dios San Martín showed up. He told me Baigorrita had said I should pay his brother no mind and that I should come to his tent. He then offered a personal remark.

"That is one deep-down rotten Indian, sir."

I felt it indecorous to abandon the battlefield. I told my compadre not to worry. Caiomuta took another gurgling gulp from a flask of firewater he held in his right hand. Spurring the horse, he shouted insults to Baigorrita, calling him a thief and summoning the others to follow him. Then he fairly shot away over sands where it seemed impossible that a horse could run.

Rather than await a second dialogue, I started for my compadre's tent, but then saw that Father Marcos was with the stranger. I circled widely once then went up to them.

"So where are you actually from," I asked, "Chile, Patagones, or Bahía Blanca?"

He gave no reply.

"So you've got tongue enough to talk when it comes to begging things off of us but not when I ask you a question?"

"I haven't begged anything," he answered for the first time and with a Buenos Aires accent.

"You're too damn proud," I said. "I should take everything back I gave you."

"Take it. It's right here," he said with contempt.

I got away from there. This man was making my blood boil. I went into my compadre's tent. He was still cutting his tobacco. He motioned for me to take a seat. I sat down. They brought me the stew pot. I ate. They served my compadre lamb's kidney, hot and raw, and some cold, cooked lung seasoned with onion and salt. He offered me a bite. I accepted. The kidney was inedible. It stank like volatile alkali. But I chewed it, trying not to make faces, and I swallowed it. The lung was passable, though I would prefer never to try it again.

There being no interpreters, we exchanged only occasional words. I took the opportunity to observe the physiognomy of this impassive tobacco chopper, this patriarch of sorts. Manuel Baigorria, alias Baigorrita, is thirty-two years old. He takes his name from his baptismal godfather, a gaucho from San Luis who lived in Indian territory in Chief Pichún's time and was great friends with the chief. Baigorrita's mother was a captive from El Morro. She still lived there not so long ago. She had been rescued though I am not sure when. Baigorrita is of medium size and has predominantly Spanish looks. He has big, round, shining black eyes, a turned-up nose, a regular mouth, thick lips, and a short, wide chin. Were he slightly different-looking, he could be an Arab.

He is quite a ladies' man, a gambler, and he is poor. He has a reputation for being both brave and gentle and enjoys military prestige among the Indians. His habits are simple. In nothing is he ostentatious, not even in outfitting his horse. Several times he spoke tenderly of his mother and expressed his wish to go to Morro to visit his relatives.

Caiomuta is his younger brother on his father's side. He and Caiomuta are enemies. Caiomuta is rich, as crooked as Cato, as drunk as Bacchus, and as bad as Satan. He is insolent, violent, audacious, generally hated. Yet he is strong, for there is a small circle of scoundrels who follow him blindly and help him perpetrate his iniquity.

I was concluding my study of my compadre's facial traits when San Martín came in. He exchanged a few words in Araucan with Baigorrita and, after drawing me aside to say he had something to tell me, he withdrew.

"See you later," I said to Baigorrita, who, without interrupting his tobacco chopping, answered with an "Adió." (Like the Negroes, the Indians generally drop the final *s*.) I went to see what San Martín wanted.

"Sir," he told me as soon as I got near him, "the man is a spy for Calfucurá."

"And what is he after?"

"He came to see what you are doing here. Over there they are afraid you are going to set these Indians against those Indians."

"And did you tell Baigorrita this when you spoke with him just now?"

"No, sir."

"Well, alert him."

San Martín obeyed. I stayed and pondered the cautious foresight of Calfucurá, the great politician and warrior of the pampas, as feared for his power as he is for his wisdom. News of my arrival at the Ranquel settlements had reached him through Mariano Rosas, who had also consulted him as an ally by reason of kindred race. He had answered that peace was desirable and that there should be no hesitancy in sealing and keeping it.

At the same time he had sent a secret emissary.

Would learned statesmen have proceeded differently?

Is modern diplomacy more sincere and less untrusting?

You, Santiago, live in Europe, birthplace and governing seat of Richelieu, Mazarin, Walpole, Alberoni, Talleyrand, and Metternich. Europe, source of our standards.

You tell me.

 THE DAY HAD been rich in impressions. The sweet, melancholy afternoon was passing. The sun's fire no longer burned. The evening breeze blew cool, buffeting the lush grass, the green and florid clover, the aromatic pennyroyal. It drew mild, balsamic fragrance from the fields, swelling the atmosphere with a delicious exhalation as it passed. The cattle plodded back to their grazing ground.

My body needed rest. My stomach clamored for a criollo roast. We had some nice, fat meat the mere sight of which stirred the appetite. I ordered a good fire built with room for everybody around it and issued a friendly call for the assistants to bring large logs of *chañar* and thistle. There was a branch hut full of old cowhide, useless gear, throw-away thongs, and corn cobs. I took a look, ordered it cleaned out, and got ready to dine like a prince and spend a first-rate evening.

My thoughts were placid, like those of a carefree boy running and playing on avenues of splendid, myrtle-shaded, green, and vibrantly colored gardens. My troubles had flown; they, too, are mere notions.

I am wont to miss them.

The sun lowered its radiant brow behind the heights of Quenqué. The clear horizon and cloudless sky foretold another lovely day. The stars began to twinkle timidly in the firmament. The evening shadows slowly engulfed the vast, endless desert panorama, and by the time night had fully spread its great shroud, the fire was blazing. Thick, yellowish *caldén* logs screeched as they burnt and the weaker thistle sparked festively, as if to celebrate the power of the element consuming it.

The men sat around the camp fire in two haphazard circles. Behind either Franciscan and each officer was an assistant. The sprightly Calixto Oyarzábal stirred the fire, tended to the roast, drank mate, and let the one-liners fly unchecked. Had the friars not been there, he might well have seemed a jocular Vulcan among the flames, encircled by the damned. The flames, rippling in the wind, singed his chin, sending him into pirouettes and gesticulations, which, to complete the picture, drew uproarious laughter from his audience.

My eyes popped out of my head at the sight of the roast. I was thinking of Rembrandt's brush and palette when a familiar voice spoke to me from behind in a respectful tone, "Good evening, everyone!"

It was Juan de Dios San Martín.

"Good evening, my friend. Sit down if you like," I said.

"Thank you, sir," he replied, "but I cannot right now. I came to tell you that Baigorrita says the horses should not be left where you have them at the moment. He has heard that some Indian thieves are about to strike and it would be better if you corralled them."

I could not agree to this just then; the animals needed to eat and eat well. Yet, between them suffering further and me losing them, the decision was clear.

"Tell my compadre that if he says there is danger then I will round them up," I said after an instant's reflection.

"That would be better," said San Martín.

I ordered Major Lemlenyi to make sure Camilo Arias understood that the horses were not to sleep out in the open but in the corral. San Martín left and returned again.

"Baigorrita says the corral has a gate," he said. "You need to cover it with branches and put a guard there."

I gave the appropriate orders and as Calixto just then called out, "We're ready over here!" I again invited my compadre's messenger to sit down and join us. He accepted, took his place around the fire, and we started in on the roast. While we were making it disappear, we put some corn on the embers for dessert.

A pack of hungry dogs had formed a third row around us. When they saw that we didn't treat them as the Indians did, they pushed forward, and more than one of us had his meat snatched as he brought it to his mouth. In fact, our uninvited guests got so friendly that we finally had to chase them off with sticks.

"I'll tell you, man," I said to Juan de Dios San Martín, "they don't respect anything here. Do you think they would dare steal my horses right out of Baigorrita's corral?"

"Of course they would, sir. These Indians are real thieves. Why, just the other day Baigorrita lost his horses and wound up on foot," he answered.

"And what did he do about it?"

"He went out and rounded them up."

"So stealing from one another is a way of life here?"

"That's how they live. It's become a vice with them."

"And what do they do with what they steal?"

"Sometimes they eat it, other times they gamble it away, other times they will take it and swap it at Mariano's or at Chief Ramón's, or they will go to Calfucurá's with it or just up and head for Chile."

"And are the thieves punished?"

"Sometimes, sir."

"But what does an Indian do who has been robbed?"

"That all depends, sir. He can bring his complaint to the chief or find the thief himself and force from him whatever has been stolen."

I asked him a few more questions before reaching the conclusion that justice was administered two ways: through the authority of the chief or at the hands of the victim. The first way is the less usual of the two. In the first place, it means the chief must have someone find out who the thieves are, what the actual deed was, and prove it, all of which takes time. Secondly, the agents whom he commissions for this task let themselves be bought off by the thieves. Finally, this procedure yields the judge no benefit. The second way is followed more generally.

For example, let us say that someone steals a string of mares from an Indian. It was so-and-so, says the Indian, either guessing or because he knows it. He counts the number of fighting men he has in his household, recruits his friends, they all arm themselves, and raid the thief, taking back the stolen horses and everything else they can grab. Ordinarily, there is no struggle because the vindicators of justice outnumber the thief's party. All resistance to force is pointless, especially if one is not in the right. Next they render an account to the chief, who takes a share of whatever has been seized as indemnity. This makes all subsequent demands of him futile, a waste of time. If an Indian comes to the chief and says, "I stole ten mares from so-and-so and last night he came and took those ten and fifty more," the chief will answer, "Why did you steal, then? Go ahead and rob him again and take back what he stole from you."

Upon reaching this part of my inquiry into Pampa justice, I asked Juan de Dios San Martín a question. "When they rob one of the poorer Indians who doesn't have much family and few friends, and the thief is stronger than he is, what can he do?"

"Nothing," he answered.

"What do you mean nothing?"

"Sir, it is no different here than among the Christians. The poor get the worst end of it."

Calixto Oyarzábal chimed in here, burning his fingers and his mouth with a piece of roasted meat rolled in ashes.

"Colonel," he said, "the poor are like our army horses. Everybody rides them."

This remark, or comparison, drew the delighted and general approval of our whole party. And, indeed, there is nothing comparable in wretchedness to what we Argentines call the *caballo patrio*.

Let us say, for starters, that he is missing an ear, a disfigurement which gives him the same unsightly look anybody would have, say, who had no nose. He is always a skinny horse, and if he is not skinny he has a big gall on his withers or his back. He is either lame or weak with age, or hipshot or high in one quarter. He has a docked tail or else a huge knot in his tail. He is poorly brushed-out and if his mane is long there is a whole patch of burrs in it. If he happens to have both eyes, one of them is clouded. He has neither a good trot nor a good gallop, or canter or prance. And yet, everyone who finds him rides him, nor has it ever been recorded that a *patrio* could say as he died, They never gave me a beating. Everyone who ever climbed on his back has laid the strap on till the *patrio* dropped. Oh, if the *patrios* lying buried by the thousands in the open country, their carcasses a kind of postdiluvian fauna, should ever rise like specters from their unknown tombs and speak, what they wouldn't tell! What ideas they could provide for the defense and safety of the borders! Poor *patrios*. Everyone has blamed something on them. They alone have kept their silence. They have suffered, suffer still, and will suffer their impious fate with stoic resignation. Poor *patrios*! Not a soul but has grumbled and reviled the nation since the day there were *patrios* in it.

Not a soul, that is, but the *patrios* themselves.

We cooked the corn and ate. With supper over, conversation went on for a while longer and then each one of us turned his thoughts to making his bed. Mine was a splendid one. They had taken some hides and used them to make curtains in the hut, so that the cool night air could not discomfort me. I went to bed.

After they made up the Franciscans' and the officers' beds, the assistants took over the fire and had themselves a good roast. I was lulled to sleep by their chitchat and by the sounds of carousing coming from my compadre's tent. He and his women and a few intimate friends were savoring to the utmost the firewater I had brought them. Several times I awoke with a start, thinking I was seeing the face and hearing the voice of the Negro with the accordion. I was fast asleep when Juan de Dios San Martín approached my bed and woke me.

"Colonel!"

Fearing my compadre might have the Mariano Rosas treatment in mind for me, I kept still.

"Colonel, Colonel!" repeated San Martín.

I said nothing.

He approached the bed of one of my officers.

"The colonel is sound asleep," he said, "and he can't hear me. I came in to tell him they just ran off some thieves who were fixing to steal his horses. He should send more men to the corral."

Seeing there was no risk in admitting I was awake, I called for four assistants to reinforce the guard around the corral. I asked Juan de Dios San Martín what Baigorrita was doing.

"He is enjoying himself," he answered.

"Good," I said. "Make sure no one gets me out of bed."

"Nothing to worry about, sir. Baigorrita has ordered me to see to it you're not disturbed. He does not want you to see him stewed. He is ashamed. That is why he waited until nighttime to begin drinking."

I sighed. There was something that would not let me get comfortable, so I tossed and turned a bit before falling back asleep. A body at last gets used to anything and I got several hours of uninterrupted sleep.

Life passes unnoticed, as I have already said. Yet not every day is the same, nor every night. Were this not so, living would be the greatest torment of all. Happily, there are contrasts in human existence. Imagine a man who does nothing in life but enjoy himself, a man for whom every bite is a succulent one and who knows nothing contrary. I ask you, sage reader, as you perhaps curse your own star, if you would trade places with him. Oh, but the hungry know not what it is to be opulent and yet sick to the stomach. A certain English magnate, sitting down to a sumptuous meal, was approached by a beggar. The beggar implored the rich man to pity his wretched state and consider that he was dying of hunger. "Get away from me," answered the magnate and he answered well. "You are hungry and say you have a miserable lot. I am the one with the miserable lot. I sit before a feast and cannot get a bite of it down. When it doesn't sicken me, it cloys."

That is why the most talented and interesting women are the ones who though often renewed are seldom spent.

I meant to say that the second night in Quenqué had not been like the first. No sooner did the roosters crow than I awoke, called Carmen, and asked him for some mate. While he built the fire, heated the water, and steeped the brew, I went over my night's impressions. I had had a dream, an extravagant dream, as all dreams are, regardless of what the great dreamers have had to say about the matter. My imagination had taken a Carlos Joliet novel, a Venetian repast, my lunch in Baigorrita's tent, and other reminiscences, and made a veritable imbroglio of it all. In my dream I was attending a dinner. Every dish served was human flesh. The guests were Christians disguised as Indians and the whole scene took place both in Quenqué and at Héctor Varela's house. The host was a woman, Concordia, daughter of Jupiter and Temis. Around her had gathered the principal men of Argentina, each wearing a Pampa headband bearing a motto. Mitre's read, *Tout ou rien*; Rawson's, *Frères unis et libres*; Quintana's, *Sempre Diretto*; Alsina's, *Remember!*; Argerich's, *Liberté*; Sarmiento's, *Lasciate ogni speranza*.[1]

There were many other guests, I could still see their faces as if in a daze, but I could not remember who they were. Some were eating! Most, however, refused the human flesh with repugnance and horror.

A great orchestra of what seemed to be wind instruments, trumpets made of newspaper, played a military air, and a chorus sang such as one might hear echoing from a crowd of people in a public square:

> *There is no hope for nations! Search the page*
> *of many thousand years — the daily scene;*
> *The flow and ebb of each returning age,*
> *The everlasting to be which hath been,*
> *Hath taught us nought or little.*[2]

Carmen arrived with the mate and roused me from my retrospective meditations.

Just then a cannon went off.

It was electric lightning striking a dry tree trunk, a frequent phenomenon in the pampas.

 BAIGORRITA AROSE VERY early and went to the lagoon to bathe and remedy the excesses of the previous evening. His guests and the Indian women did the same. All looked fresh and perfumed upon returning, their cheeks and lips painted and beauty marks daubed on to their cheekbones.

The Indian women cleaned the tent, gathered wood, built a fire, skinned and dressed out a cow, and set about cooking the noontime meal. Baigorrita and his friends saddled the horses that were hitched to the post, mounted them, and for half an hour rode them under strap a league at a time over the harshest, bumpiest terrain. My compadre returned alone, turned his horse loose, saddled another one, entered his tent, sat down, rolled cigarettes, and proceeded to smoke. Juan de Dios San Martín came to ask me on his behalf how I had spent the night and whether I had lost any horses. I answered that I had spent it quite well and that as soon as I had eaten I would go pay him a visit. San Martín relayed this message and returned with word that my compadre was glad to know I had spent a pleasant night and wished to invite me to his tent. New visitors were expected and he wanted them to meet me. I would have my meal there if I had nothing better to eat. I was speaking with San Martín when an Indian arrived with a message from Caniupán and a gift. He sent greetings—he lived a league and a half from there—and a *patai* ball mashed with toasted corn and as big as a forty-eight-mm cannonball.

I treated the messenger with all the cordiality he deserved, making certain small gifts to him after gathering contributions from the soldiers and officers. I thanked Caniupán for his attention and sent him a Crimean shirt which I had brought along especially for him, as well as sugar, tobacco, mate, and paper. I promised I would visit him later in the afternoon.

I went straight to my compadre's tent. He sat there calmly, surrounded by his children and smoking. Never once moving from where he was, he insinuated with the gentlest, kindliest smile that I take a seat. Scarcely had I gotten comfortable when he spoke to my godson.

"Your godfather," he said to the boy. "Blessing."

The little Indian came over to me somewhat shyly. I opened my arms and drew him the rest of the way to me, took his little hands, which in obedience to his father he had joined together, stroked him, and sat him down beside me. To his "Give blessing, godfather," I answered, "May God make you good, godson." His mother, who spoke Spanish, spoke to him from beside the fire.

"What's your name?"

He gave no answer. She repeated the question in Araucan and, eyeing me warily, he replied, "Lucio Mansilla."

Pleased with this, my compadre broke into a smile. The mother, the Indian women, and the captives celebrated the reply as they went about their cooking. One of the coyest among them said, "A little Colonel Mansilla."

My compadre called Juan de Dios San Martín over, who then spoke to me.

"Baigorrita says when will there be a baptism."

"Tell him any time at all, right now if he likes, before any visitors arrive." He agreed to this and I called Father Marcos, who came at once. My compadre had San Martín ask him if he would do him the favor of baptizing his son.

"It would be my great pleasure," said the father.

He left and returned with Friar Moisés Alvarez, they donned their robes, we knelt and said the Our Father while those captives who knew it joined in chorus and my godson was baptized with the name Lucio Victorio.[1] When the ceremony was over, Baigorrita thanked the Franciscans and asked them to stay for a meal.

At his signal we were served. There were two kinds of stew, beef and mare; same for the roast. I had mare, as did my compadre. The friars had beef. New visitors began to arrive as we ate. All were accorded the same treatment as we had been. Some we knew from the day before, others were newly arrived. Baigorrita introduced me to each of them successively. There were interminable embraces and handshakes, all the usual questions and answers. My compadre explained what it means among the Indians to give the godfather's given name and surname to the godchild. It amounts to placing the child under the godfather's guardianship for life. It means the godchild is obligated to love the godfather always, to respect him in everything, follow his counsel, never take up arms against him under pain of provoking divine wrath. The godfather for his part accepts his obligation to look on the godson as his own; to educate, succor, counsel, and lead him down a righteous path, also under pain of drawing the wrath of God.

Two beings were taking on a single identity by virtue of a solemn vow. For this same reason, Baigorrita spoke to me of the gaucho from San Luis known as Manuel Baigorria. He wished to be given permission to visit him. I told him that as soon as peace was established, there would be nothing to stop him from having that pleasure if Mariano Rosas allowed it. I added that Baigorria was not a good man, that indeed he had proven himself both a bad Christian and a bad Indian, having betrayed both. Baigorrita said he was not unaware of my reasons, but that for better or worse he was his godfather, whose name he carried, and that he could not but love him. I told him that these sentiments honored him because they proved his loyalty. They honored him all the more, I said, in so much as he agreed that his godfather had been unfaithful to his duties and to his word.

Several of the visitors approved of my observations. Then, gently, clearly, and simply, the Franciscans explained the meaning of baptism. They said that upon being baptized one entered into the grace of God. God, they said, was eternal, immense, and merciful; was possessed of infinite power and did things too great to be understood by men. It was his will that all men should love one another as brothers, that they neither kill, steal, nor lie; that those who marry do so with one woman only; that those who have children educate them and teach them to work for a living; that to be a good Christian it was necessary to bear these things in mind at all times. Juan de Dios San Martín translated the Franciscans' reasons, and all present listened with rapt attention. My compadre promised to raise his son by the law of the Christians, that he would not marry several women, not even two, and that he would teach him to work for a living.

More visitors arrived. We held a long conference and I explained the peace treaty celebrated with Mariano Rosas. Everyone asked me a question who wished to do so. Baigorrita told me through Juan de Dios San Martín to be patient and Camargo urged me not to falter in answering the questions. When the query was an impertinent one, Camargo would buzz in my ear, "Tell them how many mares come with the treaty, sir."

"But Camargo," I answered, "what does that have to do with the question?"

"Nothing, sir, just answer what I told you. I'll tell you afterwards how they operate here."

This was a farce. They were talking apples and I was answering oranges. And the result was always the same.

"All right, whatever Baigorrita wants to do is fine."

My compadre would then bow his head in a sign of assent. Meanwhile, Camargo, who knew the lay of the land, would murmur through his teeth to me.

"You see, sir? All they want to do is make Baigorrita think that they can talk, too."

This charade went on for at least four hours. One by one the great tribal dignitaries disappeared until at last I found myself tête-à-tête again with my compadre, who then told me that the entire treaty seemed a good one to him. He wondered, though, who would hand his share of it over to him. I told him that Mariano Rosas ought to do that. Both Baigorrita and Ramón had empowered Mariano to negotiate. He agreed and we concluded with a request by him that I make precise arrangements for this with Mariano, as half of everything the government would be giving out fell to him. I promised him that I would.

My godson, the future chief Lucio Victorio Mansilla, never once moved from my side throughout the conference. When I saw him nodding I rested his head on the back of my seat and he fell asleep. It was siesta time. I lay down without a further word to my compadre and slept until my own restlessness awoke me. My body was boiling. I got up, left the tent while my compadre stayed to have a smoke. One of the Indian women was picking fleas off of him as I left. I changed clothes, reflecting as I dressed that my dream to have myself proclaimed emperor of the Ranquels was well worth the trouble of all this sacrifice.

"*Lucius Victorius, Imperator,*" I murmured. What a nice ring it had to it. But then onomancy spoke in my head: Fool, it said. I looked at the palm of my hand, considered its lines. Then chiromancy spoke to me: Fool! it said, twice. I saw a flock of parrots cross over. I watched this and then ornithomancy spoke: Fool! it said, three times.

A vision of my country passed like a cloud of fire through my mind and so lovely did it appear to me that I blushed, ashamed that I had as yet done nothing great or good or useful for her.[2]

I ordered a horse saddled and went to visit Caniupán. I galloped half an hour and arrived at his tent. I was about to dismount when San Martín, who was accompanying me, stopped me.

"Not yet, sir. The custom is different here."

An Indian came out of his tent and hushed the dogs, who had heralded our approach.

"Good afternoon, brothers," he said.

"Good afternoon," answered San Martín.

"Would you like to dismount?"

"We will do that," answered San Martín, and turning to me he said, "Now it is time, sir. Go ahead and dismount."

I started forward and he stopped me.

"Please come forward," said the Indian.

"Let's go, sir," said San Martín, answering the Indian as well, saying, "Here we go."

I tried to hobble my horse and San Martín said, "Not yet, sir."

"Why don't you tie your horses?" said the Indian.

"We will do that," answered San Martín.

"Sir," he said, turning to me, "let's tie the horses and go in."

We tied them and entered the tent. Caniupán was seated. He arose, greeted us with great fanfare, and bade us be seated.

"Have you come to stay?"

"No, I have only come for a while," I answered.

San Martín explained the question to me. Had I said yes, they would have ordered my horse unsaddled at once, the Indian women and captives would have rolled my gear into a bundle and set it aside as if in sacred safekeeping.

Anyone who wants to may approach an Indian's tent, but he can neither get off his horse nor enter the tent unless asked to. Once the offer is made, the hospitality lasts an hour, a day, a month, a year, a lifetime. Anything that comes into the tent is scrupulously cared for. Nothing is lost. It would dishonor the house, which assumes responsibility for everything except the horses. Be the guest familiar or a stranger, they warn him of that one thing.

They will say, "You can't be too careful, even in your own place."

And it is true. Never does an Indian refuse hospitality to a wayfarer. Whosoever calls at his tent, be he rich or poor, is admitted. If instead of passing through it turns out the traveler is staying, the head of the house asks nothing in exchange for food and shelter—and gives nothing else, for that matter—except that the traveler take part in the raids.

Caniupán's tent was perfectly built and kept. His wives, squaws, and captives were clean. They roasted a lamb and made stew and dinner from it in nothing flat, and they fed me. The Indian performed the host's honors with charming grace and ease. I would have gladly stayed there a couple of days. The sheepskin on the seats and beds, the blankets and ponchos—all seemed freshly washed, were neither stained nor soiled and had no burrs in them. He introduced all three of his wives to me, his four children and several relatives, except for his mother-in-law, who lived with him but with whom, as custom dictated, he did not get along.

I spent a very entertaining afternoon, ate good lamb roast, excellent *patai* for dessert, had a drink of firewater and, as evening began to fall, took my leave and returned to Baigorrita's tent. I found my compadre where I had left him, sitting and smoking. Several Indian women from thereabouts were waiting to pay me a visit. They were going to sleep with me, that is, spend the night near my camp fire just as Villarreal and his family had done when I was held up at the shore of the Calcumuleu Lagoon. It is a custom in these parts.

Camargo was not there. Several Indians had taken him to a dance that afternoon. He had gone with my permission without asking me for it. When I asked for him I was told he had ordered them to let me know that with my permission he was going out to have a good time. This was a true gaucho message. I ordered some mate brewed and regaled my visitors as befit the occasion. There were four of them and they had gotten fairly painted up. They were led by one María de Jesús Rodríguez, who spoke Spanish as well as I did. Her name came from her godmother. She was not Christian. I forgot to mention that among the Indians godparenthood is not contingent upon baptism.

But let us leave the visitors and gather at the camp fire. The quadroon is talking with my helpers and I hear him saying that he knows Julián Murga. This piques my curiosity.

 I APPROACHED THE fire unseen and stood there so as not to interrupt the quadroon. The horrid and deformed face of Calfucurá's spy stood out against the firelit tableau.

He was telling his story.

He never knew his mother and father. He was originally from Buenos Aires and had fought with Colonel Bárcena, a man of bloody and repugnant renown.[1] He had been on many campaigns and witnessed, if not performed, deeds of unheard-of cruelty. He was at Caseros, as well as the siege of Buenos Aires and Azul with General Rivas. From there he deserted. He wandered for some time making trouble. He stabbed a man to death at a roadhouse, made his way to the Indians, was a merchant for a time in Patagones, passing as a Picunche, and there met Colonel Julián Murga.

Now, I grew up with Julián and love him dearly. Our childhood memories will stay with me forever. In our barrio, San Juan, as in every barrio, there was a ringleader. Ours was Julián. Tavernkeepers, shopkeepers, shoemakers, and old ladies all trembled when we came around. We were the scourge of the Negro who sold pastries, the bakers, the milkmen. We had our arsenal of stones for them and an array of nicknames that still survive. We chased the neighborhood dogs and cats to death and ran all the way into the backyards to steal chickens. We left no door knockers in place, no freshly painted foundation, whitewashed wall, or new windowpane unscratched or unbroken. The local crazies detested us, the constables and nightwatchmen chose to stay on our good side.

We went around in disguises frightening old ladies, preferably our own aunts. The stable boys in every household we knew found us abominable and the servant girls put up with us. Julián showed promise from the time he was a boy. He was daring, inventive, strategic. Every prank he thought of was heroic. One time he made up his mind to jump off of a roof ledge and broke his leg doing it. Another time he thought of setting fire to a tavern by throwing a cat soaked in tar and wine spirits through the door. That one started a serious uproar. We had the city divided into sections. We would hit this one one day, that one another. We might steal the boots out of Chandery's window at night and the umbrella on display at the umbrella shop, and in the morning Chandery's would be featuring umbrellas and the umbrella shop boots.

Those companions were the forerunners of what our childhood squadrons would become in later years. The betrayals and breakdowns our plans gave away! The cowardice that undermined them! Certain avid mothers even planted spies among us. Oh, the boys, the boys! Today's boys are tomorrow's men. Take note of their qualities, good and bad. Watch their temper tantrums, their bursts of generosity, for sooner or later they will be your merchants, your priests, colonels, generals, presidents, and dictators. Mankind at bottom remains the same to the grave. Nothing unsettles the mud on the ocean floor.

I went to the camp fire and said good evening. Everyone except the quadroon stood up. They made a place for me and I sat down. The spy had told his life with a candor and a cynicism that showed how familiar he was with crime. To rob, kill, or die was all one to him.

"So you know Colonel Murga," I said.

"Yes, I know him," he answered.

He didn't alter his posture, didn't even move. He knew the rules here; we were all equal. He could be unattentive, even disrespectful.

"What does he look like?"

He described Julián's face and build.

"Where did you meet him?"

"In Patagones."

He explained in his own way where that was.

"And how do you get to Patagones?"

"By the road."

"By what road?"

"By the road that goes out of Calfucurá's."

"And how many rivers did you cross?"

"Two."

"Which ones?"

"The Colorado and the Negro."

"Do you know how to read?"

"No."

"What's your name?"

"Uchaimañé." ("Big eyes.")

"I mean your Christian name."

"I've forgotten it."

"You've forgotten it?"

"Yes."

"Do you want to go with me?"

"What for?"

"So you won't have to live the miserable life you've been living."

"Will they make me a soldier?"

I did not answer.

"It's not so bad living here," he went on. "I do what I want and have enough to eat."

"You're a bandit," I said, and rising I left the camp fire and got ready for bed.

The talk broke up. The quadroon remained beside the fire like a salamander. Half-starved, the dogs surrounded him and jumped on the leftovers from supper. They were snarling, biting each other, taking food away from one another. The spy remained motionless among them. He took a bone they were fighting over and gave it to one of the skinnier ones, petting it as he did so. As I watched I sank into deep moral reflection. Here was a man who had not had so much as a word, not even a gesture of attention, for me, a man who for all his pitiful nakedness bore himself arrogantly, and now this act of generosity, this gesture of compassion for a hungry soul and that hungry soul was a dog.

I had judged him a worse man than he was.

So much for our judgment. It's no less imperfect than our nature. If it doesn't fail because we think everybody else inferior to us, it fails because we have not studied others closely. And if it does not fail for either of those two reasons, it fails because we, in our lack of charity, fail to bear in mind the words of The Imitation of Christ: "If you have some good quality, believe better things of others, so that you may preserve humility." [2]

Who was this man? An unknown. What kind of life had he led? An adventurer's. What had been his theater, what spectacles had he beheld? Battlefields, killing, and robbery. What notion had he of good and evil? None. What were his instincts? Was he intrinsically bad? Could he be moved to compassion by the hunger or thirst of his fellow creatures? Having spied him through the darkness as he sat beside the dying fire, taking pity on a dog so weak and lean that it seemed damned to stand hungrily by while its friends feasted, I found it impossible to doubt. Would I be any better than this man, I wondered, if I did not know who had brought me into the world; if I had been neither educated, guided, nor counseled; if my life had been an obscure, fugitive one; if I had hidden among barbarians and adopted their customs and laws and changed my name; if I had become so brutalized as to forget my given name? Had I never lived in society or been taught since reaching the age of reason to identify my personal well-being with the general well-being, which is the basis of our morality, would I be better than that man? If it were not for fear of punishment, which sometimes is reprobation and other times torture by law, would I be better than that man? I asked myself yet a third time.

I dared not answer. Nothing has ever seemed so audacious to me as Jean Jacques Rousseau exclaiming, "I only know my heart and men. I am not like the others I have seen and daresay I do not resemble anyone else in existence. If I am worth no more than they, neither am I like them. That nature has acted well or badly in breaking the mold in which she cast me cannot be known except by reading me."

I took a last look at the camp fire. The quadroon was stirring the fire mechanically with one hand while petting the skinny dog with the other. The dog was sitting on its hind legs with a chunk of bone held between his extended forepaws. He bit into the bone until it cracked, looking restlessly left and right all the while, fearful lest he have his prize snatched from him. A flickering flame lit the deathly face in a patched chiaroscuro. I felt sorry for him. It didn't seem such an ugly face.

The air was cool.

I went up to him.

"Aren't you cold?" I asked.

"A little," he answered, looking straight at me for the first time and giving his protégé a resounding slap. The dog had growled as I approached, baring its fangs. It was perfectly calm all around us.

Everyone was asleep and there was nothing to be heard but the cadent breathing of my people. Just then the moon came breaking through a black shroud, eclipsing the light of the last embers of the camp fire. Its glimmer illuminated that silent scene, where civilization and barbarism commingled as all my company of officers, friars, and soldiers slept peacefully alongside the reeking, tattered tent of Chief Baigorrita.

Careful lest I step on anyone's head, body, or feet, I sought the place where they had set my saddle and gear. It was at the head of my bed. I found a woolen poncho, returned to the camp fire, and gave it to Calfucurá's spy, whose greasy feet the dog was licking.

"Here," I said, "cover yourself."

"Thanks," he said, taking it from me.

I was about to sit down and continue questioning him—the quiet was perfect for that—when I heard several horses galloping and voices shouting, "Where him Colonel Mansilla?"

The spy stood up. He wore a huge knife half under his sash. I looked at him. His face showed curiosity but no ill intention.

"What's all the shouting about?" I asked him.

"Sounds to me like they're drunk," he said.

"See if you can make it out," I said.

He turned his ear to the shouting, which grew closer. I could not clearly perceive what they were saying. It was no longer my name that rang in the silent night, but Araucan echoes.

"What are they saying?" I asked. I thought I heard a familiar voice.

"It's Camargo," he answered.

"Camargo?"

"Yeah. He's got some drunk Indian with him. They're almost here now."

Sure enough, they slowed their horses down and came to a halt behind Baigorrita's tent. Camargo stood before me in an instant.

"Colonel," he said with his foul breath, "go to bed. Go to bed right now!"

"Why, man?"

"Caiomuta is very drunk."

He then took me by the arm and pushed me toward the hut where my bed was.

"Go to bed, sir," said the spy as well.

I flew into my bed.

Caiomuta had entered his brother's tent and woken him up.

They were speaking heatedly in their language. I understood nothing at all. I was calm but wary. Suddenly a man tripped on my legs
and fell on top of me.

"Hey!" I shouted.

"Excuse me, sir," said Camargo, recognizing my voice.

"What are you doing, man?"

"Quiet, sir," he answered in a low voice. Then, dragging himself
along on all fours he approached Baigorrita's tent, staying close
enough to my bed to be able to speak to me without raising his
voice.

"What a scoundrel that Indian is," he said.

"What's going on?"

"He's telling Baigorrita that he wants to kill you."

"And what is my compadre saying?"

"He just busted his chops and said he dares him to try."

At that moment Baigorrita shouted, "San Martín!"

Camargo was laughing so hard he had to hold his stomach.

"Oh, that is one bad Indian," he said. "He can't get up on account of his brother busted his chops so bad. Serves him right.
Know what, sir? That pack of thieves stole my stirrups. I had to
give them everything and ride back bareback. I don't even have a
set of reins. I put half a bit on my mount, that's it."

"San Martín, San Martín!" shouted Baigorrita.

San Martín came, entered my compadre's tent, and spoke with
him. My name was repeated several times.

"He says he should take care of you," explained Camargo. "He
says not to make noise and if Caiomuta starts any trouble, they
should kill him."

So drunk was Caiomuta that he could not get himself up from
the spot on which his brother's formidable arm had laid him
out. Camargo crawled out like a reptile from where he was and
stretched out at the foot of my bed and begged my pardon pro-
fusely for having returned a little too cheerful. He told me again
the story of how they had robbed him. The Indians were a bunch
of poltroons as he well knew, he said. That is why he didn't fool
around with them. He said it was Caiomuta who made them steal
his silver stirrups from him. He had had to scare this information
out of an Indian, threatening to kill him if he didn't tell him the
truth. The Indian was so scared of him that not only did he tell him
everything, but he also gave him a skin full of firewater he had
stashed away for some time. The stirrups would show up the next

day, he was told, and if they didn't he should ride back to Mariano's bareback, which would shame Caiomuta because you just don't steal a guest's belongings.

I could not get to sleep. I could hear Caiomuta roaring and was alert. San Martín approached my bed and looked closely at me.

"What?" I said.

"Nothing, sir. Just go to sleep. There's nothing to worry about."

"Thanks," I replied.

He said good night and left, going directly into Baigorrita's tent. At this point, the Indian who had come with Caiomuta, who had fallen on the ground and stayed there after failing to dismount successfully, got back on his feet.

"Where him Camargo?" he asked.

Nobody answered.

"Him Camargo big murder," he said.

Nobody answered.

"Big murder!" he shouted.

Camargo woke up and let an oath fly at the Indian, who had no answer.

They stayed there like that for more than an hour.

I finally fell asleep.

Suddenly I woke up, startled.

Something soft, damp, and warm lay atop my house.

 THE MOON HAD completed its path across the sky, the stars shone faintly through ashen clouds, a chaotic darkness reigned. I opened my eyes and saw nothing. Something was pressing on me hard, stopping my breathing. A glutinous, fetid substance ran down my face like a profusion of sweat. A great, throbbing bulk oppressed my chest, confusing its heartbeats with my own. Another weight lay on my torso and something, perhaps arms, was thrashing about. Startled, fatigued, my restorative sleep interrupted, I was confounded by the darkness. I heard something like a grunt and felt as if a giant rolling pin were turning on my outstretched humanity. I could not get my arms out from under the covers. They were pinned on both sides. With an effort I managed to free one of them. Groping with a certain inexplicable fear, as one will enter a dark room at night not knowing where the furniture is, I touched something like the face of a heavily bearded man with a three-day stubble. It felt like a bladder made of sandpaper. I freed my other arm and, still searching, brought it to the height of its opposite. I felt something like the mane of an animal. Then, feeling around with both hands at the same time, I found another round thing which I knew beyond all doubt was a human head. A whiskey-like liquid ran down my face like the last sputter from a spigot. I was gagging. I called out for Camargo in anguish but he could not hear me. I thought I was dying. I did not know what was smothering my senses. I gave what felt like a head a hard shove with my two hands. I made a triangle with my knees and with a heave sent the oppressive weight rolling. "*Peñi*, brother," it cried.

I stood up, like don Quixote in the scene with Maritornes, and saw a body rolling at my feet.[1] I called for Camargo again, this time at the top of my lungs. He bolted up, came to my bed, and when I said, "What is that?" pointing to the bulk there, he crouched, took a look, and burst into laughter.

"It's the drunk Indian," he said.

I could see what had happened. His friend of a short while before had tripped and fallen when passing our entrance. He had rested his face on mine and bathed me in his drool and his alcoholic eruptions. I had to call Carmen, had to wash and change clothes. The light of dawn was near. I ordered a fire built and water heated and went to sit by the fire.

The quadroon and the dog were still there, sleeping.

I greeted the dawn with mate in hand. My compadre arose as the last morning stars were vanishing. He called San Martín, issued his orders, and a moment later Caiomuta was on his way out of the tent in the arms of four Indians. He looked like a dead body. They slung him lengthwise over the horse, arms and legs dangling, and sent the animal and its master homewards with a whack of the riding strap.

My compadre came straight to the fire and said hello as he sat down beside me. He asked me if I had slept well. I had, I said. I gave him mate and a cigarette. Saying no more, he took them both and left. Several times during the few minutes he was there he stared indifferently at the quadroon, who now woke up and, saying good morning, got to his feet. "Have a seat," I said, passing him a mate. He did so and drank.

More of our congregation began to arrive at that moment. My aide Rodríguez spoke to the quadroon as he took his seat.

"So you know how to write, eh?"

The man made no answer. Ensign Ozarowsky spoke.

"He doesn't know how to write. He was just acting like he knew. Those were just lines he was making." He went on to describe how the previous day he had seen the quadroon behind the kitchen with a pencil and a mysterious air, making like he was taking notes from what he could overhear. But the whole thing had been a pantomime.

Calfucurá's spy was some character!

When he realized they were talking about him he left. The dog went with him. It had found a man who seemed like an Indian and who spoke a language it knew. It would stick with him out of gratitude.

Dogs are more loyal than men; men are more generous than dogs. This arrangement will do so long as there is no other planet to emigrate to. Yet the human race has much to learn from the canine and vice versa.

I remembered that this was the day set aside for the great council.[2] I called San Martín and had him ask my compadre what time we would be getting under way. When the sun passes high noon, he answered. I gave my orders and the morning was taken up in getting ready. When everything was in order I went to Baigorrita's tent, entering as if it were my own. I had noticed his people moving about and was curious to know what was going on.

The hour was close at hand.

My compadre hardly budged from his habitual apathy when he saw me. He was cutting tobacco with Rodgers's razor again. He could see in my face that I had something on my mind, so he called San Martín, who asked him for me if it was not time to saddle the horses. He answered that we had time enough yet. It was only two gallops from there to Añancué, the boundary line of his land. He had already sent for the horses and was having a cow brought so my people could eat some meat before leaving. However, it was going to take a long while to get the cow, which was far away.

"You mean my compadre has no fat cows here?" I asked San Martín.

"No, sir, he's very poor."

"Very poor?"

"Yes, sir."

"And how much does a cow cost?"

"It has no price."

"What do you mean, no price?"

"If it's for sale, it depends on how many more they have. If it's to eat it costs nothing. They don't sell their food here. Whoever has the most, that's who you ask for it."

"So, whoever has a lot today will soon wind up with nothing left to give, right?"

"No, sir. Everything given out has a payback."

"What do you mean by a payback?"

"Well, sir, anyone here who has a cow, a mare, a goat, or a sheep to give away, collects later. Someday the one who is receiving will have some to give."

"And what does a rich Indian do if twenty poor Indians ask him for something all at the same time?"

"He gives all twenty of them something with payback and gradually gets it back."

"And if all twenty die, who pays him?"

"The family."

"What if he has no family?"

"Then his friends."

"And what if he has no friends?"

"He cannot help but have friends."

"But not everybody has friends who will pay for them."

"They do out here, sir. You can see that there are newcomers in every tent who live off of what the owner gets for them."

"What if they suddenly lost their desire to pay?"

"That never happens."

"But it could happen."

"Yes, sir, it could, but if it ever did, the first time they needed something no one would give it to them."

"I imagine every Indian has a long list of debts and debtors."

"They spend their whole day talking about what they have given and received with payback."

"And they never forget?"

"An Indian never forgets what he has given or what he has been offered."

"You said that when a cow is for sale it has a price."

"Yes, sir."

"Explain that to me."

"By sale, sir, I mean that a person who has something trades it with someone who has something else."

"So, then, if an Indian has a pair of silver stirrups and nothing to eat, and he wants to trade the stirrups for a cow, he trades them. Is that it?"

"No, that is not how it is done. They would give him the cow with payback and he would give the stirrups with payback as well."

"What if an Indian has a pair of silver spurs and wants to trade them for stirrups?"

"He trades them with or without payback, depending on the deal."

"And do they trade the same way with the Chilean Indians?"

"No, sir. They trade with the Chileans the same as the Christians do, unless they are related to them."

"And what about with Calfucurá's Indians and the Pampas?"

"Same thing, sir."

"Do they sue each other here?"

"That certainly happens, sir."

"And how do the Indians settle their differences?"

"They name judges."

"And what if they don't agree with the ruling?"

"They have to agree."

These barbarians, I said to myself, have established the law of the gospels—for your sake today, for mine tomorrow—without resorting to utopian socialism. They have solidarity, trade value on transactions, credit for the pressing needs of life, judgment by civil jury. You need specie for unequal trade here, credit for food. It is the opposite of what obtains among the Christians. The hungry do not eat if they lack the means. Clearly, then, institutions are the result of custom and of need. It would be exceedingly wise of legislators to keep this in mind when fashioning laws. Let those who so often seek their yardstick in other nations of alien race, religion, and tradition take these observations to heart.[3]

As I carried on my soliloquy, the Indian who bilked me out of my beaver-skin gloves appeared. He was somewhat drunk. He made some flip remark when he saw me. He sat down beside me and asked me for my silk neckerchief. I refused. Its disappearance would be tantamount to a signal. However, I finally had to give in. It was an insignificant piece of clothing and who was to say what my compadre might think if I were unwilling to part with it. You can expect anything from a suspicious Indian.

What pleasure it gave this Indian to receive the kerchief! He immediately put it on and set it just as I like to wear it. Then he pulled his hat back on. He was still feeling uppity, and now turned his praise and admiration to my long goatee. Big, nice, he would say, running his filthy hands along it. I wanted to stand up but he would not let me. He laid on me like four wet blankets, nor was it within

my powers to tell him that all this horseplay was darned annoying.
I knew my compadre found it highly amusing and that he had great
respect and affection for him besides. The Indian was hugging and
kissing me. He would look me up and down and shout, "That Colonel Mansilla, him bull."

It was the greatest compliment he could give me. To be a bull is
to be every inch a man.

Not knowing what else to do for me, he struck upon the idea of
braiding my goatee. This was the other sign I had agreed on with
Camilo if any real danger should ever threaten me. How could I let
the Indian have his way? He was stuck on his idea and I began
seriously to worry, and with good reason. You will recall, dear
Santiago, the arrangement I had with Camilo in case the Indians
should refuse to let me leave. I could understand that they would
take the kerchief. Any Indian might decide to ask me for it and I
had set myself up for that. But that anyone should then want to
braid my beard as well, that was inexplicable, extraordinary.

Certain things simply cannot be foreseen. Napoleon was right:
in war you must lay two-thirds of what happens to calculation and
one-third to chance. I could not conceive of a betrayal because
Camilo's boys were all good, reliable men. They must have gotten
together to talk about the sign, I reasoned, some spy overheard
them and now they are setting a trap to see what I will do.

The Indian was relentless. Let the chips fall where they may, I
thought. Let him braid my beard. I was careful to keep my back
turned to the entrance lest Camilo walk by, see the sign, and light
out for Villa Mercedes with a false report for General Arredondo.
I was on edge. The horses were due any moment and with them
Camilo, who as agreed upon had not seen me for days. There
would be no way of warning him. The Indian refused to let me out
of the tent. More annoying and burdensome than a jealous woman
in love is a drunken man.

The cow my compadre had sent for arrived, delivering me from
danger. They asked him if they should dress it out and roast it. He
said yes, and had them tell me we could saddle our horses any time
now. I got up, unbraided my beard and, over the Indian's repeated
protestations of "Don't go, friend," left the tent.

Three horns sounded the call and moments later the riders began to arrive. They were on good horses and were dressed in their
best finery. One of them wore a complete lieutenant colonel's uniform and stood there in his bare feet.

My people were ready. They brought the horses over and we

saddled them. I said a tender good-bye to my godson. How strange the ways of sympathetic hearts: teardrops ran down the little boy's face. We mounted and departed at full gallop and soon scattered. The quadroon came with us. The dog from Baigorrita's tent followed him. Several groups of Indians joined us along the way and when we got about to Poitaua it was already late. I drew in my reins to wait for the Franciscans. My compadre did the same. An eagle sat perched atop a carob tree, peering north. Baigorrita had San Martín tell me this was a good sign. The eagle was pointing the way. Had it been looking south, every one of those Indians would have turned around and gone back.

The Franciscans presently arrived and we moved on at a trot. I was going to tell them the Indians' superstition about the eagle and have a good laugh, but then I remembered that I do not eat where thirteen are seated or kill spiders at night.

There is a world in which all men are equal—the world of our misgivings. The most level-headed of us is a barbarian. If this is not so then tell me, reader, why you despise so-and-so.

IN PITRALAUQUEN WE again halted our march. Iridescent flamingos hailed our arrival with a resounding ovation of roseate wings, vanishing into the colorless ether in random waves.

My compadre and his newly arrived Indians were on such poor mounts that he asked me if I could please lend him a few horses to get to the settlement line. I ordered they be given to him and then told San Martín it seemed incredible to me that Baigorrita did not have more horses.

"He's almost been left on foot after last night," he said.

We rested a while and then moved on. As I mounted my horse, I stole a pack of tobacco from the Indian who had taken my gloves. He had it tied to his tethers.

Run with the wolves and you soon learn to howl.

I told my compadre about it and he laughed heartily, applauding the idea as well as the laugh the rest of them would have on the Indian when they found out I had robbed him.

We were going at a full gallop. We were some two hundred in all and took up half a league because of the disarray in which the Indians ride.

The sun was setting in awesome splendor. Like darts of fire, its rays scattered the shrouds laboring to hide it from us, tinting the sky a lively hue as they glanced off to the opposite hemisphere. The bands of waterfowl rent the air in raucous flight, honking as they returned to the lagoons where they kept their eggs. How incredible the number of snow-white swans of supple, silken neck; spotted, broad-billed geese; regal ducks with feathers as blue as lapis lazuli; black ibis of hooked beak; dark, tiny-footed curlews; austere, gray-winged woodcocks. There are thousands of these birds in any lagoon and how they brighten the pampas.

The pleasures that await the hunter there!

Picture this: a number of soldiers gathered eight thousand eggs in one day. They had already taken more than that in the week leading up to this feat.

Oh for a rifle!

We entered the hills. Night fell and we galloped on. The dust and the dark engulfed the trees in deep blackness. They rose up like ghosts as we approached. We could not see each other at close range, but only led each other on. My horse was a superior one. I took the lead and got lost. I drew in my reins, came to a halt, listened closely in the direction it seemed those preceding me would be coming. I could hear nothing. What danger was I in? In reality, none. A tiger could do nothing to me. My horse would have kept me clear of him. Our tiger, the Argentine jaguar, does not attack like the Bengalese tiger, but only when chased. Anyway, the mountain had been scorched by the heat and the tigers live in the tall grass. What, then, had overcome me? Dark of night. Shadows hold a certain solemn something for me. Alone in the darkness I feel overwhelmed. I can control myself, but I shake. Dogs and the dark are my two greatest nightmares. I love men and I love the light of day, though I have been capable of greater madness for women. I cannot say what it is that terrifies me when I am alone in a dark room, going down the street at late hour, or crossing the wooded hills. Nor what it is I feel when climbing the slippery sides of the mighty Andes on the steady back of a wary mule. Yet I do feel something terrifying, something not of the senses but of the imagination, that poetical, mystical, fantastic, ardent, cold, limpid, nebulous, transparent, opaque, luminous, somber, cheerful, and sad region which is everything and nothing, which is like the sunshine and the penumbra, which nurtures and destroys, forges its own chains and breaks them, engenders and devours itself, intones tender dirges one day, takes golden plectrum in hand the next and sings for joy, loves freedom today, tomorrow lies prostrate before an odious tyranny.

Ah, if we could but fully know all that we feel! Would that our impotent nature could cross the forbidden threshold between the finite and the infinite! Would that we could penetrate the abyss of the psychological world as surely as we can reach the remotest stars with a telescope! If we could separate the rays of the human gaze as a solar spectrum filters the beams of the great luminary: if we could sound the heart as we do the stormy shoals of the sea!

Would we be happier?

Happier . . . !

Are we in fact happy? [1]

If we constantly talk about happiness it is because we have some notion of it. Define it for me, then. I want to know, need to know, must know. It is my right. Yes, I have a right to be happy as I have a right to be free. And I have a right to be free because I was born free.

What is freedom? Is it not the power to act or not to act, the faculty to choose? Is it not the exercise of my conscious, reflective, deliberate, calculating will, whatever good or ill I may hope to derive from it?

How dare you rule out my definition. Why would you object to it? Because it is not a juridical one, liberty being the power to do that which will not harm another? I must caution you that I speak not as a legalist but as a philosopher, and that I acknowledge your distinction.

Agreed, then. Freedom is just that: my rights running parallel to yours, an abstraction which might lend itself to graphic formulation.

My rights: _____

Your rights: _____

But then one right superimposed upon another is no right at all. It is abuse or tyranny. I have the right to speak, as do you. If I impose silence upon you and do not myself observe silence, I oppress you. I have the right to work for myself, as do you. If I make you my slave, I tyrannize you.

We agree. If happiness is not absolute it is relative. Unlike good and evil or right and wrong, it is objective and subjective, depending on circumstances, character, aspirations, and endless other accidentals.

I understand. You are trying to tell me that a Trappist monk, a derelict and unbelieving Trappist monk, may live as peacefully in his retreat as I, a clean-minded believer, do amidst the hustle of society.

Precisely.

What recourse is then left to those of us who tumble fatefully through life's whirlwind?

To take it as it comes, resign yourself to it.

Conformity may suit the slave.

Do you think you have said anything with that?

If I didn't I would not have spoken.

I must warn you, nevertheless, that you are slave to your passions.

And what do you mean by that?

I would merely remind you that God is inscrutable and that your inability to define something satisfactorily in the abstract does not prove the inexistence of that thing. In a word, it was unreasonable of you to ask so despondently if we are in fact happy.

Consequently, just because I cannot define what I experienced in discovering myself lost in those hills, it will nevertheless still be thought of as fear.

How long did this go on? A matter of seconds. Perhaps if it had lasted longer I would have been able to define it. I was baffled and did not know what to do. My horse walked in any direction it pleased, I was disoriented and it was all the same to me whether I went one way or another. I had wandered this way and that for a moment when I heard a herd of horses near, very near. Doubtless my own emotions had kept me from hearing them sooner.

There are times when, depending on one's spiritual disposition, the buzzing of a fly or the whisper of a leaf can sound like a tempest. There are other times when we fail to hear the blast of a cannon. In battle I have seen frightened men, men panicked and overtaken by terror, flee headlong towards enemy lines. They neither recognized those speaking to them nor heard what was said to them.

I meandered back to the road, joined a group that was galloping by and followed. We came to an escarpment. Through errant clouds borne on a light, easterly breeze there shone a few stars, telling us we would have light when the moon came out. We reentered the darkness.

We happened on some barrancas with nitrate lagoons that looked like mirrors of burnished silver. We climbed the dunes. As we reached the crest of one of them the wandering queen of the heavens showed her white face, plunging it into the motionless surface of the lagoons and sending forth a burst of diamantine lights.

The buglers sounded a call. Never had the horns of war echoed in my ears with such solemnity. It was like the trumpet call of Judgment Day. Its vibrations rippled each upon the next as they traversed the void.

Baigorrita's cornets answered. We had reached the border line and called a halt. A parliamentarian arrived and spoke and spoke some more. He was answered reason for reason. Another came after he was dispatched, then another, each with the same protocol until at last the son of Mariano Rosas arrived and invited us to advance. We marched and, after passing along a vast beach where the Indians play *chueca* after their great juntas, we arrived.

 MARIANO ROSAS AND his people were camped in a hilltop clearing. It was a laborious climb to the top. The horses sank to their flanks in the spongy sand. Every step they could manage was a victory as again and again they fell and stood up. Shaking, they would make an arduous effort and fall again. Under strap and spur, their limbs would stiffen as they drew their front legs up and out all at once and dragged themselves until their hind legs came free. They sweated, panted, stopped, wheezed, and climbed. At times we had to dismount, tug on their reins, and rouse them into action.

"Heeyaaaahh!" we cried.

A brave and powerful animal is the horse.

We came to the top of the hill. There, beneath two spreading carob trees, the commander-in-chief of the Ranquel tribes had seated his royal personage. He held solemn parliament with the chiefs and Indians from near and far as they arrived one by one at the meeting place. He received each of them with the same consideration, asked all of them the same questions, knew them by name, knew where they came from, their grandparents' names, their fathers', wives', and children's names, and explained to each of them the reason for the junta to be celebrated the next day.

They each answered in kind and after answering took a seat in a line. On his right sat the most notorious captains and elders, among them one Estanislao, the object of much attention. He had

come a great distance from the border between Baigorrita's and
Calfucurá's land.[1] Perhaps seventy years old, he was tall and bent
under the weight of his years. His long white hair fell slack and
even to his shoulders, giving his wrinkled, sun-baked face a pleas-
antly venerable appearance. He wore a *paisano*'s garb: Pampan
poncho and waistcloth, Crimean shirt, fringed breeches, coltskin
boots sewn at the toe. He wore no hat. A broad blue and white
headband adorned his brow. He required the assistance of two robust Indians to get off of his horse. Once dismounted, he was given
a pair of crutches of crude *chañar*. They all cleared a path for him
as he made his way forward to Mariano Rosas, who arose and with
a lively and effusive display of affection opened his arms in welcome. The chiefs and captains holding seats of importance moved
to their right, giving the elder the place of honor. The barbarians
were paying him respectful homage in the wide open desert under
starlight and it made me realize that respect for those who have
preceded us in the trying and scabrous journey through life is innate to the human heart.

I have the worst opinion of those who do not bow reverently
before the aged. Whenever I meet an old person, be he friend or
stranger, I instinctively step aside. Whatever his condition, whether
of stately bearing or not, whether dressed in opulent raiment or the
enemy's dirty rags, a head hoary with life's winter always fills me
with a religious respect. Who knows, I ask myself as he passes,
how many times his heart has been unjustly wounded? Who can
say what sorrows have torn his soul apart? Who is to say he is
not many times over a victim of contempt, even after laying his
dearest interests upon the altar of homeland and friendship? Who
knows what unspeakable calamities may have befallen him before
he reached old age? Who is to say he has not nursed an illusion
of happy last years in a comfortable home with a solicitous and
tender wife and children, only to be cast from his family for his
foolish ways or his damnable luck. Who can say whether this
sickly, tremulous existence, this flickering star of dying light—a
sunset on a hazy day—might not need a little social consideration
if he is to draw another breath of life?

The young and the aged are like the two poles of the earth: opposite but the same. In the former there is a pristine candor, in the
latter a harmless feebleness.

> *Last scene of all,*
> *That ends this strange eventful history,*

Is second childishness and mere oblivion;
Sans teeth, sans eyes, sans taste, sans everything.[2]

No one faces the threshold of eternity with a curse on his lips for his brothers. Whether from fair-mindedness or fear, all regret the wrong they have done or the good they have failed to do when the quadrant of time marks the solemn moment between being and not being.

Oh the aged! The aged! Do not, I repeat, do not fail to step aside for them, look at them, salute them. It takes so little to please those who stand with one foot on the last step in this world and the other in the doorway to eternity, awaiting the fatal instant with neither rancor nor hatred in their heart.

Estanislao had a long dialogue with Mariano Rosas. Baigorrita's turn came next and after him the rest of the captains and Indians of importance accompanying him. I extended personal greetings to the chief and took my seat beside my compadre. As the ceremony did not concern me, I allowed myself a respite. The gallop had jogged my stomach and aroused my appetite. I tried to abandon the field but Baigorrita was growing impatient with all the tell-me-this and have-you-heard and asked me to stay. He said I should wait for him and we would camp together. I ordered the horses to be turned out far from there and in a safe place. I then told them to make camp nearby, on a thickly wooded hill, and to have a fire, some stew, and a roast waiting for us.

They made sure I had mate to drink while my compadre performed his courtesies. Hilarión passed me a delicious piece of pie baked over the embers and I, rather like a spoiled, candy-eating child with visitors around, gobbled it up when they weren't looking.

We all have some indelible memory of certain scenes in life: a splendid dinner at the Club del Progreso; a dinner in La Plata; a picnic; lunch on board a ship. I cannot forget a certain piece of pie cooked under ashes and passed quietly over to me by Hilarión.

"I've been saving this one for you, Colonel," he said.

The sharp eye of Mariano Rosas caught this. Figuring I was hungry he had a couple of roasted pigeons passed to me. It was Dr. Macías, in fact, who carried out the order, as I found out the next day. Poor Macías! I will soon enough have occasion to take up his story. Oh, but how sad it was to see him! We had never been friends, but I felt for him that special closeness of schoolmates that often binds two hearts more tightly than blood itself. Whether in the bosom of one's homeland or on foreign shores, and whatever the storms that have tossed our life's ship of hope, the presence of an old schoolmate is as good as a talisman.

I could see the talk was not about to end; it threatened to go on until midnight, judging by the number of personages who had yet to exchange greetings. I could see, too, that the Negro with the accordion was nearby and preparing to give us a serenade, so I made a sign to my compadre. He answered that he could not leave yet, that I should go ahead. He would join me later.

Mariano Rosas was fully engaged in a remarkable display of memory and oratorical skill. I motioned to him that I was leaving, he motioned back that that was fine, that this was no affair of mine anyway. I stood up, made my way through the thick wall of a crowd that was listening to the parliament. I called my assistant, who brought me my horse. I put my foot in the stirrup and was preparing to mount when I heard grating chords being played behind me. It was the Negro with the accordion! As I swept my right leg around I kicked him in the chest with my left foot, which sent him sprawling. I took off at a gallop. The artist was stewed.

I rode to the hill where my people were camped. Their fire blazed as brightly as an Inquisition bonfire. I wanted to jump over it, as the boys will jump over the fires of tar and wood shavings on the feast of San Juan. Some temptations are irresistible. I spurred my brave horse, cleared the fire, and scattered everyone but left the roast, the stew, and the kettle standing, which earned me a warm ovation. Pleased with this victory, I dismounted with uncustomary agility, took my place around the fire, and started in on some mate.

My compadre still not arriving, we ate supper. I had some set aside for him and before retiring called for a report on the condition and whereabouts of our horses. There were more than twenty of us around the fire, talking about who knows what, when there suddenly came a thundering of hooves. "It is Baigorrita," said some. The riders stopped nearly on top of us. A firm, manly and, to me, unknown voice hailed, "Good evening!"

"It is Chañilao," said some.

"Good evening," said others.

"Climb down if you like," I said, pretending not to have noticed who he was, though I had seen his face perfectly well by the glow of the fire. Chañilao climbed down. Speaking in Araucan and jingling his enormous spurs, he walked over to me with an air of great indifference and sat down next to me. I did not move.

No one except the Indians knew him. He was a tall, thin man of prominent, marked features and fair, slightly sunburned skin. He had long, chestnut brown hair with a blond hue to it, penetrating blue eyes and a broad, sharply chiseled brow. His nose was straight in the classical Greek style and his full lips stood out on his small mouth. He had a pointed, upturned chin with a dimple on it and was smooth-skinned. He had easy manners and dressed like a rich gaucho. He wore a fine Panama hat, silver spurs, and a long knife, also of silver, which was strapped to his waist. He used a gold-tipped riding strap and had a great rolled cigar in his mouth. Ignoring me, he spoke with several Indians, affecting a most conspicuous air and tone of superiority, a studied one, it seemed to me. I motioned to my assistants with one finger over my mouth so that they would not say who I was. I had them pass him a mate.

"Where is my friend Camilo Arias?" he said as he took it.

Just then we could hear my compadre Baigorrita coming.

CHAÑILAO IS THE renowned Manuel Alfonso, a Córdoba gaucho who once lived on the border of Río Cuarto.

He has been with the Indians for years.

There is no braver, no keener scout and guide than he.

He carries a topographic map of the frontier provinces in his head. He has crossed the pampas thousands of times in every direction, from the sierra of Córdoba to Patagones, from the Andes to the shores of the River Plate. There is no river, stream, lagoon, ravine, or grassland in that vast territory that he does not know well. He has opened new *rastrilladas* and frequented the old, abandoned ones. He knows hidden water holes where horses and travelers can slake their thirst on the perilous journey across the pampas. He has ridden with the Indians on their most daring forays, and if they have come back safely it has often been his cunning and intrepidity that saved them. His constant treks, day and night, fair weather or foul, rain or thunder, sunshine or clouds overhead, have made him so practiced as to foresee meteorological phenomena with barometric, thermometric, and hygrometric precision. He is a human compass needle. His gaze marks the true course, and the possible course, with quadrantal accuracy.

He speaks the Indian language as well as the Indians do, has a wife of his own and lives with them. He can break a colt, swing a

lasso, hurl the bolas, and rope a steer. He knows the cattle planta-
tion life as well as any landowner, has done business with Rosas
and Urquiza, and been taken prisoner many times, only to escape
by his own wits and temerity. Shortly before the battle of Cepeda,
he and twenty of his Indians were captured near the Buenos Aires
border. He alone outsmarted the guards and got away.

When the Indians are invading or attacking, he is their oracle.
An untrusting sort, he lives in Inché, thirty leagues farther south
than Baigorrita, whose Indians he rides with. He has a following
and is a captain, which says it all with regard to this unquestionably native Argentine specimen.[1]

Chañilao is not bloodthirsty; he has lived alternately among the
Christians and the Indians. He has friends in Río Cuarto. Camilo
Arias, my faithful and inseparable companion, is one of them. The
last time Chañilao emigrated from there it was on unwarranted
suspicions about him. That is our country for you: our policies
tend to make enemies of our friends, pariahs of our countrymen,
secretaries, ministers, and ambassadors of those who have fought
us. We are generally fair with our own, always weak with our adversaries. We tolerate the temporizers, but never those whose conscience stands on honor and duty. On them we turn a bitter, scath-
ing criticism. Character is the worst part of patriotism as far as the
halfway crowd is concerned, which has a flair for recruiting nobod-
ies, seducing traffickers and speculators, but not for admiring talent and probity. They are better at giving in than at imposing their
will through moral rectitude. They prefer those who knuckle under
to those who stand emboldened on the pedestal of their beliefs and
cry out: This is what I believe!

Oh, if only the country were not desperately short of breath! If
only every heart weren't convinced that we must get the land ready
before thrusting the fecund seed into her! And if only the sword
weren't lethal, and if only a truth written in blood weren't a fratricidal conquest.

Camilo had spoken at length to me of Manuel Alfonso, whose
few remaining affairs he had tended to the last time the gaucho had
fled the frontier. He harbored a warm respect for him that the *paisano* always professes for a gaucho, for any but a bad gaucho, that
is. Camilo had taught Alfonso how to work in the fields, and as he
held the Indians in mortal contempt, had fought hand to hand with
them many times, losing two brothers in two raids, he entertained
the illusion of drawing Alfonso out of his lair.

Camilo Arias is the same as Manuel Alfonso in one sense, his opposite in another. Camilo is as smart as Alfonso, knows his way around just as well, rides as well, and is just as brave. But he is no adventurer. Camilo is a gaucho *paisano*, but not an outright gaucho. They are two different types. The gaucho *paisano* has a home, a set place to stay, work habits, respect for authority, whom he will always side with, even against his better judgment. The real gaucho is a wandering criollo. Here today, gone tomorrow, he is a gambler and troublemaker, an enemy of all discipline who flees from military service when his turn comes, takes refuge among the Indians if he knifes someone, or takes up with the *montonera* if it comes around. The *paisano* has an instinct for civilization and imitates the city man in dress and custom. The gaucho loves tradition and detests the gringos. His pride are his spurs, his silver trim, his leather sash, his knife. The *paisano* removes his poncho when coming into town, the latter enters town showing off his best finery. The former is a laborer, teamster, cattle driver, cowboy, ranch hand. The latter hires out for branding. The former has been a soldier several times, the latter was once part of somebody's outfit and made his break first chance he got.

The *paisano* is always a federal, the gaucho is no longer anything at all. Because he has suffered more than the collar and frock coat crowd, he has also become disillusioned sooner. He votes in the elections because his commander or the village mayor tells him to. So much for universal suffrage. He quickly drops any complaint he may have; he considers complaints—and rightly so—a waste of time to pursue. In short, the former is useful for industry and labor, the latter a dangerous inhabitant anywhere. If he singles out a judge it is because his instinct tells him fear will drive a judge to give him fair treatment. There are instances of him wounding or killing to avenge unfair treatment. The *paisano* comprises the Argentine social mass, the gaucho is disappearing. Those living in their cocoons in the great cities have seen the gaucho's world through a peephole. Those who long to see foreign lands instead of traveling their own; who have crossed the ocean on a steamer; who know where Riga is but cannot say where Yavi lies; who have experienced the feverish pleasure of eating up the miles on a locomotive, having never known the primitive thrill of a ride on a horse-drawn cart; for all those kinds of people, the gaucho is an ideal human being.

They have never seen one.[2]

Liberty, progress, immigration, the long, slow palingenesis we have gone through these past eighteen years, are driving him to extinction. The day we realize we have a mass of soulless people who believe in no one and in nothing; a people scattered across immense plains without churches, schools, roads, or laws, nothing that effectively protects them, nothing that prepares them for self-government or popular suffrage, nothing that teaches respect for the foreigner who has come to share everything with us except our pain, because that is not what drives us; a people, in short, having nothing but some strong men with a gun or a gown who oppress or exploit; the day all that sinks into our heads will no doubt be the day the gaucho disappears altogether. Only then will we have a people, properly speaking; a people with heart, conscience, conviction, passion. Our country must cease to be a myth, an abstraction, so that all can understand and love her with the same perfervid love. Certain fanaticisms are necessary and should be created if they do not exist.

Manuel Alfonso again asked for Camilo Arias.

"Have him called here," I said.

The gaucho did not so much as look at me, though he now knew who I was. No doubt intending to calm me down, he decided to ask a question.

"So what are we supposed to make of all this peace talk? All of a sudden we are all friends and the *porteños* are invading Calfucurá."

"Look, pal," I answered, "you don't talk that kind of bull around me. If you don't like peace, just move somewhere else."

He turned around to look at me, beating the ground mechanically several times with his riding strap.

"I'm only saying what I have heard," he replied.

"Well, I still say it is a bunch of barbaric bull."

He looked harder at me and answered only with a malicious smile. A bad old boy, this one, it seemed to say. I was spoiling for him and I'd be done for if I let up now. He was one of those slick gauchos.

"And this is my camp fire," I added, as if to say I don't want people saying things I don't like.

"And who are you?" he said, still toying with the strap and staring into the fire.

"Find out," I answered. Just then I heard a familiar voice at my side.

"At your service, sir."

It was Camilo Arias who had come when I had him sent for.

"You have a friend here," I said, pointing to Manuel Alfonso.

The *paisanos* are generally on the cool side. They said hello as if they had seen each other the day before.

"Let's go," said Camilo.

"C'mon," answered the gaucho, standing up. He said good night and left.

It all had me seriously concerned. That a man as smart and as familiar with the Indians as he; a man with the standing he enjoyed for all the favors he had done them; that a man of his know-how and courage should come out with words like those at my camp fire, revealed the worst kind of intentions.

Manuel Alfonso had not yet climbed on his horse when my compadre Baigorrita appeared. He climbed down and sat beside me. I asked for his supper, they brought it to him, he took out his knife and spoke.

"Knowing Chañilao?" he said.

"That's him right there," I said, pointing to him. He had just rolled a cigarette and that instant was lighting it as he rode off.

"Right there," said my compadre.

"Something wrong?" I asked San Martín.

"I'd say so," he answered.

Baigorrita was more pensive than usual. His questions, exclamations, and somber air had me convinced that Manuel Alfonso had not come to my camp fire to talk about peace and Calfucurá without a reason. What could it be? On the eve of a great junta any untoward development was alarming.

"Is something wrong, compadre?" I had San Martín ask him.

"Yes, compadre," he answered for himself.

He then spoke with San Martín, who relayed to me that Mariano Rosas had told him many things about me. He had said that while camped in Calcumuleu I had treated the Indians very badly and had had a number of insults passed on to him. He also said that I was very arrogant.

I told him everything that had happened.

"There is some intrigue here," he said through San Martín. "It is because they see we are friends."

Now I understood everything. While I was in Quenqué they had set me up in Leubucó. My compadre finished his supper. He and I were the only ones still sitting at the fire. The rest had turned in.

"Let's go to bed, compadre," I said.

"Good," he answered.

I called Carmen, who showed me to my bed. It was beneath a beautiful *caldén* tree. I was sitting there when an Indian woman rode up, dismounted, and approached me.

"I have to speak to you," she said in a mysterious tone.

BEFORE DAWN THE next day I already knew in rich detail the intrigue that had developed in Leubucó while I was in Quenqué. News of Baigorrita and I being compadres had had an adverse effect on Mariano Rosas. So sacred is this relationship to the Indians that Mariano was alarmed by the budding friendship now sealed by the baptism of his ally's oldest son. Those surrounding him, far from allaying his fears, fed them, warning him not to be caught unawares, to be on guard. My conduct was publicly censured. I was accused of having treated the Indians discourteously from the day I arrived in Aillancó and of failing to announce my trip in advance. My niggardliness was compared with Father Burela's magnificent cargo of fifty loads of beverage and criticized. I was no good, they said. I had imposed the peace treaty on them by sending an ultimatum. I had brought along an instrument with which to measure land because the Christians were preparing an invasion. The treaty had no other purpose than to occupy the Indians in order to win time.

Father Burela seemed aloof from these rumors but had not reproved them, either. Because he had no part in the junta, he was on Mariano Rosas's side. He had been with him the night before, was acting very much the cohort, and appeared cross at Baigorrita for having made me his compadre, a remarkably strange complaint coming from a priest.[1]

My diplomatic horizon loomed gloomy indeed.

The person who had taken the trouble of coming furtively to me with this news of what had happened in my absence believed we would be having an unruly council and wished to prepare me for it. Chañilao's malicious statements made the situation even knottier. Before coming to my camp fire, he had gone to where Mariano Rosas was holding parliament. Speaking with him and others he had spread his news about and spawned an atmosphere of distrust.

Day was breaking when a messenger arrived from Mariano

Rosas. He wanted to know how I had spent the night and advise me that we would move out as soon as the sun came up. A cornet would give the signal. I said that I had spent the night uneventfully, that I was glad to know that he and his people had slept well, and that I was at his disposal. I sent for Camilo Arias, then ordered that the horses be rounded up. My people got on their feet and prepared to leave. While they were bringing in the horses we heated water and had mate.

Camargo inspired trust. I told him what had happened with Chañilao, what took place in Leubucó during our excursion to Baigorrita's settlement, and what Mariano Rosas had said in the meanwhile. When I asked him for his candid opinion, he gave it unhesitantly. The man's heart is not wanting in nobility. I felt reassured by him though not completely. Every world has its mysteries. He perhaps better than anyone knew those of his world. The fact that he did not come back from Quenqué empty-handed proved as much. He had made them give back the stirrups they stole from him in Caiomuta's tent, and the rest of the things he had thrown contemptuously at the Indian to humiliate him and foul up his scheme.

The horses arrived and with them Camilo. I ordered the former saddled and while this was being done conferred with the latter about his interview with Manuel Alfonso. They had slept together but had not reached an understanding because the gaucho did not care for me. They had separated as friends.

A cornet sounded.

Baigorrita's bugles answered, we mounted, and began to move in a dispersed march. We soon sighted Mariano Rosas's people atop a ridge. They sounded a halt, muster, and fall-to, all of which were obeyed much as a disciplined troop would have done it. We assumed battle formation with Baigorrita, myself, and my group at the head of the line and advanced in that same order. Mariano Rosas and his Indians performed the same maneuver. The two lines marched towards each other, some three hundred from each side.

The sun was rising at that moment, bathing the azure sphere in its light. The atmosphere was diaphanous. The remotest objects seemed well within sight, as if a short distance away. The sky was clear. Only the odd, pearly cloud sailed along the void with ponderous majesty. The morning's mild breeze barely rustled the golden grasses. The dew had sprinkled the land with a vast mantle of rich and varied pebbles.

When the two advancing lines were within fifty meters of one another, the bugles and cornets sounded a halt and the two Indian parties whooped their mutual greetings, palms beating lips. As their echoes died on the breeze all fell silent and the cries began anew. No one was armed. All rode excellent horses, wore their best clothes, and displayed their handsomest silver finery and smartest gear and leather. Mariano Rosas sent an Indian forward. Baigo-rrita followed suit. They placed themselves at an equal distance from each line, exchanged their reasons and returned to their re-spective points of departure. The two chiefs had now greeted each other and invoked the protection of God that they might deliber-ate wisely. The bugles and cornets sounded attention, orders were called out in Araucan, the second file of each line took two steps back, and those facing north turned to their left. They sounded a march and the two lines formed wings. Mariano Rosas sent an In-dian forward who approached me and spoke in his language. Ca-margo acted as my interpreter.

"General Mariano," he relayed, "says you should dismount and present yourself to Father Burela."

I thought I must be hearing wrong.

"And present myself to whom?" I asked Camargo, perplexed.

"To Father Burela!" he answered.

"Father Burela?" I exclaimed, looking at the Franciscans and my officers. "You cannot be serious."

"Tell him," I went on, "to tell Mariano that I do not have to greet Father Burela. I represent the President of the Republic here. If anything, it is Father Burela who should be greeting me."[2]

The messenger left and I sat there grumbling. I was indignant. This all stemmed from the intrigue that had gone on in Leubucó. The messenger returned, insisting as before that I present myself to Father Burela. I gave him an extremely sharp answer. I would sooner cut out of there with my people, I told him, and let the junta go on without me if that is what they wanted. I added that I was in no mood for joking.

The Indian relayed my answer.

Baigorrita had heard everything I said through Camargo and had him tell me we should get off our horses.

Mariano Rosas was not visibly altered by my answer. When he had conferred with his counselors his ambassador returned for the third time.

"The general says you would be greeting everybody."

"That is another thing entirely," I replied. With that I ordered all of my party to dismount, myself first.

Mariano Rosas and his party did the same.

Another Indian came forward and spoke with Camargo, upon whose instructions the ceremony began. Mariano Rosas and his party were in wing formation, as were Baigorrita and my party. That is, my left stood face to face with Mariano's right. We started out to the right marching several steps toward the east, then turned and followed north until we stood perpendicular to Mariano Rosas's left, which remained still. The angle thus formed, the greetings—vigorous handshakes and embraces—began. We filed before them, so that when Baigorrita shook hands with Mariano Rosas and I with Epumer my tail, militarily speaking, was embracing the last Indian in Mariano Rosas's party. We then continued filing by until the last of my assistants had hailed Mariano Rosas, whereupon we returned to the places from which we had first dismounted.

Mariano Rosas and his party at once advanced twenty paces. Baigorrita, myself, and my party simultaneously did the same, forming two squadrons. The two cavalry lines formed a circle in which the vanguard, right, and left wings of each were in conversation with the other. Mariano Rosas and his people dismounted. Baigorrita and I and our parties were now enclosed in two concentric circles, the outer one formed by horses, the inner one by Indians.

All of these moves were carried out in silence and in order. Clearly they were part of a familiar procedure. None of the Indians hobbled or tied his horse in the straw beds. The reins were simply left hanging, nor did the gentle animals ever move from their places.

Mariano asked all present to be seated. We took our places on the grass, which was still damp from the evening dew. No one laid down a poncho or saddle blanket. We all folded our legs Turkish style. Mariano Rosas gave me use of his interpreter, José, who took his place between us. The parliament began. I was under the unpleasant influence of what I had heard the night before and was still bristling at the aborted attempt to get me to greet Father Burela. Resting my elbows on my knees and covering my face with my hands, I prepared to hear Mariano Rosas's opening speech.

The interpreter informed me that the speaker was not yet addressing me.

The commander-in-chief began his talk and went on a long while, sometimes moderately, other times heatedly. He lowered his voice almost to inaudibility, then raised it to a shout. He waved his arms with his eyes fixed on the ground before him or looking skyward. At times, when reaching what must have been the sublime heights of eloquence, his head would shake and his body shudder as though in an epileptic seizure. President, Arredondo, Mansilla, horses, sugar, tea, tobacco, silver, and other Spanish words floated frequently through his oration.

His audience alternately approved and disapproved. When they approved, the orator lowered his voice. When they disapproved he would shout like a madman. He finished his inaugural speech amidst enthusiastic acclamation. Now it was time for the debate. The chief began by invoking the name of God. He protects the good, he said, directing his words to me, and punishes the wicked. He then spoke to me of the loyalty of the Indians, of the peace they had known in other times. If it failed, he said, it was through no fault of theirs. He gave me a course in freedom as practiced among them. This was why, he said, the principal captains and most important Indians by reason of fortune or age had been called together. They would say whether they liked the treaty. He was only doing their will, his duty being to safeguard their happiness. Never would he impose his will on them. It does not work among the Indians as it does with the Christians, he said, where the commander commands. Finally, he asked me to read the articles of the treaty relating to the quarterly distribution of mares, etc., etc.

I was preparing to answer when I heard them shouting derisively at Dr. Macías, who had taken a rifle I gave to Mariano Rosas and gotten himself mixed up with the chief's people.

"Get out of here! Get the doctor out!"

Poor Macías bowed his head and walked away in resignation, the laughing stock of the wilier Indians and of some Christians.

I reached into my pocket, took out my memory book, found the excerpt from the peace treaty and, attempting to mimic Ranquel oratorical custom, began my speech. I explained the treaty point for point. I spoke of God, the Devil, the land, the stars, the sun, and the moon. I spoke of the loyalty of the Christians, their desire to live in peace with the Indians, help them in their needs, teach them to work, and make them Christians that they might be happy. I spoke of the President of the Republic, General Arredondo, and myself.

It was my first speech.

It may be that among Christians I would have been applauded. I realized what effect my rhetoric and actions were having on the barbarians when I looked at the Indian who stole my gloves from me in Quenqué. He had put them on again and was fast asleep beside me.

Beyond any doubt we are destined to run an endless gamut of disappointments on our complicated journey through this beguiling world. Let the fanatics talk all they want. A fool can never be a hero, for the word hero awakens a sense of grandeur and implies intelligence. I was not born to be a ministerial orator, least of all among the Indians and that's all there is to it.

 MARIANO ROSAS DEMANDED that I reread the articles stipulating how many mares, how much tobacco, sugar, and mate, etc., would be allotted. He wanted all the Indians to hear for themselves what sort of peace treaty was going to be signed. This last phrase, "going to be," considering that the treaty was already signed, ratified, and exchanged, was a truly original Ranquel touch. I had heard it not once but several times and it did not sit well with me at all. The mood of the Indians was not at the moment a favorable one for me to score oratorical points. Moreover, the council appeared to be turning into a meeting to approve or reprehend the chief's conduct. I gathered as much from something he said several times. "I am now going to tell my Indians," he said, "what we have settled on and whatever they decide, that is what will be done."

I had been warned of this the night before.

I conceded, reading yet again those articles of the treaty of greatest concern and interest to them.

Food will ever be a primordial chapter for the human race.

"Not enough! Give more!" shouted several voices in Araucan. I knew what they were saying because certain Christians then said it in Spanish, provocatively, and added a few yeahs to back it up. Noting this, Mariano Rosas lectured me on the poverty of the Indians, demanding more mares, mate, sugar, and tobacco.

The Indians are poor because they do not like to work, I countered. They would be as rich as the Christians if they could learn to love work. I also told them I could not commit to more than the amount agreed upon, which was not a little but a lot.

"Too little! Not enough!" several of them shouted.

"Now do you see?" said Mariano Rosas, no longer using a brotherly tone of voice with me. "They say that what you are giving is little."

"I can see that," I said, "but it is not a little. On the contrary, it is very much."

"More, more, more," cried several voices together, more numerous than before. I addressed them, reading yet another time the articles detailing the allotment of mares, etc. I compared it with what Calfucurá's Indians were to receive and thus proved to them that they would be getting more.

"Tell me this isn't true," I said when no one contradicted me. Then, seizing my opening, I loosed oratorical thunderbolts on Calfucurá.

"He has broken the peace," I said. "He is a real bandit who does not fear God and works in bad faith. He found out that Mariano Rosas is receiving more through this peace treaty than he and so has again become the Christians' enemy, claiming that the Ranquel Indians have been given preference. But all that is just to see if he can get as much from this treaty as my brother Mariano Rosas and I have arranged for *his* Indians to get."

I laid as much stress on the word "brother" as I could and looked in Mariano Rosas's direction. "So you can see," I shouted with all the volume I had and in my best Indian mimicry. I wanted them to hear me and felt my style was winning them over. "So you can see that the Ranquels are preferred over Calfucurá's Indians."

Mariano Rosas asked me how many mares the Indians were allotted by the treaty. He was actually asking when the treaty had gone into effect. Evidently it was and was not a treaty. I answered that the Christians were bound by the treaty from the day the President of the Republic had signed it. He said he thought it began the day on which he returned it to me signed. I said no. He then asked when the President of the Republic had signed it. I gave him his answer, whereupon he added up the days and told me how much we owed them. At this point I explained what I had already gone over with him in Leubucó, namely, what the President, Congress, and budget are. I said that the government could not immediately furnish everything agreed upon. In order to provide the money, Congress must first decide if the treaty was right for them. I was complying with my orders in explaining all this, not that it was a simple task to make these barbarians understand our complicated constitutional apparatus. At any rate, I continued along those lines.

"Some things will be furnished to you on a running account," I said. "The rest will come when Congress approves the treaty. This is the President's way of showing the native inhabitants that he means them well."

It dawned on me as I made these observations that there was a perfect similarity between the Indians' discourse and my own. Mariano Rosas, I reasoned as my voice went on working, has signed the treaty. I, too, thought that was the end of it. Now it turns out that this council can nullify it. Precisely the situation with the President and the Congress. An identical case, is it not? The extremes meet.

I expected an appeal from Mariano Rosas but several Indians beat him to it.

"What if Congress does not approve the treaty?" they asked. "Will that mean no peace?"

Put yourself in my shoes, Santiago, and tell me you would not have been lost for an answer. I told them that would not happen. The Congress and the President are very good friends and the Congress is bound to approve and give him all the money he needs.

"But Congress can disapprove, can't it?" asked Mariano Rosas.

I didn't dare admit this was true because I would risk confirming their suspicion that the Christians were only trying to gain time. I resorted to oratory and mimicry, gave an extensive, fiery, sentimental, and emotional speech. I do not know if I was inspired, but then I must have been (or they did not understand me), for I noted certain currents of approval.

Eloquence has its secrets.

I always recall, when I see a crowd moved by resonating, euphonic, dazzling diction, a certain preacher from Catamarca. He was giving a sermon on Good Friday. There was a boy hidden under the pulpit who was whispering it to him. The priest had reached the most touching part, the moment when the Redeemer is about to expire, the Pharisees having finished him. The martyr's agony had begun to wrench tears from the congregation. Bitter sobs resounded in the temple vault. The preacher was moved as well and lost his train of thought. He looked under the pulpit to find that the boy had fallen asleep. He could not possibly continue speaking, so he turned to mimicry.

Quasi sermo corpis, Cicero has said, and this time it proved true.

Sorrow rose in the church like a tide. With a little help the crisis could be induced and the picture would be complete. Lost for words, the preacher put his arms and lungs to work. He gestured and shuddered and gave out wrenching cries. Panting and over-excited and lost in their own moaning and groaning, the congregation could hear nothing else. They could see, feel, and reason that the preacher had reached a sublime peak and they drowned him with wailing and lamentation. The sacred effigy bowed its head for the last time, all shuddered under the wave of sorrow, and the preacher disappeared.

At a recent banquet given for journalists by King Leopold, it was the man from *La Liberté* of Paris who garnered the most applause.[1] "Let *La Liberté* speak," they called out over and over, and so he rose to his feet. The lights, the wine, the laborious digestion of a sumptuous meal, and the conversations had left everyone somewhat lightheaded. This was a smart young writer, I should add. "Gentlemen," he said in *sa majesté*'s presence, "let's have a round of applause!"

Which was as far as they let him get. He began to move his head, wave his arms like oars, and the applause and the hurrahs grew.

"Liberté!" he said, and there was more applause, more hurrahs.

"Egalité!" Twice the applause, twice the hurrahs.

"Fraternité!" Triple the applause, triple the hurrahs.

There are certain ploys one must not abuse. I tried not to exhaust mine. When I saw that my audience was convinced that the President and Congress would not be likely to fight over a pittance, nay over a million or more, I turned the meeting over to Mariano Rosas, who proceeded to ask me by what right we had occupied the Río Quinto. This had always been Indian land, he said. His fathers and grandfathers had lived near the Chemecó, the Brava, and the Tarapendá lagoons, along Plata Hill, and in Langhelo. The Christians, he added, are still not satisfied. They want to stock up (his exact words) on more land. These accusations and appeals found an alarming echo in the crowd. Several Indians tightened the circle and moved in closer to hear my answer. I felt it cowardly to silence my conscience and sentiments, even before an audience of barbarians. With my elbows resting as always on my thighs, my face in my hands and my eyes turned downward, I began to answer. The land, I told them, does not belong to the Indians but to those who make it productive by working it. The chief stopped me right there.

"How can you say it is not ours? We were born here."

I asked him if he thought the land where a Christian was born belonged to that Christian. He said nothing, so I continued.

"Government forces have occupied Río Quinto for the greater security of the border. However, those lands do not yet belong to the Christians. It is everyone's land and no one's. Someday when the government sells it, some one or two or more people will own it and they will raise cattle on it and grow wheat and corn. Are you asking me by what right we stock up on land? I would ask you by what right you invade us to stock up on cattle."

"It is not the same," several of them said, interrupting. "We do not know how to work. No one has taught us how to do this like the Christians. We are poor. We have to go on our raids to live."

"But you steal what is not yours," I said, "because the cows and horses and sheep you bring back with you are not yours."

"And your Christians take our land away from us," they said.

"That is not the same," I answered. "In the first place, we do not recognize that land as yours while you do recognize that the cattle you rob is ours. In the second place, you cannot live off the land unless you work it."

"Why haven't you taught us to work after you took away our cattle?" observed Mariano Rosas.

"That's right! He's right!" yelled a number of voices. A dull murmur floated along the circle of human heads. I looked quickly and saw more than one face glowering at me.

"It is not true that the Christians have ever stolen your cattle from you," I said.

"It certainly is true," said Mariano Rosas. "My father has told me there were many animals roaming the Cuero and Bagual lagoons in other times."

"They came from the Christian cattle ranches," I countered. "You are all ignorant and do not know what you are talking about. If you were Christians, if you could work, you would know what I know. You wouldn't be poor, either; you would be rich. Listen to me, barbarians. I have something to say. We are all children of God, all Argentines. Are we not all Argentines?" I asked, looking at some of the Christians. The word pierced the tender fibers of patriotism and drew my audience out like magic.

"Yes, we are Argentines," they said despite themselves.

"And you are Argentines, too," I told the Indians. "And if not, what are you?" Now I was shouting. "I want to know what you are. Answer me. What are you? Will you say you are Indians? Well, I too am an Indian. Or do you think that I am a gringo?[2] Listen to what I have to say. You know nothing because you cannot read. You do not have books. You only know what you have heard from your fathers and grandfathers. I know many things that have happened before this time. Hear what I say so that you will not live in error. And don't tell me that what you are hearing is not true, because if I ask any of you the name of your grandfather's grandfather, you will not have an answer for me. Yet we Christians know these things. Hear now what I have to say.

"Many years ago the gringos disembarked in Buenos Aires. In those days the Indians lived where the sun rises, on the shores of a very big river. The gringos who came were all men. They brought no women. The Indians were simple. They did not know how to ride horses because there were no horses here. The gringos brought the first mare and the first horse, and cows and sheep. What do you think of that? See how you know nothing?"

"That's not true," some of them shouted. "Him not tell truth."

"Don't be barbaric, don't interrupt me, listen to me," I said, pressing on. "The gringos took the Indians' women from them, had children by them, and that is why I say that all those born in this land are Indians, not gringos.

"Hear me well.

"You were very poor then. The sons of the gringos, who are the Christians, us, Indians like you, taught you a number of things. We taught you to ride horses, to rope and hunt with the bolas, wear a poncho and a *chiripá* and breeches, heavy boots, spurs, and silver trim."

"That is not true," interrupted Mariano Rosas. "There were cows and horses and everything else here before the gringos came and it was all ours."

"You are wrong," I said. "The gringos, who were the Spaniards, brought all those things. I will prove it to you. You call the horse *cauallo*, the cow *uaca*, the bull *toro*, the mare *yegua*, the calf *ternero*, the sheep *oveja*, the poncho *poncho*, the lasso *lazo*, the herb tea *yerba*, sugar *achúcar*, and many other things just as the Spaniards did. And why is it that you do not call them by some other name? Because you didn't know these things until the gringos brought them. If you had known them before, you would have given them another name. Why do you call your brother *peñi*? Because before the fathers of the Christians came you already knew what a brother was. Why do you call the moon *quien* and not "moon" as the Christians do? For the same reason. Before the gringos came to Buenos Aires, the moon was in the sky and you knew her."

Faced with this irrefutable ethnological argument, an irascible Mariano Rosas asked me what all this had to do with the peace treaty.

"When did I ask you to tell me these things?" he said.

"And what do all your questions have to do with the peace treaty, which you have already signed? Do you suppose I came to the council for you to approve it? You already have approved it and you have to abide by it."

"And will your people abide by it?" he asked.

"Yes, we will," I said. "You have our word of honor as Christians."

"Then why if the Christians have word of honor did Manuel López have two hundred Indians' throats cut when he was at peace with them? Why if Christians have word of honor did your uncle Juan Manuel de Rosas order one hundred fifty Indians' throats cut at the Retiro barracks when he was at peace with the Indians?"[3] (I am quoting him almost verbatim.)

"Yeah, what about that! What about that!" shouted several Indians.

The council was beginning to look for all the world like a popular uprising and I was no longer the ambassador but the accused.

"Don't ask me to settle those scores," I said. "Other men did those things. The president we have now is not like others that we have had before. I haven't asked you about the slaughter of Christians that the Indians have committed whenever they could." Then I threw the ball back into Mariano Rosas's court.

"What do the slaughter that López and Rosas ordered have to do with the peace treaty?" I gave him no time to answer. "You," I went on, "have killed more Christians than Christians have killed Indians." I made up every slaughter imaginable and added them to the ones I could actually remember.

"*Winca! Winca* lying!" cried several of them, and here and there around the circle a sort of clamor began.

This was the worst symptom.

Several of my assistants had retired to the shade of a carob tree.

The sun was burning like fire and the talk had been going for several hours now. There was no one left with me except the Franciscans and my adjutant Demetrio Rodríguez. Clearly the situation was growing more dangerous. I looked at my compadre Baigorrita, who sat there like a statue. I could not draw his attention. I looked around for other familiar faces to ask them with my eyes to quell the restless spirit of the mob. They all sat there speechless. If they looked at me at all they did not see me. "You see," said Mariano Rosas, "we Indians are very few and the Christians many. An Indian is worth more than a Christian."

I nearly let that one go unanswered, but rather than lower my flag, I made up my mind then and there to be heard. They can kill me, I thought, but they are going to hear me out.

"That was a barbaric thing to say, brother. All men are equal whether Christian or Indian, because all are children of God." Then I turned to Father Burela who, like a ghost at a banquet, was watching the turbulence with never so much as a look or word of support for me.

"Let this venerable priest speak," I said. "He is here among the Indians in the name of Christian charity. The government and the rich people of Buenos Aires have given him money to ransom the captives. He can tell you that what I have just said is true."

The reverend gave no answer. He wore a long face and his lips were drooping. His eyes were open wider than usual and his nose was inflamed. He was sweating bullets and was as pale as wax. What a contrast he made with Father Marcos and Father Moisés, who said nothing because they could not speak, had not been asked to. Yet their kindly faces wore an evangelical peace bespeaking the generous concern one friend feels in seeing another compromised by a stiff challenge.

"Let Father Burela speak," I went on. "He has no sword and you cannot help but trust him. Let him say whether the Christians hate the Indians."

The reverend gave no answer. His face looked to me like that of a man under sentence. No doubt his conscience had his tongue tied, the hypocrite.

"Let Father Burela speak," I insisted. "He knows whether the Christians want the Indians to live together in peace and give up their shiftless ways as Coliqueo's Indians have done who now live near Junín."

The reverend gave no answer. Then, whether it was the horses spooking, whatever it was—I don't know—but I felt something like a shudder go through the crowd. I will confess I feared an attack. Redoubling my energy, I continued.

"I am the representative of the President of the Republic here," I said. "I can promise you that the Christians will not go back on their word. If you keep your part of it, the peace treaty will be honored. You can back out of your part of the commitment but sooner or later you will come to regret it, as will the Christians if they deceive you. I have not come here to lie. I have come to tell the truth and the truth is what you are hearing from me. If the Christians should abuse the good faith you show them, then you would be right to take revenge for their falseheartedness. In the same way, if you do not show me and those accompanying me our due respect and consideration, if you do not allow me to return or you kill me, the day will come—mark my words—when the army will put you all to the sword for being traitors.⁴ And in these immense pampas and these lonely forests there will be no memory, no sign that you ever lived here."

Camargo came over to me at that moment.

"Talk about what they will be getting with the treaty," he mumbled in my ear.

"And what else do you want the Christians to do?" I said. "Are you not getting two thousand mares to give out to your poor? And sugar, tobacco, paper, firewater, clothing, oxen, plows, seeds to plant, and money for the chiefs and captains? What more do you want?"

After a long silence, Mariano Rosas addressed the gathering.

"We are all set then," he said, "but we want to know how much of each thing you are going to give us. Go ahead and speak, brother." And turning to the Indians he said, "Now listen closely."

Once more I enumerated the provisions of the treaty. At last calm was reestablished and the council appeared to be coming to an end. I took the renewed mood of goodwill as an opportunity to dispel any and all motives of future resentment, explaining that my presence there did not insure peace. I was a representative of the government and a subaltern of my superior officer, General Arredondo, with whose permission I now sat before them. They must not think, I said, that because another officer should replace me the peace was thereby altered. No, that officer would have to abide by the treaty and carry out the orders that the government gave him. I told them they often mistook the officers with whom they had their dealings for the government. At no time was my absence from the frontier to be the basis of any complaint or of a refusal to observe the agreement faithfully. Be they near or far, I told them, they would always have a friend in me, one who would do everything in his powers on their behalf if they deserved it.

Mariano Rosas rose from his place.

"It is over, brother," he said with the friendliest smile in the world.

For nine consecutive hours the friars and I had been sitting in the same position in the same place. When we tried to get up our stiffened legs would not obey.

We had to ask for help.

We got up.

Mariano Rosas said that certain Indians of importance would like to speak with us privately. I was hardly in the mood for a conference, but what was I to do? I accepted.

My first interlocutor was the old man with the crutches. We sat down face to face on the ground, called for our respective interpreters, and the talk began. The old man was a most recalcitrant conversationalist. He spoke of his forebears, of the services he had rendered, his wisdom and patience, the leagues he had ridden to come to the council, this world, the hereafter, and so forth. When I thought he was about to say it had been a great pleasure to meet me, he played his ace.

"I have listened carefully to all of your reasons and do not like any of them."

"Well I'll be damned," I said under my breath, "if the old man doesn't want to stir up some trouble." Several Indians had formed a circle around him and were voicing their agreement with what he had just said. I seized the moment to speak. I told him I was very glad to have met him and that I was deeply sorry that an elder as respectable, as experienced, and as worthy of the Indians' appreciation as he should have troubled himself to travel so far to see me. If he should ever pass through Río Cuarto, I said, it would be my great pleasure to receive and regale him in my home, and now that peace had been made and they would be receiving so many things—and I ran off the entire list to him—we should all regard one another as children of the same god.

The Indian repeated word for word everything he had said the first time and topped it off as before.

"I have listened carefully to all of your reasons and do not like any of them."

I did the same, repeating my answer. We went at it for a good long while. Nine times he said the same thing, nine times I answered the same as well.

The old man gave in.

Other personages followed him. I had to speak with them all. They all said almost the very same thing and to all I gave almost the same answer. God took pity on me. After eleven mortal and unforgettable hours such as I have never spent before nor hope to spend in the rest of my days, I was delivered from bothersome people. That one day was worth all the others and bear in mind that I have only painted it in broad strokes. To render it in all its color I would need the framework of an entire book.

I was tired and had had enough. I stretched out on the soft grass and watched pensively for a while as the Indians scattered like flies in every direction, disappearing as swiftly as happiness itself.

 WHILE THEY WERE bringing in the horses, I rested and thought a while about the strange council which I had just attended. I was lost in thought when my compadre Baigorrita appeared. He had accompanied Mariano Rosas a certain distance on the road to Leubucó and then turned back with the intention of spending the night in Quenqué. He came to where I was sitting, dismounted, sat down beside me, and spoke through San Martín. He said he was leaving now and that I should not wonder that he had not spoken in my defense at the junta. Mariano's Indians were the reason why. If he had stood up for me, they would have said he was more a friend of mine than of theirs. He said there was much *reason in my reasons* and that the men of experience knew this, though none so well as Mariano Rosas, who nevertheless had acted as he did because if he had not his Indians too would have thought him more a friend of mine than of theirs. I should go now and not worry; Mariano was my friend. I could count on him, Baigorrita, any time and for whatever I might need. Wasn't that, after all, why we called ourselves compadres?

This language was a revelation to me. I began to see why my compadre had been so indifferent, withdrawn, and churlish during the council. It was a diplomatic gambit. He knew perfectly well the steps he must take and had a part to play.

The smoke had been greater than the fire as it turned out.

I still wanted to know if these disciples of Machiavelli would have allowed me to be sacrificed had the *populus barbaro*, exasperated by the reasons in my nonreason, laid hold of me. I was anxious to speak with Mariano Rosas to see if he would be as frank with me as Baigorrita had been, who was his ally and at the same time his rival in the righteous struggle for prestige among the Indians.

San Martín capped my compadre's thoughts with a personal comment.

"That's the way the Indians are, sir. Baigorrita is one of the main chiefs, so he has to be very careful with Mariano Rosas. The Indians are very jealous and untrusting. If you want to stay on their good side you must not appear to be a friend of the Christians."

Baigorrita interrupted. He said through San Martín that it was late. He wanted to get going. My horses finally made it in. I ordered a quick change of mounts and a moment later we abandoned the border line. I directed my party to proceed slowly along the road to Leubucó. Camilo Arias, an assistant, and I headed south in the company of my compadre. Several Indians accompanied him, among them the one with the crutches. He introduced me to some who had not visited with me in Quenqué and I had to endure their greetings, handshakes, embraces, and requests, and when we reached the place where we had spent the night before the council, we said good-bye.

Baigorrita's farewell was as cold as his reception had been cordial.

We galloped away in opposite directions.

I gave my horse free rein and was contemplating the green solitude of those grasslands in silence when I heard galloping behind me. I turned around without slowing down and saw a group of riders, Baigorrita among them, running to catch up with me. I stopped. Something was happening. My compadre rode up and San Martín said, "Baigorrita says he has come for the final embrace and the final good-bye."

And so we embraced.

The Indian hugged me effusively and when we loosened our embrace he took my right hand vigorously in his own and, shaking it hard, said, "Adiós, compadre! Amigo!" His face fairly beamed warmheartedness.

"Adiós, compadre! Amigo!" I said and again we separated.

I left at a gallop and was hurrying my horse to see if I could reach my people before the sun set when a rider caught up with me. It was San Martín. Baigorrita had sent him to say good-bye once more. He said he sent his fervent best wishes for my happiness, reminded me I had said I would visit him again, and lest I forget for a moment that I was dealing with an Indian, asked me to send him some silver spurs. I answered everything properly, dispatched the messenger, and continued on my way. I soon rejoined my people. There were several Indians spread out ahead of us. I recognized Mariano Rosas among them. His oldest son rode alongside him. When he heard my horses he turned around and, seeing it was I, stopped.

"Good afternoon, brother," he said in a markedly amicable tone. I had never seen him in such friendly spirits.

"Good afternoon, brother," I answered with deliberate dryness.

"How has it been with you?" he went on. "Get those partridges out for my brother here," he added, addressing his son, who proceeded to take two excellent cooked martins and some bread pies out of the saddle bags.

"It has been all right, brother."

He took the partridges and the pies and handed them to me.

"Eat, brother."

He was wearing a particularly devilish expression. It seemed the Indian was laughing to himself. I took the partridges, passed one to him, gave half a pie to the friars, and split the rest with him. We trotted along, munching in silence.

"Let's gallop," he said.

"No, my horses are loaded down," I said, "and I am in no hurry to arrive. You go ahead and gallop if you're in a hurry."

"What did you think of the council?" he asked.

"What did I think of it?" I said, looking him in the eye as if to say, I'll give you three guesses what I thought of it. He knew what I meant.

"It takes patience with these Indians," he said. "You have to know them. They are not very trusting and as soon as they see that someone is a friend of the Christians they think they are being deceived. They have been betrayed so many times! You saw how your compadre Baigorrita acted."

"What did he have to fear from me?" I asked.

"Nothing, not from you."

"Well, then?"

"But if I had agreed with all your reasons there is no telling what they might have said about me."

"And what if they had insulted me or tried to kill me?"

"Go on!" he answered. He took off at a gallop, yelling, "See you, brother, I'll be expecting you for supper."

"All right, brother, I'll be in Leubucó in no time. I am just going to rest a little bit in La Aguada."

The sun had all but sunken below the distant line. A broad, luminous, radiant swath of deep crimson bathed the horizon in its lovely, shifting purplish glow. Golden as they basked in it, the clusters of western clouds, like lofty moving mountains crowned in eternal snows, rose skyward in immense spirals, in formless figures of incommensurable vastness. The harsh north wind folded his wings. Soft and mild, the playful zephyrs left the traveler's brow refreshed. Grasses rippled like the unfathomed sea depths after the tempest. Rising on their pliant stems, the wildflowers splattered the fields with vibrant colors. An exquisitely mild, delicate perfume, as imperceptible as the vague memory of a first love kiss, wafted on intoxicating breezes. Glancing off the atmosphere, the sun's last rays enveloped the earth in the poetic mantle of dusk. The dying light of day mingled with night's mystic shadows to make way for the celestial wayfarer. When we reached the edge of a tiny lagoon, in whose crystalline mirror numberless water birds chirruped in chorus, the moon shone amidst flickering stars like a chaste silver-haired matron with her retinue of vestal maidens.

We came to a halt, I ordered a change of mounts and, thirsty for repose, stretched out on the soft hay and crossed my arms behind me to make a comfortable pillow. How sweet life is far removed from the din and artifice of civilization! And oh would I trade you here and now a whole day of this giddy existence for the savage pleasure of an hour in the open country.

While they were saddling the horses I thought about the day's events and, quite frankly, the Indians brought to mind what goes on in the Christians' parliaments. As the two party chiefs, Mariano Rosas and Baigorrita had the terrain covered and the vote secured. Yet each of them had paid lip service to popular sentiment. Is this not what we see all the time? Are war and peace not resolved in this manner? The people will put up with anything, will they not? They will even let their destiny be bartered away, so long as they are allowed to shout a little. Don't they make presidents, governors, and ministers who stand for certain ideas, tendencies, and aspirations, and don't the legislative bodies then do whatever they please while the multitudes watch in silence? Wouldn't the people rather be governed by justice than by that eternal and iniquitous immorality known among unscrupulous politicians as statecraft? What, if not this, goes on in the civilized world?

Mariano Rosas, his decision for peace already made when he accused me publicly of Lopez's and Rosas's atrocities; Baigorrita, under the sway of the same idea, silent and irresolute as all those gathered could plainly see: Did they not play the selfsame role Napoleon III did, arming himself to the teeth while proclaiming that *empire is peace*?

They were lying, were they not?

When Mariano Rosas and Baigorrita, having signed the peace treaty, declared in council that they would do whatever the majority resolved, were they not mimicking those who on more than one occasion have declared in Congress the opposite of what they had already agreed to with the foreigner?

I have learned so much on this sojourn!

If they had told me the Indians would teach me how to fathom humankind, I would have answered with Homeric peals of laughter. Like Gulliver on his voyage to Lilliput, however, I have seen the world as it really is on my voyage to the Ranquels.

A bunch of poor devils is what we are!

Midgets give us the proper measure of giants; barbarians, of the civilized.

It remains to be seen whether we would be happier putting pygmies in the curule chairs our magnates occupy, and trading the French buskin for the coltskin boot. So poor are the heroes and so despotically imposing the fashion of our day that we might give serious thought to the advantages and consequences of a social revolution. At any rate, yesterday's idols do not withstand criticism and in that respect are like the Ranquels, who can yet deceive the wiliest of us.[1]

On such byways did my thoughts wander until Calixto Oyarzábal approached me.

"Your horse is ready, sir."

I stood up.

"On your horses!" I shouted and with that mounted and galloped on to the great trail of Leubucó. We soon entered the hills. The sky was growing overcast. We came to a marshy clearing where fleeting, sickly lights appeared and disappeared. When I thought I was upon them they would dart away like butterflies. It was the miasmata. We were crossing an Indian cemetery and were almost at the door to Mariano Rosas's tent.

We arrived.

They had the food and music ready and were expecting me. I ate and endured the Negro with the accordion one more time. Then, finding my alleged compadre Mariano in mellow spirits, I requested Dr. Macías's release. He said yes.

We shall see later what an Indian's yes is worth. I said good-bye and left the tent. I sat down beside the fire my assistants had made and, though not especially tired, fell asleep. I was awakened by the barking of dogs. There were sounds of a woman screaming coming from Mariano Rosas's tent. I sneaked up to get a look. The chief had punished one of his wives and wanted to punish another but his son was against him, threatening to stab his father if he touched his mother. It was at once a horrible and a touching scene. They had been drinking, the tent was in chaos, and the women and dogs had taken cover in a corner. The little Indian boy and the naked little Indian girls were crying. A dying fire was the only light.

Mariano Rosas was roaring with fury.

He backed away, however, from a son protecting his mother. Judging by what I heard the next day, the boy would have been quite capable of killing his father had the latter not got hold of himself. We see, then, that even among the barbarians the beloved person who carried us in her womb, who nursed us in her bosom and rocked us in her lap is the object of sacred reverence.

I went to bed hoping and intending to sleep, but apparently by divine decree my nights in Leubucó were to be sleepless ones. Just as I was drifting off, I was awakened by an accordion serenade, complete with Negro and all. It was presided over by Mariano Rosas's four sons and it was hard to say which of them was drunkest. It was no use fighting it. There were fireworks and firewater enough for the *yapaí* to last a long while. Rather than drink it, I just went through the motions and spilled the nauseous liquid out wherever I could. At length the impertinent rabble passed out and I slipped away to an undisturbed night's sleep.

PEACE HAD DEFINITELY been attained. Popular suffrage had placed its sovereign seal on the council and suspicion had vanished.

They now regarded me as an Indian.

Many visitors came to greet me. Fair winds were blowing my way in Leubucó. Ashamed, embarrassed, the plotters begged my pardon with studied smiles and kindliness. I pretended not to have noticed their scheming. This was diplomatic terrain. I reserved punishment for a more opportune time.

I was concerned about Dr. Macías. Two years of suffering and humiliation had crushed his spirit. He expected nothing of his fellow man. Shipwrecked, a man wrestles with death as he watches the angry wave draw near that will swallow and carry him to the cold caverns of the deep. In a supreme effort he seizes a plank which others in their desperation then take from him, all in the exact instant in which the bold fisherman approaches with his boat. And so life goes. Sorrow finally dries the eyes, ingratitude numbs the heart. The unwanted truth destroys our last illusions. We are like walking mummies filing disconsolately down the dark steps of eternity. Yet something makes us tremble even as it comforts us, rattling us with a galvanizing, ineffable energy. It is hope in God, and woe to him who though he lose all faith keeps no safe sanctuary in his bones for that purer faith.

Macías could not believe I would dare demand his liberty. He never said so, but I knew it. Dejected, he mistook me for one of the chief's adulators. His attitude was a worthy one. He took every opportunity to show me that his existence was becoming more and more unendurable, but he never begged me. The poor wretch bore on his brow the marks of an intense, piercing sorrow. It veiled his bitterness. His great, dark, round eyes strayed restlessly, sometimes staring at the ground, and misting up as he remembered, no doubt, his sweet, lost freedom and fought back the tears.

Macías is forty years old. He comes from a respectable Buenos Aires family and is engaged to a young woman of English origin. His father is a well-known Spaniard in the family trade. Imagine an Arab with a large, aquiline nose and white hair and beard and you will have his portrait. He took his first studies in don Juan de la Peña's school, where I met him. Later he went on to university studies to prepare for medical school, which he completed to become a doctor. His life has swung wildly between extremes. He has been a physician, a woodsman on the isles of the Paraná, and an industrialist in El Chaco, among whose Indians he spent several years as a volunteer. There is something poetic, novelesque, and mysterious in his existence, but I must not draw the veil back any further.

Macías and I lost track of each other for a great many years. Until my arrival in Leubucó we had not seen each other since our school days. He had an unlucky gift for getting on the bad side of almost everyone in Indian country who could have made sure he received the least possible abuse. He is a strange character, both docile and indomitable, firm and versatile. He is capable of dangerous deeds, yet has no sense of personal worth, two things which explain his presence among the Indians—despite not being a captive—as well as his lack of prestige with them.

Macías was in Río Cuarto in 1867. Colonel Elía, chief of the Córdoba borderlands, had initiated peace negotiations with the Indians. Macías offered his services and departed with the proper credentials. Whether Elía was not in fact authorized to negotiate with the Indians, or whatever the reason, the fact is that our plenipotentiary was left to his own devices and his own luck. His lack of luck, or of tact—curses the both of which tend to obscure man's superlative gifts, thwart his plans, and make all his illusions vanish, as a windstorm will strip the leafiest tree bare—turned Macías the plenipotentiary into Macías the prisoner. He wrote and wrote and wrote, but his letters went unanswered. Even the soldier sent along as his assistant deserted him. Alone, having neither servant nor subsistence, a drifter, what was he to live on and how was he to escape? He was forced to accept his food from the Indians and the Christians living with them for political reasons. Either he was weak or he miscalculated or it was the easiest thing to do, I have no idea, but he sided with the latter group, then clashed with them, which left him no choice but to turn to the Indians. He befriended Mariano Rosas and rose from prisoner to *secretary*. The first notes I received from the chief in Río Cuarto were written by my old classmate.

I misjudged him from that distance.

There were so many stories going around about why he had gone to the Indians that it was difficult to remain detached from what popular suspicion about him suggested. Who can counter the opinions of those whom we know regarding those whom we don't know? Where is the head so steadfast that it can scoff at opinion and wait? Do our judgments about others generally come from direct observation? Are not the love, hate, sympathy, and antipathy we profess in fact refractory in origin? Getting named to a secretariat will net you some envy anywhere you may be—Paris or Berlin, Buenos Aires or Leubucó. Macías had excited the rivalry of the Christians. They feared his rising star. They began to scheme and were successful at it.

Though I meant him no harm, I contributed to his downfall

from Río Cuarto. As I have already explained, I misjudged him and wrote to Mariano Rosas that his secretary was no good and that his notes said precisely the opposite of what his messengers were telling me. This was true. What remained to be seen was whether or not Macías was writing what he was told and whether the discrepancies between his written messages and their spoken ones were not merely warped grammar or Ranquel diplomacy. Time, in initiating me in the ways of Leubucó, clarified this mystery for me. Macías was following his orders scrupulously, but his notes were read to Mariano Rosas by other Christians before leaving the chancery in Indian territory. Macías therefore fell from grace and favor. Those who had held him in esteem when he was secretary abandoned him, and those who had no regard for him as secretary redoubled their hostility. He was subjected to every kind of humiliation and ended up another nobody in the chief's following. He slept wherever he happened to find himself at nightfall and ate wherever he could beg a scrap of meat. His clothes were deplorable.

Poor, luckless Macías!

When I saw him all he had for clothing was a dirty, tattered shirt, plain cotton breeches, and an old red *chiripá*. What remained of a hat covered his top and his boots were all holes. His feet were ruined, his hands callused. He kept everything he owned in a leather bag: buttons, thread, pebbles, needles, sugar, medicinal herbs, tobacco, mate, paper. A four-sided gold reliquary wrapped in a piece of rag held pictures of his parents and his two children.

Poor, hard-luck Macías!

Try to imagine how it felt to see him, a high-born and well-educated man who had enjoyed life and frequented high society, reduced to this. He could not comprehend it himself! He would see me happy, festive, and content—I was pretending that things had never looked brighter—and he figured I was hardened to misfortune. His heart was atrophied with pain; he thought mine had gone dry.

Poor, luckless Macías!

The Indians spoke ill of him. As far as they were concerned he was a madman. The Christians did the same, spreading horrible stories around about him. They blamed all their vices on him. So dire was his situation that he wrote to the President of the Republic but received no answer. And, indeed, how was he to get one when his letters had been intercepted and held up?

I called Captain Rivadavia and had him ask Mariano Rosas if he was receiving visitors. I was told to go in whenever I pleased, that he was about to have his lunch. I went to his tent. He looked shaken up from the previous night, was paler than usual. He was sitting beside the fire when I came in and did not move when he saw me.

"Good morning, brother," he said. "Excuse me for not standing up. I am not so well today."

"Stay comfortable," I said as I sat down. "How was your night?"

"Bad," he said. He knit his brow the way we do when a mortifying memory has hold of us.

"What's the matter?"

"My head hurts."

"Do you want to take a very good remedy that I have with me?"

"If you know what it is I will take it."

I left and came right back with a vial of some wonderful drops I have for the corona. It was all I had for a first-aid kit. I opened the vial and asked for a pitcher of water. I poured all the water out of it except for a couple of inches at the bottom. I put sixty drops in. "Watch," I said, taking a swallow. I did not want him to be ill at ease when he took his.

"I don't mind drinking it, brother," he said and, taking the jar, downed every last drop in it.

"A little bitter, that's all," he said.

"Yes," I answered.

"And did you rest well?"

"Very well."

"Damned Indians, eh?"

"Yeah. The junta went pretty rough there for a while."

"Hey, they don't all catch on right away."

"That's for sure."

"What about your friend Father Burela? Why didn't he help you out?"

"I don't know. He seemed a little scared to me."

He smiled as if to say "a little more than a little" and, stroking one of his sons, sat him on his knees.

"What a bull, this one!" he said.

It was the son who had defended his mother the night before.

"He is a good-looking boy," I said.

"But he's no good. He was going to kill me," he said, both

pleased with, and amazed at, his son. The little Indian understood what his father was saying but paid him no mind. He perked up, yawned, stood up, spoke in his language and ducked out of the tent as only our gauchos do. Mariano watched him until he got to the door.

"Bull, brother," he shouted once more.

"How old is he?"

"He must be . . ." he signaled twelve with his fingers.

"He is still very young."

"Yes, but already a gaucho."

They brought out the meal. It was the same as always. Corn and squash stew, roast beef, and roast horse meat.

"Well, brother, I will be leaving soon so that I can start sending the rations."

"Whenever you like, brother. I only have a little left to talk over with you."

"I mean to be on my way in two days."

"Then we will talk tomorrow."

"Fine. I am going to take Macías with me."

No answer. He had refusal written on his face.

"He is not doing you any good here."

Silence.

"He is a poor fool," I said.

"Look, brother," he answered, and was about to go on when two visitors interrupted us. They made their greetings and sat down. I ate the rest of my meal and stood up to leave. "We will talk later," I said, and left the tent. I was cross.

I went straight to Epumer's to pay him a visit.

Mariano Rosas had lent me his horse.

I was received with gallantry in Epumer's tent. Calfucurá's spy, the one who struck me so oddly in Quenqué, was crouched in a corner like a clay idol. He looked at me when I came in as he might have looked at a dog.

What was he doing there?

F OR ALL ITS UPS AND DOWNS, *the grand council was a kind of climax against which the disintegration of desert society loomed portentous for Mansilla. The quixotic and often comical pilgrimage to a dubious Mecca has garnered for the narrative a multitude of stories which serve to diminish the impact of the loss of Argentina's Indian-Christian world. Mansilla's special universe — first an upbringing in the bosom of the Dictator's family, later an escape to enlightened humanism through world travel — enables him to weave a safety net into which the many redeemable and indeed superior "specimens" of the desert realm are expected to fall. His task in that regard is to assess what is worth saving by comparing it with values already familiar to his readers, although subject to question by them.*

The Argentina which Mansilla envisions would arise from a Christian civilization as open at its fringes as the "barbarians" are innately educable. Every episode in this latter part of the story juggles these imperfect terms one way or another. Doña Fermina Zárate's concubinage exemplifies it. The Indians' way of training a horse — befriending the animal and mastering it are one and the same for them — upholds it. Chief Ramón is a silversmith who has rigged himself a bellows in what for Mansilla is an impressive display of native technical ingenuity. Doctor Macías's freedom can be coaxed from Chief Mariano Rosas once the chief understands that he has been hoodwinked by the jealous Christian renegades who hate the doctor; that is, once the chief gets to the kernel of deceit.

This is docility in the good sense of the word, and it is not unlike the changes that Mansilla himself must go through. As disturbing to him as was lifting the pox-infested body of Chief Ramón's brother in Chapter 2, he all but faints away while holding Chief Mariano Rosas's daughter in his arms at her baptism in Chapter 58.

In the first instance he is performing a corporal work of mercy for the benighted barbarian. In the second, the girl is wearing a dress stripped from a statue of the Virgin in a chapel in Córdoba during one of the Indian raids. His perhaps exaggerated shudder nevertheless gets something further across about the nature of fusing the Christian body to the heathen one.

On his way back to Río Cuarto and normal military duties, Mansilla waxes sentimental for the camaraderie, the solidarity, and the deeper ties that have united him with the seventeen men who have accompanied him to the desert. Although he has points of information to make in the Epilogue, it is sentiment per se that marks the note on which Mansilla closes. The social scientist, the anthropologist, and even the career military man yield to the novelist, the intellectual, the witness. It is the amalgam of all of them that speaks through the final pages of Mansilla's shambling, improbable Excursión.

EPUMER HAD HIS tent about a quarter of a league from Mariano Rosas's settlement.

There is no Indian more feared than Epumer. He is brave in war, terrible in peace when drunk. Firewater makes a madman of him. Now it may be adulation and it may be truth, but they all say he is a good man when he has not lost his head. He lives well, luxuriously in fact. Everyone goes to his house and is well received.

They had been waiting for me. The tent was freshly swept and the floor watered down. Everything was in order. Epumer was sitting on a high seat made of sheepskin and blankets. There was another, higher one across from him that was reserved for me. The squaws stood waiting, ready to serve the food at the first sign. The captives stirred the fire. Epumer stood up, shook my hand, embraced me, told me to make myself at home, and motioned for me to sit down. When I did so, he sat down as well. The rest of the riffraff and freeloaders present did not take their seats until Epumer gave them the sign.

The conversation ambled on about Indian customs. They begged my pardon for being unable because of their poverty to present me with the kinds of gifts I deserved, though a generous, modest, and well-mannered Christian could not have regaled me any better. Epumer introduced me to his wife, Quintuiner, his two daughters, and even the captives, whose air of wholesome content-ment caught hold of my attention powerfully.

"How are you girls doing?" I asked them.

"Very well, sir," they answered.

"Don't you wish you could leave here?"

They blushed and said nothing.

"They have children," said Epumer, "and they are not looking for men."

"We are very much loved here," the captives added.

"I am glad to hear that," I said. Then one of them blurted out. "I wish all the captives could say the same, *your excellency*."

She was from Córdoba.

Epumer motioned for his wife and daughters to sit down and ordered the meal be served. They obeyed.

They were dressed in their newest and finest. The *pilquén* was of a rather fine red silk. Their necklaces and belts, bracelets and an-klets were beads. Their big triangular earrings and their brooches were of heavy, tooled silver. Oddly enough, the blanket was a woolen, plaid one. They had painted their lips and fingernails with carmine, put numerous black beauty marks on their cheeks, and shaded their lower eyelids and eyelashes. They looked very pretty. Epumer's wife especially reminded me of a certain quite elegant lady from Buenos Aires whom I do not wish to name. After all, we couldn't have that, could we? Imagine putting her charm, beauty, and sweet personality, that lithe, wickerwork figure and her so-prano voice—and how she captures the delicate accents of Cam-pagna—putting all that prestige alongside a squaw![1]

They brought the meal, chinaware, place settings, glasses, and tablecloth. We started with *pasteles a la criolla* made by one of the captives. I had two of them even though I had just eaten with Ma-riano Rosas. Next they brought out the *carbonada*. Epumer said he had inquired about my tastes. He had asked my assistant what I liked to eat. I could not refuse them and ate a plateful. It could not have tasted any better. The meat was thick and there was only the thinnest bit of fat on it. A roast followed—there was lamb and beef to choose from—then a pot of stew. For bread we had some meal cooked on the open coals. Dessert was fried corn and cheese cakes mashed with carob and served with wild wasp honey. I was so full after the *carbonada* that I refused the rest, though in vain. They insisted and I had to have some of everything. I felt sorry for them. They kept saying, "Please excuse us if it is not good—she made it," and they would point to this or that captive, who would look at me as if to say, "We did our very best for you."

What a scene it was! A copy of civilization in the open desert, on the pampas, and among the barbarians leaves an indescribable impression.

Calfucurá's spy watched all that went on with a restive, owlish gaze.

"Who is that?" I asked Epumer.

"I don't know him," he said.

"Well, I do."

"He came here a little while ago. He was hungry so we gave him something to eat."

"And you don't know him?"

"No!"

"He's a lying scoundrel."

"And what harm is a poor man like him going to do us here?"

This answer shamed me. The quadroon had the dog from Quenqué with him. I remembered that the man had a heart and was maybe even more down on his luck than I was. I changed the subject. The spy heard me talking about him and did nothing about it other than to flash me a strange look and withdraw further and further into himself.

I took out my memorandum book and asked Epumer and his family what they wanted me to send them from Río Cuarto. I wrote it down. They requested very little: cloth for blankets, needles and thread. Epumer said he wanted a silk vest.

"A red one?" I asked.

"No, black," he answered.

I stood up and took my leave. Breaching local custom, they walked me out to the hitching post. I climbed on my horse and departed. At a certain distance I turned around. They were still watching me. I waved and they answered with a flutter of handkerchiefs.

I arrived at Mariano Rosas's tent. He was sitting alone in the entrance. His visitors had left. I climbed down, tied his horse to the post, thanked him, and walked around to my quarters. Inside, the Franciscans were enjoying the pleasures of a siesta in pious restfulness. The noise I made coming in woke them. I told them of my visit to Epumer's. We talked at some length about the frank and cordial hospitality he extended today after the violent and troubling scenes of the first days. Finally, I told them I had determined to leave within two days. Father Marcos expressed a desire to remain behind and arrange for the founding of the chapel to which the peace treaty alluded. This seemed an imprudent idea and I amicably opposed it. Father Moisés gathered from my reasons that I was reluctant to leave his companion alone, so he offered to stay behind with him. This was generous of him. I pacified both of them and gave further reasons for my refusal. At length I told them they should be thinking about the baptisms they were to do the next day. I told Father Moisés to go request permission from Mariano Rosas. He sent an assistant in to see if the chief was receiving visitors. He was, and the father then left our ranch for Mariano's tent. The chief had just received other visitors. I went in behind Father Moisés.

Mariano Rosas seated the father beside him. He had granted his permission as requested and entreated him to baptize his oldest daughter. I was to be her godfather. They brought out the food, a pot of stewed mare's meat. "Father," said Mariano to the good Franciscan, "to show you that I am a good Christian and that it gives me pleasure to see men such as yourselves here, let us eat from the same plate." So saying, he set between himself and the father a plate that they were at that moment handing to him.

"It is my great pleasure," said the Franciscan, who then with no revulsion whatsoever began gobbling up the mare meat as if it were royal fare. For my part, I declined, explaining why lest they think I was upset with them. The custom in those parts at day's end is to eat as many times as the opportunity presents itself.

Some of the visitors were familiar. I struck up a conversation with them. Father Marcos for his part gave a long explanation to Mariano Rosas on the meaning of baptism. "I know that," the chief kept saying. Father Marcos insisted that the little girl they were going to baptize be educated as a Christian. The chief promised him this. When he had finished his plate, Father Marcos excused himself and left. I stayed where I was and looked for a comfortable position, which I found when I lay down. I let Mariano Rosas talk to his visitors and fell asleep. When I awoke, I was alone in the tent. I got up and found Mariano in the entrance again. I sat down beside him.

"Well, brother," I said, "do I take Macías with me or not?"

"Let's go in," he said, getting up and entering the tent. I followed him and he motioned me in ahead of him from the doorway. We sat down and he spoke first.

"Brother, the doctor better stay here."

"You had already granted me this one," I said.

"True, but he better stay."

"And what about the peace treaty, brother? Are you forgetting that Macías is not a captive and that if he insists I take him away from here I will have to demand him from you and you will not be able to refuse me?"

"I don't deny this, brother, I am just saying I will give him to you later."

"And what will the Christians in Río Cuarto say when they find out I have come back without Macías? They will say that I backed down on this demand and will rightfully complain. This compromises me, brother."

Just then Macías walked in on his way through the tent. Mariano cast an angry look at him and spoke crossly.

"You don't walk in when people are in conversation. Get out." These were his exact words. Humiliated, Macías backed away.

"I thought . . ." he mumbled.

"Get out, Doctor," Mariano said emphatically, and the poor devil left. I realized that somebody had influenced the Indian's mind and it seemed a wiser tactic not to insist. I did, nevertheless, intimate one last time.

"Well, brother?"

He looked into my eyes and said, and I quote him exactly, "Brother, that man's heart is mine."

What is going on here, I said to myself, neither answering nor averting the chief's eyes; whereupon he added, and again I quote, "That man's conscience is mine."

A mixture of astonishment and fear for Macías's life sealed my lips. The Indian stood up and took his box of archives off of his bed. He opened it, poked around in the pouches, found the one he wanted, and took some papers from it.

"Read," he said, handing them to me.

I took the papers, which were in manuscript, opened one of them, and read. Written in Macías's hand, it was a long letter to the President of the Republic. In it Macías related how it had come about that he was living with the Indians. He made a fairly vivid description of their life and gave some sense of what the Christians were about in Indian territory. They compared unfavorably with the Indians in his view. Finally, he called upon the government for restitution of his lost freedom. The letter was poorly composed; Macías does not write well. However, it did have the eloquence of suffering. As I read, Mariano Rosas cleaned his fingernails with his knife. When I finished reading I looked at him but he did not see me. I read another one of the papers, a letter much like the first one, this time addressed to the governor of Mendoza. The rest of the papers were the scratchings of a heart scarred by misfortune.

"There, I'm done," I said when I had finished reading the whole bundle.

"Now do you see?"

"Yes."

"What do you think?"

"I don't see anything against you here."

"No?" He looked at me incredulously.

"No, nothing at all," I repeated.

"Brother!" he said, suspecting something.

"Word of honor, brother, not a thing."

He could not answer and would not take his eyes off of me. I knew he was trying to probe my thoughts.

"Brother," I said, "anybody who told you these letters speak badly of you was lying."

"Read them to me, brother."

"Would you rather the father came in and read them to you?"

"No, you read them, brother."

I read them to him. It took about a quarter of an hour. I looked at him several times as I was reading. His eyes were downcast and his brow was furrowed.

"What do you say now?" I asked him when I had finished.

"I say the man is ungrateful" (his exact words).

"Why, brother?"

"Because he says those things about the Christians after they gave him food to eat" (exact words).

I did a lightning-quick sizing up of the situation and said, "You're right, brother. Let him stay, then."

"Yes," he said, "two more years."

"As long as you like," I said.

He took the papers, put them in order, placed them in their pouch, and closed the drawer.

"Tomorrow we baptize your goddaughter," he said.

"Good," I said and left, wishing him a good afternoon.

Macías was at the door of my ranch. He looked like a ghost. He had heard nothing but his heart told him what had happened. The suffering have prescient hearts; they see sorrow coming, thereby prolonging it. I looked at him with a smile meant to put him at ease. He drew a long sigh as I passed.

"I know," he said, "you didn't do so well in there."

"It is never too late, man," I said, "when luck is smiling on you."

He shook his head as though to say, "I was fooling myself."

I wanted to put his doubts to rest.

"I still haven't spoken to him," I told him.

 I FELT SO SORRY for Macías that I dreamt about him all night. It was not only an act of charity but also performance of duty for me to redeem him from captivity. Peace had been solemnly chartered, and Mariano Rosas was obligated by treaty to leave completely free to do so anyone who wished to quit the asylum of Indian territory and return home. As soon as morning came I called for Captain Rivadavia. I wanted to confer with him. He was the only man in whom I had complete trust. He had lived with the Indians longer than I had and had both their respect and that of the Christians, which was no mean feat. Also, Mariano Rosas was very fond of him. Rivadavia knew this side's customs and that side's wiles; all the strings to pull, in short, in a world where the study of the human heart is as difficult as anywhere else.

If he could not quell my doubts, who could?

I told him everything that had happened. We exchanged ideas and, as it turned out, Macías had fallen prey to a new scheme. There was no doubt that Mariano Rosas had shared the content of our conferences with his confidants and that they had dissuaded him of his determination to let me have Macías. Bound up in this were the reprisals of those offended by the content of the intercepted correspondence, as well as pride and envy. The Christians who had first sought refuge with the Indians for political reasons pretended to accept the terms of Macías's release. What they were holding in their souls is another story. It bothered them that the maligned and mortified Dr. Macías, who had purchased so dearly the scrap of meat he had been given, should be released. He was leaving and they were staying. They enjoyed the favor of the chief and could not return to the home hearth; and Macías, crazy old Macías, so often the butt of their mockery and still ridiculed before my eyes, was about to break the bonds of captivity.

They were free and would stay. He was not . . . and could go.

In truth, only a noble heart could rejoice to see a poor wretch cast the evil yoke from his neck. The galley slaves cheer the newly condemned prisoner as he joins them and deride the man who has served his time and will soon leave. They say it's a fool who smiles when all must weep, but I say it's an ingrate.

It was time to make the most of the day.

We had a number of babies to baptize: daughters of refugee Christians, captives, and Indians. I reminded the good Franciscans that we had no time to lose. We sent messengers in every direction and set up the altar in the same ranch in which we had said mass some days before. The Christian men and women with their children and the Indians with theirs arrived a few at a time. Mariano Rosas's tent was a place of celebration where everyone wore their finest and exuberance reigned. I was delighted to see those poor people instinctively honoring God. The friars were as pleased as punch. Anyone who would have come to those parts that day not knowing what was going on would have thought he had been transported to a native tribe converted to Christianity.

When everything was ready Mariano Rosas was notified and his permission requested to start the ceremony, which we also invited him to attend. He sent word back that we could begin whenever we liked. He could not be with us, he said, because he had just at that moment received new visitors.

The hut serving as a chapel was too small for the gathering we had. There were parents, relatives, friends, godfathers, and godmothers with every child. The children were frightened and all of them, big and little, were crying. It was all making a powerful impression on them: the altar, the priests in their vestments, the strange faces, the solemn air about the spectators, the constant reminders to be quiet and behave. Their mothers were in an absolute fluster. "Lord, what a child," says one. "Look at this little girl," says another. They fondled, scolded, warned, threatened, used every trick in the maternal book to quiet them, but it was not to be. The discordant choir sang on. As I watched this one-of-a-kind scene I could see past the comedy to the human tendency toward things grave and solemn. These poor women—the ragged ones as well as the rather nicely dressed; the Christians and the Indian women alike—stood before that improvised altar doing the same thing they would have done under the monumental naves of a cathedral. What sentiment swayed these radiantly jubilant weeping women as they held the fruit of their womb close to them and cried out, as I heard them do so many times, "You're finally going to be a Christian, my child"?

What sentiment?

A sentiment innate to the human heart, a sentiment which Voltaire explained in a famous phrase:

Si Dieu n'existait pas, il faudrait l'inventer.

If God did not exist, it would be necessary to invent him.

The evil thing in this world is not professing a bad religion but professing no religion at all. And oh, if the one we do profess consoles us with its morality, if like an inexhaustible font of poetry it offers us solace in tribulation and a lifeboat in the final sorrows, then what an immense boon to us to believe in, worship, and trust in God! No wonder those people felt festive and considered their children blessed to be receiving baptism. Any ceremony that would have resembled the consecration of a cult would have been the same.

Baptizing thirty or more children one after another was a full day's work. Though I did not know it, the ritual allowed for the sacrament to be administered collectively.

I breathed a sigh of relief when I found out.

My goddaughter had not yet made her appearance. I sent word to my compadre that we were waiting for her and a moment later they came and placed her in my arms. She was perhaps eight years old, the child of a Christian mother. She was light brown with a little turned-up nose and big black eyes. She was nice though a little demure. She wept like a willow for a long time and made the other little ones cry, and they had stopped. We delayed the ceremony until she at last calmed down and we could begin. Through resounding Our Fathers and Latin prayers my goddaughter stayed in my arms, quiet one minute, restless the next. She would look at me, then avert her eyes. She would smile, struggle, give up. I had only one thing on my mind. They had dressed her in her best and fanciest clothes. It was a well-cut, red brocaded dress with gold trim and lace that looked fairly nice. Having no shoes they had put little coltskin boots on her feet. Actually, they were catskin. Civilization and barbarism met and embraced in her.

Now what dress is that? Where did it come from? Who made it? This was all I could think about. I was trying to pay attention to the priest but I couldn't. I was absorbed by the dress and boots. The dress I studied very closely. It was perfectly made and cut. It had Mary Stuart sleeves and was clearly not the work of an Indian seamstress.[1] But then it could not have been a gift from a Christian either, or booty from a stagecoach robbery, cattle farm, mule team, or outlying village. No child dresses like that where we come from. My curiosity was as powerful as the incongruence between the dress and the coltskin boots. An unusual curiosity, that is. Now and then a light would go on in my head. That's it, I would say, it came from such and such a place. But then, no, no, it cannot be from there. That is preposterous. When it came my turn to say "Amen" someone had to do it for me. In my distraction the dress was all I could see and the contrast between it and the boots all I could think about.

There was a Christian from Mariano Rosas's tent standing next to me. He had a face like an outlaw, a frightening face. He was one of those repellent people just the sight of whom sends a shudder down the spine. He had never spoken a word to me nor I to him, but my curiosity overpowered my repugnance to him and I quietly asked him how my compadre had come by the dress.

"Oh that," he said in a hoarse Córdoban accent, "that's the dress from the Virgin in Villa de la Paz."

"The Virgin?" I said, telling myself I had heard wrong when in fact the man had spoken quite clearly.

"That's right," he said. "We got it on one of our invasions and gave it to the general."

I almost dropped my goddaughter when he said this. He had to hold her up. I cannot in paltry human words express the effect his tone of voice and manner—and the revelation itself—had on my nerves. It did not feel as if something was being defiled before my eyes; it was not a sacrilege I was witnessing nor was I filled with stupid superstition. I felt, rather, a phenomenal impression, was diabolically moved as when in childhood I imagined the devil shuddered when they threw holy water on him. My goddaughter María, Mariano Rosas's daughter, is bound to my life's memories by an impression so unlike any other that her dress and boots still give me a shiver. I can no longer see a Virgin without those garments taunting my mind. My goddaughter's image is crystallized in my brain and the husky voice of the bandit who set the record straight for me buzzes in my ear to this day. They are unforgettable echoes, like the roar of the rising sea when the whistling wind brings it thrashing onto the rocky shore. You hear it once in your life and you never forget it.

When the baptism ended, Father Marcos gave a brief sermon to the mothers of the new Christians, exhorting them to educate their children in the laws of Jesus Christ, the only way they could reach heaven after they died. They were all happy and thanked me for the favor they had just been granted through me. Several of the women said, "I don't know what would have become of us if it hadn't been for you, sir."

I was now the godfather of four youngsters, including Mariano Rosas's daughter. I had little to offer them, but as there is always some way to show our goodwill and good wishes, I managed to do right by them.

We dismantled the altar, put the ornaments away, and went directly to Mariano Rosas's tent, where lunch awaited us. He was as complacent as I had ever seen him.

"Now we are compadres, brother," he said. "How should we treat each other?"

"Why, just as we did before, compadre, like brothers."

"Just the same," he said, "you have my thanks." He turned to the friars. "Many Christians here now, eh?"

"How true," they answered. "God be with them all!"

They served lunch, we ate, and then excused ourselves.

"This afternoon we will finish our conversation, compadre," I said as we left.

"Any time you like," he answered.

I was on my way out of the tent when he called me back. He took off the Pampa poncho he was wearing and gave it to me.

"Take this, brother," he said. "Use it in my name. My main wife made it."

This was a gift of great significance. I accepted it and reciprocated by giving him my rubber poncho.

"If there is ever no peace," he said, taking it from me, "my Indians will not kill you when they see that poncho."

"Brother," I said, "if someday there is no peace and we meet again, I will recognize you by that poncho."

The great significance of Mariano Rosas's poncho was not that it could shield me from danger, but that it had been woven by the main wife. Among the Indians this is a token of love, like a nuptial ring for the Christians. When I emerged from his tent wearing the chief's poncho, surprise swept over every face. Suddenly the people *at palace* became more attentive and solicitous than ever.

How pathetic humanity is!

MACÍAS WATCHED as the moment of truth drew near. He stammered and sighed and let it be understood he was losing all hope. I sat down by the fire and he sat beside me. I was in good spirits, perhaps because I planned to head for my corner of the world the next day. That's the way we are, restless even in the heart of happiness. Nothing is ever enough, nothing satisfies us. And only at a late, late hour do we understand that in this sublunar world those who are content with the present, those who live unhurried by people or things, are the ones who have had the best time of it. They have narrowed the horizon of their gaze, trimmed their aspirations, and shaken the yoke of social exigency. They have, in short, subjectivized life to a point where they identify with their dinner jacket.

How many consumed in sterile combat; how many, forgetting that to be awake is to dream on one's feet and that dreams are but the novitiate of death, had visions of love, hate, glory, pride, wealth, envy, fear . . . and had them wide awake or had them in their sleep? How many, I say, would not have been happier if at the end of their road they could have said:

> Sois-moi fidèle o pauvre habit que l'aime!
> Ensemble nous devenons vieux.
> Depuis dix ans je te brosse moi-même,
> Et Socrate n'eut pas fait mieux.
> Quand le sort a ta mince étoffe
> Livrerait de nouveaux combats.
> Imite-moi résiste en philosophie.
> Mon vieil ami, ne nous séparons pas.[1]

I laughed, bantered, and caroused with everyone sitting around the fire, over whose abundant tinder an appetizing roast was turning a golden brown. Taciturn, withdrawn, and somber—the very picture of despair—the woebegone hostage cast furtive looks in my direction from time to time. He wanted to say something but dared not do so. He wanted to reproach me and could not find the right words for it. His thoughts swayed like seaweed in crosscurrents. He all but spoke, then said nothing. His eyes shone without rancor, but his lips were pressed in sarcastic remonstrance.

"What are you thinking about?" I said.

"That you're awfully cheerful," he answered.

"Go ahead and worry yourself to death," I rejoined.

"Sure, you are leaving and I am staying."

"I'm telling you it is never too late when luck is on your side."

"I don't know how you figure that!" he barked. He suddenly stood up and started to leave. Just then Calixto Oyarzábal set the roaster on its side and scraped the ashes off the roast with his knife.

"It's ready, Colonel."

"Let's eat, gentlemen," I shouted. "Come on, man," I said to Macías, "eat. You've got plenty of time to hang yourself in despair later."

He walked back, sat down beside me again, and took out his knife. The roast was getting to him so he cut himself a strip of it country style. A soup kettle was brimming over with piping hot corn and angola squash. We had that and the roast finished in a heartbeat. We were just getting to the coffee—we had no dessert—when the Negro with the accordion appeared carrying something wrapped in a rag.

"It's the accordion!" I said to myself and my hair stood on end.

"Get out of here, Negro," I shouted before he could move his lips.

"Mas'r," he said, smiling, "I'm alone."

"Then what's that?" I said, pointing to the wrapped object. "This," he announced baring two fine rows of teeth so white and even that I was envious of him, "this is cheese."

"Cheese?"

"Yes, Mas'r. The general sends it to your grace for you to eat in the name of your goddaughter, little María." Then he unwrapped the cheese and put it in my hands.

"Tell my brother I send my thanks," I said. "Now, go away!" I added, waving him off.

He obeyed and then from a safer distance called insinuatingly back to me: "Would your grace like me to come back with the instrument?" I answered him with a piece of steak bone, sparking the explosive hilarity of everyone present.

"They're going to have a dance, you know," said Calixto.

"A dance?" I said.

"Yes, Colonel."

"And where are they holding this dance?"

"In that tent over there," he said, pointing it out.

"Well, let's try the cheese, drink the coffee, and go see the fandango, Negro and accordion and all."

We finished it all off and I had Calixto find out what time the dance started. He came back saying it was about to begin, so we left the camp fire and went to the party.

This was all I needed.

My watch said four o'clock—four o'clock in the afternoon, mind you. The Indians are more sensible than we are; they sleep by night and enjoy themselves by day. As customs go, this has its advantages over civilization's way. There is no need to think about lighting of any kind—no kerosene, no candles, no gas.

The dancers were all men and it was held in the open air. The women of that land have but two destinies: to work and to procreate.

I dare not say whether the Indians are wiser in this respect than we are.

However, considering the endless foul-ups we see happening year in, year out in the mixing of the sexes—wives leaving their husbands, husbands who forget their wives, jealous lovers fighting, lawsuits for upkeep, divorces, the willful abductions of innocent maidens, all of it unheard of in Indian territory—then clearly our civilization is one serious matter.

No wonder someone is always preaching against dancing!

I can understand it being deemed essential that a statesman know how to dance. For, as Molière has one of his characters say, when a minister has taken the wrong step it merely means he hasn't learned the dance.[2] Now, I do not see why it should be essential that a doctor or lawyer know how to dance. The Indians, of course, understand that dance is an exercise that insofar as it works covertly on the nervous system is good for bodily hygiene. And, as it awakens the appetite and contributes to muscle development, they allow their women to dance together from time to time, reserving for themselves a role that we will describe further on.

The dance floor, or rather the arena, was about forty rods around. Imagine a threshing floor with posts set around it like a corral. Picture, dear Santiago, a mound of earth in the center about six feet in diameter and three feet high and you will have an idea of what I am trying to describe. The spectators were standing all around the outside of the circle. It is worth noting here that the Indians are less selfish than we are when it comes to choreography; they dance to entertain their friends, we to entertain ourselves. If we want to have our fun watching other people dance, we have to pay for it, which is another drawback of civilization.

Their instruments consisted of a kind of wooden drum with sheep's hide for a skin. They played them with their fingers or with drumsticks. The dance began with a kind of military fanfare. Then, after some shrill screaming not in time with the drums, five Indians came out in a line doing cancan-style pirouettes. They were all wearing blankets when they entered the arena. They did several turns around the mound in step with the music—it was as if they were walking on eggshells—and suddenly threw off the blankets and revealed themselves. They had rolled their breeches up to their knees and taken their shirts off. Their arms and legs, chest and face were painted red and they had ostrich feathers in their headdresses. They wore necklaces that made noise and their bangs hung down over their foreheads. They did not stop when they threw the blankets off. They shook their heads as though to identify themselves and began a series of figures without ever losing their respective places in the line.

It was dizzying to watch them gyrate around the mound, shaking their heads right and left, up and down, forward and back. Each put his hands on the shoulders of the one in front of him, except for the leader, who waved his arms about. They would break loose then regroup in a chain, trip and fall together in a coil. They yanked each other out of place, kicked each other, and were sweating torrents. They reeked of colt and made a thousand faces, kissed, bit, obscenely manhandled each other, and bumped rear ends. In short, they looked like five drunken satyrs cynically showing off their physical stamina and the lubricity of their passions. The character of the turns they made determined the drumbeat, which now and then was accompanied either by a sad song or by a low, grave one, or a burlesque, depending on what the infernal quadrille was parodying.

Fifteen of them danced in three heats. The spectators kept perfect order. They never applauded, but their eyes were glued to the dancers. It was a veritable Lyrical Palace in the pampas, sans women, sans *garçons*, sans marble tables, carbonated lemonade, and what have you.

The one advantage I saw to it was free admission.

The whole farce lasted nearly two hours. The sun was setting as, glutted with gestures, yelps, and drumming, I returned to my camp fire. Luck had smiled on me in that the Negro with the accordion was not part of the orchestra.

Night fell and as it was a cool one I went behind my hut to get out of the wind. Soon the fire was glowing and there, by its light, they told me how the Indian women dance. Fifteen or twenty of them get dressed and painted up and go into a place such as I have just described. Holding hands, they make a circle and start to move around the corn stacks quite as if playing *ronda catonga*. The spectators enter the dance area and as the women go by perpetrate all manner of indecency on them until the women can stand it no longer, break up the circle, and escape however they can.

Frankly, I find the Indians less civilized than we on this count, though there are examples in the police records of gentlemen who have spent the night behind bars for having an unduly long reach in their church pews. At any rate, the upshot of this sort of abuse and license on the part of the Indians when the women dance is that the latter now abstain from their innocent pastime, which proves that women are the same the world over.

They will forgive anything except being manhandled.

I find them to be absolutely in the right in this, though I must also declare that, though they may not use their particular advantages to mistreat us, they do ordinarily treat us badly.

 I FOUND MYSELF alone at the fire watching the embers burn. They were glowing through and through and the wind blew them to ashes just when they were most beautiful, as disappointment will shatter our fondest illusions.

My thoughts floated between two worlds. They were practical thoughts, they were chimerical. They could easily come true, they could not possibly come true. I felt strong and great. I felt weak and small. I nodded off, I woke. I wanted to leave and I had not left.

A sweet voice delivered me from all the indecision.

"Good evening," came a murmur in my ear. I turned around and in the pale glow of the last embers recognized a woman. It was my comadre Carmen.

"Comadre," I said, "what are you doing around here at this time of night?"

"Compadre, I heard you were leaving tomorrow," she said.

I motioned to her to sit down. She wore a tender expression on her face. Her shirt was fastened more closely to her neck than usual and fluttered lightly as her bosom pounded underneath. Her look betrayed a scarcely concealed restiveness.

"Is there something wrong, comadre?"

"No, compadre," she answered. She stared hard into the dying fire and smothered a sigh. Had I not been at that period of our lives at which the poet said,

> My days are in the yellow leaf;
> The flowers and fruits of love are gone,[1]

who knows what would have happened!

The wind had calmed down, the sky was blanketed with clouds, the stars shone timidly, like distant lights through opaque curtains. The fire was all tepid ashes and my visitor and I beheld each other like two shadows enshrouded in crêpe. The picture was for a moment a novelesque one: the night's silence scarcely broken by the even breathing of those sleeping nearby; the poetic solitude of the place; the thoughts that like streaks of fire or the visions of a lovelier age crossed my mind. I called Calixto and ordered him to revive the fire and brew some mate. He stirred the ashes, found some coals, cupped his hands like a bellows, and in a minute had the flames going. My comadre and I remained still a short while, listening to the water boil and the wood crackle.

Fire has an irresistible, magnetic influence on the senses and I have noticed that the heart opens in the warmth of the bright flames. The heart opens, ideas germinate unhindered, and the soul rises to great and lovely heights, borne on winds sublime and generous. This is why crime is the child of darkness.

Calixto passed me the mate. I drank some and, passing it to my comadre, said, "Why have you become so quiet?"

Her answer: a sigh.

Women, then, are the same under every constellation, the same in the mountains with their eternal snows, in the romantic forests with their elusive *urutau* and its mournful dirges, on the shores of the majestic River Plate, and in the open plains of the Argentine pampas.

They think that sighing is speaking.

I must confess that it is too mystical a language for as prosaic a sort as I.

"Please, what is the matter, comadre?" I asked her again.

"Compadre," she said, "I am sad because you are going."

"Then you would like them to keep me here and not let me go back?"

"No, I don't mean that."

"Well, then?"

"I mean that I am sorry I cannot go with you."

"Well, why don't you come and visit Río Cuarto with me?"

"Because I can't."

"Aren't you free to?"

"Free!"

"Yes, free. Aren't you a widow?"

"Oh, compadre," she said bitterly, "you don't know what my life is like, you don't know how it is here." She looked around to see if anybody had heard her indiscreet confession. There was something meaningful and mysterious in her voice. I sensed there was something else she wanted to say but that she was afraid some nocturnal spy might hear her. I got up and took a look around to make sure we were alone, and sat back down closer to her.

"There is no one here," I said.

"Compadre," she said, "don't leave without coming to my tent in Carrilobo near Villarreal. I will be waiting for you there. My sister will be there. She likes you and is trustworthy. I have something to tell you which you will be very interested in knowing. Tonight I will find out the rest of what I want to know. That is why I came here. Nobody has seen me yet . . ."

Just then we heard galloping and what sounded like the voices of drunken Indians. She stood up suddenly and said, "I don't want to be seen here." Then she slipped away in the night shadows.

I followed her for an instant until she disappeared into the darkness. I felt baffled and inexplicably apprehensive as the earth trembled under me and the cries of the besotted rabble drew closer. The light from my camp fire had attracted them. Upon arriving some of them dismounted and others stayed on their horses. Epumer was their head man. They had come from a neighboring tent where they had been imbibing. He had a flask in his hand and was pretty far gone. He spoke to me without getting off his horse.

"*Yapaí*, brother," he said.

"*Yapaí*, brother," said I.

We took turns drinking and the *yapaí* followed in quick succession. Fortunately, the firewater was very diluted and he had neither horn nor glass with him, which meant I could just wet my lips since we were forced to drink from the flask.

Since they were getting very ornery—they were in fact threatening me with a long solo binge—I spoke to Calixto.

"*Che*, it's getting cold out. Hand me my poncho."

The only one I had was the one Mariano Rosas had given me that morning. I wanted to find out what impression it would make on them to see me wearing it. Calixto brought it out and I put it on. Just as I had figured, the ploy worked beautifully.

"Colonel Mansilla, him bull!" some shouted.

"Colonel Mansilla, him gaucho!" said others.

Many of them shook my hand. Others embraced me and even kissed me with their foul mouths. Several times Epumer shouted, "Mansilla *peñi*!" As we carried on our colloquium there came the sound of a broken-down old organ and with it rhymed verses dedicated to me. It made my skin crawl and gave me fever and chills all at once and set my nerves on edge as though someone had scraped a file across his teeth. Where had that accursed Negro and his execrable accordion come from?

Why bother finding out?!

I could not stand it and, backed by the respectability which my compadre and brother's poncho conferred on me, I said good night to Epumer and his retinue. It was late, I told them I was tired. I was to leave the next day and felt like sleeping. I left them and ducked into my ranch, telling Calixto to close the door tightly and lash the leather covering with tethers. My visitors hailed me with sundry "Good-bye, *peñi*!" and "Good-bye, friend!" and "*Adiós, toro!*" They went on shouting a while and jumped over the fire with their horses till it went out and got the dogs riled and had themselves a riot and when they got tired they left.

I fell asleep to the lull of the infernal hullabaloo. All night long I had the most outrageous dreams. Just as almost all the feelings in our soul come from the sensations of the *beast*, so too do almost all of the visions of our sleeping spirit come from what we have beheld when awake, both with the eyes in our head and with those of our imagination.

I am like an ogre; I have no foreshadowings when I dream.

I am no Pindar; bees will never leave their honey on my lips.

I will never like Hesiod see nine enchantresses, the muses who inspired him.

I will never like Scipio foresee the destruction of Numancia or the fall of Carthage.

Unlike Alexander at Tyre, I will see no Hercules extend me his hand from atop the city walls.

I want the sobriety and virtue it would take for me truly to see in my dreams. Either that or Socrates errs in saying that a body sated with pleasure or gorged with food or wine gives the soul extravagant dreams. Wherefore one may conclude that all emperors, kings, presidents, ministers, and deputies—all those, in short, who ought to know what they are doing and furthermore ought to read the future, since governance is providence—should be very frugal eaters and very moderate drinkers, to say nothing of certain other things indispensable for regular digestion.

I cannot have dreams such as those I had the last night I spent in Leubucó. Either I am going to dream nonsense that will never come true, or I am going to see things nonsensically that have come true. If I do not dream I have been proclaimed emperor of the Ranquels and that I, Lucius Victorius, Imperator, have had the Indian woman Carmen crowned empress, then I will dream that the Indian dance is in vogue in Buenos Aires and that boots with the Louis XV heel have given way to the catskin coltskin boot.

Which is the sort of dream I had.

And then Plato says that the divine spirit reveals the future to us in our dreams, and Strabo[2] that dreams open the truth to us because our minds are purer, cleaner, and more active at night than during the day.

These Ancients were a bunch of first-rate utopians. I only respect them because they are old now and have died.

 MY HEAD WAS an oven when I awoke. I had dreamt so hard that my ideas were a broil and I could not immediately recall what had happened during the night. I confused real facts with visions. It was as though I had dreamt of my comadre Carmen, Epumer, and the Negro with the accordion and that what I had seen in my dreams was real.

Day was just breaking. The light of dawn came through the ranch's innumerable holes and lighted the inside with fantastic glitterings. The bed was so hard that I had gotten stiff and now had a hard time moving. The impressions of the dream persisted. I was not asleep but was seeing what I had seen while sleeping. I lay there a while like Seneca's madwoman, who, not realizing she was blind, asked to be moved to another house where one could see where one was.

I was awake and did not know it.

Good Lord! How trying it is to convince yourself you are not an emperor when you awaken having dreamt an empire! My dream of power was of such tenacious stuff that had not the barking of dogs awakened my officers, I believe I would have risen dragging Mariano Rosas's poncho behind me like a royal mink mantle. When my aide Rodríguez said good morning to me I finally cleared my head. I opened my eyes in a nervous squint. It was day and the hut was utterly bright inside. My vision of the Ranquel empire vanished from my retina though like a Chinese shadow it still passed through my mind.

It felt as if I had slept for a year. I will never know why they paint time with wings. It has feet of lead the way I picture it. I suppose that the things we most desire are the ones that take the longest to come about. Then, too, the things I like the most are too quickly over.

I called an assistant, who came and opened the door. I arose, got dressed, and walked outside. I was most definitely leaving that day and not as emperor. The former was comfort for the latter and, frankly, the Ranquel empire looked better in my dreams than it did in waking reality. They brought me word that all was well with the mounts. I told Camilo Arias to have them ready by sundown. Next I had Captain Rivadavia ask Mariano Rosas if he was available to finish our conversation. He was, and I entered his tent. He had just bathed and taken mate. An Indian woman was untangling his hair. He did not move.

"Brother," he said, "have a seat and excuse me."

"That's all right," I said, taking a seat.

"Did you sleep well?" he asked.

"Very well," I answered.

"Are you still leaving today?"

"Unless you have other plans."

"You are free, brother."

"Very well. Could you tell me what else I might do for you?"

"Brother, I would prefer you did not press me for the captives I have to hand over."

"Hand them over as you can."

"There are only a few left now."

"What do you mean 'a few'?"

"Just what I said. A few."

"I don't understand."

He then added up all the captives that he had sent back to Río Cuarto at different times. Add eight to that number, he figured, and that gives you the total agreed to.

It was an unexpected move.

What did the new peace treaty have to do with earlier captives? Was this his idea or had it been suggested to him? I tried to explore the terrain but to no avail. Circumspect and reserved, he would not show his cards. I resolved to speak to him forthrightly, the incident being of a sort that could thwart the peace plans.

"Brother," I said, "you are mistaken. The captives you sent back before have nothing to do with those you will be handing over now. Read the treaty closely and you will see."

"Yes, I know, but I was thinking that you might be able to set it up for me."

"And how would you like me to do that?"

"By telling the governors that you have received all the ones I have just said."

"And how am I supposed to say such a thing?"

"I will give you the names of the old captives."

"I cannot do it."

"Well, then . . ."

"Well what?"

"We will do as you say."

"That's right," I said. All I needed, I thought to myself, is for this barbarian to make me his instrument.

He did not answer me.

"You have something else to tell me, don't you?" I said.

"Yes, but we will leave it for later."

"Will we have time?"

"Yes, I am sure we will."

This time I was silent. There was food cooking on all three fires in the tent.

"Let's eat," he said, calling for service in his language.

I said nothing. They brought plates and utensils and placed a pot of beef stew between us. He served me a heaping plateful. I did not say a word as I ate. We had gone a good long while without looking at or speaking to each other when an Indian came in and spoke to him in Araucan in a highly charged tone of voice. Mariano answered in kind. I understood none of it, though Blanco the Indian's name did come up a few times. This piqued my curiosity but I kept still.

The Indian left. We went on in silence.

"It is Blanco the Indian," he said. "He is going around saying things about you. He says he is going to head you off."

I wondered if it was a setup to scare me into suspending the trip.

"And what is he planning to do to me?" I asked.

"Kill you," he said, smiling.

"Kill me, eh!"

"That is what he says."

"Well, tell him we will see who is who."

"I told them to tell him to quit raising hell. If he doesn't like the peace treaty, what is he doing back here from Chile? I told him the other day he better straighten out."

As he seemed to be speaking truthfully and as his face conveyed a certain animosity towards Blanco the Indian, I offered an amicable thank-you. Then we fell silent again. He was not watching me. His eyes were intent on a steak bone he was stripping with his fingers. He seemed to want me to speak to him or ask him for something and I was resolved not to do it. The Indian who had taken the message to Blanco the Indian returned, spoke a few words, and left.

"Blanco the Indian says he is going to Toay."

To Toay?"

"Yes, and he says he is going to Buenos Aires province to look for sheep. They bring a good price in Chile." [1]

"What a scoundrel!" I said.

"A big scoundrel!" exclaimed Mariano.

Again we fell silent. After a while he asked me what time I was leaving.

"At four o'clock," I said.

We remained silent until he finally spoke.

"Tell me, brother," he said, "what are your instructions for me?"

"My instructions?"

"Yes!"

"That you remember your compadre at all times."

Whereupon I stood up and left the tent.

I ordered everyone to get ready and went to say good-bye to several acquaintances residing in nearby tents. I was back in an hour. My people were ready. There was nothing left to do but get the horses together and saddle up. It was a very beautiful day. We were in for a delightful afternoon. Many were preparing to come with me. Poor, sorry Macías was leaning on a forked pole at my

ranch watching the preparations. His mournful face wore the pain
of desperation. I walked over to him.

"Trust in God," I said.

"In God!" he mumbled.

"Yes, in God," I repeated, casting him a glance in which he must
have read this one thought: He who despairs of God deserves no
freedom. I entered Ayala's ranch. He had agreed to turn over to me
a young captive boy he had there, a son of Comandante Araya who
lived in Cruz Alta. The little boy knew it and could see I would be
leaving in a matter of minutes. He was sitting beside my soldiers'
camp fire crying inconsolably because I had not said anything to
him about getting ready to go. It was heartbreaking to see him.
Ayala said he had no problem keeping his promise but that he had
to notify Mariano Rosas of it.

"I thought you notified him the other day," I said.

"Yes, so I did."

"Well, then?"

"He may have changed his mind."

"Fine. Go tell him so the boy can get ready."

He left and then returned to tell me it would be necessary to pay
two hundred Bolivian pesos in silver tokens for him.

"And what sort of tokens might those be?" I asked Ayala.

"Stirrups," he said.

I immediately ordered Captain Rivadavia to buy them from one
of the quartermasters Father Burela had brought with him. I offered a promissory note payable in Mendoza. Meanwhile the poor
captive boy was all childish exuberance as he got ready to go. Captain Rivadavia returned with the stirrups, which I gave to Ayala
who in turn took them to Mariano Rosas, only to come back with
his head hanging down.

What a world this is! The chief had changed his mind again.
Now he wanted not just the stirrups but a hundred pesos worth of
goods and a hundred in silver.

We looked for the hundred pesos and found them.

I gave it all to Ayala, who took it to Mariano Rosas. He came
back huffing. The *general*, he said, had changed his mind yet again.
I blew my top. I yelled out everything I could think of to say and
cursed and insulted Mariano Rosas. I only calmed down somewhat
when Ayala begged me to. He seemed fairly cross.

"Don't get me in trouble here," he said quietly. "Look at all the
spies around us." That finally shut me up. He pointed to some tat-

tered, slovenly Indians no one was paying any attention to. They were crouched here and there and lying on their bellies on the ground like animals.

Irritated with my own powerlessness and hurting in my soul I went into the ranch, called Araya's little boy, and with paternal care prepared him for the terrible letdown. He had been so happy before. He was so downcast and tearful now.

How quickly happiness vanishes.

I hugged him, patted him, asked him for his mother's and father's sake to be brave. I told him I would ransom him soon, an offer I was able to honor, nor did I leave his side until I knew he had accepted his misfortune.

"What do you think?" said Macías to me as I left my ranch.

"God is great!" I told him.

He sighed, and in apparent doubt of divine omnipotence said, "God! . . ."

I walked towards Mariano Rosas's tent.

The moment of departure was at hand.

Camilo Arias made a mysterious sign to me.

 I HAVE SAID before that Camilo Arias knew the Indian language though the Indians were unaware of it. If he was watching for a chance to give me a sign, it meant that he had heard something. My orders had not changed. He was to speak to me only on matters of grave and urgent import.

I wonder what's going on, I thought, as I entered Mariano Rosas's tent. I stopped. "I'll be right back," I said, pretending to search my pockets for some mislaid object. I went back to my ranch. The astute Camilo lowered his head, fixed his gaze on the ground, and walked along in apparent aimless distraction. Then in a maneuver that would look casual to anyone not wise to what was happening, he leaned against the straw walls of my ranch just as I was entering, and said, "There's news, sir."

"Come in," I told him, calling several officers and assistants as well so that he would not be noticed coming in. I issued various orders to them and when they left I was alone with Camilo.

"What is going on?" I said.

"I just overheard the Indians in a conversation."

"And . . ."

"And they are going to head us off."

"Whereabouts?"

"In the hills near Jarilla."

"What else did they say?"

"They are dying to get their hands on me. They say I've killed many Indians and I cut one of their captains in the face and he still has the scar. They say I took another one prisoner and that they took him away to Córdoba."

"Is that all?"

"No. They also said you brought me along to make fun of them."

"Do they know I'm leaving today?"

"Yes, sir, and that you're going to stay in Ramón's tent."

As he was telling me this I heard a voice that could not help but grate my nerves. It came from the other side of the ranch door.

"With your grace's permission."

I didn't have to look to know who it was. He was not playing his accordion but it was there with its notes stopped. He entered the ranch without giving me time to answer.

"The general says why haven't you come yet."

"Tell him I'm coming right now," I said.

The Negro left and I asked Camilo if the Indians who had been saying this were here. They were, he said, and I sent him away and went to Mariano Rosas's tent.

What the Indians were saying about Camilo was true. He had taken their measure several times as a common soldier, killing several of them, wounding a notorious captain, and taking yet another one prisoner. I nearly left him behind. But then I trusted him so, and he and his admirable instincts were so useful to me in the open country, that I overlooked his credentials and added him to my party. Needless to say, before telling him to get ready to go with us I had to know the real mettle of his soul, so I asked him if he was not perhaps hesitant to come with me into Indian territory.

"Sir," he said, "wherever you go, I go, too."

"And what if the Indians recognize you?"

"Sir, I have never used treachery with them."

I entered Mariano Rosas's tent. He had visitors, all of them Indians whom I knew except one, down the length of whose face ran a scar that would have left him without a nose had it slanted any further. Mariano Rosas gave me a most friendly welcome. He asked me if I was ready to leave, then pointed to the Indian with the scar.

"Do you know him, brother?" he said.

"No," I answered.

"Camilo Arias gave him that scar," he added.

"That's all part of waging war," I said.

"This is true, brother," he answered.

Finding him so reasonable, I relayed what Camilo Arias had just told me. He said nothing. However, when he then spoke with his visitors he raised his voice a great deal and sent them away with a wave of his hand. No sooner had they left the tent than he told me not to worry. "Brother," he said, "no one will be bothering you on your journey. It is peacetime now."

"I hope so," I said and, before he could say anything else, added, "Brother, my horses are ready. I would like to know if there is anything else I can do for you."

He asked me a number of questions concerning the treaty. He warned me, as a sign of friendship, of Calfucurá's planned invasion from the northern border of Buenos Aires. He gave me several messages to deliver for him. Finally, he asked me not to allow the mounted scouting parties to advance as far south as had been their custom, for this apparently alarmed the Indians who were out driving game with their *boleadoras*. They would see the party's tracks and return to their settlements stricken with fear.

I answered his questions about the treaty, offered to relay his messages, and promised that the parties would find another way to do their job. I then stood there staring at the ground, acting distracted.

"Are you leaving here satisfied, brother?"

Rather than answer, I looked at him as if to say, "How can you ask me that?"

"I have done everything I could to serve you well and to see to it that you enjoyed your time here," he said.

"I am sure that is true, but I have requested something of you and you have denied me it," I answered.

"What would that be, brother?"

"Must I really say it?"

"Please do, brother."

"I do not have Macías and you know that that compromises me."

"Macías, Macías, what do you want with that doctor, brother?"

"I've already told you. Macías is not a captive. You are obligated by the treaty to release him. He wants to go and you refuse to let him."

He stood there thinking. I watched him out of the corner of my

eye. He called someone . . . an Indian came. "Ayala," he said and
the Indian left. We kept silent until Ayala came in. Mariano Rosas
spoke to him in words I can recall almost verbatim.

"Colonel," he said, "my brother wants to take the doctor with
him. You are good and loyal men and I was planning to keep him
here two more years to make him pay for what he did to you."

Ayala said nothing. His eyes met mine.

"Colonel," I said, "Macías is a poor fellow. What do you gain
by him being here? Have a heart. If he hasn't repaid you your hospitality as he should have, forgive him. Bear in mind, too, that he
is not a captive. My brother here is bound by the treaty to set him
free. Keep him here and you compromise me, you compromise
him, and you compromise the peace we have worked so hard to
establish."

Ayala shrugged his shoulders and said nothing. Mariano Rosas
searched his eyes for an answer.

"You decide, Colonel," he said. I gave Ayala no time to answer. "Look, friend," I said, "that man is not here by free choice
and if you and your people stand in his way now, everything he
said about you in those letters my brother had me read will be
justified."

Ayala looked at Mariano Rosas as if to say, "You decide."
When I saw Mariano was wavering I stood up and shook his hand.
"Brother, I am leaving," I announced.

"Wait a minute, brother," he said. He looked at Ayala.

"What do we do?"

"Good-bye, good-bye, brother. I am leaving," I repeated.

"They can have him," said Ayala.

"All right, brother," said Mariano Rosas, standing up. He
shook my hand, embraced me, and gave renewed assurances of
friendship.

I left the tent. My people were ready. Macías was perplexed. His
mood fluctuated between hope and despair.

"Saddle up!" I shouted.

"Well . . . ," asked Macías. His eyes shone with the languid light
of a prisoner's gaze. His mind was convinced it was all for nothing.
His instinct for freedom said, It can still happen, be brave. I recalled the psalm by Fray Luis de León, *Confitemini Domino*, and
I told him,

> *Cantemos juntamente,*
> *cuán bueno es Dios con todos, cuán clemente.*

Canten los libertados,
los que libró el Señor del poderío
del áspero enemigo . . . [1]

"For real?" he said, his eyes misting up.

"For real," I said. Lowering my voice I told him to keep his rejoicing to himself.

"A horse for Dr. Macías," I shouted to Camilo Arias.

I went to Ayala's ranch, said good-bye to Hilarión Nicolai and to some sorrowful captive women, and a moment later was on my horse. When those who had offered to accompany me saw that Mariano Rosas was not moving, they stood where they were, reins in hand, and never once dared to apologize for their inaction.

My arrival had been hailed with fireworks, fusillades, cornets, and hurrahs. My departure was the other side of the coin. You could almost say I was being routed. One man alone, heedless of others, came forward to say a warm and forthright good-bye. That man was Camargo, a bandit with a big heart.

The chief behaved indifferently. My friends had disappeared. Leubucó is no different than any other place; we all know what the word friend means there. Say, friend, we tell the postal messenger, I'll give you a nice coin if you can get me to Versailles in an hour, or so says the Count of Segur about friendship.[2] Friend, said the stroller to the prowler, make any noise and they'll stick you in the armed guards. Friend, says the judge to the miscreant, you'll be set free if there is no evidence against you. Otherwise, you'll hang. Small wonder that the Arabs say that to make a friend of a man you have to eat a bushel of salt with him.

Mariano Rosas was leaning on the posts at the entrance to his tent, eyeing me with indifference. I rode up to him, extended him my hand, and for the last time said, "Adiós, brother!"

I rode out. The road I had followed in to Leubucó came from the north. I would have to take a different way to get to the Carrilobo settlement to visit Ramón. Mariano Rosas did not offer me a guide, so I departed alone, relying on the houndlike instincts of Camilo Arias. Captain Rivadavia alone accompanied me. He was then to return to Leubucó from La Verde and remain in Indian territory until the first rations arrived as stipulated by the peace treaty.

What had changed Mariano Rosas's mind after so many protests of friendship? To this day I do not know.

We galloped along on sandy terrain. I rode at the front with

Camilo Arias. My people were scattered. It was late afternoon. The sun was going down and in the distance we could make out hills. We crossed a series of dunes. From time to time I cast a look back. Little by little Leubucó was receding. It seemed like a dream to me. We reached the watering hole where Camargo had his piece of land. I met a compadre there, the Indian Manuel López. He was educated in Córdoba and can read and write. I got off my horse to wait for the rest of my people to catch up. We would be leaving together. Night was drawing near and we were about to enter the hills.

Gradually, those who had set out behind us rejoined the group. I noticed Macías was missing and asked about him. There he comes, they said. We could see the dust of a rider a short distance away. The rider arrived. I was talking to Manuel López, facing another direction. When I heard the horse stop I turned around, expecting to see Macías but . . . oh horrible, most horrible vision, it was the Negro with the accordion. He started to play his abominable instrument and I stopped him.

What was he doing here?

We will find out later.

I waited a while for Macías but he did not appear.

"They must have held him there," said Captain Rivadavia. "And I told him, too, when you were on your horse and riding and he was wasting time saying good-bye, I said, go ahead now with the colonel, pal."

We were in a deep hollow. I sent two men galloping back to see if they could spot him coming. Just as it was getting dark they returned. They had seen nothing.

We could wait no longer. I cautioned the party about the order we would ride in as we entered the hills—it would be a very dark night—and we left.

How short-lived Macías's happiness had proved to be!

 WHEN WE REACHED the foot of the hill, it was completely dark. We could not see each other at short distances. We followed a mired road whose deep, twisting ruts began to open and fan out. We halted the march, surveyed the trail we would take, and settled on a system of signals in case anyone should get sidetracked in the thickness. This was the most feasible way of proceeding. A cool southerly wind was blowing, immense groups of dark clouds swiftly traversed space, floating like form-less phantoms on the colorless expanse of the void. The lightning flashed earthward like fire darts. The thunder's imposing roar and deafening peals shook the ground and reached our ears like the report of distant cannon fire.

The storm was nigh upon us.

Raindrops were falling. The wind blew, then twisted, then was still. It blew again, whirling about and whipping the dim forest with raucous impetus. The horses moved about in circles and the metallic cowbells mingled their sound with the wind's harmonies. I was wavering between carrying on and camping where we were. I called Camilo Arias and asked him if he thought it was going to rain. He looked at the sky, considered the movement of the clouds, and sniffed the wind.

"If the wind dies down, it will rain. If not, it won't."

"Should we go on, then?"

"That would seem best to me. The animals will suffer less in the hills, because if it does rain there will be hail."

"Won't some of the horses get lost?"

"They won't move. We will find a clearing somewhere and keep them in a closed circle."

"Have you found the path through?"

"Yes, sir."

"Are you sure?"

"Of course I am!"

"Wouldn't it be smart to carry torches with us?"

"That would be good, sir."

"All right, then. Have them tie us some straw bundles and oil."

He withdrew and was back in a minute with word that every-thing was ready. Our *paisanos* do certain things with remarkable dispatch. The torches they made were of dry grass tied to the ends of some long sticks.

"Let's go!" I shouted, "and take care not to wander from the path. Stay in a line, and if anyone gets separated or strays, whistle twice. We will answer by clapping our hands. Follow the light!" I got in line behind Camilo Arias, our human beacon, and we filed forward. The trees doubled over as the hurricane blew. Pounding electrical discharges fulminated the black sphere in rapid flashes. The lightning snaked horizontally from high in the sky to low in lines both straight and oblique, surprising certain remote stars between its light and its shadows. The harsh, incessant din of thunder jarred the impalpable aerial mass. The nocturnal wayfarers turned their souls inward as though warned by visible material signs of an approaching danger. We heard an echo that might have been thought to rise from the bowels of the earth if those lying in eternal rest were to loosen wrenching cries of deep despair. We heard it several more times. Sometimes it seemed to come from behind, other times from ahead, now from the right, now from the left. The road made endless twists and turns as it searched for the least quaggy terrain and skirted the most thickly grown places.

"It's a man's voice," said Camilo.

"Do you suppose somebody is lost?"

"He would whistle if he were, sir."

"An Indian, then?"

"He could have met up with some tiger. They're so afraid of that!"

The wind was easing up. Thick raindrops began to fall.

"It is going to rain, sir."

"Let's stop here, then."

We were in a small clearing. The wind ceased altogether. When two clouds traveling in opposite directions collided the downpour started, dousing our torches.

"On the double!" I shouted. "Hobble the lead mares and everyone be on the lookout."

Torrents of rain fell now. We could see each other in the glow of the lightning. The horses were calm and nobody was missing. Now and then we would hear the mysterious echo. It seemed to be near, then it would be far off. Finally, everyone could hear it.

"That is not the voice of an Indian," said Camilo.

"Then what is it?"

His ears, like his eyes, never deceived him. He remained attentive and said nothing. The echo reached us again and then died under a thunderclap.

"What is it?" I asked.

"Just give me a minute if you would, sir."

We could hear nothing. Though lightning flashed, thunder rolled, and rain fell monotonously around us, we were engulfed in a profound stillness.

Again, the echo.

"They're screaming," said Camilo.

"Screaming what?"

"Just screaming, sir."

"But what?"

"They're screaming, 'Heeeeeyyyy!'"

"Maybe it's somebody rounding up animals."

"I don't think so, sir."

"Listen! Listen!"

The water was letting up and the wind was gathering new strength. The sky was clearing, the clouds thinning, the thunder and lightning retreating, the night cooling. A purer and more soothing air opened our lungs with the promise of fair weather. The rain stopped and the sky cleared. With the stars shining, a pretty moon peeked out. Now the echo of someone shouting became distinctly audible.

"It's a Christian," said Camilo.

"Answer him."

"Heeyyy!" several said at once.

"Hello," he seemed to say again.

There was no doubt about it. It was a Christian lost in the forest, and who was to say since when. He could hear the bells on the lead mares and was desperate for help. "Who's there?" called some. "Over here," said others, and so it went for a while. We could only make out the last syllables of the echo of each answer he called out.

"It must be some escaped captive who heard our cowbells and figured it must be us," said Captain Rivadavia. This struck me as very sound conjecture.

"True," I said, "they don't use cowbells."

There were no mysterious cries now. I ordered the men to whistle. Several of them did so at once but drew no answer. There we were, our ears pricked up, when suddenly the glow from a flame lit the picture we formed—a circle of men around a tufted and formidable hawthorn tree. The ever ingenious Camilo had, by dint of much huffing and puffing on some tallow and straw, managed to start a fire in the hollow of a rotted-out half-charred *chañar*. The light must have been visible from afar despite the trees. Several men then called out together: "Heeyyyy!" A voice answered something unintelligible. We continued telegraphing in this manner, the improvised lantern burning and my people's echoes lost in the forest. Suddenly there came a voice that several of us thought familiar.

"It's Dr. Macías," said Camilo.

It was indeed his voice, or another indistinguishable from it. "Hurry! Some of you go out and signal to him," I said, cautioning them not to lose sight of the fire. We could still hear the voice.

"It's the doctor, sir," said Camilo. "His horse is about done in, too," he added.

"How can you tell that, man?"

"You can hear him laying that strap on. Just listen, sir."

I didn't have his extraordinary hearing.

"Macías!" I shouted. "Macías!"

"Lucio! Lucio!" came the answer. It was he.

"Over here!" cried the men I had just sent out.

Macías appeared. He was soaked to the bone.

"Well what is this all about?" I said.

"I fell behind what with saying good-bye to some friends and all. When I left Leubucó your party was about one league ahead of me. I could see your dust cloud and didn't want to hurry my horse. You were just at the start of the hills when I climbed the last dune. I misjudged the time, it got dark, and I got lost."

"Who were the friends you had to say good-bye to?"

"Some Indians who fed me a few times."

"And what about Mariano Rosas, did you say good-bye to him?"

"Why, sure. He didn't treat me so badly."

The slave is in ignorance of his condition until he breathes the air of freedom, I thought. I got ready to march again. They were holding supper for me in Carrilobo at Villarreal's tent.

"Sir," said Camilo, "the doctor's horse is dragging its feet badly."

"Give him a new mount."

An instant later we were on our way. Leaving the forest, we came to broken, grassy terrain. As we stepped along we flushed out the martinets, who spooked the horses with the flutter of their swift and sudden flight. The sky was clear and serene, the moon and stars shone like diamonds. The only traces remaining of the thundershower were a few faraway clouds. Then we glimpsed some fires that looked just like lightning bugs on a black night. This was very eerie at this time of night and in the desert.

The Argentine gaucho knows the wherefore of every open-country phenomenon. By day and night alike, he is an element in his own right.

"Those fires must be in some tent or other," said Camilo. "We're seeing them through the door or through a crack in the walls."

"How can you tell?"

"Why, the flames are not moving. The wind is not hitting them."

Our horses suddenly stopped as we were talking. We had come

to the edge of a great ditch. Observing the terrain closely, we saw that there was a big cornfield in front of us.[1]

"Villarreal's tent is around here," said Captain Rivadavia.

"You can hear dogs barking," said others.

We skirted the ditch in the direction Captain Rivadavia had indicated and came upon another watermelon and squash patch. It was hard to find the path that led to the tent, but the barking of the dogs and the fires took us in and out of vegetable patches until at last we found it. We arrived at the tent. Villarreal, his wife, and his sister were waiting for us. It was ten-thirty. They gave us a most ingratiating welcome. I did not wish to stay; it was very late. They insisted, however, and I had to give in. We entered the tent, a large, comfortable one with a ceiling and paint-daubed walls. Three large fires were burning within.

"Sir," said Villarreal's wife, "we held some roast lamb for you until just a minute ago, but then seeing how late it was and how you still hadn't gotten here, we thought you wouldn't be coming until tomorrow, so the boys ate it all and now they're *having a good time*. There is nothing left but cold cuts and some corn mush. Sit down! Sit down! Make yourselves at home."

We seated ourselves around one of the fires. While we dried and ate, I ordered our mounts changed. I was not hungry. However, Lemlenyi, Rodríguez, Ozarowsky, and the Franciscans seemed gastronomically quite animated. They brought out some boiled chicken and a lovely pot of some very nicely prepared cornmeal mush, ember-baked bread cakes, and roast squash. From one end of the tent came the sound of the inebriated bunch. Almost all of the niches were empty. In the one behind me slept an old woman, her head resting on her skeletal and wrinkled arm. One of her cartilaginous breasts lay bare. It was sickening.

Dinner commenced. When she saw I was not eating, Villarreal's wife gave me a sign and got up and left. I followed her and when we were both outside she confided her message to me. Her eyes were shining as only a woman's will when a mischievous thought crosses her mind.

"Carmen is expecting you."

"And where is my comadre?"

"There."

She pointed to a nearby tent. I called for a soldier to come with me. I admit it: I was afraid of the dogs. So, while my companions filled the precious pits of their stomachs, I made my promised visit.

A man must keep his word with women even though women are so often perfidious and bad. Things must have some purpose to them.

 MY COMADRE CARMEN lived with her mother, her daughter, an old Indian, and some chickens and dogs. She was awake, waiting for me. The rest were all asleep. We talked about what concerned us and in half an hour separated, perhaps forever. I had kept my promise to visit her before leaving Indian territory and she had kept hers, divulging certain plots against me she had happened to discover. Our farewell was, like all farewells, a sad one.

As I made my way back to Villarreal's tent I gave some thought to what a woman is. I recalled the pleasure they had given me and exclaimed to myself, "They are adorable!" I recalled how they had made me suffer and said, "They are abominable!" As I studied and analyzed them I found them physically perfect, spiritually monstrous.

Oh the hair, the eyes, the mouth, the skin, the elegance of some of them. They are as comely as Niobe, worthy of an Olympian god's love. Any mortal would give a hundred lives for them if he had a hundred to give, and dying yet find death sweet after such supreme goodness.

But then what hearts they have!

They are as unshakable as rocks, as cold as ice, loud as the wind, forgetful as falsehood itself. And then there are the ugly and contrary ones. No one notices them, but just come close to them, hear them, address them. What souls they have! They are as good as charity, as sweet as cherubs, as pure as the Elysian breezes. Living by their side you can love life, for they show us that there is a beauty whose charms time cannot destroy, and that is moral beauty.

Why must they be so pretty and so bad? Why at once so graceful and yet at times so perfidious?

Why the angelic faces and the satanic hearts?

Why so repellent and yet so good, so darkly seductive though unpleasant on the outside?

Why the flawed faces and the exemplary hearts?

Why has God made something as contradictory as an adorable yet bad woman? If his power is so great, why should that which we love most be capable of enticing us with its gaze and intoxicating us with its accursed breath, like those poisonous and richly tinted flowers? What, was it not enough that there should be bad men? Was it really necessary to complete the worldly inferno by making women demonic?

I would have made all women the same.

Do not all roses give off the same utterly mild and gentle fragrance?

Things that are beautiful should be so at all times and in every way.

So went my soliloquy when a human rumbling something like a growling of dogs caught my attention. I stopped. I was just two steps away from Villarreal's tent. I listened, heard garbled sounds in Araucan, looked in that direction, and beheld a repugnant spectacle. There was some horse grease set in a hole in the ground for a lamp, and the only light it gave off was a reddish glimmer. Inside the entrance to the tent, the vicious and debauched rabble was savoring with intimate abandon the last vaporous gasps of a saturnalia begun at daybreak. Men and women, young and old were mixed and tangled together. Their thick hair disheveled, their shirts torn, their greasy blankets loose. Some were half-dressed, others naked; no modesty in the women as they vomited; no shame in the men as their white spittle ran; dirty, painted faces, a gleam of lubricity in every still-conscious eye; a languid gaze coming from those about to pass out; reeking, grumbling, shouting, cursing, laughing, crying, lying all over each other; splayed, curled up, outstretched—it sickened like a seething heap of reptiles.

It humiliated and horrified me to see humanity in such a state. I entered the tent. My people were ready. Only Villarreal, his wife, and his sister-in-law were not drunk. They had hot water and everything else ready to make me some mate, so I had to sit for a while. Villarreal could neither accompany me to Ramón's tent nor send anyone with me because his whole crowd was reeling drunk and he could not leave his family. I called Camilo Arias and while I drank some mate he learned the way to Ramón's. A savvy Indian, Villarreal went over every feature of the land we would be crossing. He noted what quagmires we should avoid on either side and what wetlands to stay away from. Some dunes should be skirted, others climbed. Certain tents and crop fields would mean we were near the chief's settlement.

Once Camilo had everything down, I said good-bye to Villarreal and his family. They all embraced us warmly and wished us a happy journey in Spanish. As they walked us to the hitching post they begged a thousand pardons—and the best-bred people in the world would have done no less—for the shabby hospitality they had dispensed.

As it was a lovely night and we had no hills to cross over, I had the horses turned loose ahead of us so that our own mounts would step livelier. I also cautioned Camilo to stop every ten minutes, lest not hearing the cowbells we get lost. "Forward march!" I shouted and they moved out. As I stopped for an instant to light a cigarette, a shadow came up beside me. I recognized a woman.

"I brought you this," she said, placing a small paper package in my hands.

"And what is this?" I asked.

"A keepsake."

"A keepsake?"

"Yes, a Pampa sash. I embroidered it myself."

"Thank you. You shouldn't have gone to the trouble."

She drew a sigh. "The trouble!" she said with a tender lilt and a kindly reproach in her voice.

"Good-bye," I said, drawing my horse to me.

"Good-bye, good-bye!" said Villarreal and his wife.

"Good-bye! Good-bye!" I answered. As I galloped away I was mumbling to myself, "Women know how to love unselfishly and forget, too." They are neither angels nor demons. They partake of both natures at the same time. When they are good they are incomparable. When they are bad they are execrable. And yet, for all their failures, contradictions, and follies, our existence would without them be like a night march through a land of ice under a moonless, starless sky. Yes, sooner or later everyone ends all the frenzied moments the same way:

> *Yes! my adored, yet most unkind!*
> *Though thou wilt never love again,*
> *To me 'tis doubly sweet to find*
> *Remembrance of that love remain.*

> *Yes! 'tis a glorious thought to me*
> *Nor longer shall my soul repine,*
> *Whate'er thou art or e'er shall be,*
> *That thou hast been dearly, solely, mine.*[1]

The cowbells hanging on the horses were my guide back to my party. My horse was riding spiritedly; he could smell in the air that he was headed for home. I came to the foot of a rather elevated sand hillock and met up with Camilo Arias, who was waiting for me. As I could hear the jingling but not see the horses, it occurred to me something was amiss.

"What's going on?" I asked.

"Nothing, sir. I took the precaution of waiting for you here. We are going to cross that dune. It has a lot of slips and falls and is easy to get lost on."

"All right, let's go," I said. "It is well past midnight. We don't want to waste any time."

He started the climb and I followed. The horses were making a supreme effort to get to the top, sinking up to their flanks in the soft, breaking sands. But they were getting there, little by little. We reached the edge of the crest and just when I thought I was over the top, I found myself at a deep hollow from whose bottom flowed a pure and crystalline mirror of water. The horses' reflection shone in it as they drank and the moon lit the wild and poetic scenery from a clear, blue sky. We marched on, climbing and descending. Suddenly, despite our precautions Camilo Arias announced that we were lost. I called a halt. "So find the trail," I told Camilo. We dismounted and waited. A moment later our equestrian pilot was back.

"It's over that way."

We marched.

The night was growing overcast. Rain seemed likely as the moon drifted behind the clouds. We descended to a saltpeter bed, one so combed with trails and so thick with thorny brush that the horses scattered and confusion ensued. From all sides came the sounds of cowbells and of the drivers whistling to the horses that had strayed farthest. We had to spread out as well. The paths were very twisted and the horses would not follow each other. The saltpeter bed seemed as white as the still surface of a frozen lake. It groaned awfully beneath the hooves of the hundred horses crossing it. The horses were sinking into the quagmire, climbing over the broom plants that abound so in the pampas, rearing back when spooked by the jack-o'-lanterns streaking every which way like a phosphorescence.

The night sky darkened. The moon went down among broad, marbled clouds with somber majesty and the stars barely shone through the watery veil covering the skies. I crossed the bed. Some had already crossed and were waiting on the shore. Others were just now completing the crossing. The same went for the horses; not all of them were in yet. I waited a while as they searched in vain for the road. When I saw they could not find it and that Captain Rivadavia and others were nowhere in sight, I ordered the grass set on fire. It was damp and we had no tallow, so that did not work. We called out, nobody answered. We whistled. Utter silence. I sent three scouts out. Two of them gradually made their way back, having seen and heard nothing. The third one was still out and answered from nearby. He had been wandering around in our vicinity for quite a while.

The rain clouds threatened to let loose any minute.

"Let's march in the general direction we're going," I told Camilo, "until we reach a higher level than this. We will find the rest of the horses and riders when day breaks."

As we marched the dogs barked.

"There's a tent over there," said Camilo.

I looked in the direction he was pointing and saw nothing but darkness. "Let's stop here, then," I said, "and meanwhile someone go find out where Ramón's tent is."

He sent two riders ahead. They came back saying we were going the wrong way. They said the road was off to the left, that is, to the east, and that we were very near Ramón's tent. We would see it as soon as we crossed a ravine. We changed course and marched on in the direction he had pointed and soon came to a low-lying quagmire.

"This must be the ravine," said Camilo. "We must be close."

Among the stray group was a dog of mine named Brazil. He had been in the Paraguayan campaign in the Twelfth Line Battalion with me and now was bravely following me on this excursion. He was an exceedingly intelligent criollo hound, part greyhound and part hunting hound. He was strong, good-looking, light, and smart. He was good at hunting armadillos, buck, and ostrich and was a sworn enemy of the fox, the only animal whom he did not always outsmart. Everyone loved, petted, and took care of him. The soldiers knew his bark as well as they knew my voice. We were crossing the ravine when we heard certain doglike echoes.

"It's Brazil!" said several of them at once.

"Captain Rivadavia must be there," said Camilo Arias. We followed Brazil's barking and found them soon enough. There were

still some missing, however. Captain Rivadavia and those following him had waited hopelessly to be reunited with my group and
then simply resolved to stay where they were. They had been waiting awhile when I got there. We marched on and when we reached
some vizcacha holes Camilo Arias observed that we must be near
some tent. Vizcachas are always a sign that human population is
nearby. Brazil chased them away and sniffed out a trail that horses
and riders had made.

"Rufino Pereyra must have come through here with his horses,"
said Camilo when he heard the dog. A moment later the barking
grew louder as other canines joined in. Surely we were about to
arrive at Ramón's tent, or at someone's. We followed the barking
and when we came to a large corral, Rufino Pereyra and his horses
appeared. The lead mare had lost her cowbell in the broom shrubs
at the saltpeter beds.

We were now where we wanted to be. I approached the tent. An
Indian came out and told me that Ramón and his whole family had
been awake and holding dinner for me until midnight. He added
that Ramón was somewhat indisposed and could not get up, so we
should dismount, find a comfortable spot, and make ourselves at
home. We did so, and I settled into a spacious outbuilding where
Ramón had his silver forge. We took care of the horses and went
out into the garden, gathered plenty of corn and squash, and built
a fire. We ate supper and went to bed happy and content, as if we
had come to spend the night in a prince's palace.

How true it is: the art of happiness consists of suiting your desires to your means and of desiring only those pleasures that are
possible to have.

Camilo Arias had not left my side.

 A CERTAIN NEGRO proverb says sleep has no
master.

We all slept perfectly well. In our fatigue we
found Chief Ramón's dwelling a delight. It was
eight o'clock in the morning when I awoke. My
cohorts were still snoring with enviable lung power. I called an assistant, asked for mate, and stayed in bed awhile just enjoying the
pleasure of doing nothing, which as pleasures go is as censured and
frowned upon as it is generally sought after. According to a friend

of mine, an egregious and not at all vulgar poet, to do nothing is to rest. He holds that the day is made for that purpose and the night for sleeping.

Ecclesiastes, who knows more than my friend and I put together, says this:

The fool foldeth his hands together, and eateth his own flesh. Better is a handful with quietness, than both the hands full with travail and vexation of spirit.

I examined by the light of day the bed in which I had slept so comfortably, so à la Balzac as it were, slept as if furnished with all the appurtenances: big down pillows and silken comforters. It was a few badly stretched colt pelts and some sheepskin, and the head of the bed was a mortar covered with cushions.

I looked around.

In all my time in Indian territory I had slept under no better roof. Chief Ramón's tent beat all the others. My lodgings were a wood and straw hut some thirty-five feet long, twelve feet wide, and nine feet high. It was spotless. Along one side was the forge and beside it a crude wooden table and an iron anvil. I have already said that Ramón is a silversmith and that this craft is common among the Indians. They make spurs, stirrups, halters, breastplates, rings, bracelets, brooches, and other feminine and masculine adornments such as rings and tinderboxes. They melt down the silver, purify it in a crucible, hammer it into the desired shape, and then chisel it. They favor Chilean taste in their silvercraft.[1] They enjoy commerce with Chile and bring all sorts of articles back from there to trade for cattle, sheep, or horses.

The forge was comprised of a parallelipiped of crude adobe. It had two bellows and clearly work had gone on there the day before; the ashes were still warm. There was wood charcoal in a leather sack and several cutting instruments, hammers, and broken files on the table. The strange design of the bellows absolutely enthralled me. Before examining their construction I struck up a dialogue with myself.

"Let's see now," I said. "Proud spokesman of civilization and modern progress in the pampas that you are, how would you go about making a bellows?"

"A bellows?"

"Yes, a bellows. Isn't that what the Royal Spanish Academy calls 'an instrument for gathering and releasing wind,' though it would have made more sense and fit the situation better to have said 'an instrument designed on certain principles of physics to gather air by means of a valve and release it with greater or lesser force, as determined by the person using it, through a shaft located at one end'?"

"I see, I see."

"Well, then, if you see, tell me. How would you make one?"

"Uh, well . . ."

"Aha! Another poor, fatuous, nineteenth-century fool, a dilettante, a dolt who refuses to admit to his lack of genius."

"Who, me?"

"Yes, you. Here you are in the miserable tent of an Indian whom you've called a barbarian a million times, whose extermination you have preached every imaginable way in the name of your compassionate and much trumpeted civilization, and you're beaten and won't confess your ignorance."[2]

"Ignorance?"

"That's right, ignorance."

"I suppose I should feel humbled."

"Yes, be humble and learn once again that the world is not to be studied in books."

I bowed my head, walked over to the forge, took the bellows by the two horizontally parallel handles, pulled, released, and a cloud of ashes arose. It was ugly, but it accomplished the desired effect, releasing a current of air strong enough to inflame the live coals. The whole thing was Ramón's exclusive invention. From a dried and rubbed cow's paunch he had made a sleeve three feet long and a foot in diameter. He tied it with thongs, forming three large, contiguous pockets. He put half of a rifle barrel in one end and plugged the other. He had the rifle barrel lodged in the wall and lashed to a stake. Naturally, by pulling and squeezing until the pockets were flat, the air entered and exited with the same effect that any other bellows would have had. I considered the time it would have taken me, with all the benefits of civilization at hand, if necessity or a love of the liberal arts had prompted me to make a bellows. It was just dawning on my that I might have to admit defeat when a fair-haired, white captive boy from twelve to fourteen years old came in to the lodge. He saluted me with complete respect and called me "Mas'r."

"Chief Ramón says can he see you now," he said. "How did you sleep last night?"

I told him I was at the chief's disposal and could see him then and there if he wished. I also told him I had slept very well. The captive left and a moment later Ramón walked in, looking like an overdressed *paisano* and so clean it was a pleasure to lay eyes on him. As accustomed to work as his hands were, they seemed like those of a gentleman, with their impeccably clean, evenly rounded fingernails—not too short and not too long.

He did not stand on ceremony. On the contrary, he treated me like an old friend, repeated that I should make myself at home and that he was at my disposal. He said that they would be bringing me my lunch and that he would introduce me to his family later. He left, returned forthwith, and sat down. They brought the meal, the invariable corn, squash, stew, roast, etc.

This was all done with the greatest care. I had not sampled such a flavorful broth in the longest time. During our meal we talked about agriculture and cattle. The Indian was well-versed in everything. His corrals were large and well-made, his crop fields were vast, his cattle tamer than any other. Ramón's love for the Christians is widely known. Indeed, it is his tribe which has the most of them. One of his wives, with whom he has three children, is none other than doña Fermina Zárate of Villa de la Carlota. She was captured as a young woman perhaps twenty years old. She is old now.

The poor woman was standing right there.

"She is a good lady," Ramón said in front of her. "She has stayed with me for many years and I am very grateful to her. I told her she can leave whenever she wants to and return to her homeland and her family."

Doña Fermina looked at him with an indefinable expression, a mixture of affection and horror, a look that only an observant and penetrating woman could have understood.

"Sir," she answered, "Ramón is a good man. If only they could all be like him, then the captives would not suffer so. Why should I complain, anyway. I figure God knows what He is doing." Saying this, she broke down and wept openly.

"She is a very good lady," said Ramón. He stood up and went out, leaving me alone with her. Doña Fermina Zárate has unnoteworthy features. There are many women of her facial type, though her brow and eyes reveal a certain patient abidance of the decrees of providence. She is less aged than she believes herself to be.

"Why don't you come with me, ma'am?" I asked her.

"Oh, sir," she answered bitterly, "what am I to do among the Christians?"

"Reunite with your family. I know them. They live in Carlota and they all cherish the memory of you and weep for you."

"And what about my children, sir?"

"Your children . . ."

"Ramón will let me leave. He really is not a bad man. At least he has treated me well since I became a mother. But he doesn't want me to take my children with me."

I couldn't bring myself to say: Leave them here. They are the fruit of violence.

They were her children!

"Besides, sir," she went on, "what kind of life would I have with the Christians after being gone from my village so many years? I was a young, nice-looking girl when they captured me and now look at me. I am old. I look like a Christian because Ramón lets me dress like one, but I live like an Indian. And frankly, I think I am more Indian than Christian, although I believe in God. I'm telling you, I commend my children and family to Him every day."

"You believe in God despite being captive?"

"What fault of His is it that the Indians got me? If anything it is the Christians' fault for not taking care of their women and children."

I had no answer for her. Such lofty philosophy on the lips of that woman, the retired concubine of that barbarian, humbled me more than the soliloquy about the bellows.

A young and lovely, wasted, filthy, and ragged woman entered. She spoke with a Córdoban accent.

"Are you by any chance Colonel Mansilla, sir?"

"Yes, I am, young woman, what do you want?"

"I came to ask you for a favor. Could you get the fathers to let me kiss the cord of Our Father Saint Francis?"

"I'd be glad to." I called the holy men. They came. When she saw them enter, poor, wretched Petrona Jofré fell to her knees before them and took Father Marcos's cord first, and then Father Moisés's cord, and gushing with fervent emotion kissed them over and over. The good Franciscans, seeing her in such anguish, exhorted her, stroked her paternally, and managed to quiet her down, though not entirely. She wept like a baby.

It broke my heart to hear and see her.

She gradually calmed down and told us the brief and touching story of her sorrows. Doña Fermina confirmed all the details. She was from Cañada Honda, was Cruz Bustos's wife, and the poor woman's life had been a veritable *via crucis*. She belonged to an Indian named Carrapí and he was the worst sort of person. He was frantically in love with her. She heroically resisted his lecherous advances. Hence her ordeal.

"I'd sooner let him kill me, or I will sooner kill him, than do what that Indian wants," she said with wild energy.

Doña Fermina shook her head.

"See what a life this is, sir."

I felt desperate. What else can impotent sympathy awaken in us? I could do nothing for this unfortunate woman, had nothing to give her. All I had left were the clothes on my back. I did not have so much as a handkerchief. Doña Fermina related that Carrapí did not want to sell her out of captivity and that a Christian was making a bid on her. The Indian was asking twenty mares, sixty Bolivian pesos, a cloth poncho, and five red breechcloths for her.

"And who is this Christian?" I asked.

"Crisóstomo," she answered.

"Crisóstomo?"

"Yes, sir."

This was the man who had ridden his horse between the two Franciscans in Calcumuleu, the man who exasperated me so, who gave me food to eat afterwards and told his interesting story.

Plainly, the bad ones have a heart as well.

Pascal has said it: Man is neither angel nor beast.

He is an indefinable being. He takes pleasure in doing evil, enjoys doing good.

Consoling words amidst all this.

 INVITED INTO RAMÓN'S tent, I left doña Fermina Zárate and Petrona Jofré with the Franciscans and entered. The chief's family was comprised of five concubines of different ages, one of them Christian and the other four Indians. He had seven sons and three daughters, two of them past puberty. These two and the head concubine were dressed in their finest to welcome me.

There is no Ranquel Indian richer than Ramón. He is after all a cattleman, a laborer, and a silversmith. His family lives lavishly. They had brooches, earrings, bracelets, and necklaces to display, all hammered and chiseled from pure, solid silver by Ramón, and richly woven Pampa blankets and sashes.

The two oldest daughters were named Comeñé and Pichicaiun. Comeñé's name means "pretty eyes," from *come*, "pretty," and *ñé*, "eyes." She is the older of the two. Pichicaiun means "tiny mouth," from *pichicai*, "little," and *un*, "mouth." They had painted their lips, cheeks, and fingernails carmine, shaded their eyelids, and painted many small black beauty marks on their faces. Both of them had very appropriate names; one of them was distinguished by a very pretty and very small mouth, the other by her big black fiery eyes. They were both in full physical bloom, and anywhere in the world a man of good taste would have looked at them a good long while with pleasure.

They welcomed me with charming diffidence.

I sat down, Ramón sat beside me, his main wife and daughter facing me. The two young Indian women knew that they were pretty. They flirted just as two Christian girls would have.

Ramón is quite a conversationalist. He would not let me talk with him and the interpreter bungled his reasons as well as mine.

"Spañol! Spañol!" shouted Ramón. The fair-skinned, fair-haired captive appeared, took his orders, and left. When he came back he was carrying plates and utensils.

Dinner was served.

I had just eaten but it would have discredited me to refuse the invitation, so I ate. The captive never took his eyes off Ramón, who controlled him even as he looked at him.

"What's your name?" I asked him, thinking that "Spañol! Spañol!" meant something in Araucan.

"Spañol!" he answered.

"Spañol?" I asked, looking alternately at Mora and Ramón.

"Yes, sir, Spañol," said Mora. "That's what they call some of the captive men."

"Spañol," confirmed Ramón, who had understood my question.

"But what was your name in your own land?" I asked the captive.

"I don't know," he replied. "I've forgotten it. I was very young when they brought me here."

"Where are you from?"

"I don't know."

"He won't know anything, sir," said Mora. "That's why they

call him Spañol. When he gets older they'll give him an Indian name."

"Is that the custom here?"

"Yes, sir."

"Ask Ramón what *spañol* means."

"*Spañol* means 'from another land,'" answered Ramón.

As we were discussing this, Captain Rivadavia appeared and spoke into my ear. Crisóstomo had just arrived from Leubucó, he said, and as he was leaving there they were saying that there had been an invasion around San Luis. After relaying this news to Ramón, I asked for permission to leave, retired to my quarters, and a moment later sent Captain Rivadavia on his way with a sharp letter for Mariano Rosas. Citing the peace treaty, I demanded that the invaders be punished and told him I would expect his answer in La Verde, where I would arrive by afternoon. Ramón came over to express his displeasure at the news. He said that it was most likely Wenchenao and called him a gaucho thief. He asked me what time I planned to get underway. I answered in the gaucho style: as soon as the sun gave the first signs of rolling over. In other words, after twelve. He pointed out that that would give him time to skin a good fat cow and some sheep for fresh meat. I told him not to bother, but he said to me it was his duty and no bother at all. He said it seemed strange to him that Mariano Rosas had allowed me to leave Leubucó without meat.

We had in fact left empty-handed, resolved to eat the mules. I had made a firm resolution not to ask for food. It was understandably a matter of pride in a land where sustenance is not bought, a land where one asks for something *with payback* when one is in need. They brought a fat cow and two sheep and I had my people butcher them. Then I stepped into Ramón's forge with him, where he spoke to me as follows:

"I am a friend to the Christians because I like work. I wish to live in peace because I have something to lose. I want to know if this peace will last and if I can take my Indians to the Cuero, where the land is better."

I answered that it greatly gladdened me to hear him speak this way; that he thereby proved he was a man of sound judgment.

"I know the reason why," he added. "Don't you think I would like to live like Coliqueo? But only when the others go. They frighten easily. It is going to take a long time for them to learn to like the taste of peace."

"Then you believe it is better for you to live together than scattered about?"

"Sure I do," he said. "When you're all far apart you lose in every way. There's no trading that way."

Visitors arrived and I had to receive them. Ramón's father, a feeble septuagenarian, was among them. He told me his life and services, pondering his own merits with a cynicism worthy of a civilized man. He said he had abdicated governance of the tribe and left it to his son because Ramón was like him. He made me a thousand offers, a thousand overtures of friendship, and finally asked me for a baize-lined cloth jacket.

They announced that the roast was ready. I had the horses brought in and reminded Ramón that I was planning to leave, to which he replied I was master of my own decisions. How could I be thinking about leaving, he said. Couldn't I visit a little longer? He and a few friends would very much enjoy accompanying me a good ways. I thanked him for the courtesy and told him again there was no need to trouble himself, no need for ceremony, and he told me it was no trouble to do one's duty and that we might not meet again.

I had no answer to that.

I considered for a moment that the winds were much more favorable in Carrilobo than in Leubucó and that Ramón had no Christians around to adulate him. He was, I noted, the most radical of the Indians in custom, the one whose welcome most adhered to Ranquel ways, and the most dutiful and gentlemanly one upon my return. I capped my thoughts with a question: Does contact with civilization perhaps corrupt primitive good faith?

I heard the cowbells as the horses arrived. I ordered everyone to saddle up and turned to Ramón.

"Well then, friend, what would you like me to send you?"

"I need things for the silver forge," he answered.

"I'll send them," I said, taking out my notebook.

"What are they?"

"An anvil."

"Right."

"A hammer."

"Right."

"Tongs."

"Right."

"A wheel."

"Right."

"A narrow file."

"Right."

"Pincers."

"Right."

"A crucible."

"Right."

"A burnisher."

"Right."

"A whetstone."

"Right."

"Tincal."

Ramón had been calling out the words thus far. He had pronounced them well and did not need an interpreter. When I heard him say tincal I asked him, "Tincal?"

"Yes, tincal."

"Give me the Christian name for it."

"That is it. Tincal."

I was about to say that that might be the Araucan name, but I remembered the lesson I had just learned, my humiliation before the bellows, my humiliation before doña Fermina as she held forth like a seasoned philosopher. So, rather than say that, I asked him if he was certain.

"Yes, it is tincal. That is what the Chileans call it." He got up, went over to the forge, put his hand inside a leather pouch and, unwrapping what he took out, passed it to me.

"This is tincal," he said.

It was a bitter, whitish substance something like salt. I wrote down tincal but was sure it was not a Spanish word. When I returned to Río Cuarto, one of the first things I did was to find a dictionary. I had tincal on the brain. I found it. "Tincal," it said, "see borax."

"Praised be God," I cried. I knew what borax was. I knew it was a kind of salt found on the bottom of certain lakes. I knew that in metallurgy they use it for fusing, soldering, and as a reactor. Thank God, I repeated, for He punishes with neither stick nor stone.

All our flaunted wisdom, all our reading and study, and what do we do with it? We despise a poor Indian, call him barbarian and savage; demand his extermination because his blood, race, instincts, and aptitudes cannot be assimilated to our empirical civilization, which though it calls itself humanitarian, righteous, and just yet kills by the sword those who live by the sword; which bloodies itself out of selfishness, greed, self-aggrandizement, pride; which raises a sharp-edged sword over all of us in the name of the law; which, in short, upholds the law of the talisman because if I kill I in turn am killed. That is the way it has been since there have been Brennuses around to tip the scales of justice with their money.[1]

Meanwhile we reject that barbarian, that savage, that Indian as if we did not all spring from a common stock, as if the human plant were not unique in its species. When we least expect it he will show us our arrogance. He will prove to us we live in ignorance, that our egregious vanity has pierced the nebulous darkness of the heavens with the telescope, shrunken distance with electricity and steam, and indeed may soon fly. But that it will never annihilate so much as a simple particle of matter, or pluck from man the recondite secrets of his heart.

Everything was set to go.

I said good-bye to Ramón's family, whose daughter, contradicting local custom, embraced us and clasped our hands. They gave silver rings to some of those accompanying me.

I started the march at once. Ramón and fifty of his people rode with us at the sound of bugles. He was riding a bay he himself had broken in. It seemed like a vigorous animal.

"I am no slacker, friend," he told me. "I break in my own horses and I like the Indian way of doing it better than the Christian."

"You mean you do it some other way?"

"That's right."

"And how is that?"

"We don't mistreat the animal. We tie it to a stake and try to coax the fear out of it. If it doesn't let us come near we don't feed it. We stroke it before we ever get on it. Then we saddle it but we don't get on until it gets used to the seat and doesn't feel tickled any more. Then we put a bit on it. That's why our horses are so spirited and so gentle. The Christians teach theirs more things, like trotting nicely, but we tame ours better."

Even in this, I thought to myself, the barbarians can give lessons in humanity to those who despise them.

Ramón had accompanied me about a league's distance.

"This is far enough," I said, coming to a halt.

"Whatever you like," he answered.

We shook hands, embraced, and separated. His party saluted me with a hurrah.

"Adiós, adiós," some called out together.

"Adiós, adiós, amigo," shouted still others.

And they rode south and we rode north, enveloped in whirl-winds of sand that darkened the horizon like a black curtain.

I calculated arrival at La Verde by sundown.

I reached a grassy field and called for a momentary halt. The sand was choking us.

 THE DUNES OF LA VERDE were in sight and it is probable that another traveler in my circumstances would not have stopped. But experience is the mother of wisdom and I laughed at some of my officers, who, when they saw the destination so near, mumbled, "Now why would he stop here?"

They had not traveled the four corners of the earth as I had, on a sailing ship, on a steamer and a locomotive, in a cart, on horseback, on foot, by coach, on a litter, on an elephant's back, by camel, in a balloon, on a donkey, on a sedan chair, on the back of a mule, and on the back of a man.

As with readers, so with travelers: too much haste is a shortcoming. Both need bear in mind that unvarying movement has the same effect on the spirit as unvarying intonation does on the ears. Voltaire has told us: *L'ennui naquit un jour de l'uniformité.* Whenever I hear something read aloud very quickly I remember one story and whenever I ride a horse in the Argentine pampas I remember another.

In a play by Sedaine[1]—it may be *Rose et Colas*, I'm not certain—there is a very long scene between two villagers. The chronicles tell us that in their hurry to get through rehearsal as fast as possible, the actors went too quickly and found nevertheless that somehow the scene did not feel any shorter. They asked the author if he would mind cutting some of it out.

"Say the lines more slowly," he answered, "and that will make it seem shorter."

The same goes for riding a horse across a country at a gallop. Everything seems far away, nothing comes clearly into view. You reach the end of a day's ride overwhelmed with fatigue, having enjoyed none of the pleasant natural sights. And that's if you get there at all. Sometimes you stay out on the road somewhere. Once a traveler was crossing the country at an open gallop. It was late and the sun was setting. He came across a gaucho and asked him what time he would arrive at such and such a place.

"If you keep galloping you'll get there tomorrow," the gaucho told him. "If you just go along at an easy trot you will get there soon enough."

"And how many leagues is it from here to there?"

"About two."

"And if it is as close as that, why will it take me longer to get there if I ride faster?"

"Well," said the *paisano*, as he looked compassionately at the man's horse, "if you keep pushing that old mount of yours, it's going to drop out from under you." Whereupon the traveler promptly reined in and continued at a trot.

The application of my maxims in any season of travel, by day or by night, in fair weather or foul, on the vast solitude of the desert, has always yielded optimal results. I have always arrived on the scheduled day without leaving tired horses behind or physically or morally fatiguing those accompanying me.

My rule was inflexible.

I would part at a trot, gallop for a quarter hour, rein in, canter for five minutes, trot another five, then gallop another quarter hour, and finally stop. I would dismount, rest for five minutes and let the horses rest, before resuming the march with the same inflexible regularity whenever the terrain would allow it. The tinhorns following me liked to complain that I was always changing the pace and always stopping. First of all, they had not stopped to think about it. Secondly, once their bodies are warmed up, they are most comfortable with the gallop. I am sure, however, that the horses, being better judges of this than the riders, said to themselves, "God bless this colonel" every time they heard the word *halt* and the order to take out their bits.

Let me repeat: it goes the same for traveling as it does for reading. The longest readings are those in which there is no variation of cadence or diction. The author of the tragedy *Leonidas* had invited several of his friends to hear him read a new composition. They were eager, and when it was time for the reading there were twelve select judges, some of them academics, gathered in comfortable armchairs. At a table facing them sat the poet. The author was to read his own works. He possessed the gift of writing magnificent verse but did not know how to read it aloud.

He read in a sepulchral monotone.

The audience endured the torment for the first half hour, applauding the first two acts. As he finished the third act he noticed there was not the slightest hint of approbation. He looked up from the manuscript to discover that the entire auditorium had fallen fast asleep. He understood what had happened, so he turned off the lights and, rather than continue reading, began to recite the rest of the work, which he knew by heart, in the dark. Well, reading aloud and dramatic recital are two different arts. They all wake up shouting, "Bravo! Bravo!" but the author does not stop. His friends think they are dreaming or that they've gone blind, because when they open their eyes they can't see anything. They come to their senses after a moment's scare and the scene ends with this useful lesson: Monotony will put your best friends to sleep.

I had my reasons for delaying my arrival in La Verde, where in any case I only wanted to meet Captain Rivadavia or some envoy of Mariano Rosas, but not to stay. When I had finished reckoning the distances with my mental compass and when my watch said it was time to renew the march, I ordered the bits put back in and the cinches tightened. When it came time to move out, we spotted two clouds of dust to our rear. They were following our tracks and the one closer to us was smaller than the one whirling farther behind. Some said it was somebody chasing an ostrich. Others, a doe being run down. Camilo Arias said it was nothing of the sort, only an Indian chasing down something that was not a country animal.

My officers and I conjectured as we watched, and even the Franciscans, who were turning into gauchos, hazarded a guess or two.

By now we were mounted.

I wavered. I wanted to get going and I wanted to find out. Camilo Arias, whose eyes could drill through space, so to speak, and touch objects, then spoke with his customary self-assurance.

"It is an Indian running down a dog."

"Brazil must have gotten away," said several excited voices at once.

"Poor fellow," said the two Franciscans. "I'm glad for him." Then they looked at me reproachfully for what I had done in Carrilobo.

My sin was not such a great one, however.

I was talking with Ramón in his tent when valiant Brazil—the dog, that is—came meekly over to where I was and lay down next to me. He looked at me as if to say, "So when are we leaving this place?" He was wagging his tail like a feather duster all the while, the way we might smile affably or pat someone warmly on the back when we want to neutralize the effect of some stinging remark.

I don't know if I have mentioned that over and above his good looks, Brazil was a stout and solid cur with a shining bright yellow coat. I do, however, recall saying when at my compadre Baigorrita's settlement that it truly is a dog's life for the dogs that live with the Indians. They are all so hungry you can see their ribs. They look as if they have no flesh or blood. You would think to see them that they were fossil inhabitants from an antediluvian era when Plutonian chills froze all but the spiraled ammonite and the long-necked, broad-headed pterodactyl.

Ramón took an instant liking to our magnificent Brazil, whose stoutness stood in contrast with his emaciated dogs, like a Paraguayan prisoner beside a fat-jowled soldier of Río Grande.

"What a nice fat dog, brother," he said. "And pretty, too. My dogs are so skinny!"

"It must be you don't feed them, brother," I said.

"Not true!"

"Well, what do you give them, then?"

"Leftovers."

Leftovers, I said to myself, and recalling that the Indians drink even the steaming blood of the cattle they kill, I thought: I wouldn't want to trade places with these dogs. I recalled that I had once envied certain little long-haired, moist-eyed pooches whom certain high-society ladies and others not so high madly adore, even to the point of sleeping with them. That is humanitarian progress for you in the nineteenth century. At this rate, there will be dogs named Monsieur Bijou, Mister Pinch, and señor don Barcino by the year 2000.

So I turned to my interlocutor and said, "That is not enough."

"These dogs of mine are a bunch of mongrels," he answered. "Why don't you leave me yours so he can breed here?"

What could I say? "I suppose so, brother," I said. "Go ahead and take him, but have them tie him up right now, otherwise he will never stay in this tent. He'll come with me."

Ramón called and three captives came at once. He spoke to them in his language. They tried to rope Brazil by the neck with a lasso they had but it was no use. The dog bared his sharp white fangs, snarled, curled back, and nervously drew his tail in close. The timid captives did not dare move in on him. It looked to me like the poor wretches understood freedom better than I and that they respected the animal not out of cowardice but out of a vague and uncertain feeling of love.

I had to be my faithful companion's henchman myself.

Brazil looked at me when I went to take the lasso in hand. He rolled on to his back, paws in the air and chest out as if to say, go ahead, kill me if that's what you want to do. As I put the rope around his neck I glanced at myself in the pupil of his eyes, which seemed crystallized, and what I saw was horrible. Had my word of honor not been at stake, I would have considered myself contemptible. Brazil humbly allowed himself to be tied to a stake. When he tried to bark I gave him a severe look and a gesture of silence and he stopped. With all the coming and going the animal knew instinctively that his freedom was gone. When he saw me leave without him he broke into heartrending yelps. I could not begin to say how long he went on barking. Ramón probably got tired of hearing it and let him loose once we were far away. Brazil probably also said at that point, *Ils vont, l'espace est grand*, but I'll catch up with them. And he probably took off after us, fleeing a land where those of his species had made him forget the high regard in which he held the human race.

All eyes were on the two clouds of dust coming swiftly toward us. Suddenly, the closer one condensed. "They've roped him with the bolas!" shouted Camilo Arias. I was persuaded that it was Brazil and will confess that Camilo's words had the same effect on me as seeing a comrade in peril and glory fall prisoner in battle.

The good Franciscans were pale, my officers and soldiers sad. There was nothing to be done for Brazil.

"Let's go," I said, taking off at a gallop.

"And leave him here?" cried the Franciscans.

"Come on, let's go," I said, and an idea took hold of my mind, mortifying me for a long while. Why, I wondered as I considered Brazil's fate, should a sensate being, one who feels hunger, thirst, heat, and cold, in short, who feels pain as well as sensual pleasure, not have a soul just as I do? So deliberating, I tried to grasp the philosophical reason why people will say: That man is a real dog. But never when a dog is wild and bad: That dog is a real man.

Are we not the oppressors of all that breathes, including our own race?

Will morality ever be an exact science?

Where will it all end if comparative anatomy, philosophy, phrenology, biology, etc., register progress as extraordinary as that which physics and chemistry make with each passing day? Where, if the material world no longer holds anything recondite for man?

What is there left for him to discover?

Electricity, the lens, and steam power have opened the earth and the sea's abysses to unfathomable depths. Man has discovered luminaries in the remote, invisible heavens and his voice travels thousands of leagues with stunning and magical speed.

And so I drifted along, daydreaming, when, unprompted by strap or spur, my horse stopped before an obstacle.

We were at the foot of the La Verde dunes.

 THE READER IS already familiar with La Verde, in whose deep, circular basin there flows cool, limpid, and abundant fresh water. All those entering or leaving by the Cuero and Bagual roads stop to water their horses there and cool off a few hours beneath the dense branches of the carob trees, the *chañares*, and the buckthorn that grace the slope leading in sharp drops down to the lagoon's edge. Green reeds, yellowish cattails, and the blade-like reed mace of semicylindrical leaf grow in dense cover there while hidden frogs and toads chant their eternal monotonous celebration of the inalterable peace of these hushed and solitary regions . . .

As I reached the sandy crests of the dune with my people, a small group of riders coming from Leubucó appeared at a right angle to where we stood. This must be Captain Rivadavia's answer, I thought and, spurring my horse, shot down the hill. In a matter of minutes I was in possession of his letter. Mariano Rosas had read my diplomatic protest and, versed as he was in public affairs, offered to chase, apprehend, and punish those who my sources said had been marauding near San Luis even as I held open council with Baigorrita's, Ramón's, and Mariano's notables. This in compliance with the peace treaty.

Promises do not help pay, but they always help one out of a spot and if the Indians are tireless in making requests, they are no slackers either in making promises, which is more or less how the whole world is run. Individuals are no different than nations in tapping the arsenal of human perfidy for excuses and reasons for going back on their sworn word. And the multitudes in either hemisphere always let themselves be led around by the nose by ambitious schemers and impostors who exploit and rule them. Yesterday it was Napoleon III, the risen champion of nationalities, victorious at Magenta and Solferino, proclaiming the Italian Federation. Today it is Bismarck who cries out for gallophobic Germanism. Tomorrow it will be another Peter the Great in the name of Pan-Slavism who will make the most of Muscovite turbulence, the ignorance of the serfs, and religious fanaticism.

In America we had Rosas, Monagas, and López. They all knew how to strike the mysterious and magnetic chord that mystifies the people. Meanwhile, liberty and universal fraternity remain a beautiful utopia, a holy aspiration of the soul. Individual man and collective man go their different ways under one master today, another tomorrow, from hegemony to hegemony, and who is to say whither they are bound . . .

Perfection and perfectibility seem two great chimeras.

We ramble along and falsehood is the one truth we possess. It is as if God had willed a great barrier erected before human conscience that would stop it whenever it made bold to penetrate the dim limbos of the moral world.

The sun was setting majestically, the horizon was cloudless and sharp, the blue sky was taut and glossy. Here and there could be seen a cloud glazed in rainbow colors and hung high in the gigantic vault. A richly oxygenated breeze blew soft and cool. The cattails swayed gracefully on their supple stems. Mirrored in the clear waters of the lagoon, they leaned until their ivory tufts were damp. They might have been naiads of white and comely countenance, who moisten the tips of their flowing hair and behold themselves in distracted infatuation in the serene and liquid mirror.

Sure signs from sky and earth augured both a pleasant night and a day as lovely as the one that had just transpired. It was therefore crucial to make the most of the few remaining minutes of light. I cannot say what vague and false premonition burdened my breast with anguish. Was it that I would soon separate from my companions, men who had shared with me on that strange pilgrimage all the deprivation, all the fatigue, all the hazards surrounding us, and which I sometimes overcame with patience and other times with audacity and an indifference to life? [1] Or was it that with the danger past my mind was now turning deep within itself, absorbed in the contemplation of its own specters?

Have you never been through a heroic ordeal where you saw death up close but stayed serene and only later felt something like a shudder and it was fear of what had happened?

Have you never grappled with death, overcome it, and felt immediately after the crisis had passed a nervous shiver, as if some inner echo were calling it impossible?

Have you never dashed to save a beloved object on a cliff's edge and felt, when you knew it was safe again, a kind of lightheadedness? And did it not teach you that this existence is supremely good despite the thorns they pierce and harm us with when the sojourn is harshest?

Have you never kept vigil for hours on end at the bedside of a loved one, your mind overcome by the idea of life, swayed by fond hopes? And the convalescent's livid face, those shining eyes, did they not strike you as the specter of death, so that only then did you grasp the terrible arcanum that lies between being and nonbeing?

If you have, then you will understand the impressions of my soul, which were so different at that moment from what they had been before, in that very same place, when unarmed and unannounced I set out, ready for anything, towards the heart of the tent settlements with a handful of spirited men.

At the bottom of the dune there was a sort of twilight, while on the crest the sun's last rays still shimmered. Endless flocks of water birds flew overhead on their way to distant nests, their wings beating in noisy, random arcs. Refreshed, our horses splashed in the water at the lagoon's edge, rolled in it, nipped here and there at the most tempting tufts of grass, and whinnied, their heads pointing north, their ears pricked and stiff like a quadrant needle marking the direction to follow. I called the good Franciscans and my officers and told them I had resolved to separate from them.

It is a lie that discipline kills affect. It does accustom a man to masking his feelings, however, even the most tender and honorable ones. Too often are they taken for hardhearted those who must abide by the terrible law of passive obedience, a law that keeps the soldier divorced from the citizen and, contrary to the spirit of the century, remains set, like an unmovable monument to slavery. Nor is the generous tide that has cradle-rocked the civilized world since the fall of the Roman empire enough to shake it. That is why the greater the servitude oppressing him, the greater the soldier.[2]

Upon receiving orders to form two groups, the most numerous of which would follow the well-known Cuero road and the smaller of which, headed up by me, would take the unknown road past the Bagual Lagoon, a tinge of sadness showed in the men's faces. No one answered back and all hurried to get ready for a night march, but I knew that more than one of those hearts was sorry to be leaving me. It was not only the secret sympathy that binds men together irrespective of their position. It was also a certain love of the unknown, that special gift for combat and struggle which belongs to the male of the species and makes a life appetizing when that life is not consumed in monotonous effeminacy and pleasure.

Once my orders were carried out and my instructions were recorded in Major Lemlenyi's memory book, the two groups formed. I said good-bye to Lemlenyi, the Franciscans, Ozarowsky, to everybody. Then, after repeating the same thing several times like a tiresome old crank, I climbed on my horse and rode off followed by the four companions in my group. Lemlenyi's group preceded me. Our mounts were fresh and easily climbed to the crest of the dune by the great northern trail. We said good-bye one more time from there. Lemlenyi and his group took the right branch, I took the one on the left to the west. "Careful you don't gallop," I shouted one last time as I pressed my knees into my own horse's sides to make him step a little more lightly. A seasoned animal, he started to trot. My two backup horses took the front and the sonorous clink-clink of their bells in the profound silence of the pampas felt like a good sign to us riders. It buoyed our spirits.

The horses from either group neighed mightily to each other. Why are they separating us, they seemed to ask. My group looked back several times until the distance and the dust clouds rendered the northbound group invisible. They trotted on towards Loncouaca, where the permanent and abundant waters slake the thirst of men and animals alike. They probably did the same thing we did, looking back several times to try to see us. Brave compañeros! It remains for me to say before I lose sight of them altogether that they made the crossing without incident, following my orders strictly. They were quite hungry and trotted two days and two nights until arriving at Fort Sarmiento. The Franciscans were so rattled by the trot that they almost fell to pieces. Despite their gentle temperament they called the whole ride an infernal one and several times asked why they shouldn't be allowed to gallop a ways.

"First," said my officers, "because the orders are to march at a trot, and second because if we gallop we won't get there in two days."

Father Marcos claimed his horse was superior. The officials countered with something designed to raise his hackles a bit, which I don't think the Order of the R. F. Saint Francis is opposed to. "So was the Moor that roughed you up last time," they told him. That march is engraved in the memory of those who made it. There is not one of them who does not agree with the theory I set forth in my previous letter concerning the rumblings that went on with La Verde in sight.

The night shadows slowly engulfed space. The changes in the terrain disappeared in the darkness. We floated in a gloomy void. It was like on the first night of Genesis, as the country folk say. The sky was hooded, the starlight could not pierce the great opaque clouds that covered the heavens like an immense mortuary shroud.

We had been trotting and galloping for several hours. A short distance away there appeared a black point, blacker than the black night. It lay along the way we were following, rising like a colossal phantom. A noise heard nowhere but in the pampas, along the shores of the lagoon, was becoming more and more perceptible. We were about to arrive at the Bagual Lagoon. The phantom was a brush-covered dune. The peculiar noise was the nocturnal chirring of the birds, their eternal innocent murmured love song sung in the tall grasses that shelter them from the chilly damp.

The Bagual Lagoon is a strategic point along this road, as is the La Verde lagoon along the other. It rarely dries. Water is easily brought to the surface and there is nothing else noteworthy about it. It has the common, basin shape of pampa watering holes. Only when the weary and parched deserter or the bandit seeking refuge among the Indians reaches the Bagual, the sound of a galloping posse still drumming in his ears, can he finally breathe free and easy, dismount, and stretch out to take the restless slumber of the fugitive.

Coming from the tent settlements it is the opposite. The organized party of raiders, large or small, the gaucho Indian working at his own risk, whether alone or not, the captive risking his life to get away—they all stop here.

Once in the Bagual dunes, no one who is coming looks back, whoever is leaving looks only ahead. It is a veritable Rubicon, not only because of the distance separating it from the tent settlements, but because of its topographical position, the point being that whether you are coming or going on the Bagual road, there is never a lack of water, that most formidable enemy of traveler and mount on the desert of the Argentine pampas. To the south and advancing toward the tent camps, Ranquilco and the Colorado Dune, which lie along the road, offer safe grazing and water.

It was still early, I had had a good gallop and, there being no reason to hurry, I marched on towards Agustinillo to see if I could arrive there before the moon came out. We were galloping across the winding paths of a scrub-covered hill, when we noticed five dark shapes to the left and right of the road.

"What is that?" I asked Camilo.

"Horses," he said.

"Well, let's get them," I said.

We fanned out, led the animals out of the grass, and added them to our own.

Whom did they belong to?

That night I came to understand why our gauchos have an irresistible tendency to appropriate whatever they find when out on the road. I mumbled Proudhon's aphorism: "Property is theft."

"They must be Indian horses," Mora said.

"Robbing a thief is no crime at all," I said.

Suddenly we heard whistling. I pulled on my horse's reins and slowed the pace of the march. The whistles were coming from different directions.

"That must be the Indians now," said Mora.

"What Indians?" I asked.

"The ones from Jarilla."

"And why are they whistling?"

"They must have heard us and don't know what it is."

I trusted Mora and called a halt. Fearing an ambush, I prepared to fight and had my four companions dismount. I reasoned that if there were more of them than of us, we would be stronger standing on the ground, and if they didn't mean us any harm they would approach to see who we were. And indeed, no sooner had we dismounted than seven Indians armed with lances appeared. At the same moment the moon began to break through a mountain of clouds like a luminous silver blade.

I told Mora to speak to them in their language, which he obediently did. The Indians advanced cautiously, their horses turned sideways to us. Camilo Arias then said, with that wonderful instinct of his, "They are afraid."

"Speak to them again," I told Mora.

Obeying, he spoke again, and the Indians cantered toward us with their lances poised. They stopped about twenty meters away from us.

"Who giving permission go through here?" they said.

"Who giving permission be around here?" said I.

"Who him being?" they countered.

"Colonel Mansilla, *peñi*," I added.

When they heard this the Indians lowered their lances and approached us unafraid. We greeted one another, shook hands, talked a while, returned them the fine horses we had stolen from them—they were their horses, after all—and gave them a few belts of anisette and all the mate, sugar, and tobacco we could give. One of my assistants, Demetrio Rodríguez, gave his poncho to one of them who was almost naked. At last we said good-bye, parting like the world's best friends.

"Who were those Indians?" I asked Mora.

"They are from La Jarilla," he said.

"What about the one who had his face covered and wasn't talking? Who could that have been?"

"That was Ancañao."

Ancañao was an Indian gaucho who had pulled off a daring raid along my frontier line. I was in Buenos Aires at the time. He got as far as the Tala de los Puntanos Lagoon, where he took and seriously wounded a private of the Seventh Cavalry, who was carrying a communiqué for Río Cuarto.

Of such matters we were conversing when the moon at last tore free from the shrouds that had held her full splendor in check, spilling her light on the white sheet of a vast saltpeter bed. Innumerable glittering silver lights burst forth as if the earth were sown with brilliants and sapphires. It was a most lovely spectacle. The moon, the stars, the opaque clouds themselves were reflected in that immobile mirror. The effect was that of a sky upside down. The tracks from the last raiding party that had passed through were still imprinted on the crystalline ground. I halted for a moment to taste the salt. It was excellent. The Indians who live nearby gather it in great quantities and use it for cooking without subjecting it to any prior preparation.

We marched on. Soon we were in Agustinillo, camping on the edge of a pretty lagoon in the shelter of great *chañar* trees. I had my bed made as close as possible to the fire because it was cool out. Then I took my tired limbs and tried to doze awhile now that we were completely out of danger. It was impossible to sleep. Predisposed as it was to meditation, my mind simply would not suffer itself to be subjugated by matter. I was thinking about the extraordinary scenes that a number of days ago had been an ideal and

I spoke to myself in the mute and solemn language in which the voice of the spirit speaks to us in moments of intensity: man's misery arises from seeing his designs frustrated and from living by conjecture, for reality is the supreme good and the supreme beauty. Indeed, between the dreamt ideal and the fulfilled one lies a world of pleasures that can only be properly savored by those who have longed for a thing and set out to do it and after great pain and suffering achieved it.

What after all are virtue and happiness if not the science of the real?

Plato has said apropos of the beautiful:

"The soul that has never perceived the truth cannot take on the human form."

Like the sage, then, let us be glad that the truth is so salutary and that we harbor hopes of someday finding the effective substance of all, so that all will not remain symbol and dream.

EPILOGUE

THE SUN HAD NOT YET begun to dissipate the crystalline dew shed by a serene night on the loamy carpet of the pampas, and we were already up and riding to make the most of a cool and terribly pretty April morning. This was necessary if we wished to avoid spending another night on the road.

I did not have to mind the horses as much as those who had taken the Cuero road. The Bagual route is strung with pleasant lagoons boasting permanent water supplies. There is always excellent grazing on the vast grass flats around them, and where the broken and hilly land winds into deep hollows there is shade and firewood. All this lonesome, uninhabited land has a grandiose future. In the solemn and majestic language of silence, it calls out for muscle and work.

When will its rose-colored dawn glow?

When indeed!

Alas, when the Ranquels have been exterminated or placed on reservations, Christianized and civilized.

I have tried to give a sketchy idea throughout the preceding pages of the lives, ways, and customs of these Ranquels. How many of them are there? From eight to ten thousand souls, including some six to eight hundred Christian captives of both sexes, children, adults, young and old people.

On what do I base this? On certain observations I have made with my own two eyes, on data I have gathered, and on a certain very simple statistical calculation. The three tribes of Mariano Rosas, Baigorrita, and Ramón, which constitute the great Ranquel family, are comprised of those same three chiefs, two minor chiefs, Epumer and Yanquetruz, and fifty-nine captains, whose names are as follows:

Caniupán, Melideo, Relmo, Manghin, Chuwailau, Caiunao, Ignal, Tripailao, Millalaf, Quintanao, Nillacaóe, Peñaloza, Ancañao, Millanao, Pancho, Carrinamón, Cristo, Naupai, Antengher, Nagüel, Lefín, Quentreú, Jacinto, Tuquinao, Tropa, Wachulco, Tapaio, Caoimuta, Quinchao, Epuequé, Yanque, Anteleu, Licán, Millaqueo, Painé, Mariqueo, Caiupán, José, Manqué, Manuel, Achauentrú, Güeral, Islaí, Mulatu, Lebín, Guinal, Chañilao, Estanislao, Wiliner, Palfuleo, Cainecal, Coronel, Cuiqueo, Frangol, Yancaqueo, Yancaó, Gabriel, Buta, and Paulo.

Each one of these captains leads ten, fifteen, twenty, twenty-five, and even thirty Indian braves. By Indian brave I mean a healthy and robust male from sixteen to fifty years old. If each chief, sub-chief, or captain can arm on the average twenty Indians, that gives a figure of one thousand three hundred. This figure concurs with a further, undeniable fact, namely, that Mariano Rosas and Ramón each have six hundred Indian braves and Baigorrita a few more than that.

These eight to ten thousand souls occupy a zone approximately two thousand square leagues in area, between 63° and 66° south latitude and 35° and 27° east longitude. Its natural boundaries could be stated as the Laguna del Cuero to the north, the end of the Salado River to the south, the same river to the west, the pampas to the east.

Some four to six hundred tents are scattered about within that vast perimeter. Each one comprises a family, which is never fewer than ten persons, nor is any tent without at least one captive man, woman, boy, or girl. This, then, gives us a population of some four to six thousand souls, though it should be noted that this figure is based on the minimum number of persons in a family. If, then, the figure of four hundred to six hundred tents were thought to be an exaggerated one, the population of four to six thousand souls would remain the same, as ten persons per family is an understated figure. Every tent that I have seen had upwards of twenty persons in it.

Now, statistical principles tell us that every ten thousand souls will easily yield one thousand members for the armed forces. Granted this, the figure of one thousand three hundred Indian braves becomes a reasonable one for determining the population of the Ranquels. Be that as it may, the sad reality is that the Indians are out there, constantly threatening the property, homes, and lives of the Christians. And what have the Christians or the government or civilization done in behalf of this forsaken race, which by the cruel law of necessity is compelled to rob, kill, and destroy?

What have they done?

Let us hear the barbarians speak.

One day while I was conversing with Mariano Rosas I spoke to him as follows:

"Brother," I said, "the Christians have so far done everything they could and from now on will do all they can for the Indians."

There was visible irony in his expression when he answered.

"Brother, the Christians have killed us whenever they could, and if they can kill us all tomorrow they will. They have taught us to wear nice ponchos, drink mate, smoke, eat sugar, drink wine, and wear heavy boots. But they have not taught us how to work or made their God known to us, so what service do we owe them?"

I would have liked Socrates to be inside of me at that moment to see how he in all his wisdom would have answered. For my part, I examined my conscience and said nothing . . . I had thus far done my duty within my humble sphere and as best I understood it. Yet, my personal conduct neither should nor could be an argument against the humble objections of the barbarian. I will never tire of repeating it: There is no greater evil than an unmerciful civilization.

That is how one famous historian rebuked his own country, censuring its policies as conqueror of India.

The Ranquels descend from the Araucans, with whom they maintain close kinship and friendly relations. They are somewhat narrow in the brow, have prominent cheekbones, short, flat noses, large mouths, thick lips, noticeably sunken eyes at the outside angle, thick, abundant hair, sparse mustache and beard, more developed sight and hearing organs than ours, copper-colored, sometimes sallow skin, medium height, broad backs, strong limbs.

These characteristics are being lost, however, as they cross with our own race with a resulting gain in stature, elegance of form, whiteness, and even sagacity and activity. In a word, the Ranquels are a solid, healthy, and well-constituted race having none of that *semitic* persistence that checks the tendency in other races to cross and mix. Their predilection for our women proves as much. They find them more beautiful than the Indian women, which could induce us to state that the aesthetic sentiment is a universal one.

I once exchanged these words in conversation with an Indian:
"What kind of woman do you like better, an Indian or a
Christian?"
"Well, Christian woman."
"Why?"
"Christian, her whiter, taller, nicer hair. Christian her prettier."

Would it be good or would it be evil to conquer the Ranquels,
whose physical and moral physiognomy we now know, in order to
absorb and meld them, so to speak, into the criollo mold? In our
day it seems to be beyond question that the fusing of the races im-
proves the human condition. What women did our forefathers the
Spaniards bring when they arrived in America? Did the Mother
Country do with her colonies what the governments of France and
England did with theirs? Did she send shipments of prostitutes?
Did not the conquistadores have to marry the native women and
begin to breed among their own only after the first generation?
And if this is so and all of us Americans have Indian blood in our
veins, why the constant cry for extermination of the barbarians?
The facts observed with regard to the physical constitution and intellectual and moral faculties of certain races are too isolated to
allow any sweeping conclusions when one is talking about con-
demning entire populations to *death* or *barbarism*.

Who can say at what point a race of people must come to a halt
as a result of its own nature?

What order of truth is within the grasp of some races, beyond
that of others?

What are the practicable functions which the organs of any such
people may perform that another people will never accomplish?

What are the virtues proper to this or that form of organization?

Has phrenology perchance spoken its last word?

Are there not nations as barbaric, slavish, and vicious as the rest
living among the most perfectible races?

We are horrified that the Ranquels sell their women and that
they visit terrible raids upon us to capture and appropriate our
own. Yet, among the Hebrews in the Patriarchs' times, the groom
paid the father his *mohar*, did he not? And among the Arabs, was
a widow not part of the estate or wealth left by the deceased husband? And didn't the Romans have their *coemptio*, that is, purchase, and *usus*, in other words possession of the woman? And did
Saxon law not have the *mundium* and other such customs? And

what about the Visigoths with their *arras*, which were like a nuptial fee that replaced outright purchase as in earlier times? And did the Franks not pay their spouse's father the spouse's value, which he and his daughter then shared?

If there is anything that is impossible to determine, it is the degree of civilization to which each race will attain. Moreover, if there is any theory designed to justify despotism, it is the theory of historical fatality.

The calamities that afflict humanity arise from hatred among the races, from age-old preoccupations, and from the lack of benevolence and love. Therefore the most efficacious means of dissolving the antipathy ordinarily observable among certain races in countries where privilege has created two social classes—the oppressors and the oppressed—*is justice*. However, this word will go on ringing empty so long as the declaration that all men are equal is offset by the sore reminder that equal services and virtues have not merited equal reward, that equal vice and crime do not go equally punished.

Though I rode on and on, it was clear I would have to spend another night on the trail.

Early the next day I reached the banks of the Quinto. I had ridden two hundred fifty leagues, seen an unknown world, and dreamt . . .

April in its glory beautified the green scenery of Villa de Mercedes, where the slender poplars and melancholy weeping willows grow myriad and full.

The day was calm, my soul was glad.

We laugh openly when we ought to be more taciturn or groan. How unfeeling we are!

And then in a lucid moment we finally let out the bitter cry: Oh God, no! . . .

Yet I love pain and even remorse because they bring me to my senses.

NOTES

CHAPTER I

1. Each installment of the serial was intended as an open letter to Santiago Arcos, the son of a prosperous Chilean merchant and a professional adventurer near and dear to both Mansilla and Sarmiento.

2. Mansilla's map does not include Nagüel Mapo, which lay to the south of Chief Baigorrita's settlements in what is today the Gobernación de la Pampa, nor does he mention the ostrich egg challenge in the chapters relating to his visit with the chief (see Chaps. 43–45).

3. By calling the dubious reward of the Córdoba assignment his military fate or star, Mansilla conceals the sting of disappointment. He had labored hard to get President Sarmiento elected and hoped for a prestigious ministerial post in return.

4. This is the arid expanse of semidesert lying between the Andes to the west and the pampa grasslands and the Atlantic to the east, a kind of inland empire, at the time, of Ranquel, Araucan, and Pampa settlements, and also the refuge of a great many mixed bloods.

5. Sarmiento's government was pushing into Ranquel territory, and concessions to the Indians were subject to a maze of parliamentary hedgings and reconsiderations which Mansilla knew would exhaust the Indians' patience. He convinced his superiors that the trip to the tent settlements could serve as a way of assuring the Indians that the government was determined to comply with the terms of a treaty Mansilla himself had drawn up.

6. Whether this was historical prescience on Mansilla's part or simply a firm grasp of realpolitik, in 1879–1880 the Argentine army fanned out across the desert, marched to the settlements and, greatly aided by recently acquired Remington repeat rifles, introduced the Indians to the ideology of conquest by eradication and relocation, and themselves to a battery of fatal diseases and debilitating malaises.

7. Bartolomé Mitre was the Argentine president from 1862 to 1868, a candidate for the same office in two other campaigns, a lyrical verse writer when young, and a career military officer of uneven accomplishment. Mitre courted French, English, and Brazilian aid in the struggle to finance Buenos Aires's ascent over the rest of the nation in civic affairs. His

status as "favorite son of fortune and glory" was, by the time Mansilla wrote the *Excursión*, taken for granted, although his many foibles as a general have not been forgotten by Argentine historians.

8. General José Miguel Arredondo was Mansilla's immediate superior in the frontier command.

9. Here Mansilla carries Sarmiento's torch of the new stewardship of the land's abundant natural wealth.

10. Compilations by Pedro de Angelis of early Spanish expeditions between Argentina and Chile or from Buenos Aires outward to the pampas and beyond no doubt found their way into the Mansilla home library. De Angelis brought out two such accounts, one by a Spanish merchant named Sebastián de Undiano y Gastelú and another by Spanish Royal Navy Captain Félix de Azara, in 1836 and 1837, respectively. Both had been written in 1796 and dealt with border extension and military fortification on the periphery of Buenos Aires.

CHAPTER 2

1. Mansilla refers to Indian commissions that came from Ranquel territory to the forts prior to his expedition. Their purpose was to voice the Ranquel chiefs' position on the newly drafted peace treaty.

2. The chief of the Ranquel tribes had taken his Christian name from Mansilla's own uncle, dictator of the Argentine nation from around 1834 until his downfall in 1852. Rosas's police had captured the chief as a boy. Before escaping, he lived for several years on one of the Supremo's cattle farms.

3. Considering Talleyrand's legendary passion for intrigue and his disregard for principle, Mansilla's remark rings as less than complimentary. By the same token, the likening of Mariano Rosas to the French foreign minister and diplomat typifies Mansilla's insistence that the Indians must not be excluded from the political embroilments that accompany the achievement of nationhood.

4. In this inverted analogy Mansilla speculates on what might have happened had Mariano Rosas, through Carmen, had the shrewdness of an Hernán Cortés. Carmen's possible parallel with Mexico's Malinche also lies just below the surface.

5. Mansilla misses no opportunity to highlight both the Indians' willingness to forge allegiances and his own reputation as the peacemaker of Río Cuarto.

6. Although Mansilla finds tobacco use widespread among the Indians, there is no mention in this book of a ceremonial peace pipe in the life of the Indians as he found it.

7. "When the pox broke out among the Ranquels in Salinas Grandes in 1873, the chiefs roped off a sanitary zone where they cut the throats of all Indians arriving from affected areas. Their intention was to preserve a dividing line. The specter of morbidity terrified them. Mothers would abandon their children, and children their parents. Clearly fear overpowered filial love, leaving the infected to such shelter as providence might

afford them, with a bit of water and perhaps a tatter of clothing in the boundless desert" (Guerrino, *La medicina*, 32).

8. Sarmiento's drastic dichotomy—civilization versus barbarism— here stands neutralized by a corporal work of mercy.

CHAPTER 3

1. Throughout the book, Mansilla will by turns praise, defend, and patronize the Franciscans accompanying him as the religious arm of the expedition. Less comradely is his relationship with Father Moisés Burela, who had been sent by the Argentine government from Mendoza to the Ranquel settlements to ransom captive Christians (see Chap. 53).

2. *Lechuza, lechuzo*: owl. Mansilla is inconsistent throughout the book in his reading of omens, symbolic names, and the lore surrounding them.

3. The judicious Spaniards of Chapter 2 and, here, the noble Spaniards, are characterizations which would place an Argentine writer of Mansilla's time in a minority with respect to the former colonizer and mother country.

4. One finds Mansilla juggling the adventurousness of the first chapter with this loftier, quixotic statement of mission.

5. Mansilla had energized life at the Río Cuarto fort, creating what he viewed as an enlightened garrison at whose hub an officers club might heighten the appeal of frontier life. By mentioning this frontier club in his serial, he broadens the perspectives of his cohorts at the club he frequented in Buenos Aires. He is also interested in the regard of his military peers as he rights public misconceptions about the Indians.

6. That is, a discerning and well-pleased sort of stomach, such as the author of *The Physiology of Taste* desired for his readers and Mansilla strove to possess. Mansilla's attention to detail in matters of food, as well as his congenial and rambling style, suggest that he had thoroughly digested the Frenchman's writings.

CHAPTER 4

1. Literally, Mansilla says that the new Fort Sarmiento has "stolen" the older name from the pass. He doubts the current president's name can erase the one that time and custom have given the pass.

2. See Chapter 37 for greater detail on how the Indians retrained their stolen army mounts.

3. Through sheer repetition, "my friends the Franciscans," "the good Franciscans," and "the good and holy fathers" will become tropes as the book progresses.

CHAPTER 5

1. Throughout the *Excursión*, Mansilla plays down the fact that Juan Manuel de Rosas was his maternal uncle. General Justo José de Urquiza,

an immensely wealthy landholder from the province of Entre Ríos, led the forces that ended the Rosas dictatorship at the battle of Monte Caseros in 1852.

2. Also called the War of the Triple Alliance (1865–1870), this conflict saw Argentina side with Uruguay and Brazil against Paraguay. It was a point of no return for Mansilla as a journalist, career officer, and writer of some depth and transcendence. He recruited for this unpopular war, fought and was wounded in it, and began to organize Sarmiento's presidential campaign as the war came to an end. He also wrote and published the first of several military treatises he was to pen and sent frequent and colorful dispatches to the Buenos Aires press from the Paraguayan front. His articles irritated the conservative tastes of the high command.

3. Tuyutí was the site of the bloodiest battle of the Paraguayan War. Mansilla fought there and at Curupaití, where he was wounded in the shoulder.

4. This is possibly a cheese from a department of the same name in the province of Corrientes, which borders on Paraguay to the north and is, in any case, the setting for Private Gomez's story.

CHAPTER 7

1. As newspaper serials went, Mansilla's account of his trip to the Ranquel settlements did very well for *La Tribuna*. Some of its popularity may have derived from the author's habit of threading the names of actual comrades and friends—Irrazábal, Alvarez, Garmendia—through what was essentially a camp-fire narrative. One seldom-mentioned name is that of his adjutant, Demetrio Rodríguez, who, for reasons never made entirely clear, made an attempt on Mansilla's life less than a year after the *Excursión* was published.

CHAPTER 8

1. The Paraguayan War was never popular in the provinces and here Mansilla suggests one reason why.

2. Mansilla was in fact the most vexing ally and subordinate General Gelly y Obes ever had. Cut from a more spartan cloth than Lucio, General Gelly viewed the officer-cum-journalist Mansilla as a loose cannon who had little of the sobriety required for a military career.

3. The sense of Santiago Arcos as an intended reader has begun to slip away, especially for those not following the account since it began to run.

4. *Hamlet:* I, v, 166–167.

CHAPTER 9

1. When Mansilla was seventeen years old, his father discovered, and tried to discourage, his son's passion for French literature. "One does not read Rousseau's *Social Contract* in this country when one is the nephew of Juan Manuel de Rosas," admonished the elder Mansilla. Lucio read

and translated French for the rest of his life, however, spending his last years in Paris, where he died in 1913. The late-eighteenth- and early-nineteenth-century parlor society of empowered literati luminaries which Madame de Staël's name would conjure up still served, ninety years after the French Revolution, as something of a hallmark of the polite socialization of letters.

2. Mansilla had taken his assignment to the outpost in Córdoba seriously enough to qualify himself, after assiduous study and observation, as something of an amateur geographer. The "thousands of leagues" he told of surveying in Chapter 1 here yield a firsthand knowledge of the land (see Chap. 60, n. 2).

3. He does meet Chief Ramón first, however (see Chap. 16).

4. The red scarf, scarlet cape from the French Algerian cavalry, white gloves, and long goatee give us an idea of the figure Mansilla cut.

5. Again, it appears that Mansilla's literary cosmos has been shaped by French writers.

CHAPTER 10

1. Sarmiento draws a barb. There follows a kind of litany of the annoyances of city life.

2. An epidemic of yellow fever was to sweep through Buenos Aires in 1871, less than a year after Mansilla wrote the present chapter. It claimed, among thousands of other victims, Mansilla's eldest son, Andrés.

3. Argentina's foremost Romantic writer, Esteban Echeverría, wrote *La cautiva* in 1837. Mansilla uses the poem as a backdrop, its setting a quasi-mythical desert inferno into which he now penetrates.

4. One of the many kindred souls Mansilla found among French writers, Théophile Gautier (1811–1872), like Mansilla, wrote much of his best work while, and about, traveling.

5. One senses the transcontinental railroad, the westward homesteading explosion, and the burgeoning industrial power of the United States of the 1870s in this throwaway remark. By 1870 the United States had spent over $100 million on wars with the Sioux, Cheyenne, and Navajo. It had been only three years since the signing of the Medicine Lodge Peace Treaty, by which all territory south of the Kansas border was declared to be Indian land. However, one year after Mansilla carried out his *excursión* in Argentina, the United States suspended all treaty making with the Indians and began the exclusive use of executive orders and agreements. Argentina's President Sarmiento had celebrated in his *mensaje* of 1869 the arrival of Remington rifles from the United States. They were to be instrumental in the removal of the Argentine Indians from their ancestral lands (see Chap. 1, n. 6).

6. Mansilla's casual dismissal of the work of Thomas Malthus helps to sustain the irony of the ensuing paragraphs on war, despotism, and mindless progress. At bottom, Mansilla feels that political amorality underlies the evils which Malthus viewed as inescapable.

7. Mansilla's range of sentiment in writing about both war and progress was broad. Here a bitter irony colors his prose.

CHAPTER 11

1. In *Facundo*, Sarmiento had made much essentialist hay of the savvy trackers and scouts of the pampas. As always, Mansilla is prepared to bring any such character into the arena of his personal experience, appropriating even as he demystifies.

2. "El Chacho" was the nickname of General Angel Vicente Peñaloza, one of the more renowned provincial caudillos to rebel against the Buenos Aires–based federal government. Sarmiento led the war against El Chacho, and Mansilla's immediate superior, General Arredondo, captured and killed the rebel general in 1863. Mansilla came from a family of both unitarian and federalist sympathizers.

3. Hilario Ascasubi and Estanislao del Campo, poets and contemporaries of Mansilla, are the possible objects of recrimination here. Then, too, Mansilla's *excursión* is itself charged with a generous dose of quixotic idealism.

4. There had long been a ready market for hides, firewater, and woven goods in Chile. Indeed, overland commerce between the two countries was to a great degree the province of an Araucan-Ranquel trade network.

5. The word has survived. It refers to any armed militia, whether composed of marauders or of tightly organized resistance units, outlawed by the government which it actively opposes.

6. If Mansilla's denunciation of his own generation seems bombastic or overblown, it would be helpful to recall the devastation of life, nature, and artifact which the author decried at the end of the previous chapter.

CHAPTER 12

1. Not to be confused with El Chacho, Angel Vicente Peñaloza (see Chap. 11, n. 2), this possibly refers to a petty chieftain who survived by intimidating what hapless travelers might be preyed upon for money in the Argentine desert.

2. Although there are innumerable digressions yet to come, the narration here begins to shift from reminiscences set in wartime Paraguay and Brazil to the matter at hand: reaching the Ranquel settlements.

3. See final pages of Chapter 60 for Chief Mariano Rosas's perspective on the railroad.

4. Echeverría, *La cautiva*, I, 1–3.

5. The time referred to is the 1830s and 1840s, during the civil wars in the Argentine provinces.

6. This is perhaps a tongue-in-cheek allusion to Mansilla's own origins in the San Juan district of Buenos Aires. Betting that the next president of Argentina would be someone from San Juan would boil the possibilities down to Sarmiento, who was from the *province* of San Juan and for whom Mansilla campaigned vigorously, or to Mansilla himself.

CHAPTER 13

1. Byron, *Darkness*, ll. 2–3.

2. The magistrates in the provinces frequently pursued the gauchos' mothers, sisters, and wives. The political leverage these judges possessed enabled them to have the gauchos pressed into military service or arrested for failing to carry working papers from one itinerant cattle-ranch job to the next.

3. Not so much false as heavily alloyed and generally worthless.

4. Alessandro Manzoni, *Cinque Maggio*, ll. 43–48. Note the Cervantine irony with which Mansilla dispels his own delusions of grandeur as he discovers what he was using as a pillow. The quote from Dante, *lasciate ogni speranza*, also shows humorous self-disparagement.

CHAPTER 14

1. Mansilla was intrigued by multiple, mirrored images. One 1907 photograph shows him seated in a circle, in conversation with five identical pictures of himself. In another from the same year, five Lucio Mansillas are seated in a circle, each facing outward as if unaware of one another.

2. This declamatory salute to Napoleon via Manzoni is a premonition of the comically grandiose dreams and visions of imperial splendor which will seem to tempt Mansilla in the Ranquel desert (see also Chaps. 32 and 47).

3. Laboring to keep pedantry in check, Mansilla invokes the metaphor, but not the name, of Sisyphus.

4. The detail—a tabloid paper used to wrap food—stands in nice contrast to Mariano Rosas's use of the paper in Chapter 54.

5. Perhaps Mansilla's oft-consulted Byron.

6. Throughout the narrative, and no matter how faithfully he embraces his doctrine of carousing with the Ranquels the better to unite with them, Mansilla never seems to be the last to retire at night or the first to rise in the morning.

7. The names of Orión, the pen name of Uruguayan-born journalist and close friend of Mansilla, Héctor Varela, and Carlos Keen, rising star of the new *porteño* liberalism, would be well-known to Mansilla's readers. Varela in fact owned *La Tribuna*, in which these letters were running, and was immensely popular. Calfucurá was an Araucan chief of fearsome and legendary repute who led innumerable raids throughout the 1840s, 1850s, and 1860s on cattle ranches in the province of Buenos Aires. He was also an ally of General Urquiza at the battle of Monte Caseros in 1852 (see Chap. 5, n. 1).

For all of this, it is hard to tell whether Mansilla means that the urban, civilized way of life is difficult to attain or merely that it is easy to give up.

CHAPTER 15

1. That even at this level of instinctive horsemanship Mansilla should find himself second-guessing the Indian and in turn being second-guessed

suggests that ambiguity was not so much a literary quality of the narration as an activity, perhaps *the* activity, of the excursion.

2. Firewater was then viewed not as a gift but as a medium of exchange, an agent of diplomacy for both church and state.

3. Mansilla laces the narration with Arabian motifs frequently enough to remind his readers of some of his earlier writings. Indeed, his first travel narrative, an eleven-page article published in 1855 in *El Plata Científico y Literario*, was entitled "De Adén a Suez." The *Excursión* is, arguably, an extension of those first forays into the exotic unknown.

4. Whenever moved to do so, Mansilla will pose the conflation of Christianity with civilization as a spurious one at best.

5. Mansilla's stylized use of officious language signals a certain ambivalence on his part. He is either stressing the respectability of the chief's communiqués or poking fun at this shoddy imitation of real diplomacy. In short, it is an instance of either advocacy or of mockery, but not both.

CHAPTER 16

1. In Mansilla's simplified scheme of things, four peoples comprised the desert society as he found it: Chilean Indians, Chilean Christians, Argentine Indians, and Argentine Christians. The number of mixed-bloods among all four groups, however, was enough to blur any sharp racial distinctions.

2. On the one hand, the gesture underscores the power and extent of Mansilla's reputation. On the other it points to the scarcity of firearms and the preferred form of execution among Indians and gauchos.

3. The militaristic lexicon serves personal ends for Mansilla. His career was not on the firmest footing and displaying a mastery of military science might bolster his credibility.

4. With all the Christian refugees present and the many borrowed and cast-off army uniforms among the Ranquel warriors, the sound of bugles signaling formations must have capped an impression of a ragtag militia.

5. With extermination fever slowly taking hold of the Argentine government and spreading to the populace, Mansilla casts his vote in favor of assimilation and the preservation of Indian dignity.

6. See Chapter 2, in particular note 8.

7. "The fever they take, it makes them shake / Till they're terrible to see. / I'll leave to others the hows and whys, / But it wouldn't cause me much surprise / If their fevers are worse from eating horse, / For that's how it seems to me" (José Hernández, *El gaucho Martín Fierro*, II, 6, 847–852; trans. Walter Owen).

CHAPTER 17

1. Overshadowed by the all-powerful firewater, beet and cane sugar seem nevertheless to have been powerful agents of dereliction among the Indians.

2. Mansilla is generally careful to identify fabrics accurately. Indeed, it

was on the pretext of buying jute that his father first sent him on foreign travel. *Calamanco* was a glossy, striped, or checkered satin weave that had been popular for centuries.

3. It may also have been that tall tales were common camp-fire fare among the Ranquels and that this storyteller wanted not to convince Mansilla but to engage him.

4. Not to be confused with Patagonia, from which its name nevertheless derives, Patagones is a department within the province of Buenos Aires.

5. Its name taken from the Old French *darne* ("stupefied"), this common grass wine was once believed to have narcotic properties.

6. Mansilla probably read *On Crimes and Punishments* by Cesare, marchese di Beccaria, whose links with Manzoni render Mansilla's familiarity with both authors, as well as with their peer, Madame de Staël, more coherent as a scheme of reading.

7. Mansilla presents himself as an able negotiator who has championed the nation's sundry causes while assigned to the fort at Río Cuarto.

CHAPTER 18

1. Matías Behety was a Uruguayan-born poet and journalist who, at twenty-one years old when the *Excursión* ran in *La Tribuna*, was just coming into the limelight as a frequent contributor to that same paper. Note, also, that Mansilla is now narrating directly from Buenos Aires.

2. By "misfortune" Mansilla may have been referring to Sarmiento's refusal to give him a ministry, or to the several newspapers he started which failed. As for being seen as a buffoon in a sideshow, this was the risk which Mansilla always ran, and the price he often paid, for his flamboyance and his publicly voiced opinions.

3. The Sáa brothers, José Felipe, Juan, and José Luis, were caudillos from the western province of San Luis. Crisóstomo is referring to José Felipe, who had taken part in the battle of Pavón in 1861 against Bartolomé Mitre (see Chap. 1, n. 7, and Chap. 5, n. 1). Exiled in Chile after his defeat at Pavón, José Felipe Sáa was joined by his brothers and one thousand *montoneros*. They seized power in San Luis but in a matter of months were unseated by Mansilla's superior, General José Miguel Arredondo, at the battle of San Ignacio. It is worth noting that many of the caudillos referred to in the *Excursión* had been ranking officers in the confederate army during the Rosas dictatorship.

4. Crisóstomo's story here depicts an almost medieval Argentina, where shepherds tending the flocks of their overlords turn homeward as the church bell tolls the Angelus.

5. Details such as these—Indians bearing gifts of watermelons—and the many squash and cornmeal stews, as well as the mixed first courses which Mansilla recorded throughout the book, bespoke a society better prepared to assume stewardship of arable lands than many readers of *La Tribuna* had been led to believe.

6. Manuelita was the former dictator's daughter and, as Mansilla hardly need mention to his readers, his own first cousin.

CHAPTER 19

1. Mansilla's description of the Araucan chief recalls the warring elite of the Araucan nation of earlier centuries. By the same token, Mansilla's company might be thought of as an extrapolation-in-time of the Spanish colonial expeditions to the south of Chile centuries before, in which the Spaniards were unable to subdue the Araucan war parties.

CHAPTER 20

1. This point is overstated. The Indians clearly had the intelligence to breed their best animals for desirable traits. Whether a diet of horseflesh and the highs and lows of a cattle-raid economy encouraged such control is another matter.

2. Advocacy, more than pedantry, prompts this allusion en passant to *King Richard III*. Mansilla's point is that Indians, like Europeans, harbor dramatic thoughts.

CHAPTER 21

1. Actually, M. Jourdain wishes the love letter written on his behalf and has the Master of Philosophy recite all of the possible embellishments of his original thought. Mansilla's paragraphs here on diction and rhetoric are remarkably informed by this scene (Act II, scene vi) in Molière's play.

2. "With capes flying" was Mansilla's polite way of referring to poncho fights, altercations in which the Indians would swat each other with their ponchos.

3. The one ministerial appointment Mansilla received was a post as Argentine ambassador to Germany, Russia, and Austria-Hungary. The assignment came, however, in 1899 when Mansilla was 67 and no longer interested in assuming diplomatic obligations. He resigned in 1902.

CHAPTER 22

1. One wonders if the idealizers of the pampas (see Chap. 11, n. 3), so distressing to Mansilla, would have remembered, or known enough, to paint guanacos in the Argentine desert.

2. The motley Indian militia (see Chap. 16, n. 4) nevertheless presented its enemy with strategically conceived battle formations that have seldom been the subject of serious study among Argentine scholars.

3. Sarmiento had delighted in equating barbarian and Bedouin, as he did savage and Indian. Mansilla counters this simplification by linking Arabian and Indian alike to fantasy and exhilaration.

CHAPTER 23

1. The most famous treatise by the marquis de Laplace was titled *Celestial Mechanics*. As he did with Malthus (see Chap. 10, n. 6), Mansilla makes light of a European theoretician in order to register an ironic outlook.

2. It is difficult to know whether Mansilla means life experiences or general reading when he uses the term "social studies." In any case, his father, General Lucio Mansilla, was eighty years old when Lucio published the *Excursión*. The elder Mansilla died the following year, 1871.

3. In 1868, Mansilla was sent to San Luis and Mendoza with orders to subdue the Patriada de los Colorados, a federalist rebellion. Before Mansilla could reach the area of the rebellion, the Sáa brothers were defeated at San Ignacio by Mansilla's commanding officer, General Arredondo (see Chap. 18, n. 3). Here Mansilla meets two of the outlaw officers of the scattered company.

CHAPTER 24

1. A favorite word of Mansilla, it marks the schematic study of facial traits. Mansilla also studied phrenology, the determination of character and intelligence based on study of the skull's shape.

2. These were, in effect, the trade and migration routes of the Araucanian and Pampan nations as they then existed in the pampas, desert, and lower Andes.

3. Secrecy in this regard helped to protect both the raiding and the peaceful parties and tribes from surveillance by the Argentine army and insulated the hide, tallow, and firewater trade economy from government interference.

CHAPTER 26

1. The *enramadas*, or entranceways, were extensions of the tent built on wooden uprights and using sides of hide and a flat, straw roof. They varied greatly in size and furnishings but in any case served as a sort of foyer.

2. It was the more grotesque and degrading practices of his uncle's regime which most embarrassed Mansilla and which he most consistently repudiated.

3. The barb is aimed at the English but cuts somewhat at the Ranquels as well.

4. This may refer to the wine that Father Burela brought to the settlements. Mendoza province produces Argentina's best wines.

5. See Chapter 9, note 4. As a senior diplomat and retired general representing Argentina in several European countries in the 1890s, Mansilla was said to require five large trunks for his military wardrobe alone.

CHAPTER 27

1. *Julius Caesar*, IV, iii, 217–218.
2. See Chapter 24, note 1.
3. These trade routes and cattle trails dated back at least to the early eighteenth century.
4. Miguelito surely means the white or criollo poor, that is, the disenfranchised but not racially or culturally ostracized.

CHAPTER 29

1. "Perhaps it would have been an easier and more successful undertaking for me," echoed José Hernández, in his preface ("Carta Aclaratoria") to *El gaucho Martín Fierro*, two years after the *Excursión* was published, "if I had only set out to make people laugh at the ignorant gaucho's expense, as custom currently sanctions it in this type of composition."
2. Mansilla's nativism is a frontal challenge to Sarmiento's avid xenophilia, as well as to the liberal project of unchecked foreign investment and massive immigration.
3. Two works by François Fénelon, *Demonstration of the Existence of God* and *Dialogues of the Dead*, are possible sources for Mansilla's one-word quote.

CHAPTER 30

1. It is difficult to say whom Mansilla meant to mock here. At the same time, he seldom bothered to engage critics who saw him as superficial, impulsive, and unfocused.
2. Mansilla always kept a journal. He had begun his first one in 1850 at the age of nineteen, filled it extensively during his first travels, and then lost it while in the Paraná region in the late 1850s.
3. Mansilla perhaps views the Rosas dictatorship, by now some eighteen years dismantled, as an entrenched Sparta and Mitre qua Epaminondas as the general who, like the Theban statesman, helped to break the Restorer's (read: Sparta's) hold on the country.
4. In 1876, six years after the publication of the *Excursión*, both Mansilla and Orión (Héctor Varela; see Chap. 14, n. 7) were elected to the Chamber of Deputies in Buenos Aires. Varela was soon recalled because of his Uruguayan citizenship, an ironic reversal of fortune considering his popularity as the beloved and quintessential *porteño* here lauded by Mansilla.
5. This may be Mansilla arranging some refractory praise through Miguelito for his knowledge of the country. Renca is a tiny village in the eastern part of the province of San Luis.

CHAPTER 31

1. Echeverría, *La cautiva*, II, 113–116.
2. Mansilla had begun his military career in earnest in 1861, serving

as a captain in the northern part of the province of Buenos Aires. From that point on, his progress as a journalist and military theoretician outpaced his less-than-steady rise through the ranks. He was promoted to general in 1883.

CHAPTER 32

1. Aniceto el Gallo was one of the comic newspaper and broadside gauchos of Hilario Ascasubi. Anastasio el Pollo was a pen name adopted by Estanislao del Campo, whose *Fausto*, a parody of the opera by Charles Gounod, had appeared in *La Tribuna* in 1866. Both writers used gaucho dialect to create political satire in the anti-Rosas campaign (see Chap. 11, n. 3).

2. Few chapters offer as perfect a blotter of Mansilla's problems, likes, and annoyances as this one on music, dreams, and theatrics.

3. The obsequiousness of the Negro servant recalls the servitude of the blacks under Rosas. It also annoys Mansilla.

4. See Book of Daniel, V, 5–25.

5. The high-wheeled transport cart from the northern Argentine province of Tucumán had been familiar throughout the country, and in Paraguay and Peru, since colonial times. Its appearance here has pan-Argentine overtones, as does the image of the colossus, with its one foot in the Andes and the other on the shores of the River Plate. Note that the great but bemired city goes unnamed.

6. Southern, that is, only with respect to the Argentine border. The Pampa tribes are missing from Mansilla's list.

CHAPTER 33

1. Mansilla cannot bring himself to accept the fort's name. In 1868, Martín de Gainza had been appointed minister of war by Sarmiento, who bypassed Mansilla for the post.

2. Santos Lugares was the site of a jailhouse in Rosas's time.

3. As Mansilla tells it, the family's surname was actually Ortiz de Rozas. As a young man, Juan Manuel changed the spelling of his own name to "Rosas" to spite his mother, who had insisted that he do certain menial tasks in order to learn how to run an *estancia*. He refused, ran away from home, signed the note he left "Rosas," and never used the original spelling again. Mansilla, for his part, refused to recognize his uncle's alteration of the family surname, insisting instead on the original spelling in his writings on the Dictator.

4. This detail in the story of Mariano Rosas's escape from the dictator's *estancia* suggests a more civil hubbub of trade and traffic in livestock than is generally written into canonical descriptions of life on the Argentine frontier.

5. The red banners signified allegiance to the Rosas dictatorship and the federalism that it claimed to uphold.

CHAPTER 34

1. The song has the ring of an old *cielito*, or patriotic verse, from the era of Argentina's war for independence from Spain. The Negroes of Ravelo whom the black accordionist mentions were soldiers in the Battalion of the Restorer of Laws, that is, Rosas, who were under the command of a Negro colonel, Agustín Ravelo, and were active throughout the 1830s.

2. As a younger man and at his father's urging, Mansilla had worked in a slaughterhouse.

CHAPTER 35

1. That is, the Negro was ill-suited to rouse the scattered federalists to action. Tyrtaeus was a versifier of great power who galvanized the despondent Spartans to victory during the second Messenian War in the sixth century BC.

2. It is open to conjecture whether Mansilla did not think the women's names were important enough to record, or whether they were not introduced to him by name.

3. This argument appears in *The Physiology of Marriage*, Meditation XVII: The Theory of the Bed.

CHAPTER 36

1. Mansilla has little to apologize for here, considering the best guess of the *Grand Larousse* on the origins of the word "cancan": "Probablement de *cancan*, nom enfantin du canard, par comparaison de la danse avec le dandinement de cet animal."

CHAPTER 37

1. The way in which Rufino Pereyra has been consigned to military service, his fight with the posse, and the accusations maligning his character together would point to him as a forerunner of Martín Fierro's sidekick-in-exile, Sergeant Cruz.

2. Elsewhere Mansilla's perception of the Ranquels contradicts this view of them as handicapped by indolence. His purpose in this passage is perhaps to strike a consonant note with Sarmiento's ideas on the ennobling quality of work.

CHAPTER 38

1. Mansilla finds it unnecessary, perhaps, because he feels the chief errs only slightly.

2. Mansilla was not actually elected to Congress as a deputy until 1876, though he did count among his peers and cohorts a great many political figures of his day.

CHAPTER 39

1. Though Mansilla presents Camargo in a romantically tinted *verismo*, the marauding gauchos were in fact caught in a double bind: they could remain among the Indians as a renegade population only if they joined the raids on the Christians, and at the same time they were persecuted by the propertied Christian classes.

CHAPTER 40

1. Any gaucho soldier of some renown in the civil wars and now living among the Indians might still have his party of followers.

2. Mansilla's vision of "religion among the infidels" owes some of its coherence to orthodox Catholicism as first learned under maternal tutelage. This childhood influence may have problematized for the author any categorical endorsement of freethinking, Eurocentric liberalism.

3. Caudillos of greatly varied fortune, charisma, and consequence, there is little that unites the named and unnamed celebrities here other than the drama of national consolidation in which they all took part. From Mariano Rosas's point of view they may have been linked by the fact that, whether his people sided with them or not, the idea of obliterating the Indians only seemed to gather momentum among the people from whom they came.

4. It is interesting that the chief seems to be saying that having Christian settlements both to the south and the north of the tent camps would not bother his people.

5. That is, the article was taken from the newspaper in which the *Excursión* first appeared, the "present" paper. Mansilla does not try to wriggle out of the contradiction in which he finds himself caught.

6. Though he stops his time line at 1820, the Argentine literary historian Alvaro Yunque, in his *Calfucurá: The Conquest of the Pampas*, summarizes the advance of white culture and the tactical use of treaties in a way that undercuts Mansilla's kindly paternalism. "From the year 1580," writes Yunque, "in which the whites possess 1,220 square kilometers of pampa, until 1820, in which they possess 39,258, the advance is continuous. Civilization cannot be contained merely out of loyalty to what it has pacted with the barbarian. The Indians stand on legal reason, the civilized on historical reason. The civilized have always resolved this apparent paradox by means of violence. The treaties with the natives, who owned the land, were only delay tactics. That is the way it happened in the pampas. Neither the *huincas* from Europe nor the *huincas* from America ever seriously meant to halt their progressive-minded advance in order not to violate the rights of the barbarian aborigine. When he needed to stall for time, however, the *huinca* did not hesitate to make treaties with the Indian."

CHAPTER 41

1. This brief exploration completes the observations Mansilla began, and which he wryly cautioned his lady readers to skip, in Chapter 36.

2. It was not until Anglican missionaries came to Usuhaia in 1882 that any native population in Argentina fell victim to a tuberculosis epidemic. On the other hand, it has never been proven that the diet of horse, cow, and sheep—not to mention deer, guanaco, and ostrich—eaten raw more often than not, had any direct relation to the low incidence of tuberculosis among the Indian populations.

CHAPTER 42

1. Coliqueo was also given land in the town of Bragado, in the province of Buenos Aires, as a token of thanks for his support of President Mitre at the battle of Pavón.

2. This is further evidence for Mansilla's contention that the pampa is in fact the pampas, a region far more varied in topography and wildlife than is typically believed.

CHAPTER 43

1. That is, a warm wind.

2. The object is to distinguish between two kinds of movement, that caused by animals and that caused by swaying objects such as trees and scrub.

3. It is difficult to tell from Mansilla's narration whether there were goats and lambs in large numbers in the tent camps. In any case, the roundup he describes helps back his assertion that Ranquel customs supported a coherent way of life.

CHAPTER 44

1. "In drunkenness and revelling, in gluttony and foulness, the Emperor Vitellius spent his few months of rule" (Henderson, *Civil War and Rebellion*, 132).

2. It had been some twenty years since Mansilla had traveled with an American, J. F. Rodgers of Boston, to Benares, Delhi, the Himalayas, Egypt, Suez, Constantinople, Paris, London, and Edinburgh.

CHAPTER 45

1. See Chapter 11, note 2, concerning El Chacho. Note, as well, that the chief is arranging the marital affairs of the captive women even when giving them away to Christians.

2. A frequent theme and issue in literature both by and about native peoples throughout the Americas is distrust of the technical instruments of the white newcomers, especially as such instruments relate to the measuring of land.

CHAPTER 46

1. In Mansilla's phantasmagoria of motto-bearing personages, only one, Sarmiento, carries a pessimistic message.

2. Byron, "Ode on Venice," ll. 56–60. The poem resonates much like Manzoni's *Cinque Maggio* (see Chap. 13, n. 4, and Chap. 17, n. 6).

CHAPTER 47

1. Mansilla's biographers make no mention of his ever having assumed full godfatherly duties of the kind described in this chapter.

2. Mansilla casts his cry in the wilderness in esoteric terms, which helps him to ponder, but not to renounce, his pro-Ranquel patriotism. By "great or good or useful" he perhaps meant something beyond the scope of the "conventional" war with Paraguay, in which he took part, or the effort to bring life to the army outpost at Río Cuarto. Possibly, he hoped to look back at the "excursion" as a far-reaching accomplishment.

CHAPTER 48

1. Like most of the events cited here to profile the quadroon, Colonel Bárcena's infamous bloodbaths took place in the 1840s at the height of the provincial, caudillo-led rebellions.

2. Thomas a Kempis, *The Imitation of Christ*, I, 7.

CHAPTER 49

1. The knight-errant grapples with the formidable Maritornes in chapter 16 of Cervantes's *Don Quixote*.

2. The council is the crowning event of the entire excursion and, indeed, of the book.

3. One may wonder if Mansilla had Sarmiento in mind as he wrote this sentence.

CHAPTER 50

1. Mansilla seems to have intended the reader as his interlocutor in this somewhat confusing dialogue. It is also possible that he was giving literary expression to his fondness for multiple images of himself (see Chap. 14, n. 1).

CHAPTER 51

1. That is, land to the south and east. Mansilla's council would have been hailed as possessing greater historical import if the legendary and still-powerful chief Calfucurá had attended. Nevertheless, the arrival of

elders such as Estanislao signaled a certain extraordinary resonance to the event for the tribes.

2. *As You Like It*, II, vii, 136–139.

CHAPTER 52

1. Though often the self-styled anthropologist, Mansilla seldom goes so far as to use the word "specimen."

2. Here Mansilla is using the press to cure the urban malaise of ignorance of all that is not immediate. His enjoinder to the fortunate sons of the city perhaps prompted as well Hernández's reaction to anti-gaucho policies (see Chap. 29, n. 1).

CHAPTER 53

1. Mansilla's undisguised dislike for Father Burela lends credibility to his frequent praise for the Franciscans.

2. Father Burela may have been better than Mansilla at getting the chief to see things his way.

CHAPTER 54

1. Aside from his 1863 "Letter on the Advantages of Colonization," the infamous King Leopold had not yet made widely known his views on the treatment of colonial subjects.

2. The terms *gringo*, and later, with massive immigration, *gallego*, came to be the preferred way of referring to Spaniards or, more generally, to all white non-Argentines.

3. Luis Franco (*El otro Rosas*, 234), cites the execution of sixty Indians by Rosas at the plaza in El Retiro. Franco gives no date but does quote the description of the massacre by an eyewitness.

4. As noteworthy as Mansilla's prescience here is the grim and vaguely biblical tone which his warning to the tribes of the Argentine desert assumes.

CHAPTER 55

1. One implication is that yesterday's idols, among them Rosas, do not withstand present-day scrutiny, yet they continue to deceive. The idea that the coltskin boot might better symbolize Argentina's native character than did the curule chair reveals a side of Mansilla's thinking that he seldom voiced as a legislator and diplomat.

CHAPTER 57

1. The sarcasm necessitates the use of the derogatory "squaw" in this passage.

CHAPTER 58

1. Again, note Mansilla's attention to detail in identifying fabrics and fashion (see Chap. 17, n. 2).

CHAPTER 59

1. Pierre Jean de Béranger, "Mon habit," ll. 1–8. Considering the poem's subtitle, "Air du Vaudeville de Décence," this may be as close as Lucio Mansilla ever came to breaking into song.
2. *Le Bourgeois gentilhomme*, II, 2.

CHAPTER 60

1. Byron, "On This Day I Complete My Thirty-Sixth Year," ll. 5–6.
2. Strabo (*c*.63 BC–AD *c*.21) wrote a *Geography* that offers some aid in placing Mansilla's writings in a literary tradition. Book I begins: "The utility of geography—and its utility is manifold, not only as regards the activities of statesmen and commanders but also as regards knowledge both of the heavens and of things on land and sea, animals, plants, fruits, and everything else to be seen in various regions—the utility of geography, I say, presupposes in the geographer the same philosopher, the man who busies himself with the investigation of the art of life, that is, of happiness" (Jones, "Conflict and Adaptation," 3).

CHAPTER 61

1. Apologists for the summary expropriation in Argentina of Indian land, undertaken in 1879 by the army under the command of General Julio Argetino Roca, have often cited the livestock trade with Chile as a sign of a thriving black market that had to be wiped out.

CHAPTER 62

1. The psalm cited by Mansilla may be translated roughly: "Let us sing as one / how good is God to all, and how merciful, / let the liberated sing, / those whom the Lord has delivered from the power / of the harsh enemy . . ."
2. Yet another guiding voice for Mansilla from within French history and literature, Louis-Phillipe, Count of Segur, was a flamboyant diplomat and historian, as well as an admirer of Enlightenment philosophy, who served under Louis XV and Louis XVI.

CHAPTER 63

1. See Chapter 18, note 5.

CHAPTER 64

1. Mansilla provided a translation of these verses in the first edition of the *Excursión* but neglected to cite their author.

CHAPTER 65

1. Many of the Ranquel chiefs, most notably Calfucurá, were in fact Chilean-born Araucans. The Ranquel presence in the pampean desert was the result of a constant and uneven migration eastward from Chile that began at least as early as the building up of coastal colonial cities by the Spaniards in the sixteenth century. Handicrafts such as silver and leather invariably bore characteristics of Chilean, that is, Araucan and Mapuche, origin.

2. As he did in Chapter 50, Mansilla engages himself in dialogue.

CHAPTER 66

1. As Mansilla's phrasing suggests, there were two Brennuses. Both led the Gauls, the first in invading Greece, the second Rome. It was the latter who agreed to lift the seven-month siege of the Capitoline in exchange for ransom booty. He is said to have hurled his sword into the scales, crying "Woe to the vanquished!" when false weights were discovered in the payment.

CHAPTER 67

1. The French dramatist Michel-Jean Sedaine is best remembered for a domestic comedy, *Le Philosophe sans le savoir* (The Philosopher without knowledge), first staged in 1765.

CHAPTER 68

1. *Contempt* for life, or indifference to death, is what Mansilla seems to mean here.

2. In 1862, Mansilla had published a *Handbook of Exercises and Maneuvers for the Argentine Army*. His *Basis for the Establishment of a National Military School* followed in 1863; he translated a *History of the French Cavalry* the same year and in 1868 *La Tribuna* carried his *Groundwork for the Organization of the Argentine Army*. He had also read Rousseau, Proudhon, and Marx, and translated, among others, Alfred de Vigny and Edouard Laboulaye. That is, he was as steeped in humanistic socialism as he was in military science and history.

GLOSSARY

alpataco: a bushlike variety of the carob tree generally found in western Argentina.

boleadoras: leather-covered balls of stone or bone, either two or three, tethered to a single knot and swung and hurled for hunting or as a weapon.

calamanco: an ordinary, coarse, red-colored woolen poncho popular in the eighteenth and nineteenth centuries.

caldén: like most of the trees Mansilla names, this is a slow-growing, drought-resistant hardwood of the leguminous family and a close relative of the carob tree. It is excellent for firewood and for furniture making.

carbonada: a popular Argentine beef stew seasoned with *ají*, to which squash, corn, and rice are added before serving.

carda: scrub brush reaching some 50cm in height. It thrives near riverbanks and in wetlands.

cepo: a stocks or pillory.

chambao (or *chambado*): a drinking vessel made from cattle horn.

chañar (Gourliea spinosa): like the *espinillo*, the *tala*, and the *turca*, the xerophilic *chañar* makes excellent firewood. Its leaves are used as an anti-asthmatic in popular medicine.

charquicán: a stew made mainly of beef jerky; popular in western Argentina and Chile.

chicha: a fermented beverage, usually of corn or carob but also of *chañar*, grape, or apple.

chipá: a Guaraní word for a baked corn or mandioca flour hotcake made with fat, milk, salt, and cheese.

chiripá: a full-length, apronlike garment worn by gauchos in earlier centuries for most tasks carried out on horseback. Both the word and the article are of Quechua origin.

criollo: originally, a term for the American-born sons and daughters of Spaniards. It now connotes the native son or daughter and, by extension, the genuinely native Latin American, and especially Argentine, person, sense of humor, or outlook.

espinillo: see *chañar.*

estancia: a cattle farm, particularly one in the River Plate region.

facón: a large carving knife which the gauchos and *estancia* hands would wear in back under their sash.

gama: a female fallow deer.

gateado: of the color cinnamon bay or reddish bay.

iettatore: an evil-eyed man, bearer of ill luck, jinx.

mataco: a small armadillo.

mate: the term refers both to a small gourd and to a widely popular herbal tea drunk from it, primarily in Argentina, Paraguay, and Brazil.

mazamorra: a stone-ground cornmeal paste or mush served with milk and sugar, usually as a dessert but sometimes as a breakfast.

nandubay: a tree of the mimosa family.

ombú: a giant herb with the appearance of a tree. The *ombú* grows most abundantly in the River Plate provinces.

pago: hometown, childhood home.

patai: black bread made from dark carob fruit.

pasteles a la criolla: small, meat-filled pies.

piche: a small, frequently hunted armadillo.

porotillo: a name for any of a variety of common grazing grasses (from *poroto,* meaning "bean" or "legume").

pucherete: More often called *puchero,* this is a common meat and vegetable stew.

ronda catonga: a *ronda* is a children's game played in a circle, with the participants holding hands and reciting rhymes. The *catonga* may be a version of the game that Mansilla knew from childhood or had seen elsewhere in northern Argentina.

roto: a Chilean term roughly equivalent to "bum" or "hobo."

urutaú: a solitary, gray-crested owl found in northern Argentina and Paraguay.

villancicos: traditional Christmas carols.

vizcacha: a large ratlike rodent of southern South America.

zambo: knock-kneed.

SELECT BIBLIOGRAPHY

Abad de Santillán, Diego. *Gran enciclopedia argentina*. Buenos Aires: Ediar Sociedad Anónima Editores, 1956.

Angelis, Pedro de, ed. *Colección de obras y documentos relativos a la historia antigua y moderna de las provincias del Río de la Plata*. Reprint of 1836–1837 edition, with notes and foreword by Andrés Carretero. Buenos Aires: Plus Ultra, 1969–1971.

Balzac, Honoré de. *The Physiology of Marriage: or, Meditations of An Eclectic Philosopher on Happiness and Unhappiness in Marriage*. Translated and with an introduction by Francis MacNamara. London: The Casanova Society, 1925.

Beccaria, Cesare, Marchese di. *An Essay on Crimes and Punishments; with a Commentary by M. de Voltaire*. Albany: W. C. Little, 1872.

Béranger, Pierre Jean de. *Musique des Chansons de Béranger: Airs Notés Anciens et Moderns*. 10th ed. Vol. 7. Compiled by Frédéric Berat. Paris: Garnier Frères, Libraries, 1847.

Brillat-Savarin, Jean Anthelme. *The Physiology of Taste: or Meditations on Transcendental Gastronomy*. Translated by M. F. K. Fisher. New York: Knopf, 1971.

Campobassi, José S. *Mitre y su época*. Buenos Aires: EUDEBA, 1980.

Colquhon, Archibald. *Manzoni and His Times: A Biography of the Author of "The Betrothed."* London: Dent, 1954.

Echeverría, Esteban. *La cautiva, La guitarra y otros poemas*. Edited by Nélida Salvador. Buenos Aires: Plus Ultra, 1975.

Franco, Luis. *El otro Rosas*. Buenos Aires: Editorial Claridad, 1945.

Freidemberg, Daniel, ed. *Romances, coplas y canciones: selección*. Buenos Aires: Centro Editor de América Latina, 1981.

Guerrino, Antonio Alberto. *La medicina en la conquista del desierto*. Officer's Library, no. 718. Buenos Aires: Círculo Militar, 1984.

Giddings, Robert. "Mark Twain and King Leopold of the Belgians." In *Mark Twain: A Sumptuous Variety*, edited by Robert Giddings. London: Vision, 1985.

Gori, Gastón. *Vagos y malentretenidos: aporte al tema hernandiano*. Santa Fe, Argentina: Colmegna, 1951.

Guglielmini, Homero M. *Mansilla*. Monograph Series, Library of the Sesquicentennial. Buenos Aires: Dirección General de Cultura, 1961.

Gutiérrez, Juan María. *Estudios histórico-literarios*. Compiled and with a prologue and notes by Ernesto Morales. Estrada Collection, Vol. 12. Buenos Aires: Angel Estrada, 1940.

Henderson, Bernard W. *Civil War and Rebellion in the Roman Empire A.D. 69–70: A Companion to the "Histories" of Tacitus*. London: Macmillan and Co., 1908.

Hernández, José. *Martín Fierro: Poesía gauchesca*. Vol. 2. Introduction and notes by Jorge Luis Borges and Adolfo Bioy Casares. México: Fondo de Cultura Económica, 1955.

Hidalgo, Bartolomé. *Cielitos y diálogos patrióticos*. Buenos Aires: Ciordia & Rodríguez, 1950.

Hogsett, Charlotte. *The Literary Existence of Germaine de Staël*. With a foreword by Madelyn Gutwirth. Carbondale: Southern Illinois University Press, 1987.

Ibarguren, Carlos. *Juan Manuel de Rosas: su vida, su drama, su tiempo*. Buenos Aires: Ediciones Theoria, 1961.

Jones, Kristine L. "Conflict and Adaptation in the Argentine Pampas, 1750–1880." Ph.D. dissertation, University of Chicago, 1984.

Lanuza, José Luis. *Morenada*. Buenos Aires: Emecé Editores, 1946.

Laplace, Pierre Simon. *Oeuvres complètes de Laplace*. Paris, 1891–1898.

Mansilla, Lucio Victorio. *Una excursión a los indios ranqueles*. Edited and with an introduction and notes by Julio Caillet-Bois. México: Fondo de Cultura Económica, 1947.

———. *Rozas, ensayo histórico-psicológico*. Buenos Aires: R. Alonzo, 1973.

Martínez Estrada, Ezequiel. *Los invariantes históricos en el Facundo*. Buenos Aires: Casa Pardo, 1974.

———. *Muerte y transfiguración de Martín Fierro*. 2 vols. Buenos Aires: Fondo de Cultura Económica, 1958.

Meschia, Carlo A., ed. *Ventisette traduzioni in varie lingue del Cinque maggio di Alessandro Manzoni*. Foligno: Stabilimento F. Campitelli, 1883.

Molière. *The Merchant Gentleman (Le bourgeois gentilhomme), A Comedy in Four Acts*. Translated by Margaret Baker. New York: S. French, 1915.

Mujica Láinez, Manuel. *Vida de Aniceto el Gallo (Hilario Ascasubi)*. 2d ed. Buenos Aires: Emecé, 1955.

Neyra, Juan Carlos. *Prontuario de próceres y traidores*. Buenos Aires: Ediciones Cícero, 1990.

Orsolini, Mario Horacio. *Ejército argentino y crecimiento nacional*. Library of the Coming Day. Buenos Aires: Ediciones Arayú, 1965.

Owen, Walter, trans. *The Gaucho Martín Fierro by José Hernández*. Drawings by Alberto Güiraldes. New York: Farrar & Rinehart, 1936.

Popilizio, Enrique. *Vida de Lucio Mansilla*. Biography and Correspondence Series. Buenos Aires: Editorial Pomaire, 1985.

410 BIBLIOGRAPHY

Pradère, Juan A. *Juan Manuel de Rosas, su iconografía: reproducción de óleos, acuarelas, grabados, litografías, viñetas de imprenta, monedas, porcelanas, curiosidades, etc.* Buenos Aires: J. Mendesky e hijo, 1914.

Ramos, Jorge Abelardo. *Historia política del ejército argentino.* The Syrinx Series. Buenos Aires: A Pena Lillo, 1959.

Raone, Juan Mario. *Fortines del desierto: mojones de civilización.* Buenos Aires: Editorial Lito, 1969.

Sanhueza, Gabriel. *Santiago Arcos: comunista, millonario y calavera.* Santiago de Chile: Editorial del Pacífico, 1956.

Sarmiento, Domingo Faustino. *Facundo.* Latin American Literature Collection. La Habana: Casa de las Américas, 1982.

Slatta, Richard W. *Cowboys of the Americas.* New Haven: Yale University Press, 1990.

———. *Gauchos and the Vanishing Frontier.* Lincoln: University of Nebraska Press, 1983.

Strabo. *The Geography of Strabo.* Translated by Horace Leonard Jones. London: W. Heinemann, 1917–1933.

Thomas à Kempis. *The Imitation of Christ.* Translated by Edgar Daplyn. London: Marshall, Morgan, and Scott, 1979.

Viñas, David. *Indios, ejército y frontera.* México, D.F.: Siglo Veintiuno Editores, 1982.

Yunque, Alvaro. *Calfucurá, la conquista de las pampas.* Buenos Aires: Ediciones A. Zamora, 1956.

Zárate, Armando. *Facundo Quiroga, Barranca Yaco: juicios y testimonios.* Buenos Aires: Plus Ultra, 1985.

INDEX

Achauentrú, Chief, 12–16, 99, 129
Achiras, 5, 17, 49, 93
Agustinillo, 377
Aillancó, 76, 130, 136, 289
Alvarez, Ensign, 31–32
Alvarez, Father Moisés: opposes expedition, 14; knocked off horse, 80; in snoring duet, 86; in brush with Crisóstomo, 92; baptizes Mansilla's godson, 259–260; advocates founding chapel, 319; captive kisses cord of, 360
Añancué, 272
Ancañao, 378
Angelito (Scout): as messenger to Chief Ramón, 42; fresh tracks of, 47; trail marked by tracks of, 66–67; speculation about, 72
Araucan language: Mansilla's ignorance of, 75; parliamentary protocol of, 109; Miguelito able to speak in, 171; in dream, 175; Carmen speaks to Negro in, 187; words for courting in, 197; at junta, 294; word for foreigner in, 362–363. See also Araucan nation; Ranquel Indians (nation)
Araucan nation: migratory origins of, 3–4; and road to Leubucó, 129. See also Araucan language; Ranquel Indians (nation)
Araya, Comandante, 339
Arcos, Santiago, salutation to, 2; wager with, 3; and human

species, 13; and changes in Argentina, 46; and pacing of story, 134
Argentina, Republic of: and promise of bounty, 54; exceptional campfires of, 56; abuse of army horses in, 255–256; chief figures of, in dream, 257–258. See also civilization; horses
Argentines, as typified by Private Gómez, 28; and love of plains, 51; Ranquels hailed as, 84, 130; unselfish valor of, 215; unhygienic customs of, 242; as typified by Chañilao, 285; increasing power of paisanos as, 286; appeal to loyalty of, 298–299. See also Gómez, Private; gauchos; junta
Arias, Camilo, 41, 42, 98, 195–196, 285, 287, 340–342
Arredondo, Gen. José Miguel, 5, 161, 181, 209, 293, 302
Avila, Eloy, 40
Ayala, Colonel, 128, 166, 177, 216

Bagual Lagoon (Laguna Bagual), 160, 374, 376, 382
Baigorrita, Chief: and Mansilla's wager, 4; misconstrued letter to, 73; deference of, to Mariano Rosas, 178; and asylum for Camargo, 215; and Mansilla's visit to, 227; unceremonious wel-

come by, 236; reception in tent of, 240–243; and release of captive woman, 245; description of, 251; unwillingness of, to be seen drunk, 257; baptism of son of, 259–260; as protective of Mansilla, 269; interprets omen, 276; anxiety of, over rumors, 288; impassivity of, at junta, 301. *See also* baptism; junta; Rosas, Mariano

baptism: offer of, to Ranquels, 126; of Baigorrita's son, 259–261; as planned for Mariano Rosas's daughter, 319; collectively, of children, 323–326. *See also* children; Franciscans

barbarians, and sense of pomp, 106; and the unusual, 130; admiration of, for Mansilla, 133; and law of reciprocity, 274; unjust rejection of, 366

Bárcena, Colonel, 264

Bargas (bandit), 223–224

Blanco the Indian: depredations of, 49; scheme for foiling, 49–52; news of, from Chile, 87; reappearance of, 199–200; sworn vengeance of, 337–338. *See also* Pampa Volunteers

Brazil: Private Gómez in hospital in, 27; as agent of leveling of countryside, 46; name-changing in, 121. *See also* Paraguay, war with

Brazil (pet dog). *See* dogs

Buenos Aires: Victoria Square in, 124; contrasted with desert, 162–163; border security of, 178; Mariano Rosas's curiosity about, 218; and first gringos, 300

Burela, Father: arrival from Mendoza, 75, 128; and rumors of Mansilla's scheming, 289; with Mariano Rosas, 291; silence of, at junta, 301

burial, Ranquel customs of, 222–223

Bustos, Cruz, 79, 80–85, 207

Caiomuta, 169, 268–270, 290

Calcumuleu, 74, 90, 102, 188, 263, 288, 361

Calfucurá, 129, 287, 288, 295, 342

camaraderie: and roll call after battle, 24; poignancy of loss of, 373–374

Cañada Honda, 360

Caniupán, Chief: in confrontation with Mansilla, 85; as Mansilla's escort, 89–90; on road to Leubucó, 102, 107–108; as liaison to Mariano Rosas, 131

captives: as servants, 194; treatment of, 224–225; scheme for release of, 336–337; ransom of, 361. *See also* women

Carmen (Ranquel woman): as envoy of Mariano Rosas, 7; and safety of Mansilla, 186; on Ranquel religious customs, 221–223; as confidante of Mansilla, 331–333, 351. *See also* Gualicho

Carmen (valet), 66, 86–87, 176, 243, 257–258, 271, 289

carob: chewing of, 68; crushed, as dessert, 136; diverse uses of, 229

Carrapí (Indian), 361

Carrilobo, 129, 364, 369–371

Cepeda, battle of, 227, 285

Chamalcó, 53, 182

Chañilao (Manuel Alfonso), 283–286; 289

children: living conditions of, among gauchos, 193; as burden to unwed mother, 226

Chile: and Araucan migrations, 4; Blanco the Indian in, 49, 200; price of carmine from, 100; riding gear from, 102; as hideout of Juan Sáa, 161; tobacco brought from, 229; as origin of Mora,

231; as destination of stolen horses, 254; nature of trade with, 274. *See also* Araucan nation; Blanco the Indian

Christianity: arrival of, in Leubucó, 106; versus barbarism, 106; and treatment of Indian civilization, 134. *See also* barbarian; land; Ranquel Indians (nation); Ranquel Indians (women)

Christians, upon first meeting Mansilla, 128; as typified by Miguelito, 162; Indians' suspicion of, 296; rights of, to land, 297–298; sworn word of, 302; parliaments of, compared to Indians, 307–308; duplicity of, concerning Macías, 322; repudiation of, 383. *See also* Macías, Jorge; Mariano Rosas; Ranquel Indians (nation)

civilization: and hospitals, 44; as leveler of countryside, 46; and need for self-assessment, 193–194

Club del Progreso (Buenos Aires), 4, 183, 194, 282

Club del Progreso (Río Cuarto), 15

Cobo, Commander, 20

Colchao, Major, 245

Coli-Mula, 41

Coliqueo, Chief, 227, 301

Colorado Dune, 376

Colorado River, 4, 220, 266

colorados, 93, 145. *See also* Crisóstomo; Miguelito; Sáa, Felipe

Comeñé (Ranquel woman), 362

Córdoba (province): new borders of, 5; way of giving directions in, 16, *See also* Río Cuarto (river)

Crisóstomo, 92, 94–96, 361

Cuadril, 160

Cuero River: as best route for new railroad, 54; bleakness of surrounding land, 54–55

Curupaití, 23, 25–26

Curuzú, 26

dance, 263, 329–331. *See also* Ranquel Indians (women)

directions: way of giving in Córdoba, 16; Indians' suspicion concerning, 129

dogs: Mansilla's fear of, 167–168, 277, 350; at Baigorrita's settlement, 254; pity of quadroon for, 266; Brazil (pet from Paraguayan war), 355–356, 369–371

Donatti, Father Marcos: frontier duties of, 11; opinion of, of expedition, 12; as rider, 52; on return march, 375. *See also* Alvarez, Father Moisés; Franciscans

dreams: of conquest, 172–175; of Argentine leaders, 257–258; during last night in Leubucó, 334–336

economy, basis for, among Indians, 272–274

Elía, Colonel, 311

El Morro, 143–144, 151, 160, 162

El Pino (cattle farm), 179

Epumer, Chief, 128, 132; as host in Leubucó, 137–140; as adversary, 169–171; and visit from Mansilla, 314, 316–318

espionage, intricacies of, in Leubucó, 228–229. *See also* Calfucurá; Carmen (Ranquel woman); quadroon

Estanislao, 280–282

Federación (Junín), 179

federals: and Camargo, 123; in Negro's account, 186–187; as typified by paisano, 286. *See also* Unitarians

firewater. *See* liquor

flamingos, 230

Franciscans: Mansilla's concern for, 105; as misfits in chief's tent, 166; preparing for mass, 216. *See also* Alvarez, Father Moisés; baptism; Donatti, Father Marcos

gauchos: and knack for building
fires, 40; dwellings of, 193; as
name of praise among Ranquels,
195; traits of, as opposed to paisano, 285–287; and knowledge
of country ways, 349. *See also*
Pereira, Rufino
Gelly y Obes, General, 35–38
godfathers, Mansilla as, 7; duties
of, among Indians, 260. *See also*
baptism
Gómez, Private: origins and induc-
tion of, 20; leave granted to, 23;
return of, 25; arrest of, 29; sentencing of, 32; execution of, 34;
as apparition, 36
guadales, and travel in the pampas, 18
Gualicho (evil spirit): and first offering at parliament, 9; assumed
to be with Mansilla, 127–128;
religious significance of, 221–
223. *See also* Carmen (Ranquel
woman)
Guevara, Ensign, 27, 29, 31–33

handouts: at meeting with Chief
Ramón, 79; excessive allowance
of, 91; Indians' manner of re-
questing, 111–112; exhausted
supply of, 361
happiness, philosophy of, 278–279
Hernández, Pastor, 49
horses: as key to expedition, 12;
Indians' special training of, 18;
as opposed to mules, 18; Indians'
devotion to, 104; team-roping
of, 104–105; as measure of Indians' importance, 111; theft of,
protested, 136; free traffic of,
160; Indian way of breaking in,
206; eating meat of, 226; abuse
of, 255–256; and peace treaty,
293–295; pacing of, for travel,
367–368. *See also* Argentina;
Ranquel Indians (nation)

Indians: and argument for exter-
mination of, 46; poverty of, 294
Inés, 94–95
interpreting, art of, 231
Irrazábal, 32
Itapirú, 22, 23, 25

Jarilla, 160, 377
Jofré, Petrona, 360, 361
junta: as Indian form of parliament,
112–113; reception prior to,
280–281; greetings and introduction at, 291–292; Baigorita's
silence at, 304. *See also* Araucan
language; Burela, Father; land;
protocol

La Aguada, 307
La Esquina, 22, 37, 38
Laguna Alegre, 19, 39
land: purchase of, justified, 219;
possession of, disputed, 297–
300. *See also* Christians; junta;
peace treaty
Langheló Lagoon, 178, 219
La Tribuna (newspaper), and
plans for railroad, 220. *See also*
railroad
La Verde, 367
Leubucó: as terminus of new road,
6; first sighting of, 117; as hub
of roads, 129; as site of Mariano
Rosas's camp, 166; return to,
from Quenqué, 305; mood at,
compared with Carrilobo, 364.
See also junta; Rosas, Mariano
Lima, Father (confessor), 33
Lincoln (son of Mariano Rosas),
134
Linconao: and Chief Ramón, 8;
and pox attack, 9; at Mansilla's
home, 11; and Mansilla's request for directions, 129. *See
also* directions; pox
liquor: as gift at parliament, 8;

provided by Father Burela, 101; Ranquel consumption of, 137; at bacchanal with Epumer, 140. *See also* Epumer; Ranquel Indians (nation)

Lonco-uaca, 375

López, Manuel, 345

Macías, Jorge: first seen by Mansilla, 128–130; on consumptives, 226; sorry condition of, 282; ridiculed, 293; Mariano Rosas agrees to release of, 309; background and history of, 310–314; Mansilla's advocacy for, 320–321; second request for release of, 343; reappearance of, 349. *See also* captives; Christians

march, Indian formation of, 103

mares, distribution of, through treaty, 293–295. *See also* horses; peace treaty

mass, first in Ranquel camps, 216–218

Médano del Cuero, 46

medicine, among Indians, 226. *See also* Macías, Jorge; pox

Melideo, 128, 132

Mendoza, Private, 100

Mendoza (province), 61, 75, 128, 138, 143, 202, 211, 247, 248, 321, 339

Michaut, Doctor, 11

Miguelito (Miguel Corro): description and origins of, 143–144; love affairs of, 144–148; imprisonment of, 150–152; false confession of, 155; escape, 159–162

Mitre, General Emilio, 182

Monte Caseros, battle of, 227, 264

Monte de la Vieja, 40

Mora, Francisco: services of lent, 85; interprets parliament, 108–114; discourages asking directions, 129; interprets through Caniupán, 131; life story of,

230–232; interprets on return trip, 377–378

morality, as opposed to sentiment, 172

mules: merits of, 18; peculiar gait of, 98; arrival of, with packs, 99. *See also* horses

Multias, 194

Murga, Julián, 264

nativism: as antidote to imitation, 152–153; Ranquel law as argument for, 274

Negro (with accordion), 171–175, 186–188, 191, 215, 218, 283, 328

Nicolai, Major Hilarión, 123, 282, 344

numbers, Ranquel use of, 113–114

old age, respect for, 281–282

omens, 127–129, 276. *See also* Baigorrita; Gualicho

oratory, intonation as part of, 110; long-windedness of masters of, 116. *See also* parliament

Pacheco, don Angel, 189

Painé, Chief, 178, 182

Pampa Volunteers, 49–52

Paraguay: and Santiago Arcos, 3; Mansilla and Garmendia in, 21; Tuyutí encampment in war with, 21–23

parliament: among Indians, 8; translator's duties during, 9; rules and methods of, among Ranquels, 109–112; as compared to Christian style, 112

Patagones, 264

patriotism, appeal to, at junta, 298–299

Pavón, battle of, 227

peace treaty: first celebrated with Ranquels, 4; as motive for Captain Rivadavia's absence, 90;

as reason for expedition, 207; mechanisms of, 208–209; as basis for land purchase, 219–221; discussion of, with Baigorrita, 261; Ranquel distrust of, 289; oratorical presentation of, 293–296; importance of honoring, 302; and founding of chapel, 319; and question of captives, 336–337; and release of Macías, 343; as grounds for protesting raids, 363, 372. *See also* junta; land; parliament; Rosas, Mariano

Peñaloza, Angel Vicente (El Chacho), 48

Peñaloza (marauder), 53

Pereyra, Rufino, 200, 202–206, 356. *See also* Twelfth Line Battalion

phrenology, 171, 208, 231, 371, 384

Pichicaiun, 362

Pichún, Chief, 237, 251

Pitralauquen, 276

pox, in tent camps, 10–11

Pozos Cavados, 103

protocol: in first meeting with Mariano Rosas, 131; in greeting Ranquel chiefs, 132; for visiting tent, 262

Punta de San Luis, 144

quadroon (Uchaimañé), 264–266, 318

Quenqué, 129, 227, 288, 290, 294, 304

Quevedo, Emilio, 4

Quintuiner (wife of Chief Ramón), 317

Quiroga, 144

Racedo, Commander, 204–205

railroad: as planned by heads-of-state, 54; as foreseen by Mariano Rosas, 220

Ramón, Chief: and gesture of friendship, 8; welcome given by, 130; as silversmith, 357–358, 364–365; family and dwelling of, 361–363

Ranquel Indians (nation): migratory history of, 3; forms of conversation among, 109; drinking customs of, 137; games of endurance among, 168–169; hierarchy of rule among, 182; and slaughtering of livestock, 189; reverence for priests among, 192; use of campfires by, 193; social customs of, 197–199; and affairs of state, 218; justice among, 254–255; possible fate of, 381; demographics of, 381–383; comparative barbarism of, 384. *See also* drinking; junta; peace treaty

Ranquel Indians (women): manner of dressing of, 96–100; hair style and face make-up of, 190; courting and marriage of, 197–199; routine duties of, 258; and *pilquén*, 317; dance customs of, 331. *See also* captives; Christians; women

Ranquilcó, 376

rastrilladas, 17

religion, among Ranquels, 127. *See also* burial; Carmen (Ranquel woman); Gualicho

Relmo, Chief, 132

Renca (town), 60, 160

Riga, 286

Rincón, 8

Río Cuarto (river), 5

Río Cuarto (town), 49, 129, 130, 188

Río Quinto (river): placement of forts near, 5–6; easy crossing of, 160; Christians' right to land along, 297–298; journey's end at banks of, 385. *See also* strategy (military)

Rivadavia, Captain, 118, 123,

195–196, 200, 207, 339, 344, 372

Rivas, General, 176, 186, 264

Rodríguez, Demetrio (adjutant), 91, 215, 301

Rodríguez, María de Jesús, 264

Roqueplan, 158

Rosas, Juan Manuel de: dictatorship of, toppled, 20; theater posters in time of, 135; Mansilla as nephew of, 180; captive once maid of, 194; and slaughter at Retiro, 300. See also federals; Rosas, Mariano

Rosas, Manuelita, 96

Rosas, Mariano: messengers sent by, 91; as orator of note, 111; delays forced by, 122–125; first meets Mansilla, 128–130; food first served by, 136; drinking with, 168–171, 177, 183–184; description of, 177–178; origins and youth of, 179; vow of, 181; lassoes calf, 189; introduces family, 192; discusses peace treaty, 208–211, 219; exchange of ponchos with, 326. See also Painé, Chief; Ranquel Indians (nation)

Sáa, Felipe, 128, 161

Sáa, Juan, 215, 219

Salinas Grandes, 129

saltpeter: beds of, 41; on road to Carrilobo, 354

San Juan (district of Buenos Aires), 57, 264–265

San Luis (province): and old border of Córdoba, 5; and Blanco the Indian, 49; scouting parties near, 87; and Crisóstomo, 95; as easily reached by fugitives, 160–161; as former market, 194; origins of Camargo in, 214; captive woman from, 224, 245; word of invasion of, 363, 372. See also Blanco the Indian; captives

San Martín, Juan de Dios, 236–238, 261, 269, 272

Santa Fé, 87

Santos Lugares, 178

Sarmiento, Domingo F., 209

Sarmiento, Fort, 6, 11, 12, 228, 375

scouts: sent by Ranquels, 87; as cause of alarm to Indians, 342. See also Angelito; Private Guzmán

strategy (military): and placement of forts, 5–6; fear as component of, 73

Suárez, Mateo, 28

Tala de los Puntanos (lagoon), 378

tents: design and description of, 135, 192; Baigorrita's, 241; Caniupán's, 263. See also Ranquel Indians (nation)

tobacco: use of, among Indians, 194; making of pipes for, 229

trackers, 47–48

travel: language of, in Córdoba, 16; philosophy of, 39–40; Madame de Stäel on, 40; exacting of fees for, 53; drawbacks of haste in, 53. See also Córdoba; horses

Tremencó, 46

Tres de Febrero (fort), 11

Twelfth Line Battalion: and preparation for expedition, 15; and burial of Private Gómez, 34, 37; expert trackers of, 48; and Rufino Pereyra, 202–205; pet dog of, 355–356.

Uchaimañé. See quadroon

Unitarians, 187

Urquiza, 194, 285

Us-helo, 41

Utatriquin, 55, 59

utensils, 136

Villa Mercedes, 160, 181, 385

Villarreal (Ranquel), 96–97, 100, 352

Wada, 129
Wenchenao, 363
women: and bravery of men, 168;
    at baptism, 323–324; contra-
    dictory charms of, 351–353.
    See also dance; Ranquel Indians
    (women)

Yataití, 34
Yavi, 286

Zárate, doña Fermina, 359–361
Zárate (landowner), 94–95
Zorro Colgado, 41

DATE DUE

SEP 2 6 1997	